Media Edition



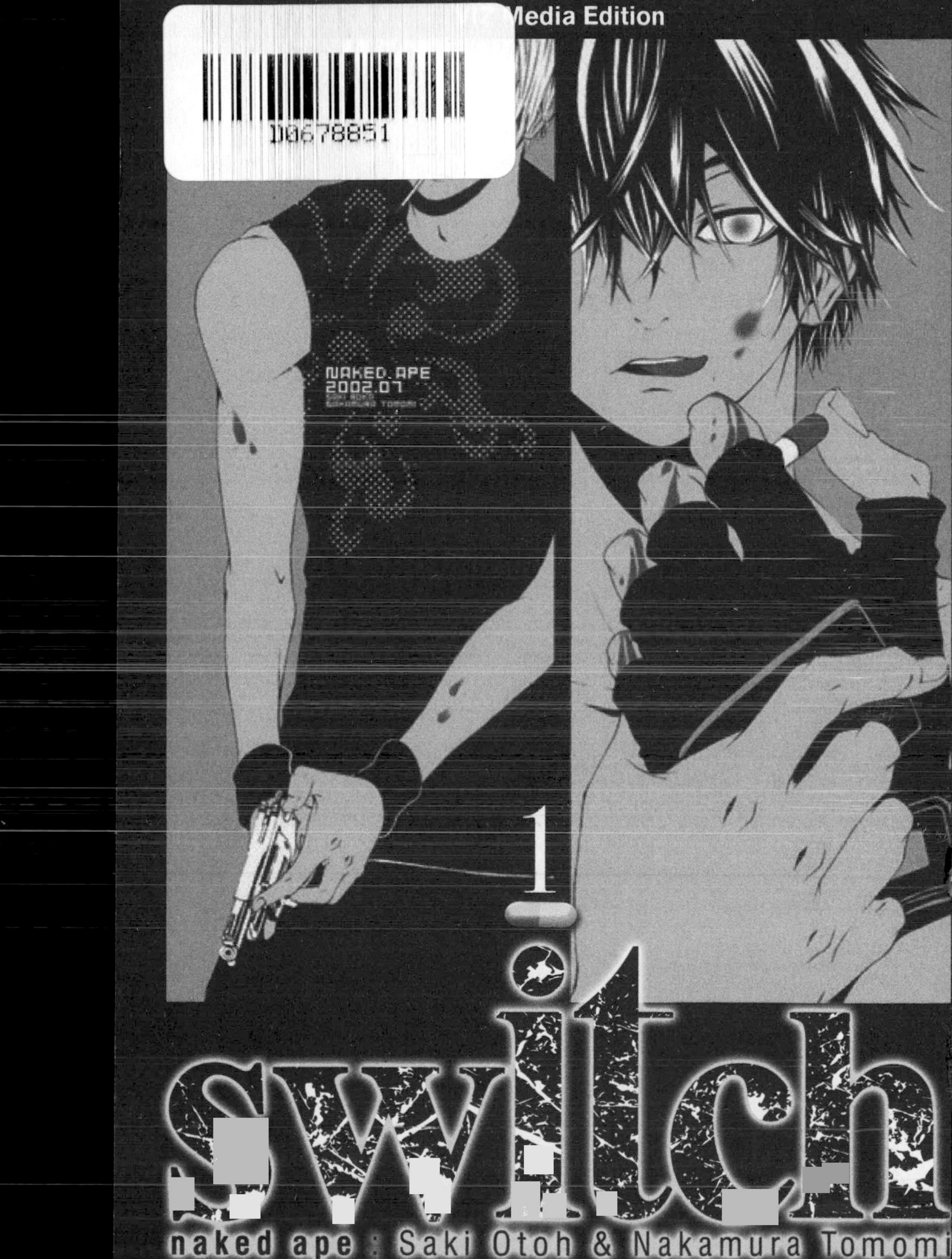
NAKED.APE
2002.07

1

# switch

naked ape : Saki Otoh & Nakamura Tomomi

# switch

## 1

## CONTENTS

Act 1 ............. 3

Act 2 ...........63

Act 3 ...........99

Act 4 ........ 139

Bonus Manga........176

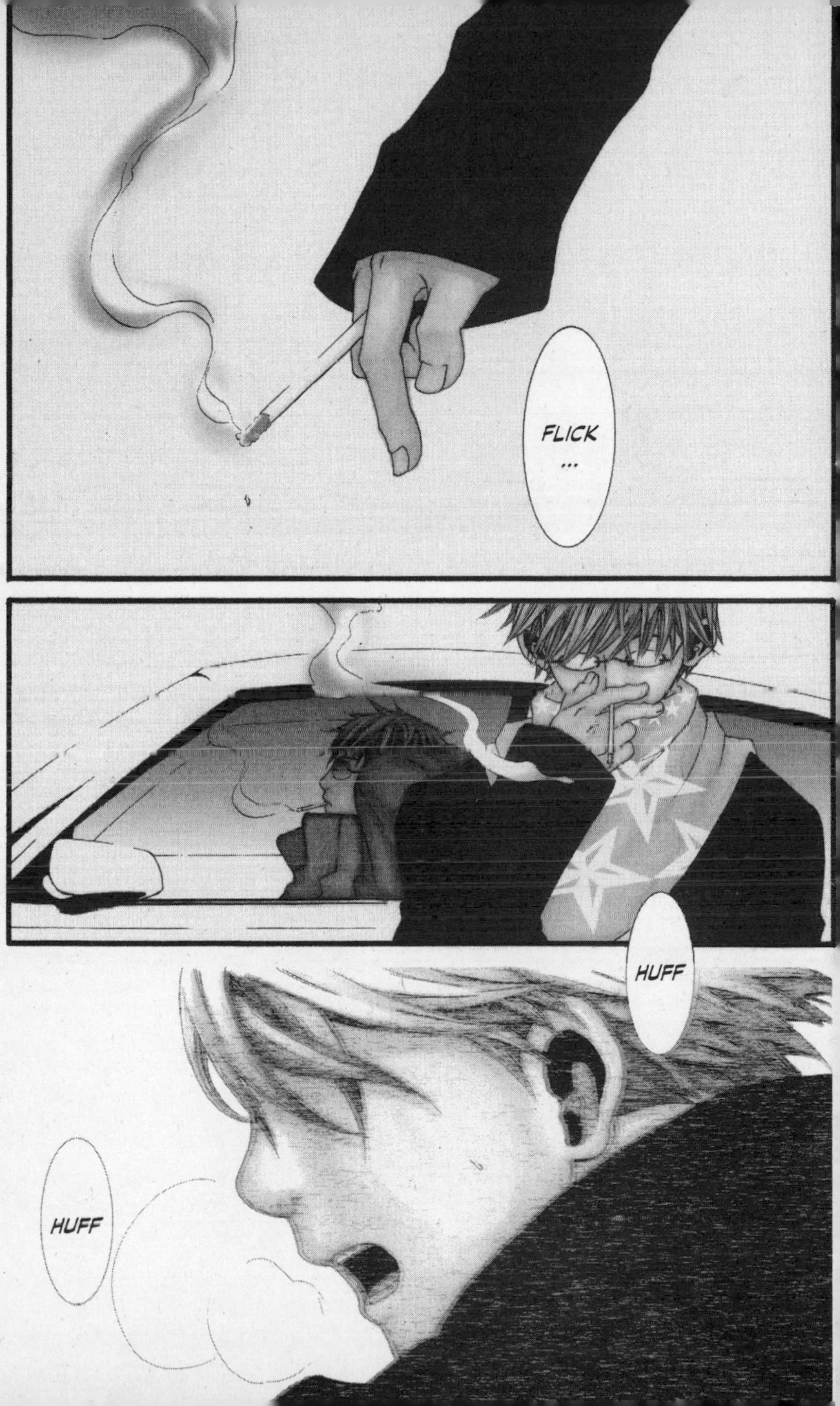
FLICK
...
HUFF
HUFF

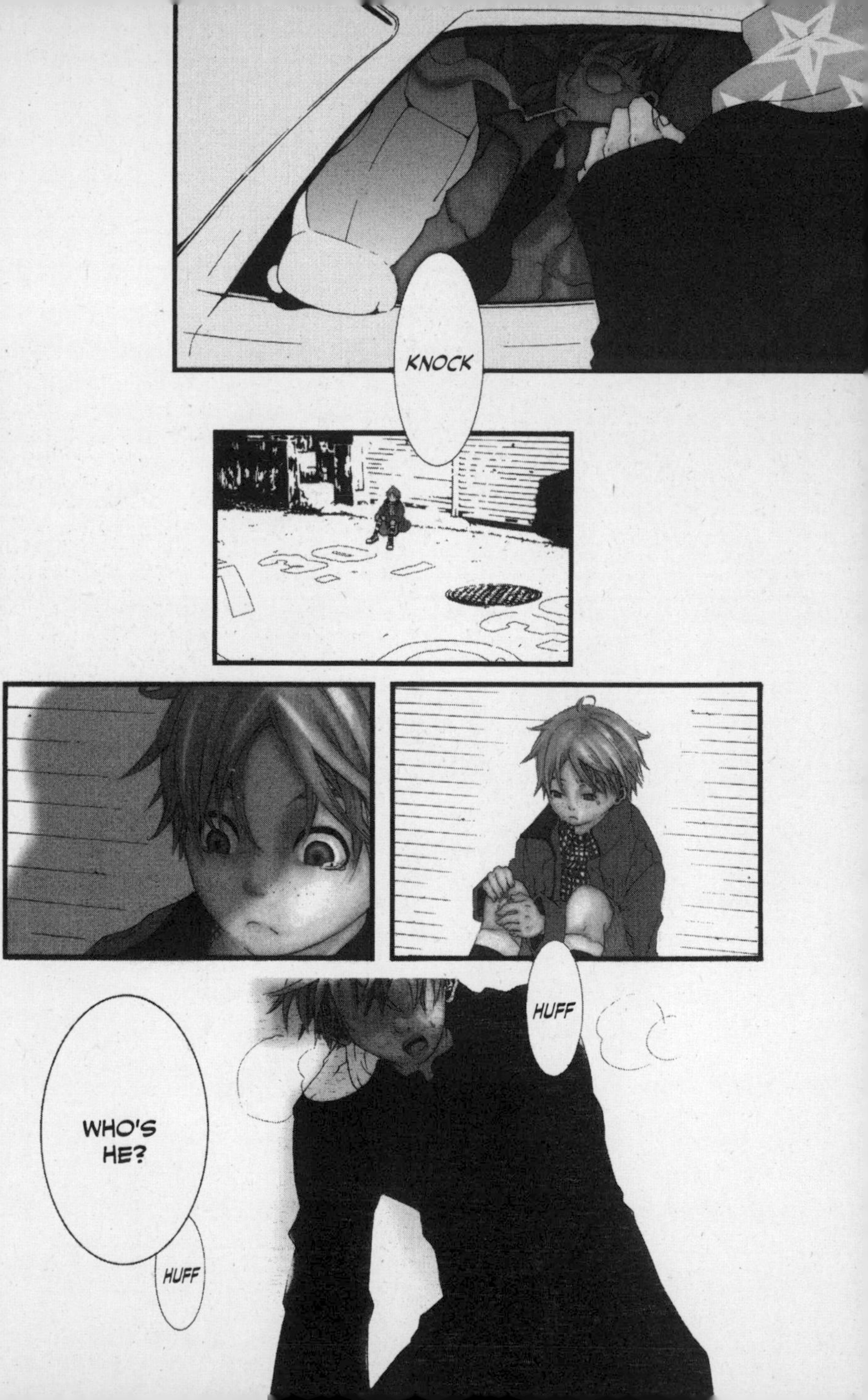
KNOCK
HUFF
WHO'S HE?
HUFF

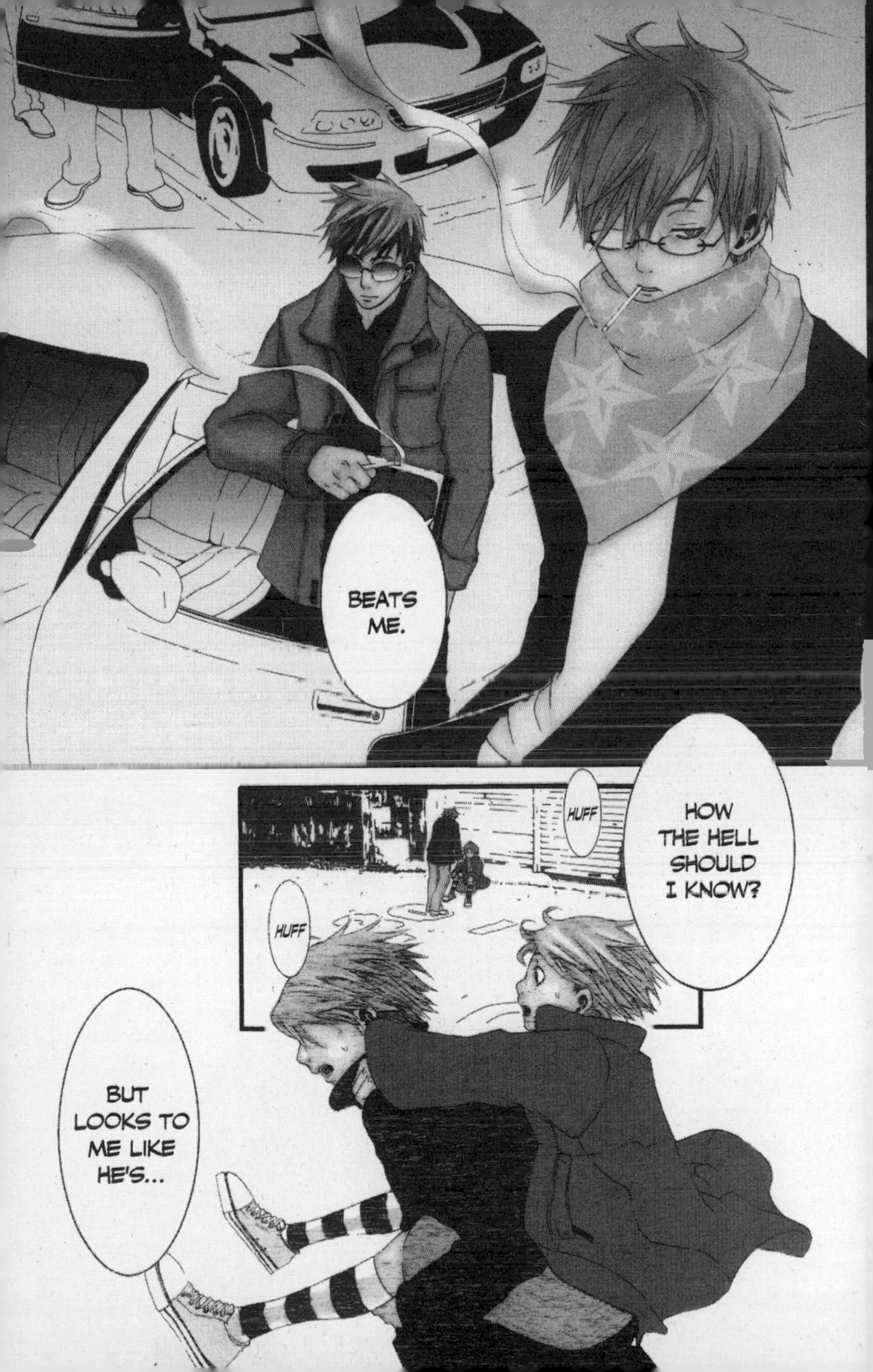
BEATS ME.
HOW THE HELL SHOULD I KNOW?
HUFF
HUFF
BUT LOOKS TO ME LIKE HE'S...

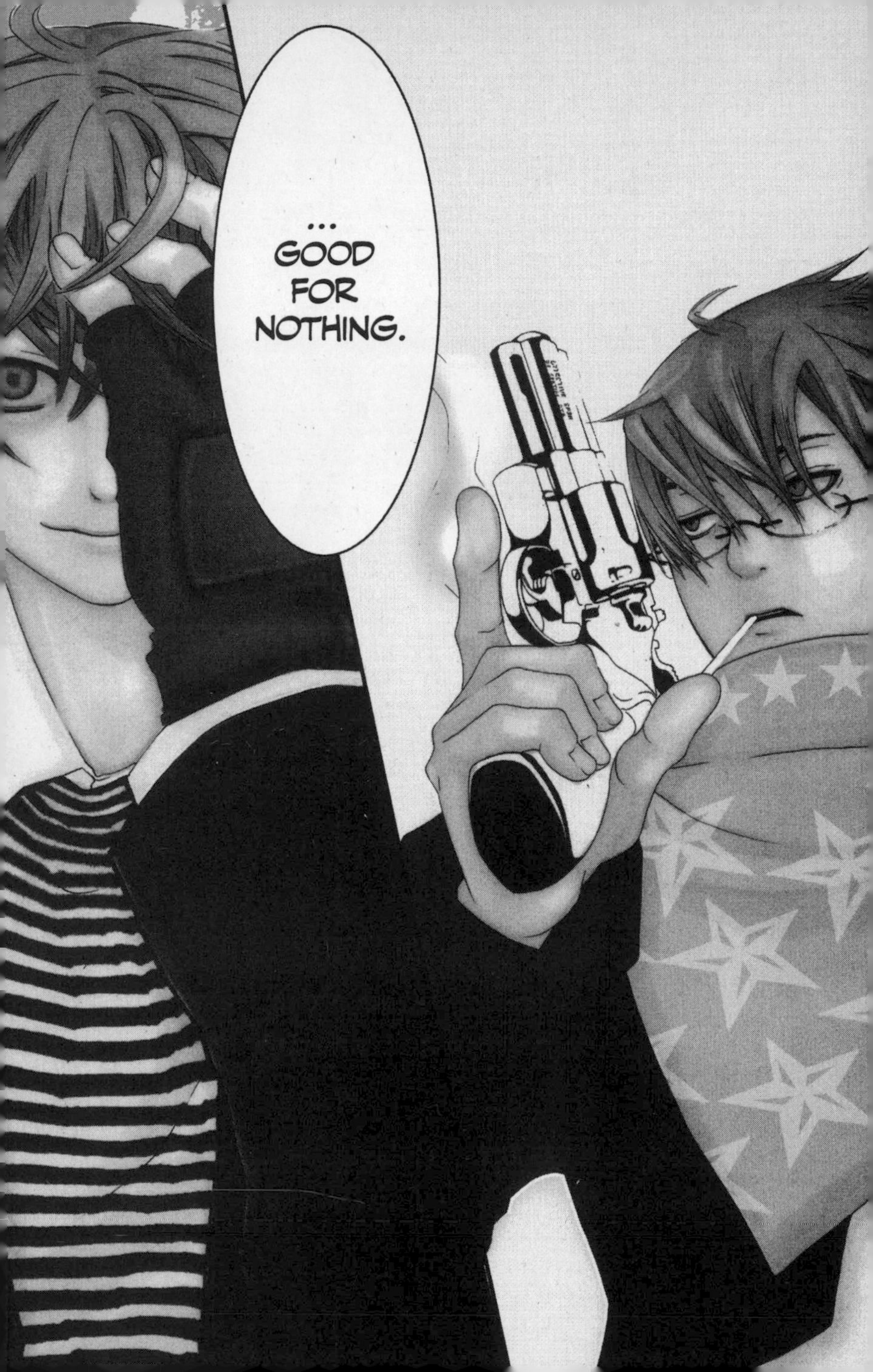
...GOOD FOR NOTHING.

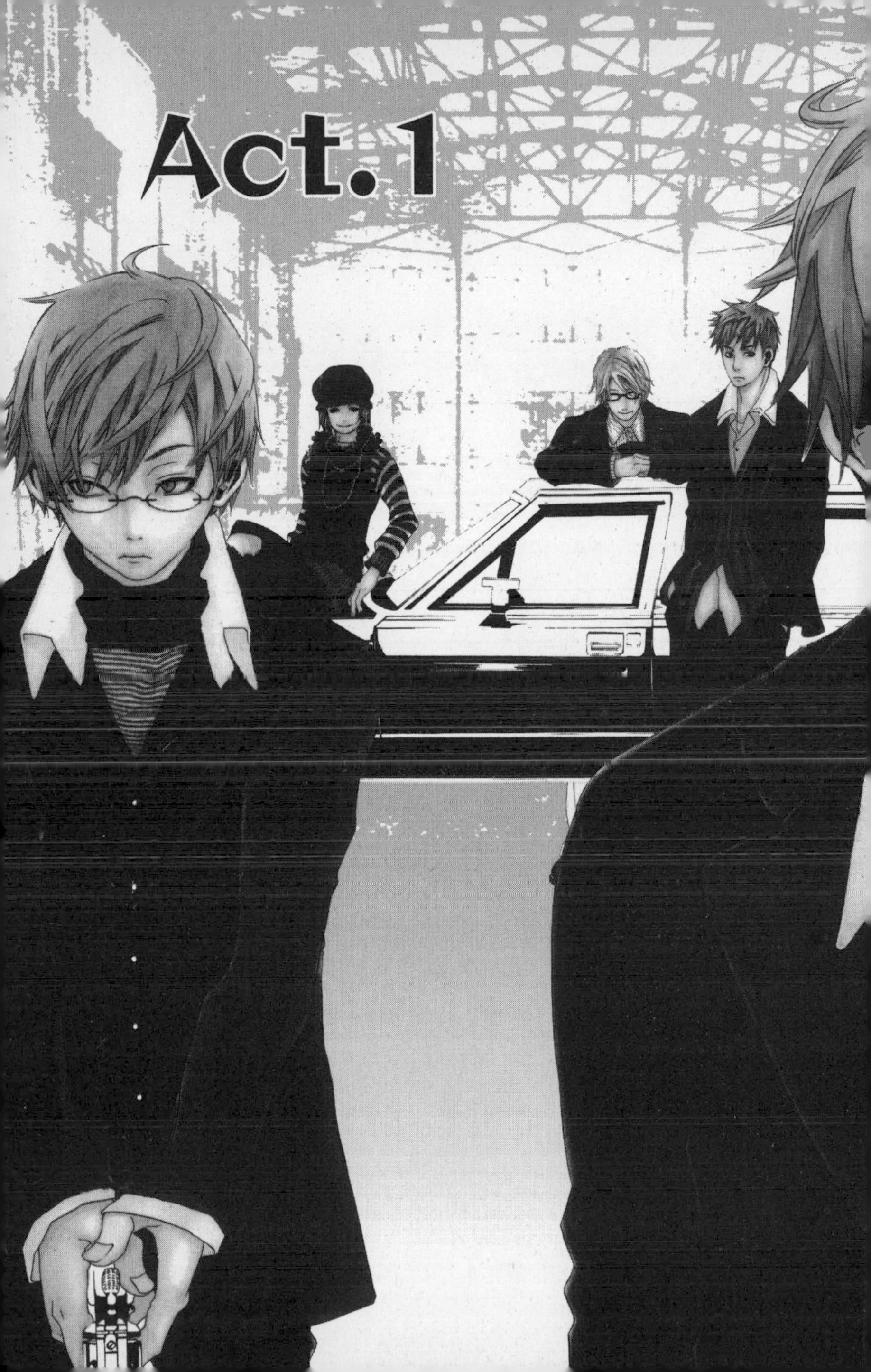
Act. 1

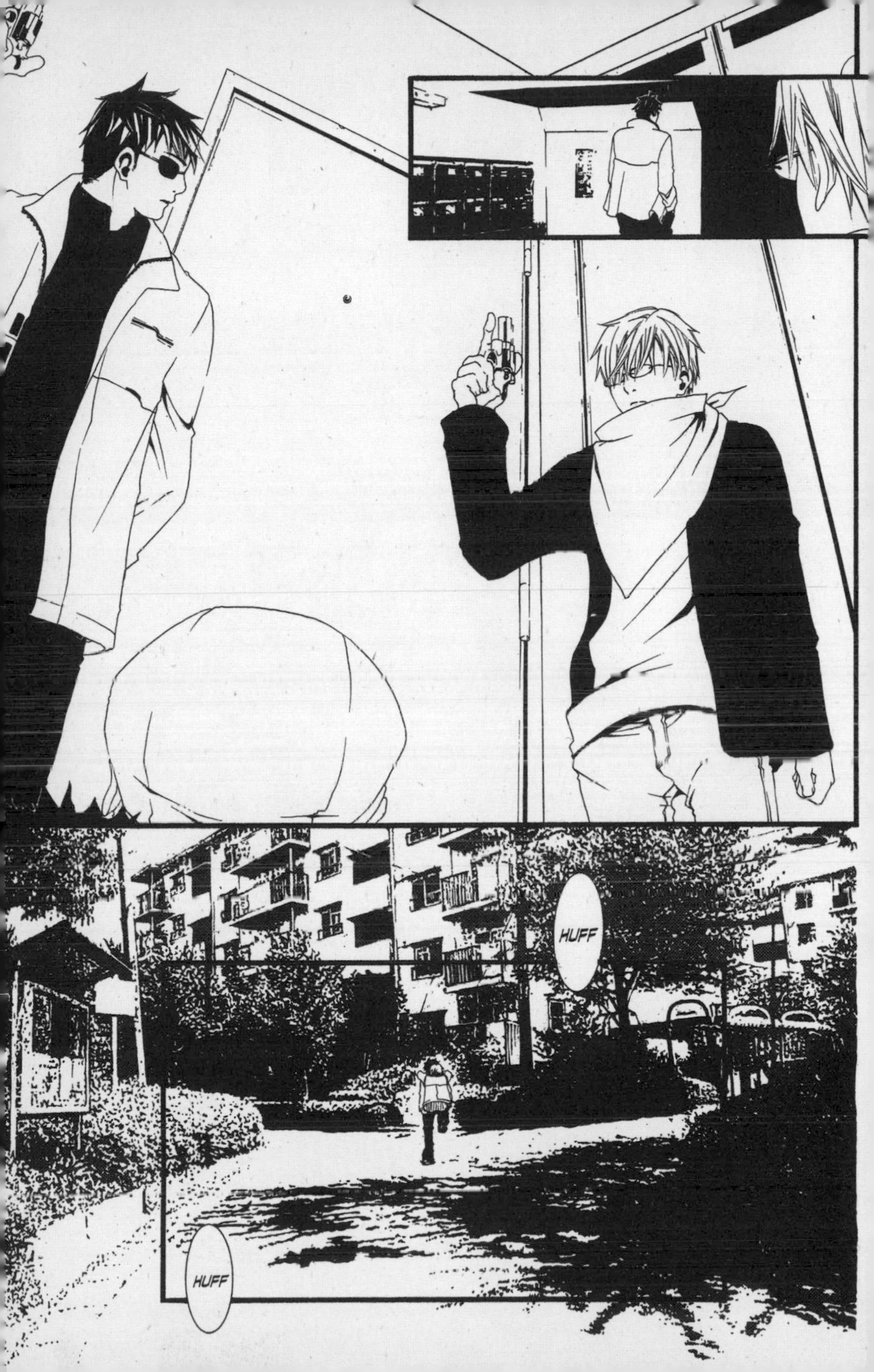
HUFF
HUFF

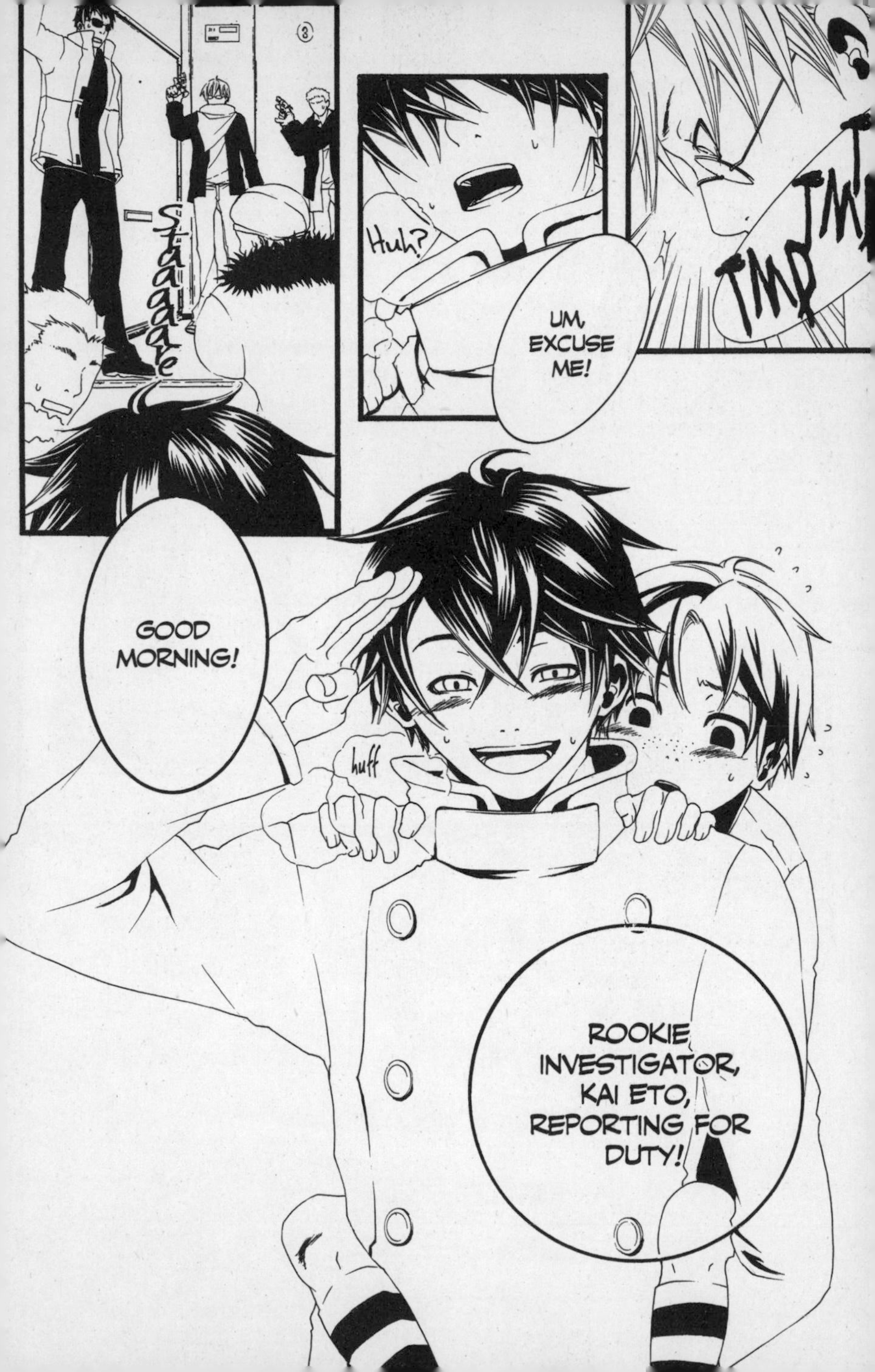
TMP
TMP
Huh?
UM, EXCUSE ME!
Staaaaaare
GOOD MORNING!
huff
ROOKIE INVESTIGATOR, KAI ETO, REPORTING FOR DUTY!

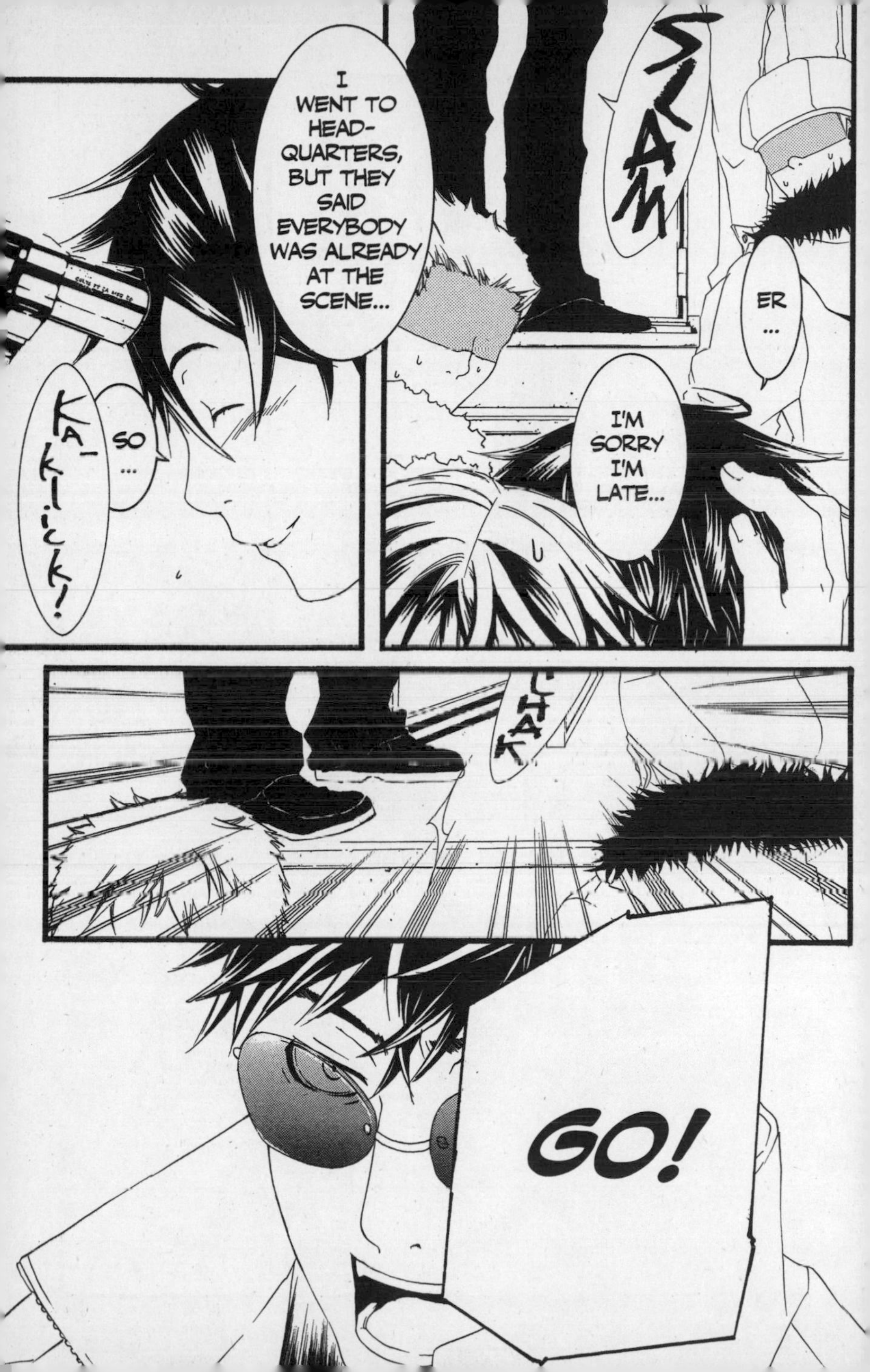
SLAM
ER...
I'M SORRY I'M LATE...
I WENT TO HEAD-QUARTERS, BUT THEY SAID EVERYBODY WAS ALREADY AT THE SCENE...
SO...
KA-KLICK!
CHAK
GO!

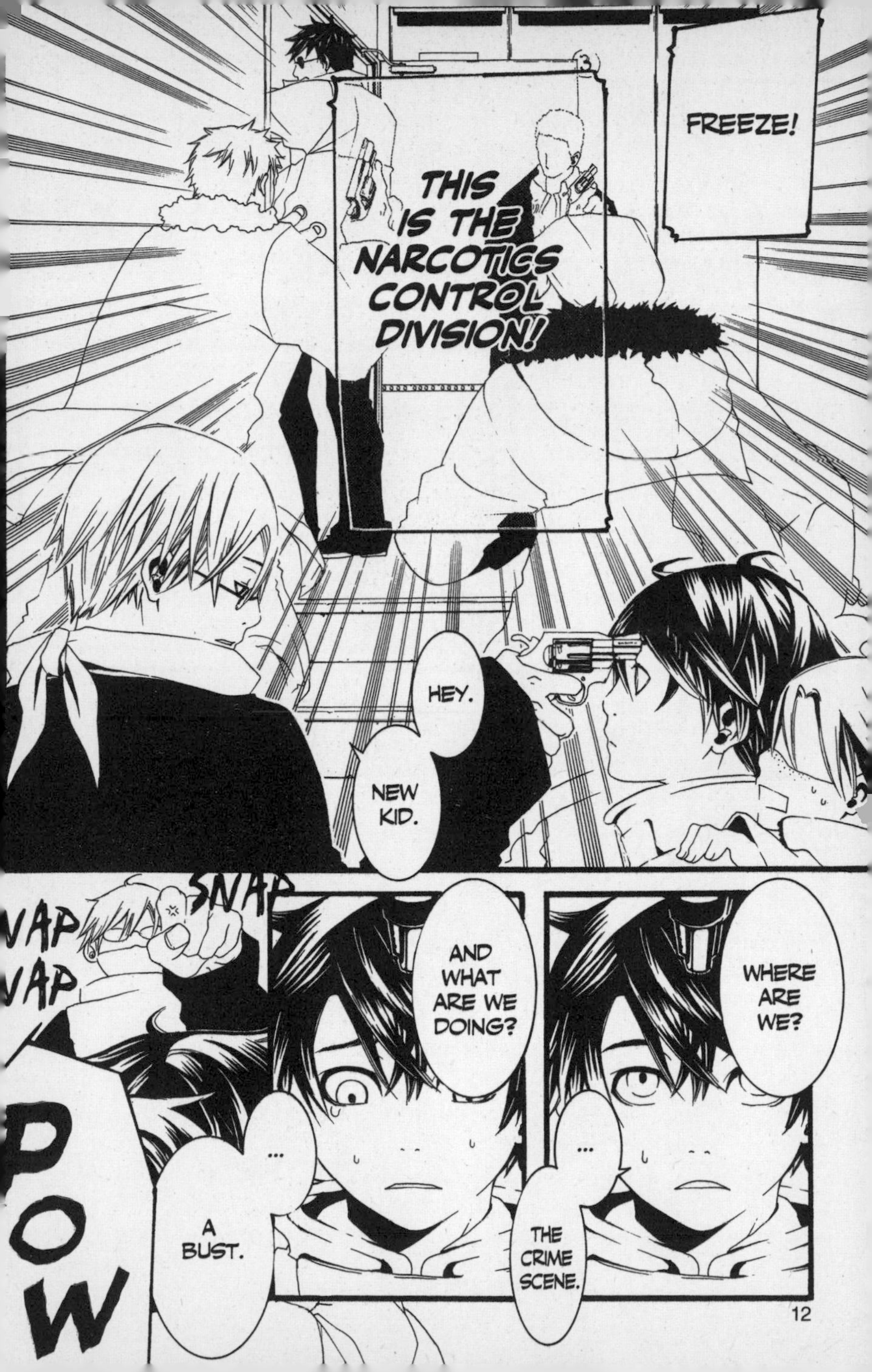
FREEZE!
THIS IS THE NARCOTICS CONTROL DIVISION!
HEY.
NEW KID.
WHERE ARE WE?
...
THE CRIME SCENE.
AND WHAT ARE WE DOING?
...
A BUST.
SNAP
POW

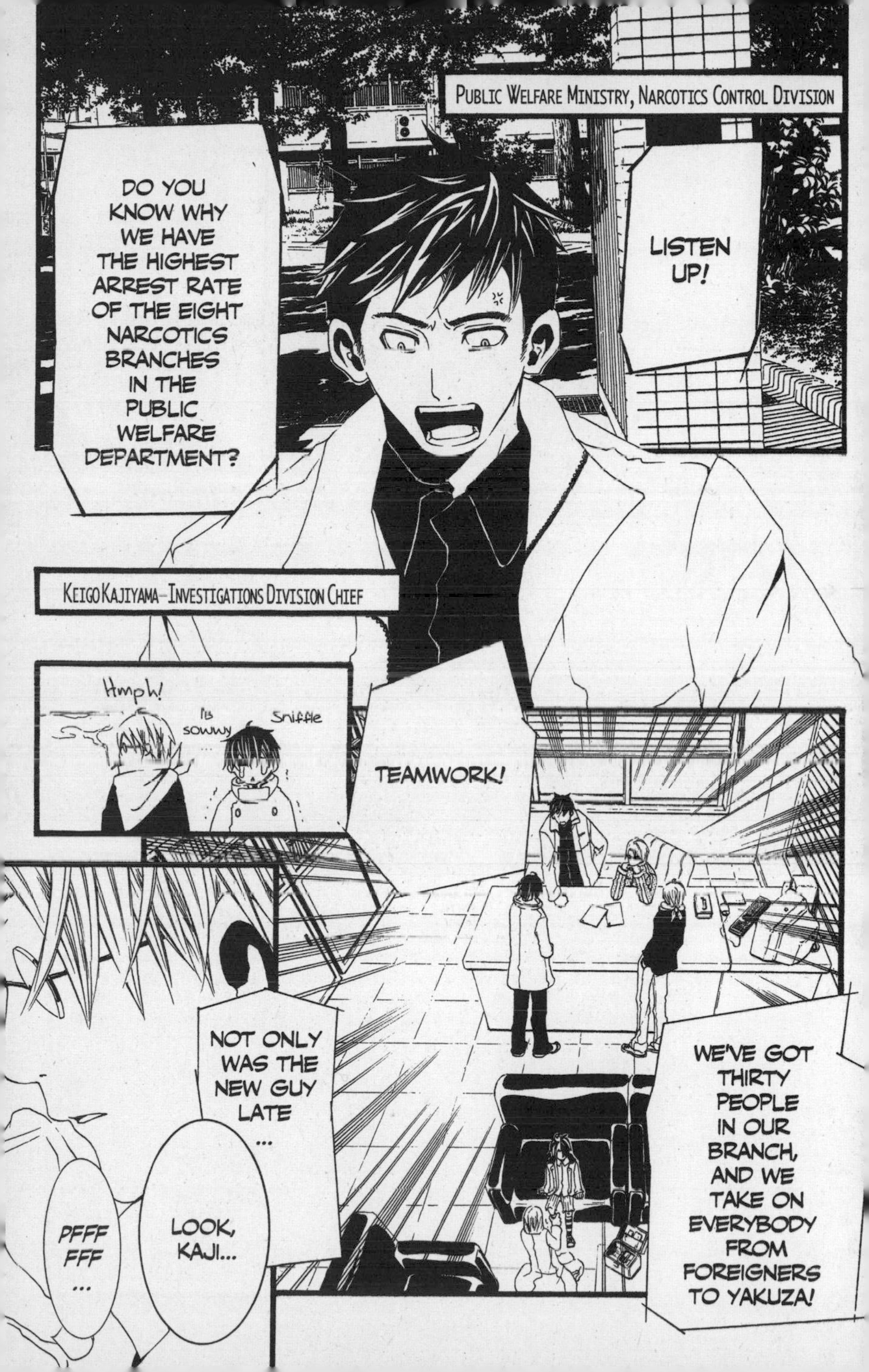
PUBLIC WELFARE MINISTRY, NARCOTICS CONTROL DIVISION
LISTEN UP!
DO YOU KNOW WHY WE HAVE THE HIGHEST ARREST RATE OF THE EIGHT NARCOTICS BRANCHES IN THE PUBLIC WELFARE DEPARTMENT?
KEIGO KAJIYAMA–INVESTIGATIONS DIVISION CHIEF
TEAMWORK!
WE'VE GOT THIRTY PEOPLE IN OUR BRANCH, AND WE TAKE ON EVERYBODY FROM FOREIGNERS TO YAKUZA!
Hmph!
I'S SOWWY ...
Sniffle
NOT ONLY WAS THE NEW GUY LATE ...
LOOK, KAJI...
PFFF FFF ...

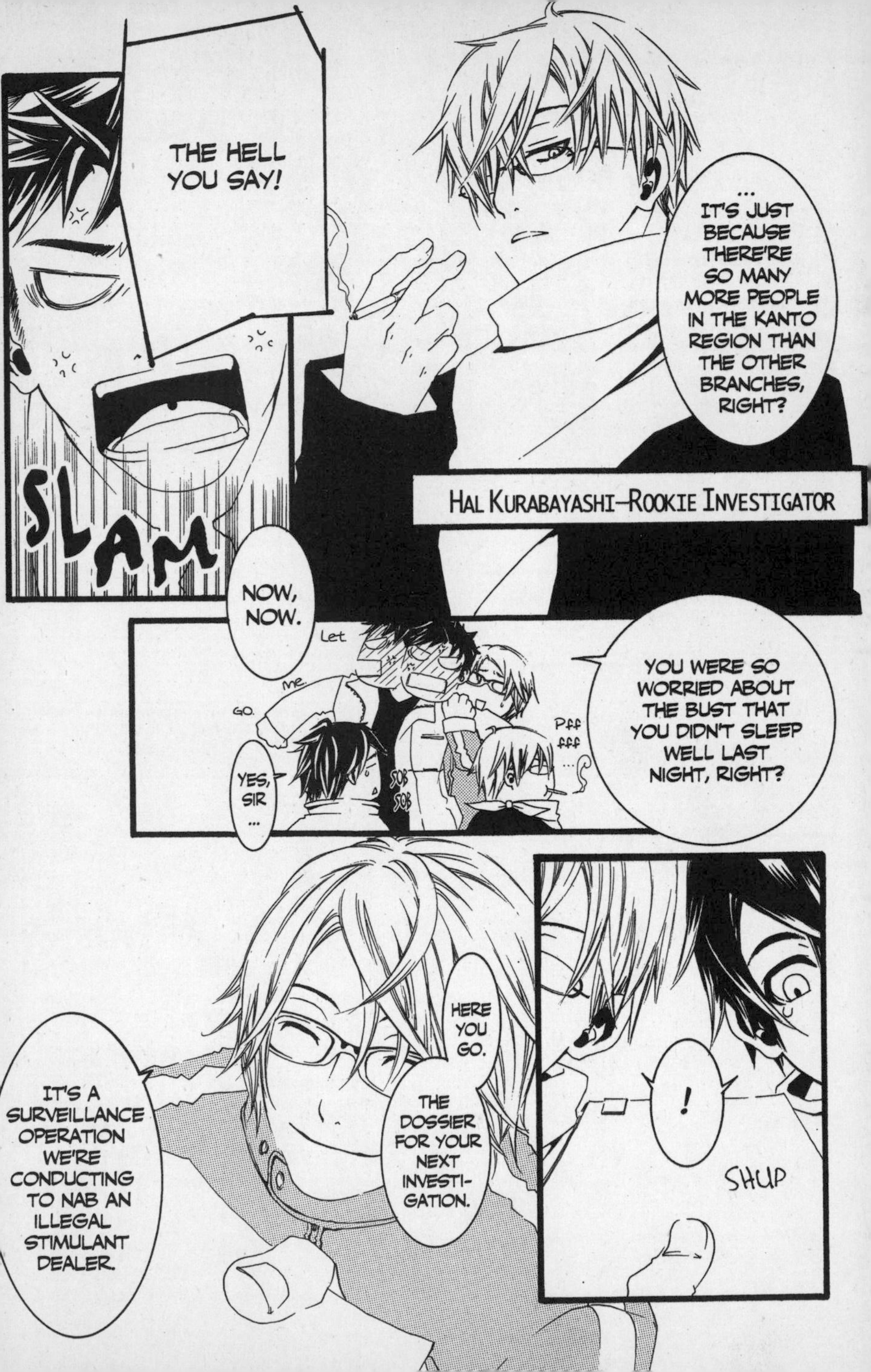
... IT'S JUST BECAUSE THERE'RE SO MANY MORE PEOPLE IN THE KANTO REGION THAN THE OTHER BRANCHES, RIGHT?
HAL KURABAYASHI—ROOKIE INVESTIGATOR
THE HELL YOU SAY!
SLAM
YOU WERE SO WORRIED ABOUT THE BUST THAT YOU DIDN'T SLEEP WELL LAST NIGHT, RIGHT?
Pff fff
...
NOW, NOW.
Let me. GO.
SOB SOB
YES, SIR ...
!
SHUP
HERE YOU GO.
THE DOSSIER FOR YOUR NEXT INVESTI-GATION.
IT'S A SURVEILLANCE OPERATION WE'RE CONDUCTING TO NAB AN ILLEGAL STIMULANT DEALER.

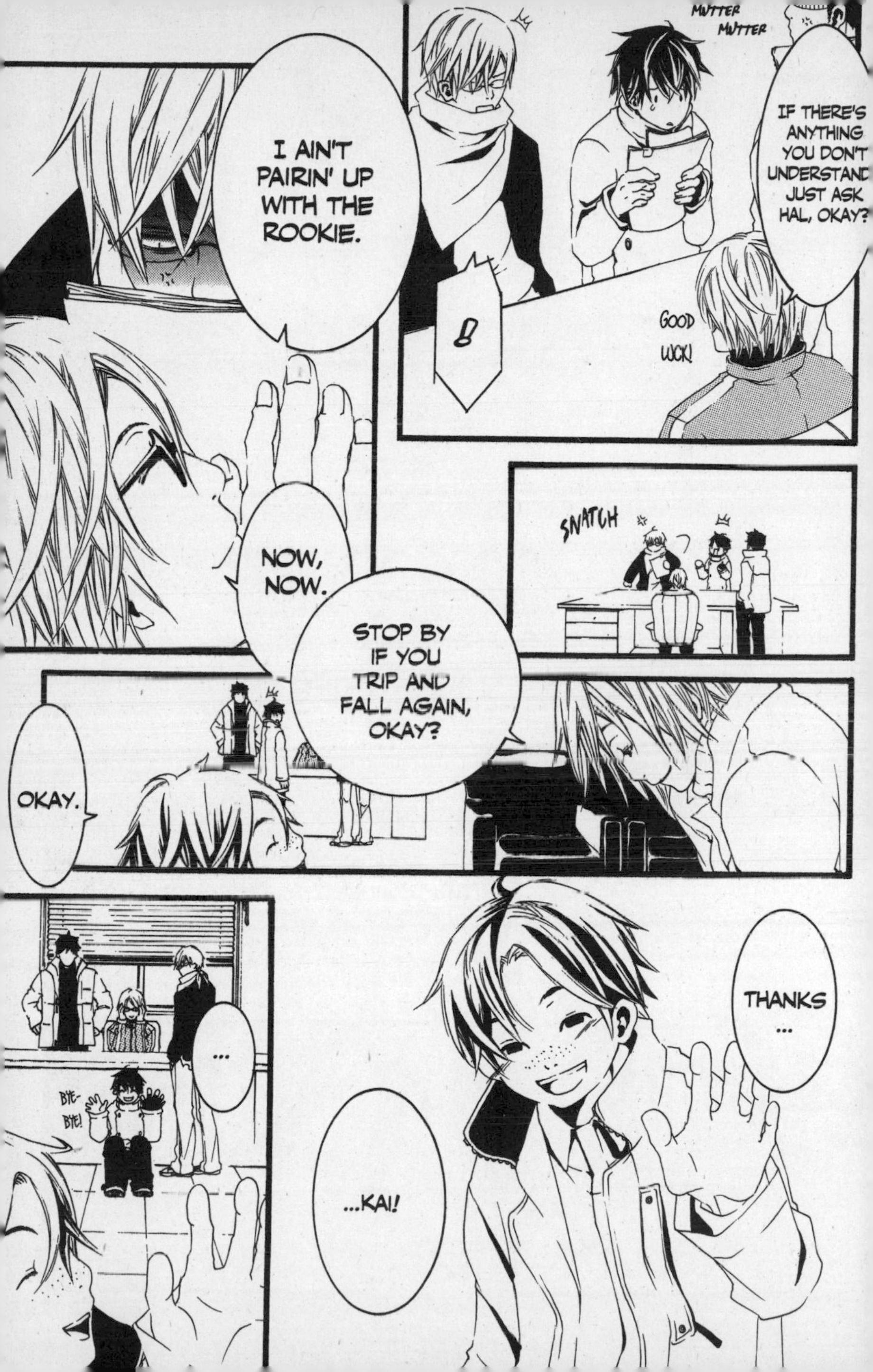
MUTTER
MUTTER
IF THERE'S ANYTHING YOU DON'T UNDERSTAND JUST ASK HAL, OKAY?
GOOD LUCK!
!
SNATCH
I AIN'T PAIRIN' UP WITH THE ROOKIE.
NOW, NOW.
STOP BY IF YOU TRIP AND FALL AGAIN, OKAY?
OKAY.
THANKS...
...KAI!
...
BYE-BYE!

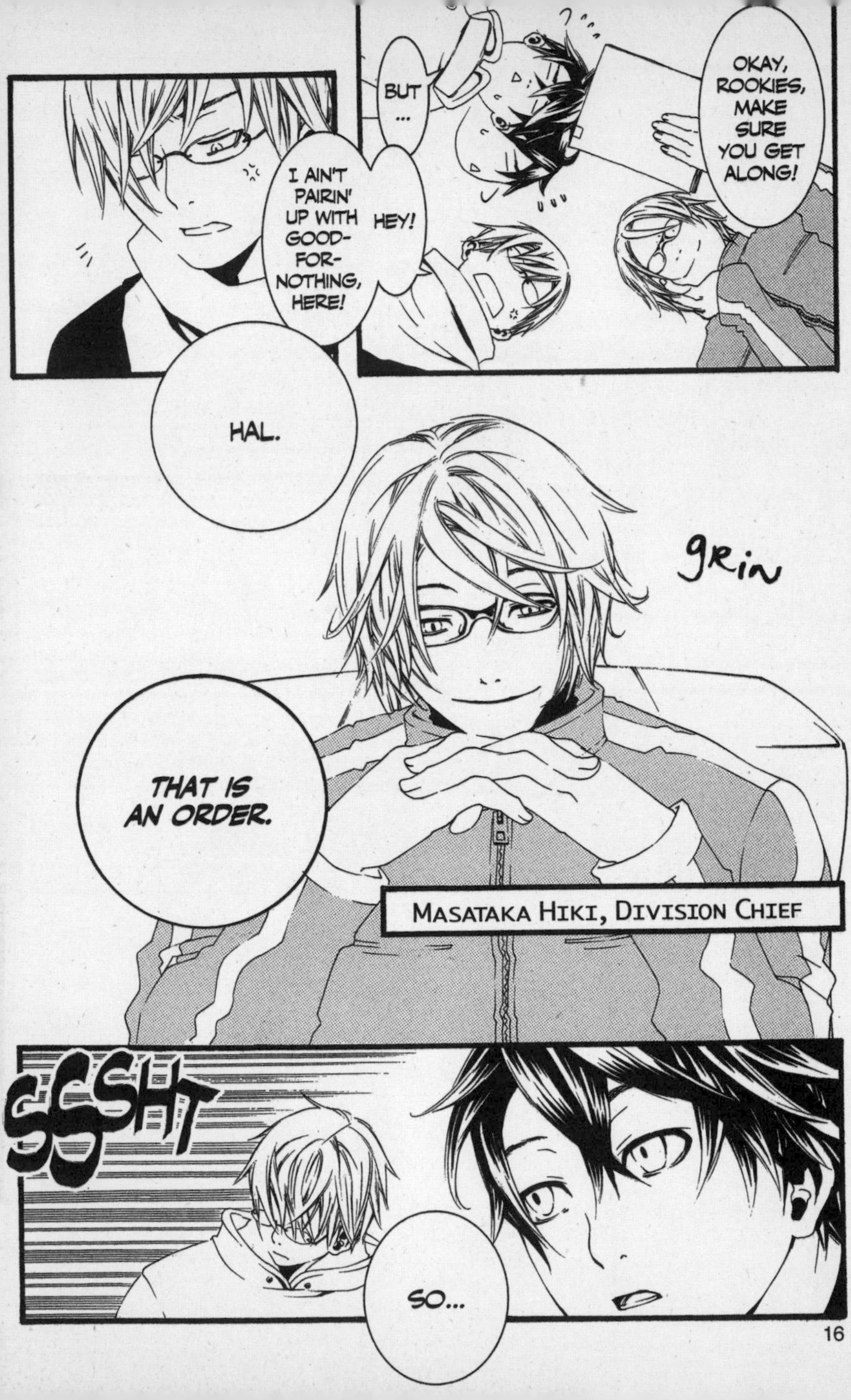
OKAY, ROOKIES, MAKE SURE YOU GET ALONG!
BUT ...
HEY!
I AIN'T PAIRIN' UP WITH GOOD-FOR-NOTHING, HERE!
HAL.
grin
THAT IS AN ORDER.
MASATAKA HIKI, DIVISION CHIEF
SSSHT
SO...

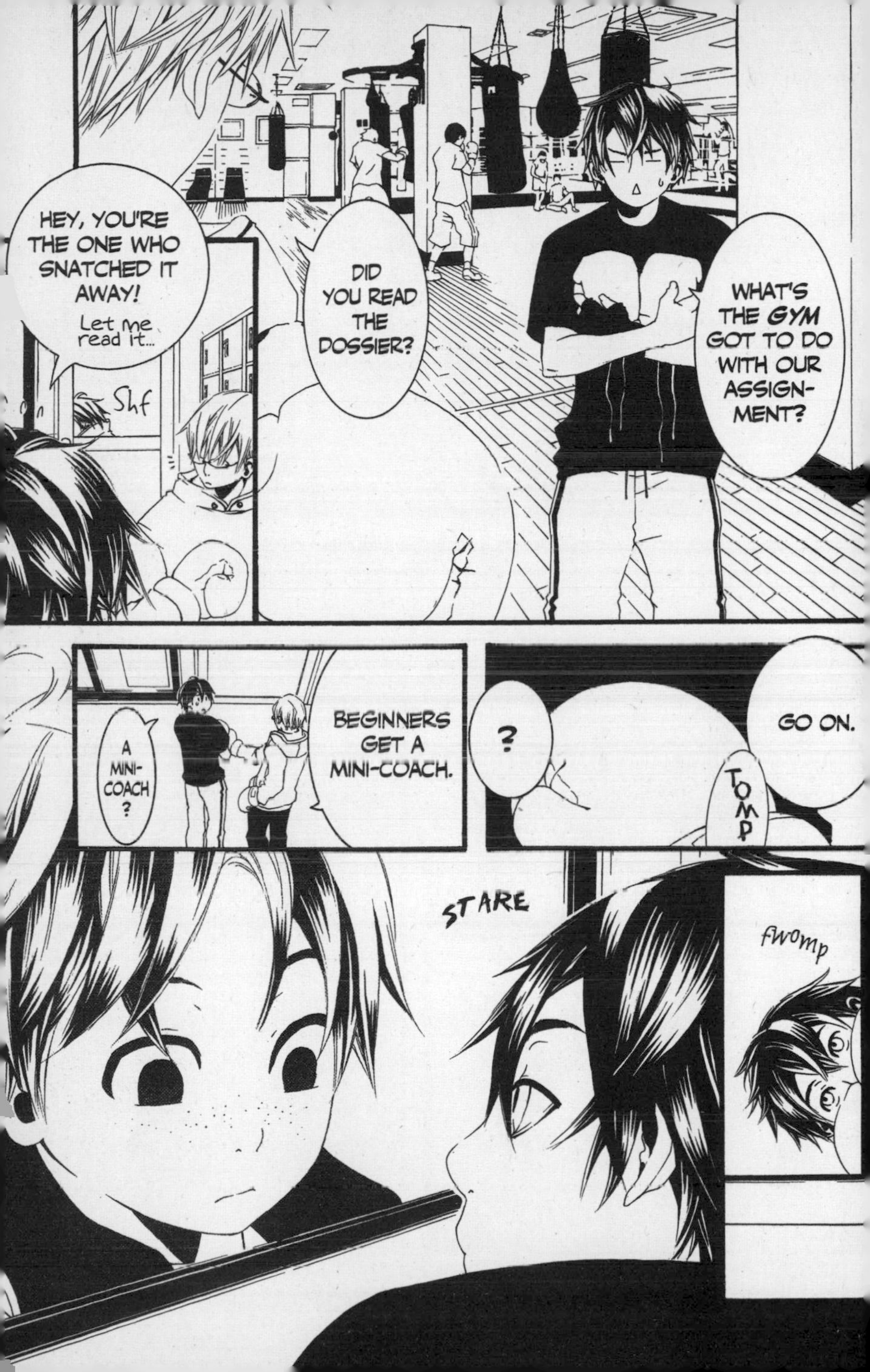
WHAT'S THE GYM GOT TO DO WITH OUR ASSIGNMENT?
DID YOU READ THE DOSSIER?
HEY, YOU'RE THE ONE WHO SNATCHED IT AWAY!
Let me read it...
Shf
GO ON.
TOMP
?
BEGINNERS GET A MINI-COACH.
A MINI-COACH?
fwomp
STARE

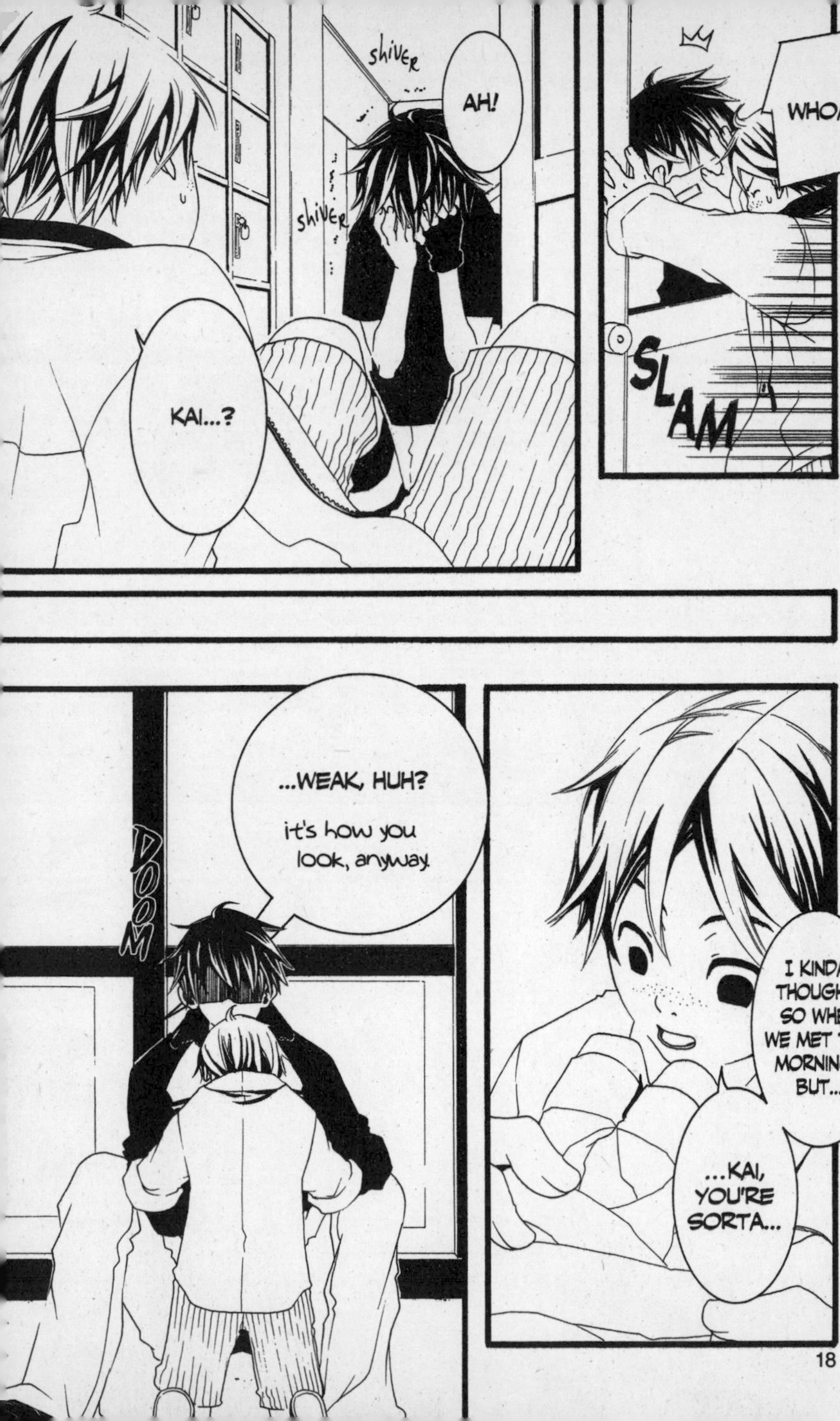
WHOA!
SLAM
AH!
shiver
shiver
KAI...?
I KINDA THOUGHT SO WHEN WE MET THIS MORNING, BUT...
...KAI, YOU'RE SORTA...
...WEAK, HUH?
it's how you look, anyway.
DOOM

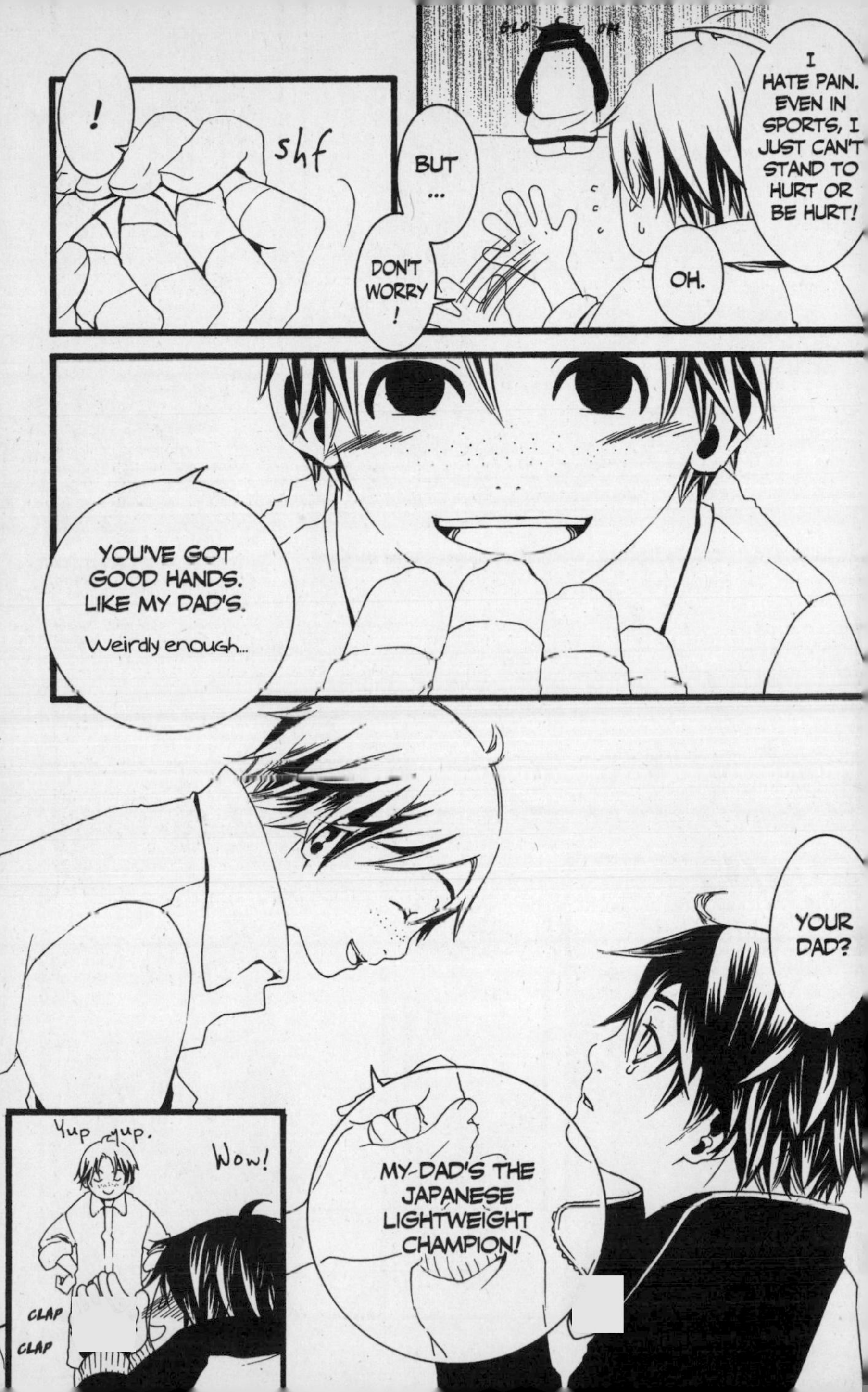
I HATE PAIN. EVEN IN SPORTS, I JUST CAN'T STAND TO HURT OR BE HURT!
GLO OM
OH.
BUT ...
DON'T WORRY!
!
shf
YOU'VE GOT GOOD HANDS. LIKE MY DAD'S.
Weirdly enough...
YOUR DAD?
MY DAD'S THE JAPANESE LIGHTWEIGHT CHAMPION!
Yup yup.
Wow!
CLAP
CLAP

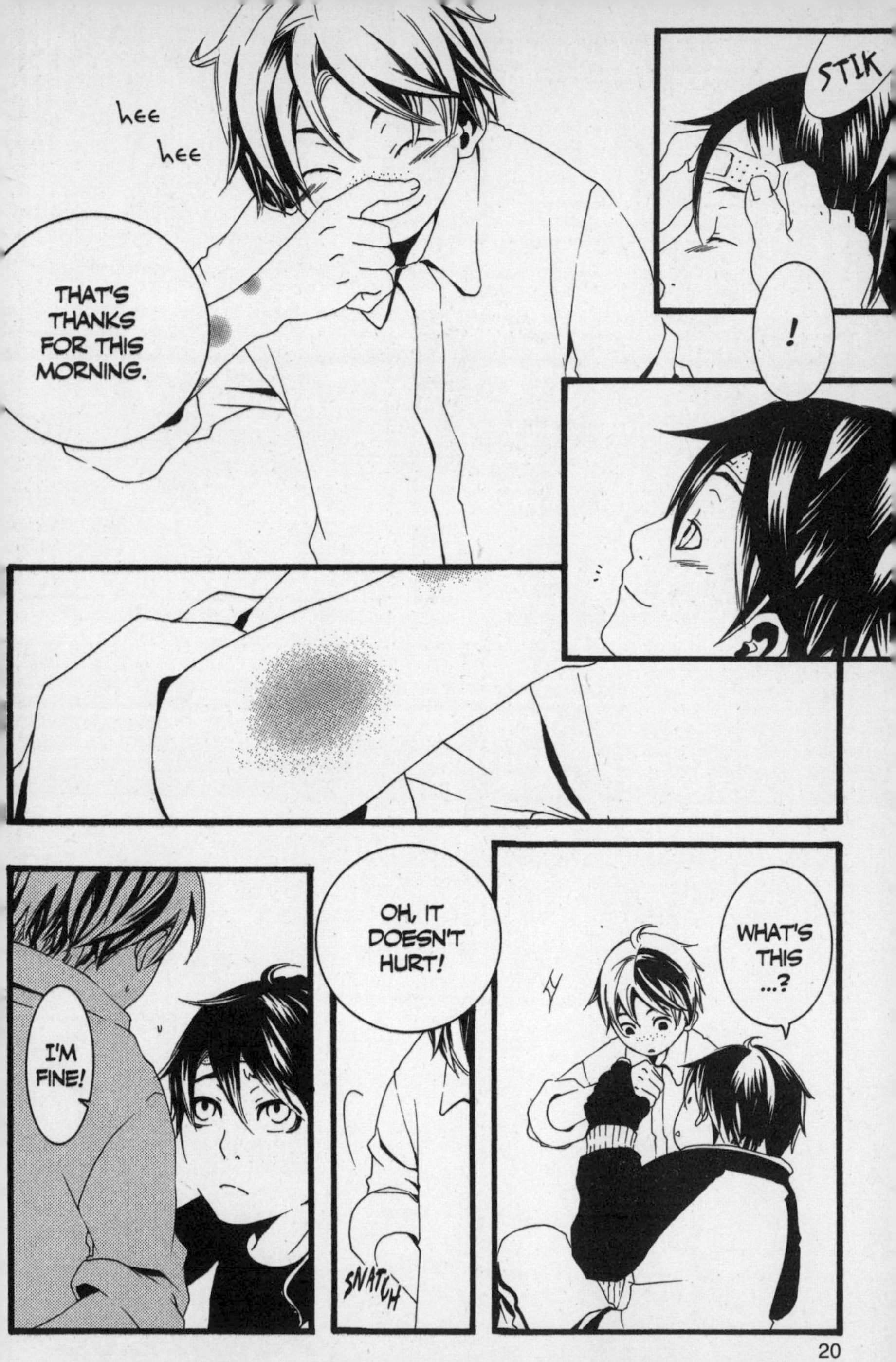
STIK
!
hee
hee
THAT'S THANKS FOR THIS MORNING.
WHAT'S THIS ...?
OH, IT DOESN'T HURT!
SNATCH
I'M FINE!

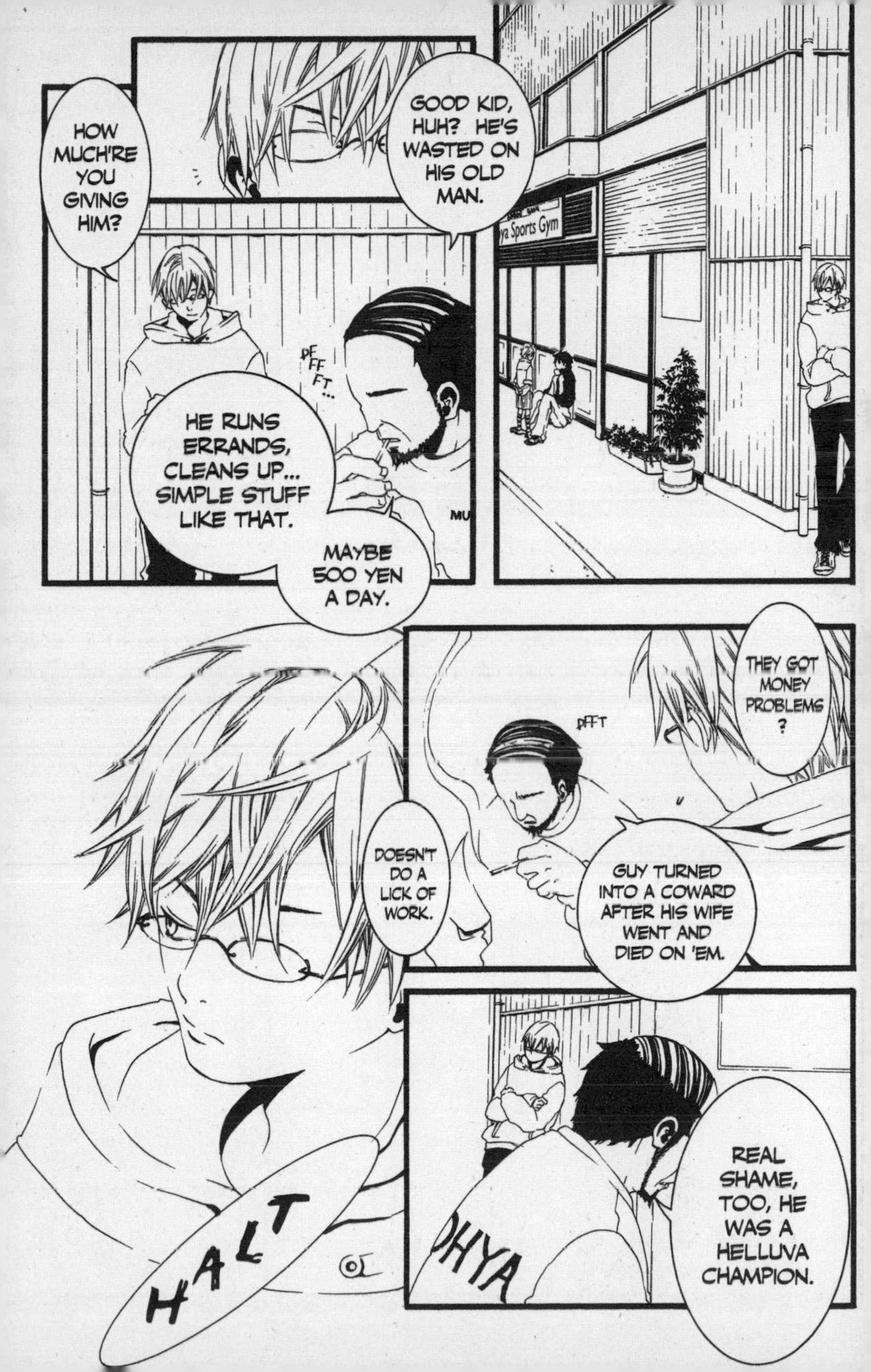
GOOD KID, HUH? HE'S WASTED ON HIS OLD MAN.
HOW MUCH'RE YOU GIVING HIM?
PFFFFT...
HE RUNS ERRANDS, CLEANS UP... SIMPLE STUFF LIKE THAT.
MAYBE 500 YEN A DAY.
THEY GOT MONEY PROBLEMS?
DFFT
GUY TURNED INTO A COWARD AFTER HIS WIFE WENT AND DIED ON 'EM.
DOESN'T DO A LICK OF WORK.
REAL SHAME, TOO, HE WAS A HELLUVA CHAMPION.
HALT

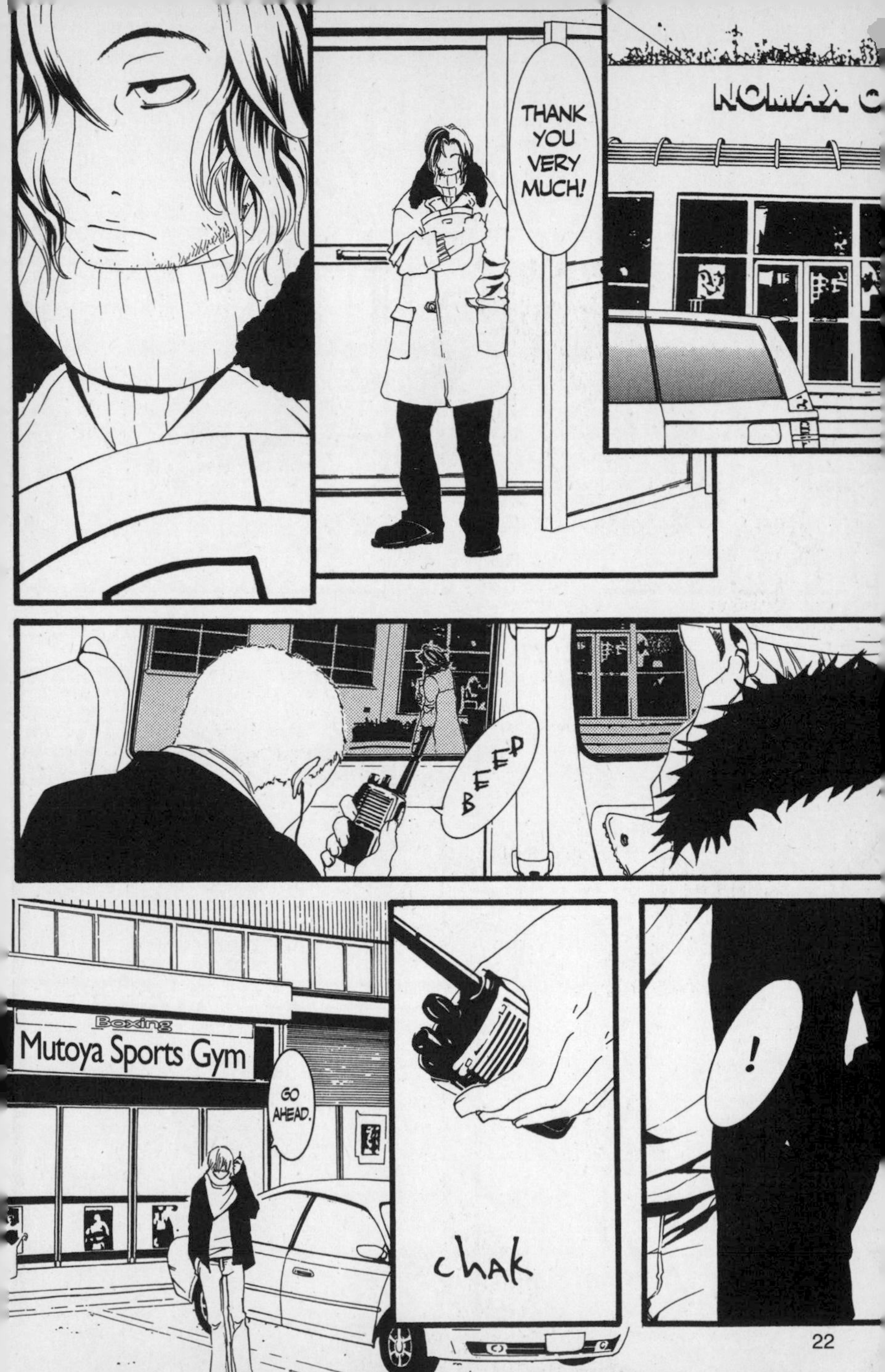
NOMAX
THANK YOU VERY MUCH!
BEEP
!
chak
Boxing
Mutoya Sports Gym
GO AHEAD.

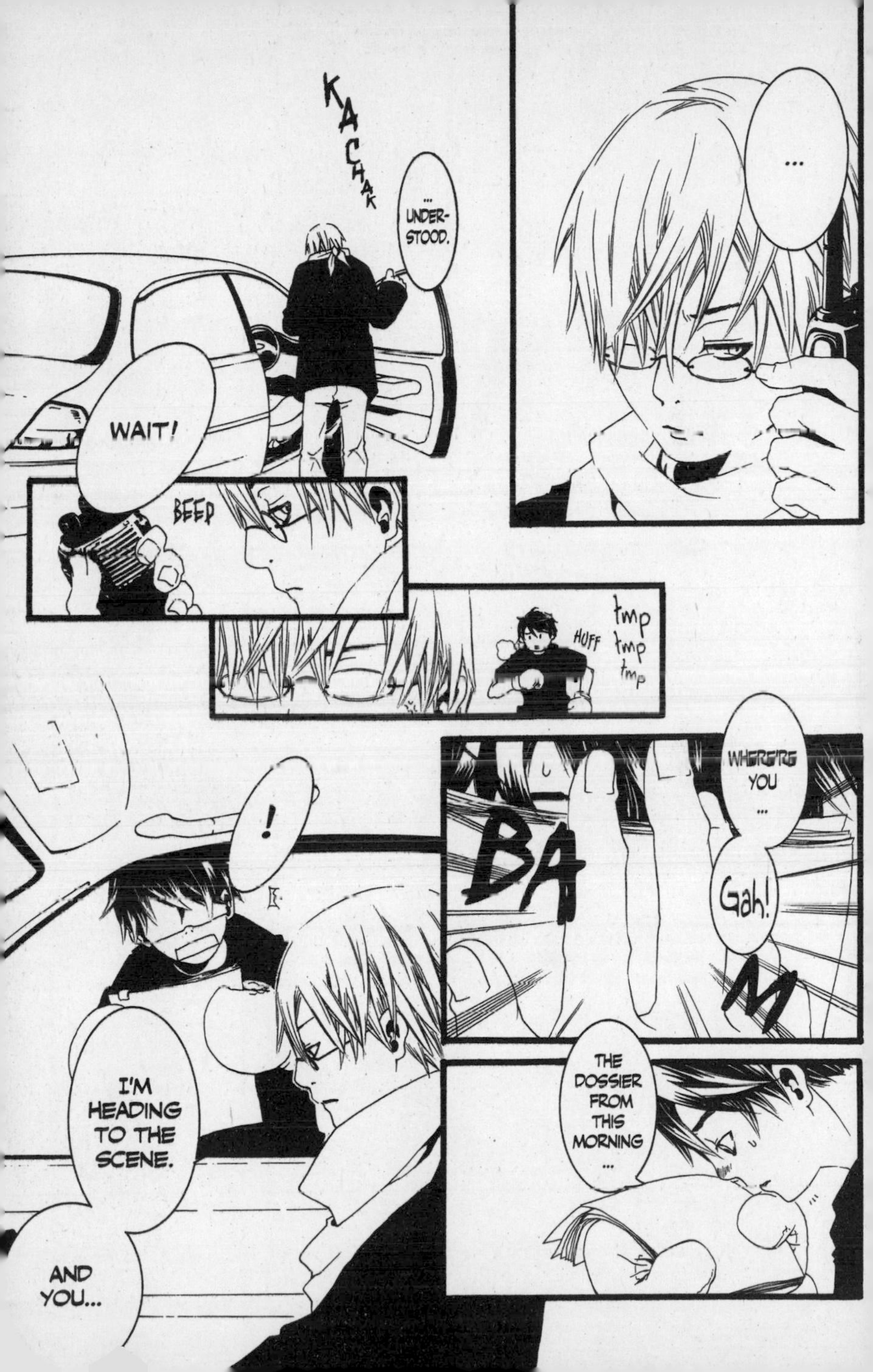
...
KACHAK
... UNDER-STOOD.
WAIT!
BEEP
tmp tmp tmp
HUFF
BAM
WHERE'RE YOU ...
Gah!
THE DOSSIER FROM THIS MORNING ...
!
I'M HEADING TO THE SCENE.
AND YOU...

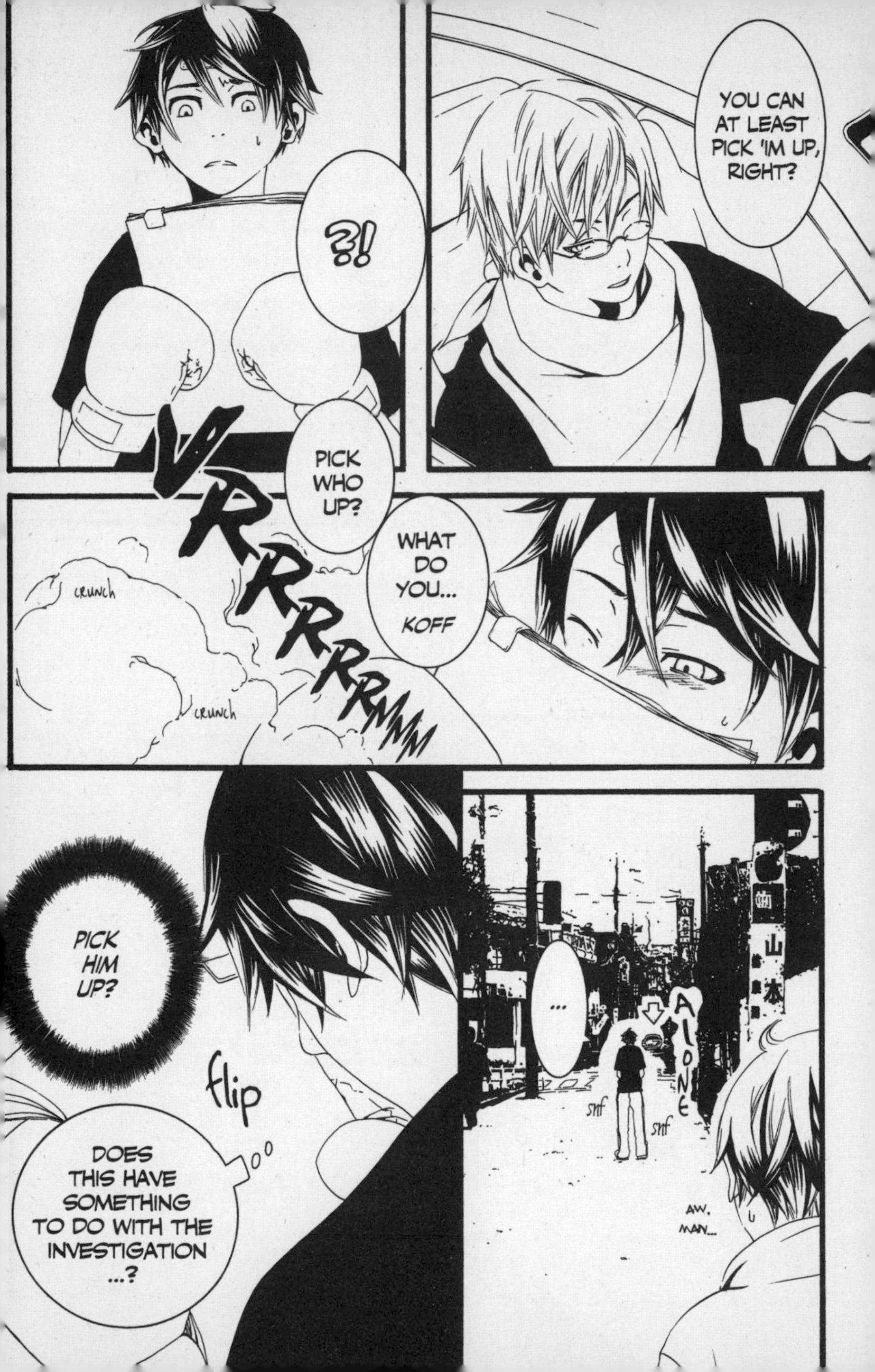
YOU CAN AT LEAST PICK 'IM UP, RIGHT?
?!
PICK WHO UP?
WHAT DO YOU... KOFF
VRRRRRRMMM
crunch
crunch
...
ALONE
snf
snf
AW, MAN...
PICK HIM UP?
flip
DOES THIS HAVE SOMETHING TO DO WITH THE INVESTIGATION ...?

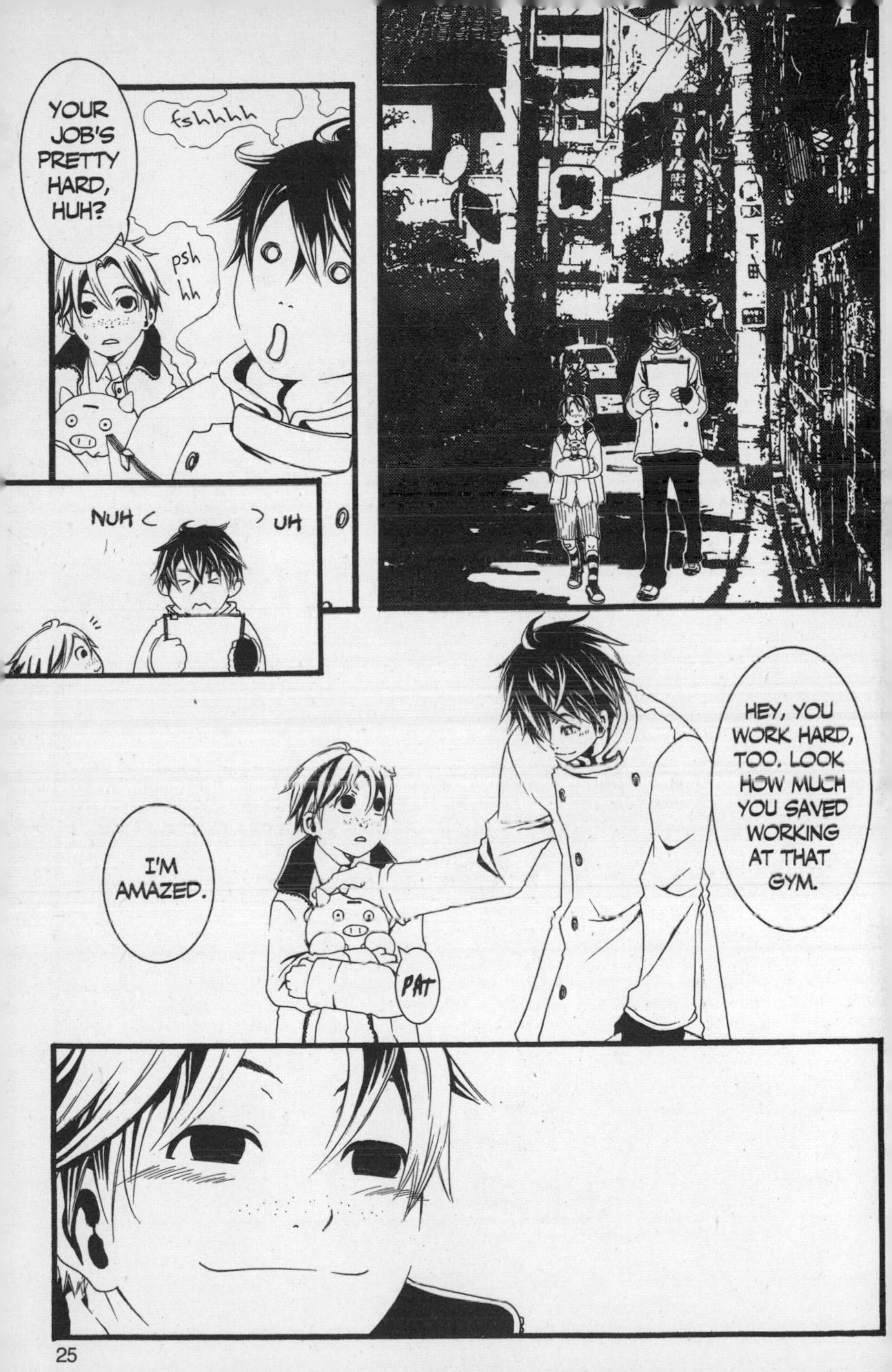
YOUR JOB'S PRETTY HARD, HUH?
fshhhh
psh hh
NUH UH
HEY, YOU WORK HARD, TOO. LOOK HOW MUCH YOU SAVED WORKING AT THAT GYM.
I'M AMAZED.
PAT

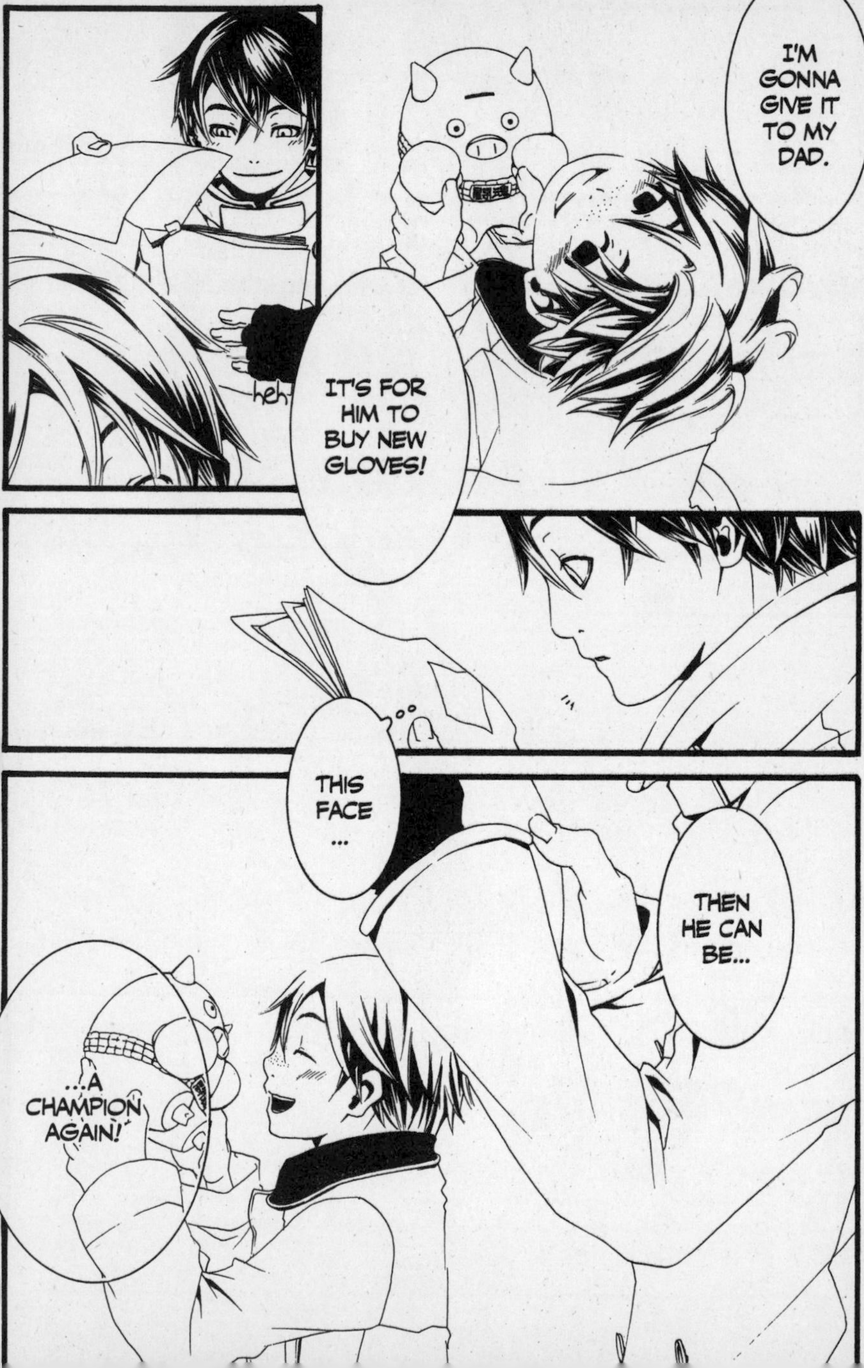
I'M GONNA GIVE IT TO MY DAD.
IT'S FOR HIM TO BUY NEW GLOVES!
heh
THIS FACE ...
THEN HE CAN BE...
...A CHAMPION AGAIN!

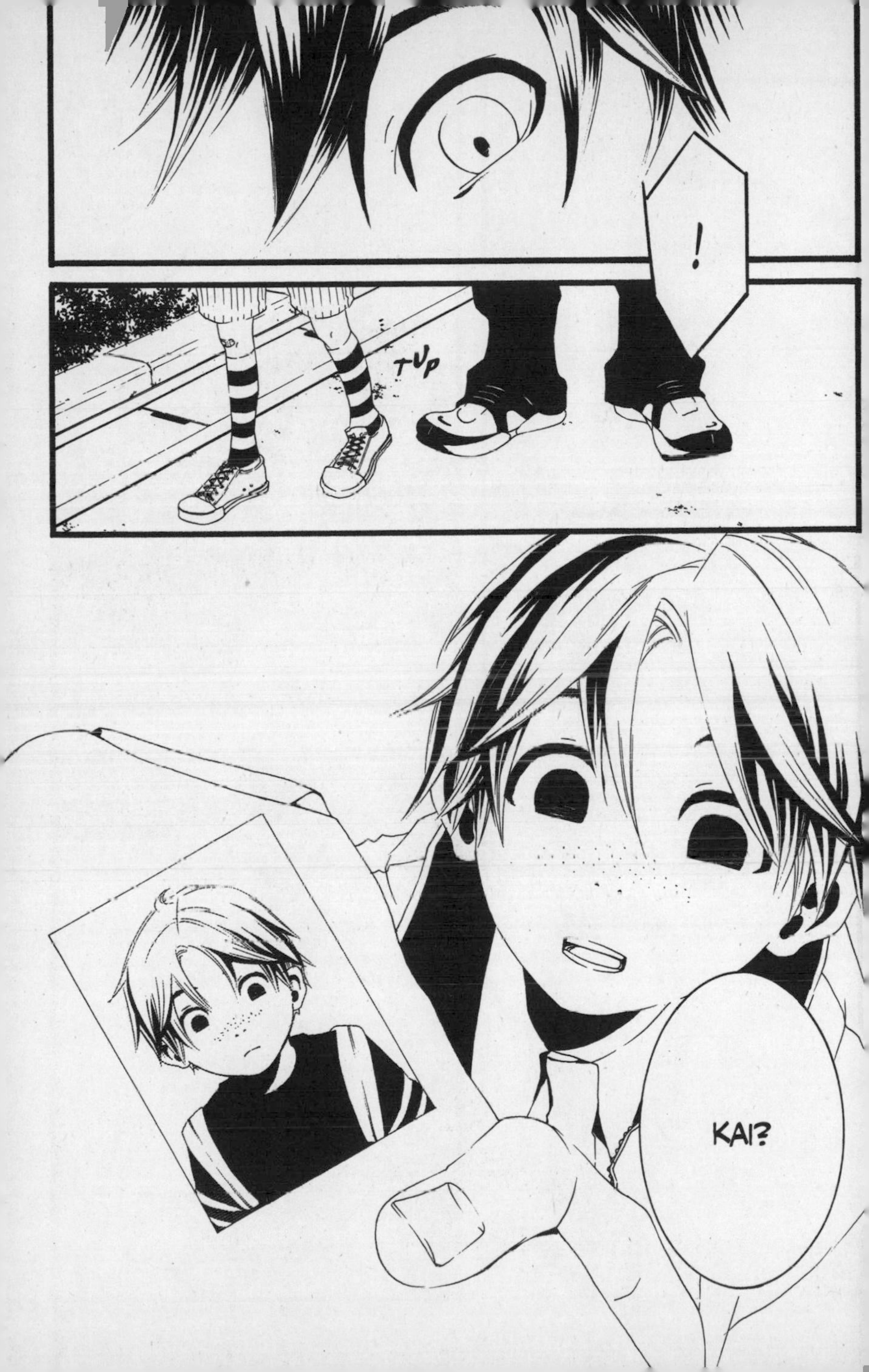
!
T-UP
KAI?

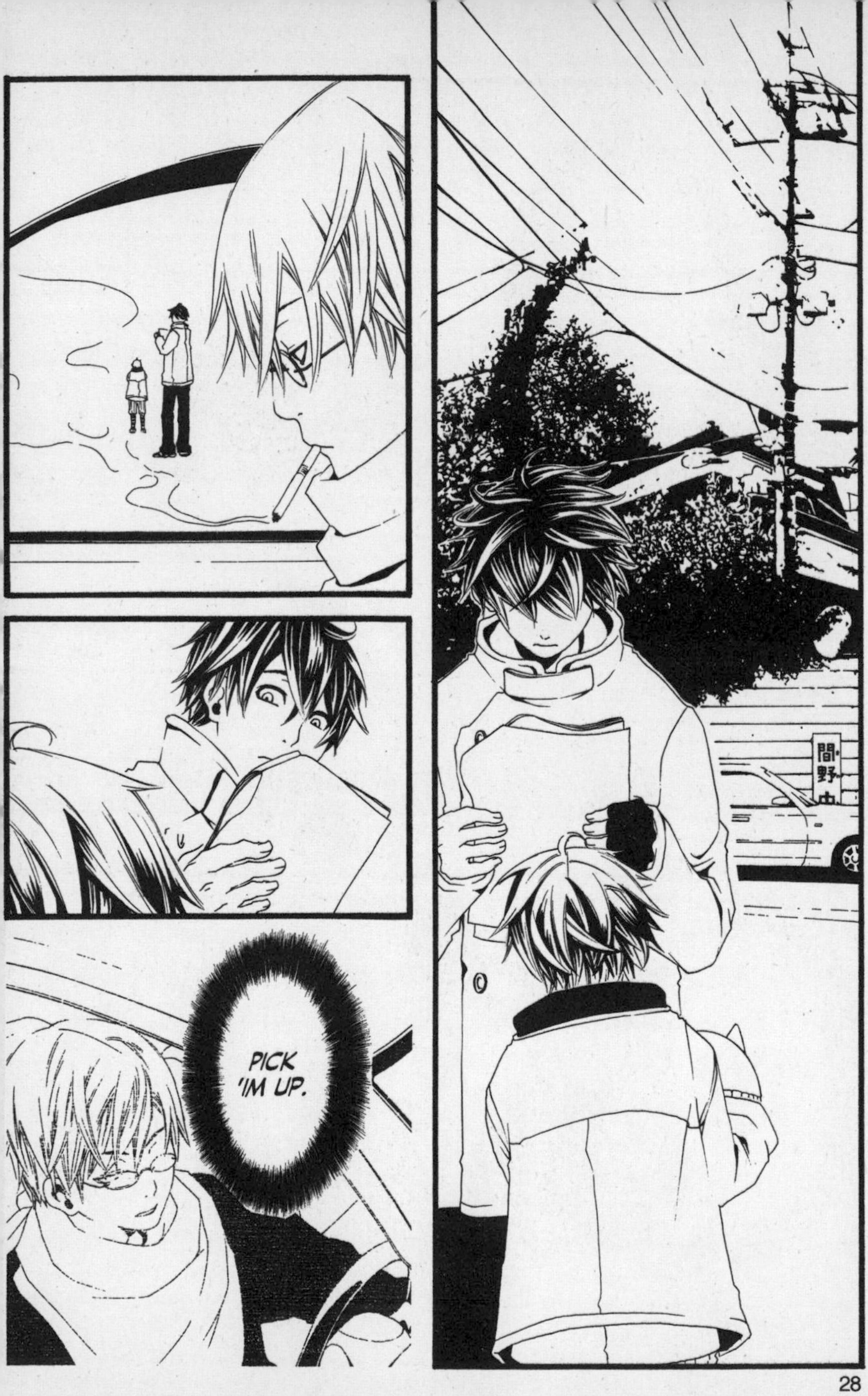
間野
PICK 'IM UP.

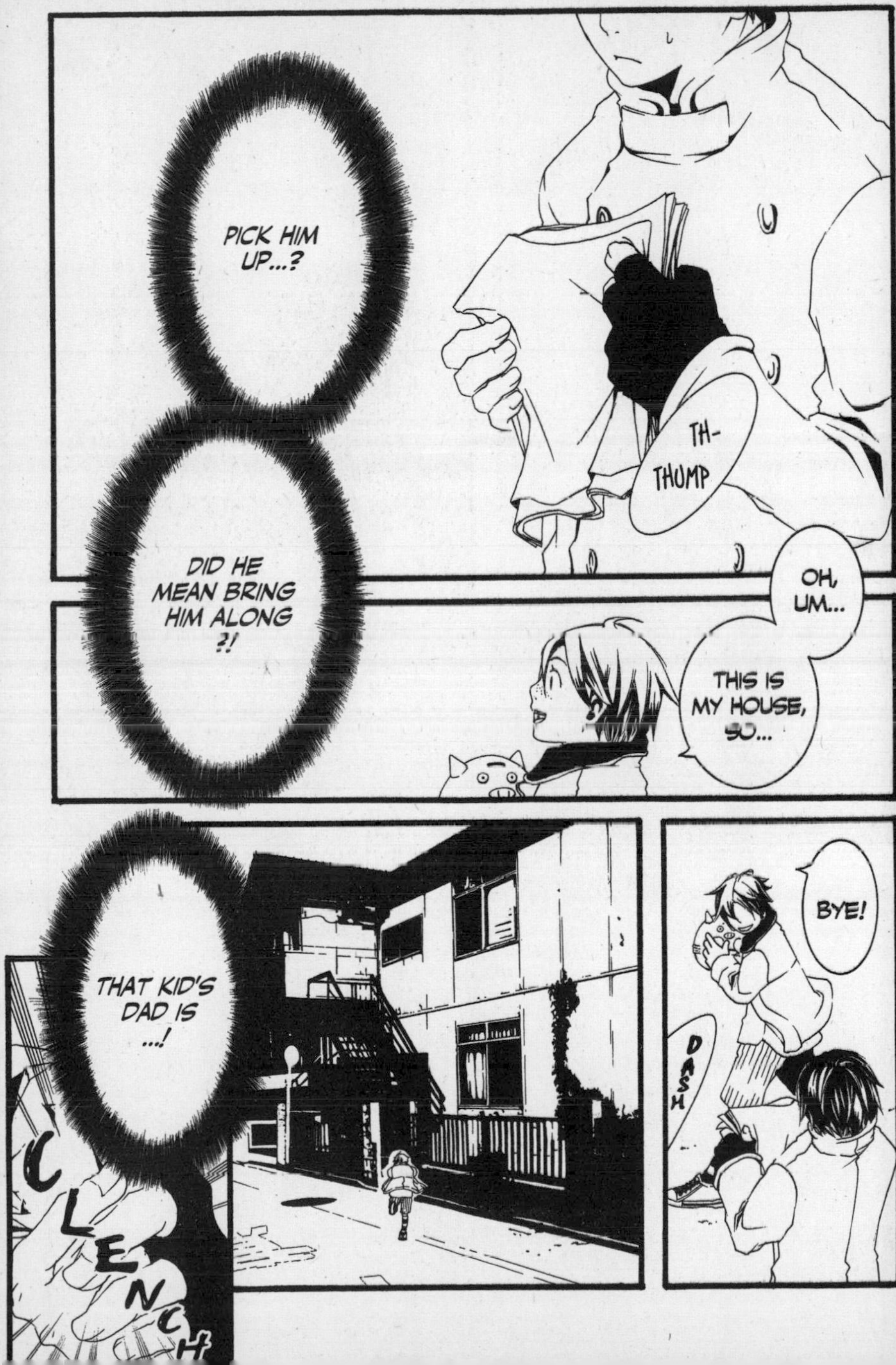
PICK HIM UP...?
TH-THUMP
OH, UM...
THIS IS MY HOUSE, SO...
DID HE MEAN BRING HIM ALONG ?!
BYE!
DASH
THAT KID'S DAD IS ...!
CLENCH

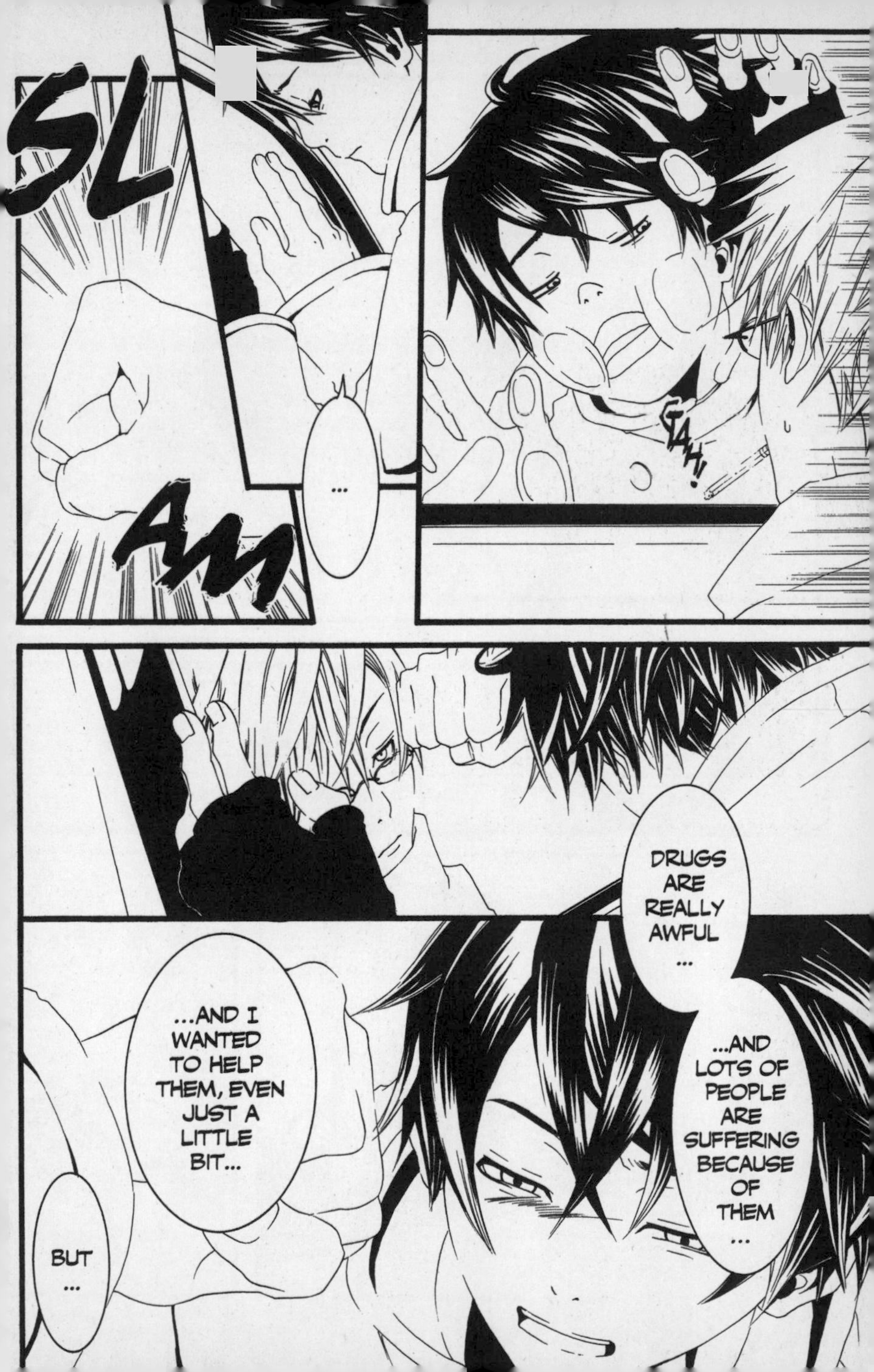
GAH!
SL
AM
...
DRUGS ARE REALLY AWFUL...
...AND LOTS OF PEOPLE ARE SUFFERING BECAUSE OF THEM...
...AND I WANTED TO HELP THEM, EVEN JUST A LITTLE BIT...
BUT...

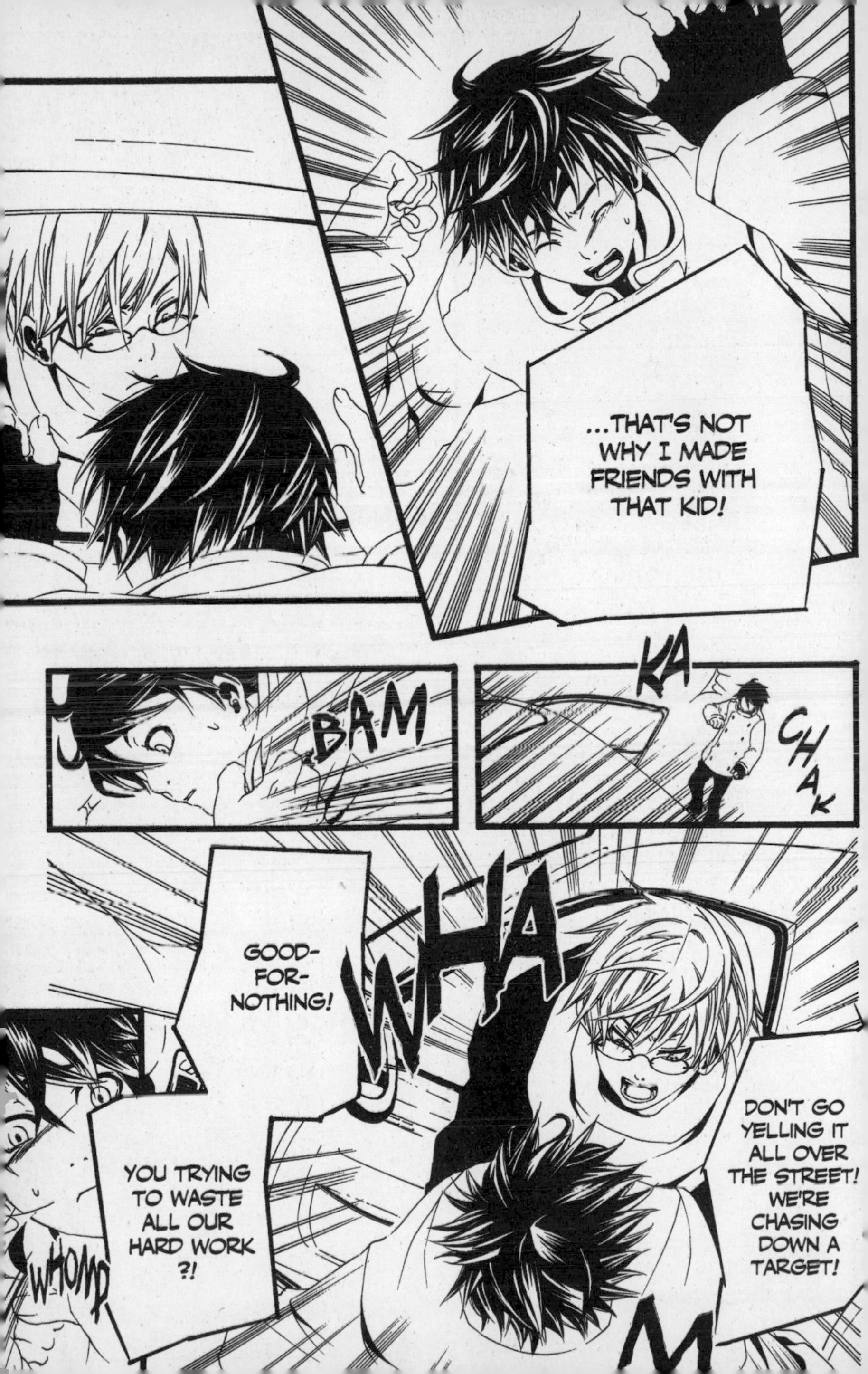
...THAT'S NOT WHY I MADE FRIENDS WITH THAT KID!
KA CHAK
BAM
WHAM
DON'T GO YELLING IT ALL OVER THE STREET! WE'RE CHASING DOWN A TARGET!
GOOD-FOR-NOTHING!
YOU TRYING TO WASTE ALL OUR HARD WORK ?!
WHOMP

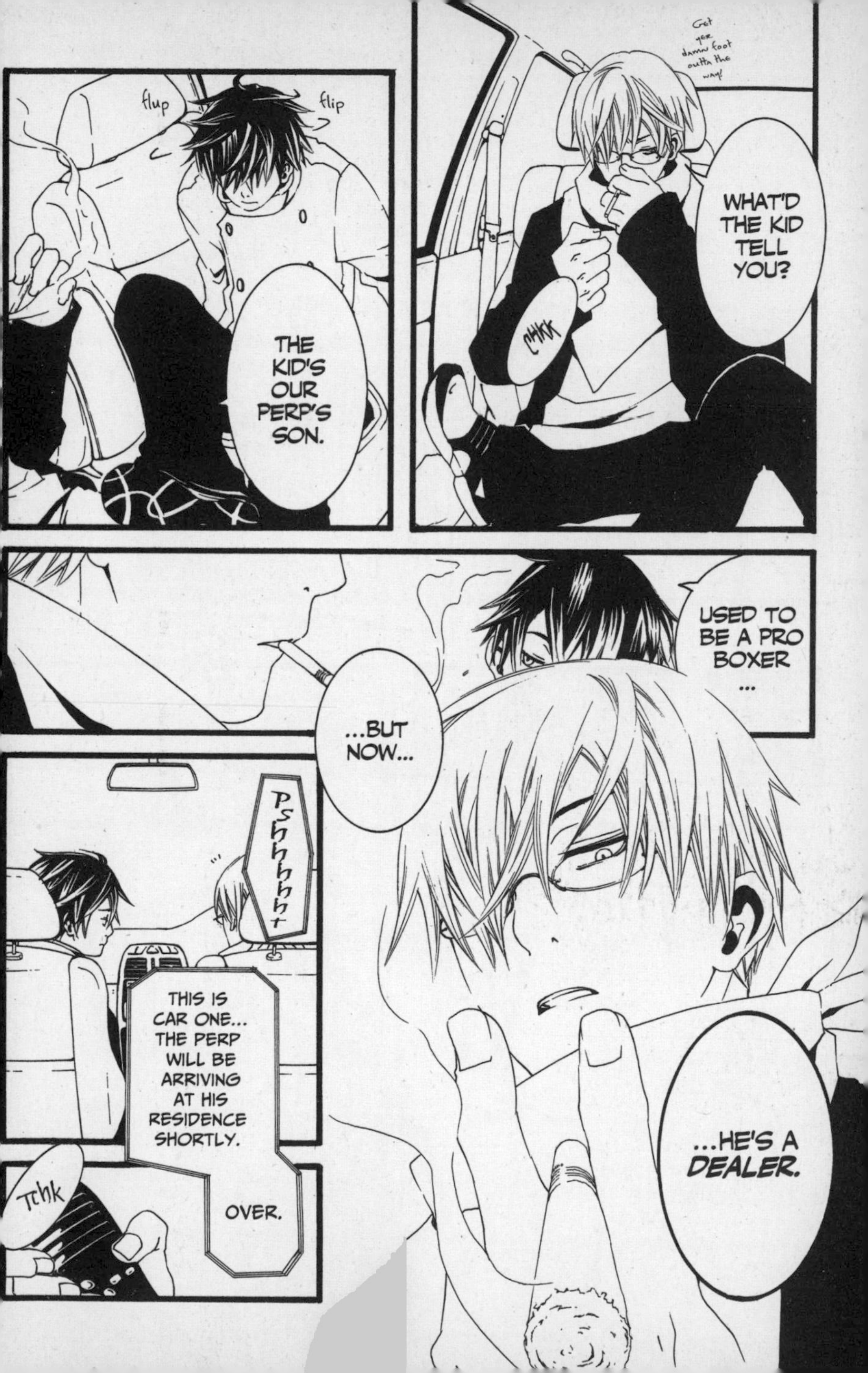
Get yer damn foot outta the way!
WHAT'D THE KID TELL YOU?
CHKK
flup
flip
THE KID'S OUR PERP'S SON.
USED TO BE A PRO BOXER ...
...BUT NOW...
...HE'S A DEALER.
Pshhhhhht
THIS IS CAR ONE... THE PERP WILL BE ARRIVING AT HIS RESIDENCE SHORTLY.
OVER.
Tchk

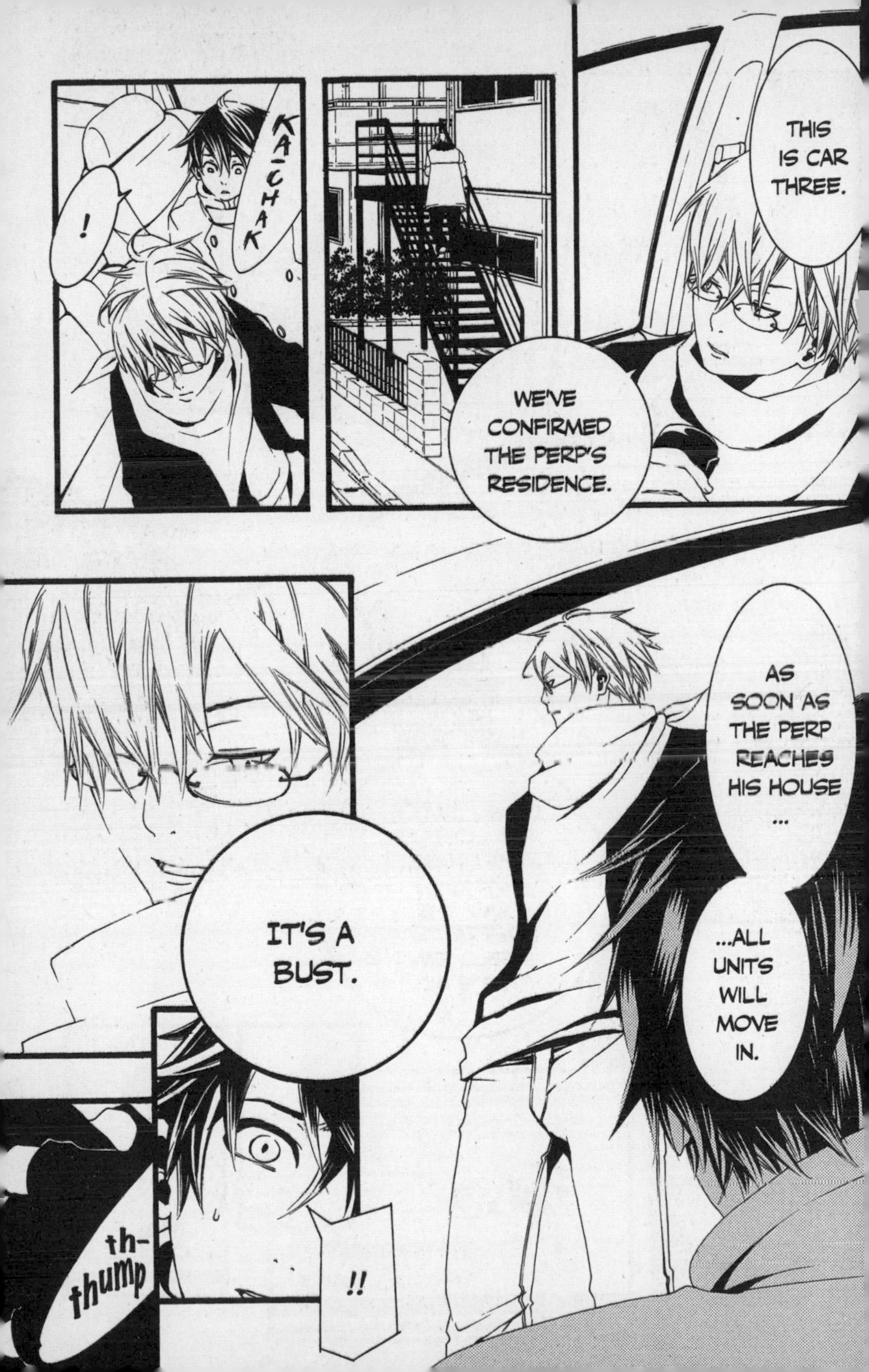
THIS IS CAR THREE.
WE'VE CONFIRMED THE PERP'S RESIDENCE.
KA-CHAK
!
AS SOON AS THE PERP REACHES HIS HOUSE ...
...ALL UNITS WILL MOVE IN.
IT'S A BUST.
!!
th-thump

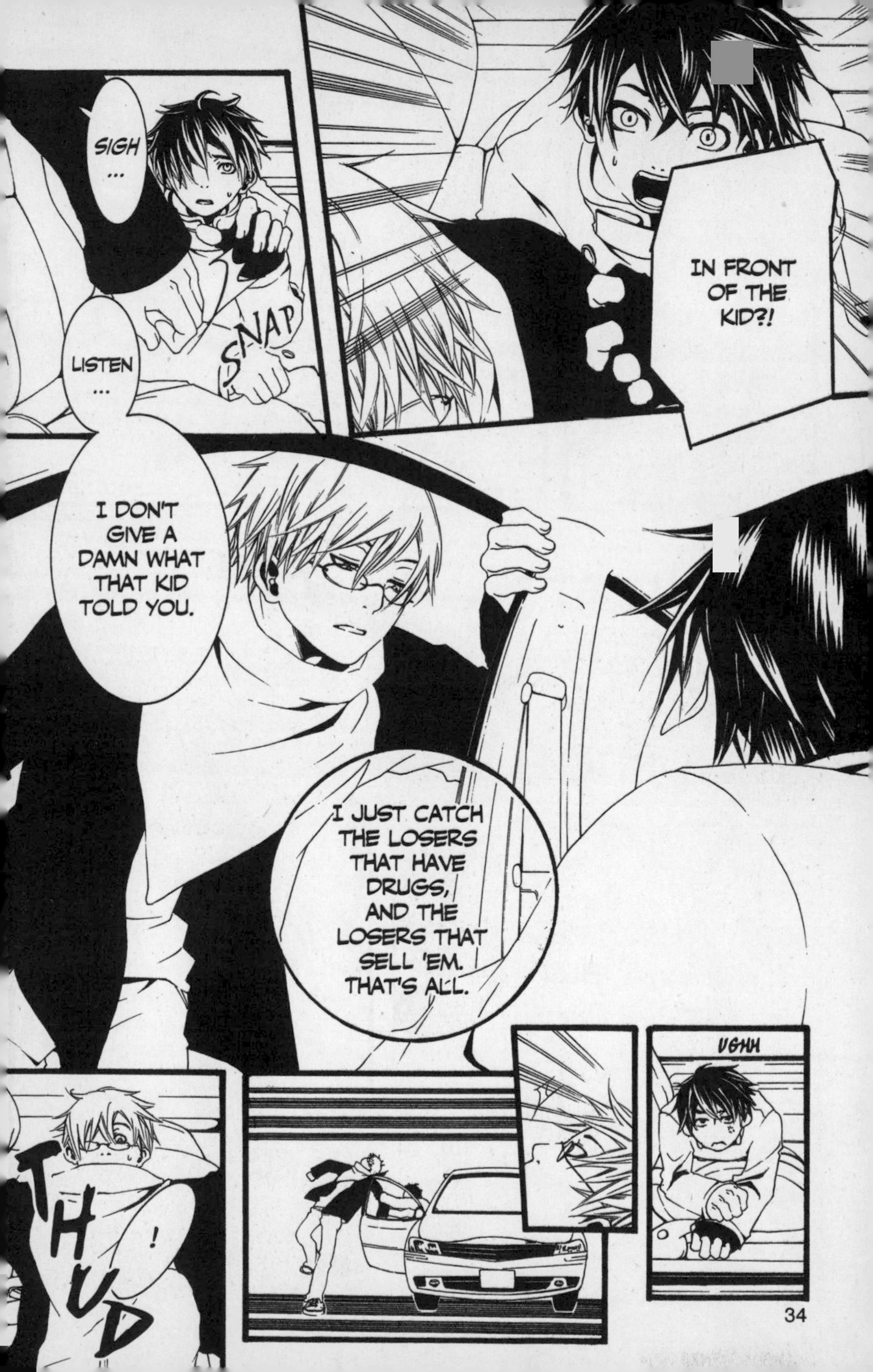
IN FRONT OF THE KID?!
SIGH...
SNAP
LISTEN...
I DON'T GIVE A DAMN WHAT THAT KID TOLD YOU.
I JUST CATCH THE LOSERS THAT HAVE DRUGS, AND THE LOSERS THAT SELL 'EM. THAT'S ALL.
UGHH
THUD
!

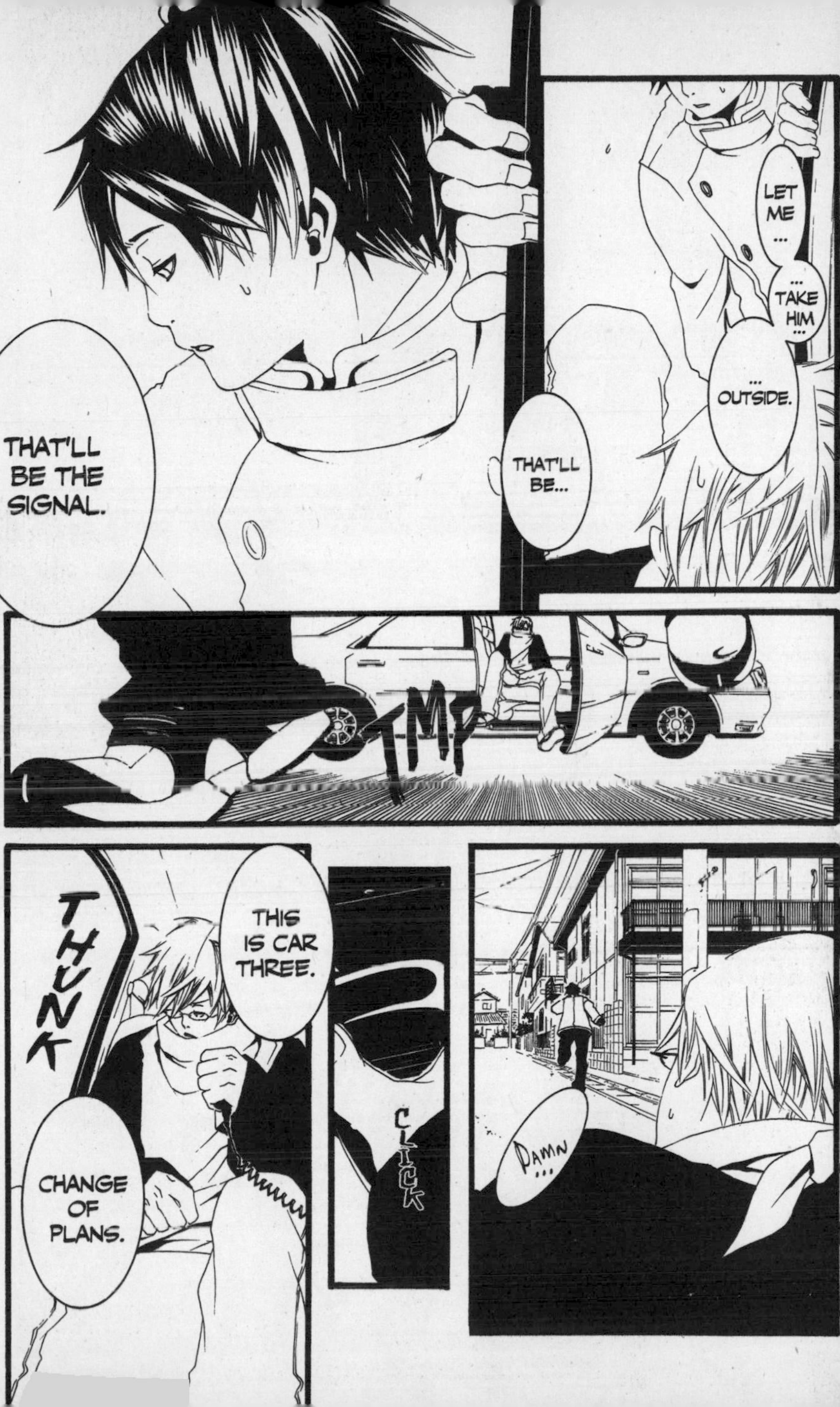
LET ME ...
... TAKE HIM ...
... OUTSIDE.
THAT'LL BE...
THAT'LL BE THE SIGNAL.
TMP
DAMN ...
CLICK
THIS IS CAR THREE.
THUNK
CHANGE OF PLANS.

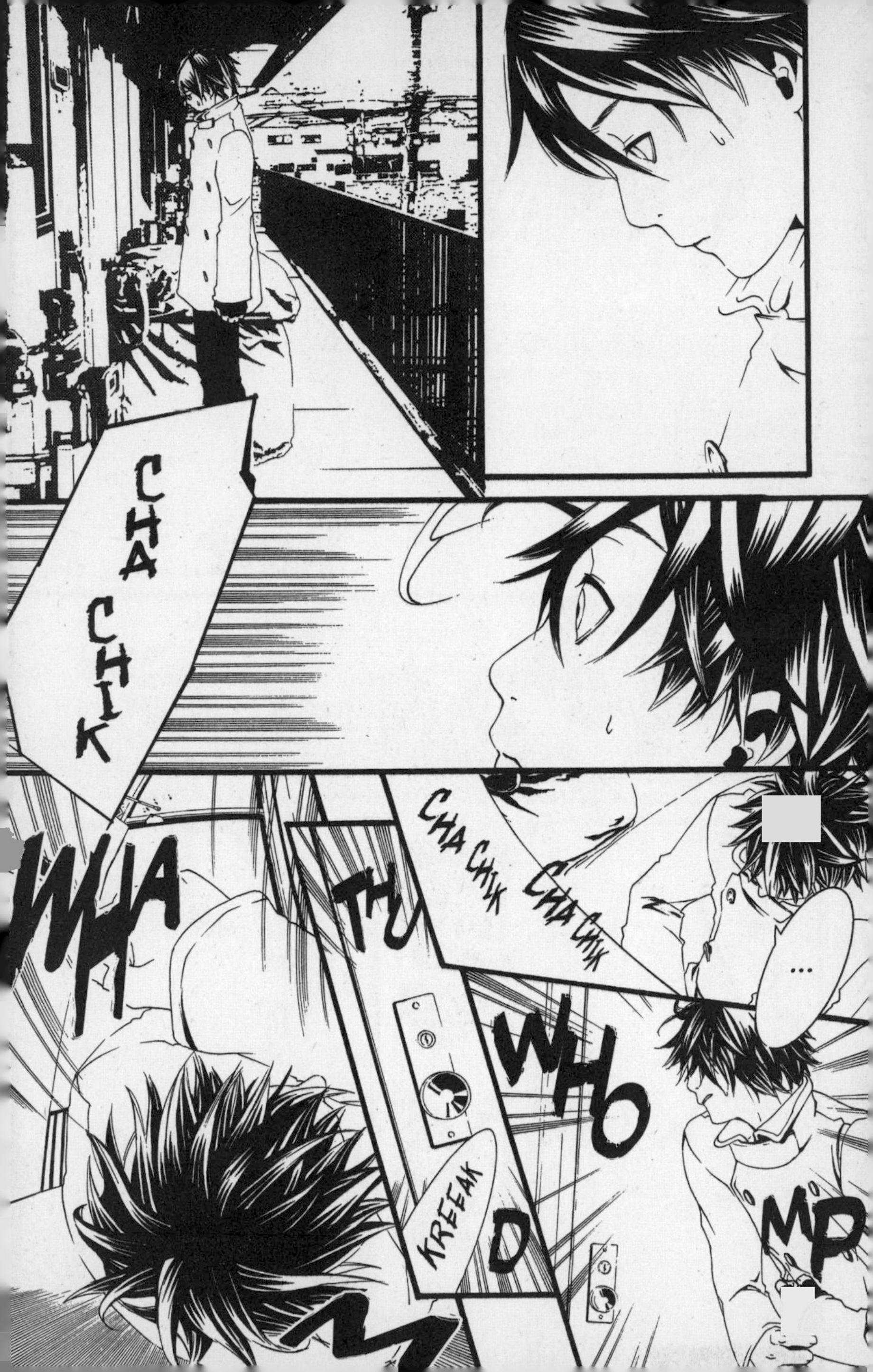
CHA CHIK
CHA CHIK CHA CHIK
...
THU
MP
WHO
D
KREEAK
WHA
M

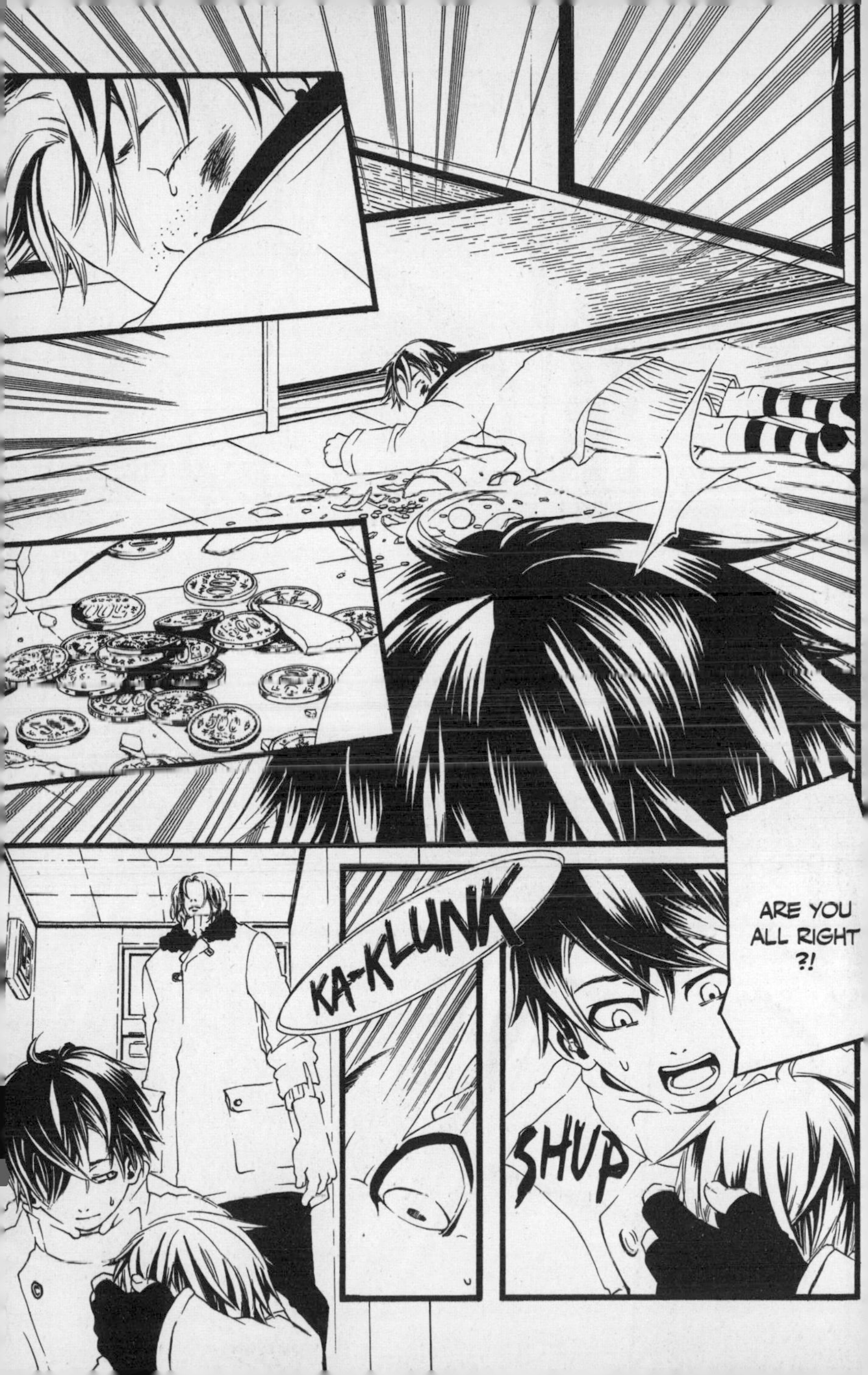
ARE YOU ALL RIGHT ?!
SHUP
KA-KLUNK

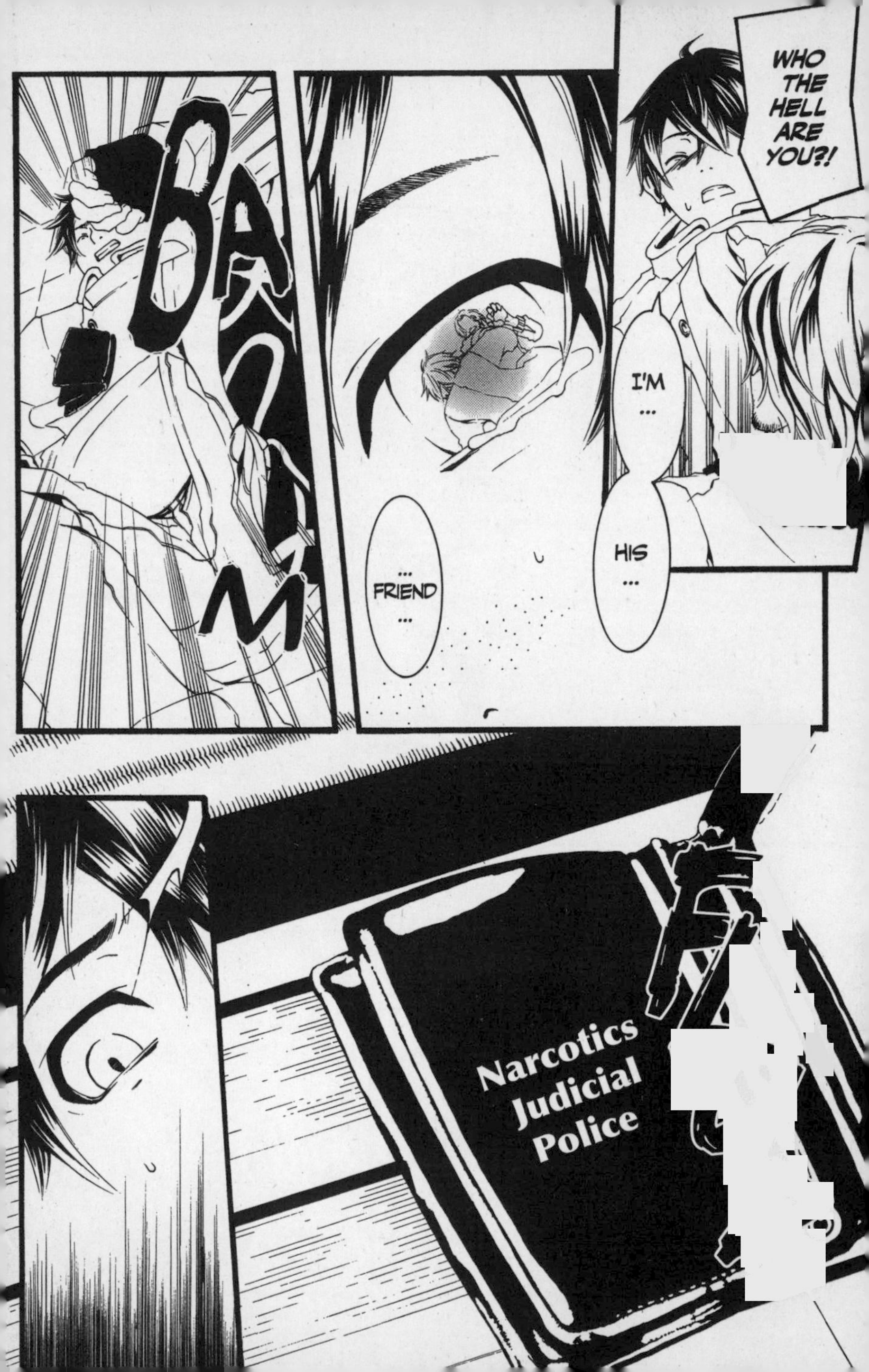
WHO THE HELL ARE YOU?!
I'M ...
HIS ...
... FRIEND ...
BAM
Narcotics Judicial Police

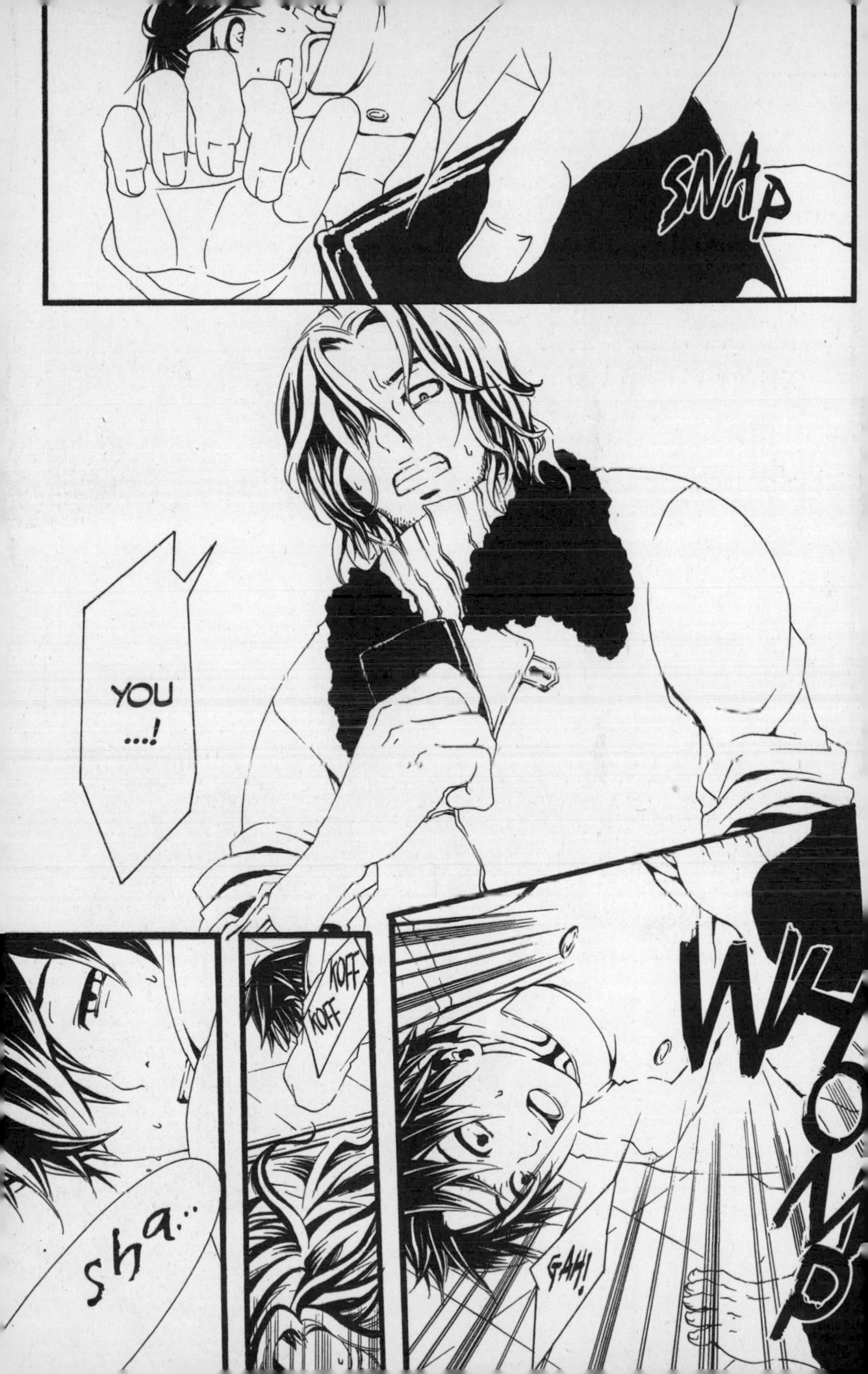
SNAP
YOU ...!
WHOMP
GAH!
KOFF
KOFF
sha...

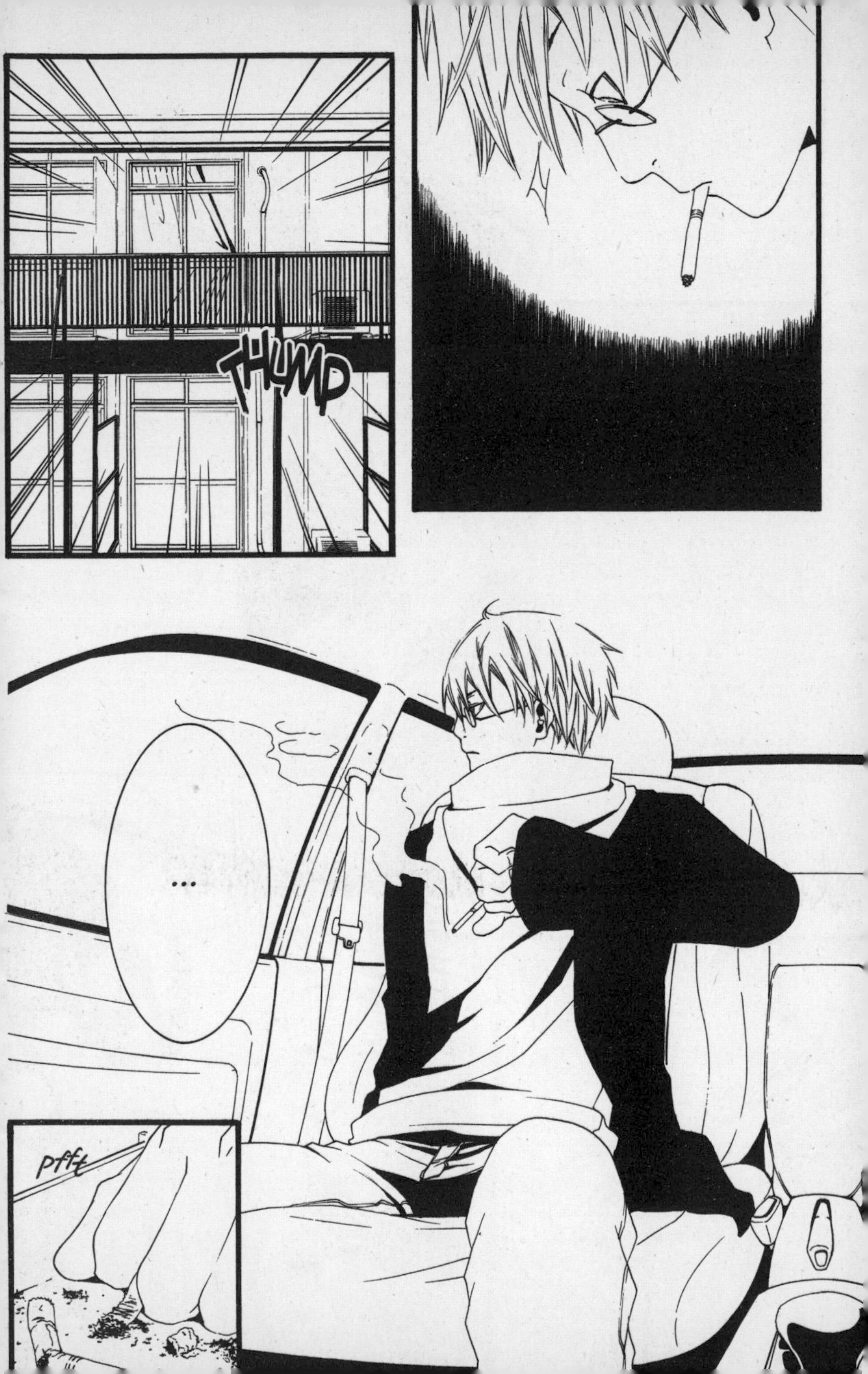
THUMP
...
pfft

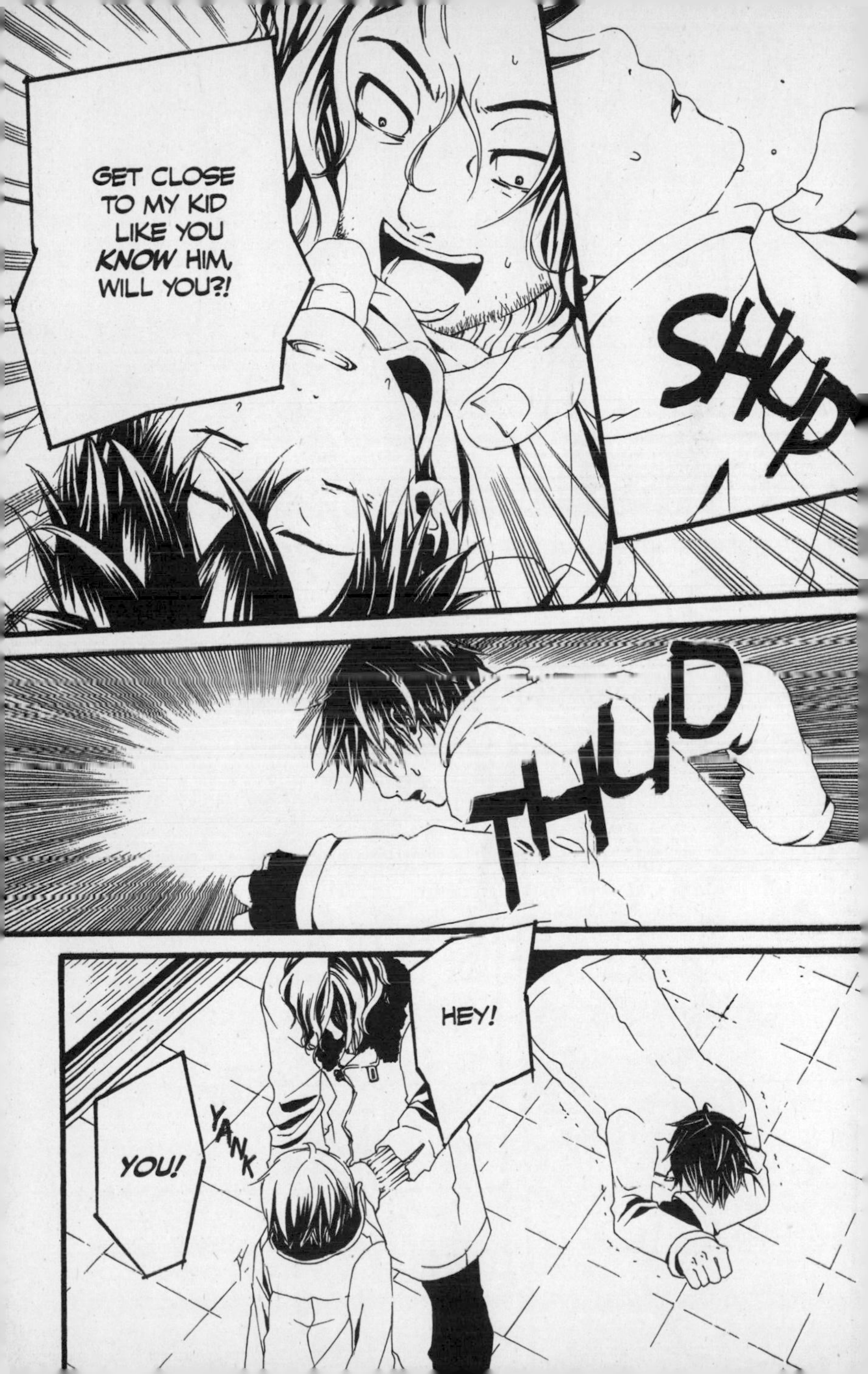
SHUP
GET CLOSE TO MY KID LIKE YOU *KNOW* HIM, WILL YOU?!
THUD
HEY!
YANK
YOU!

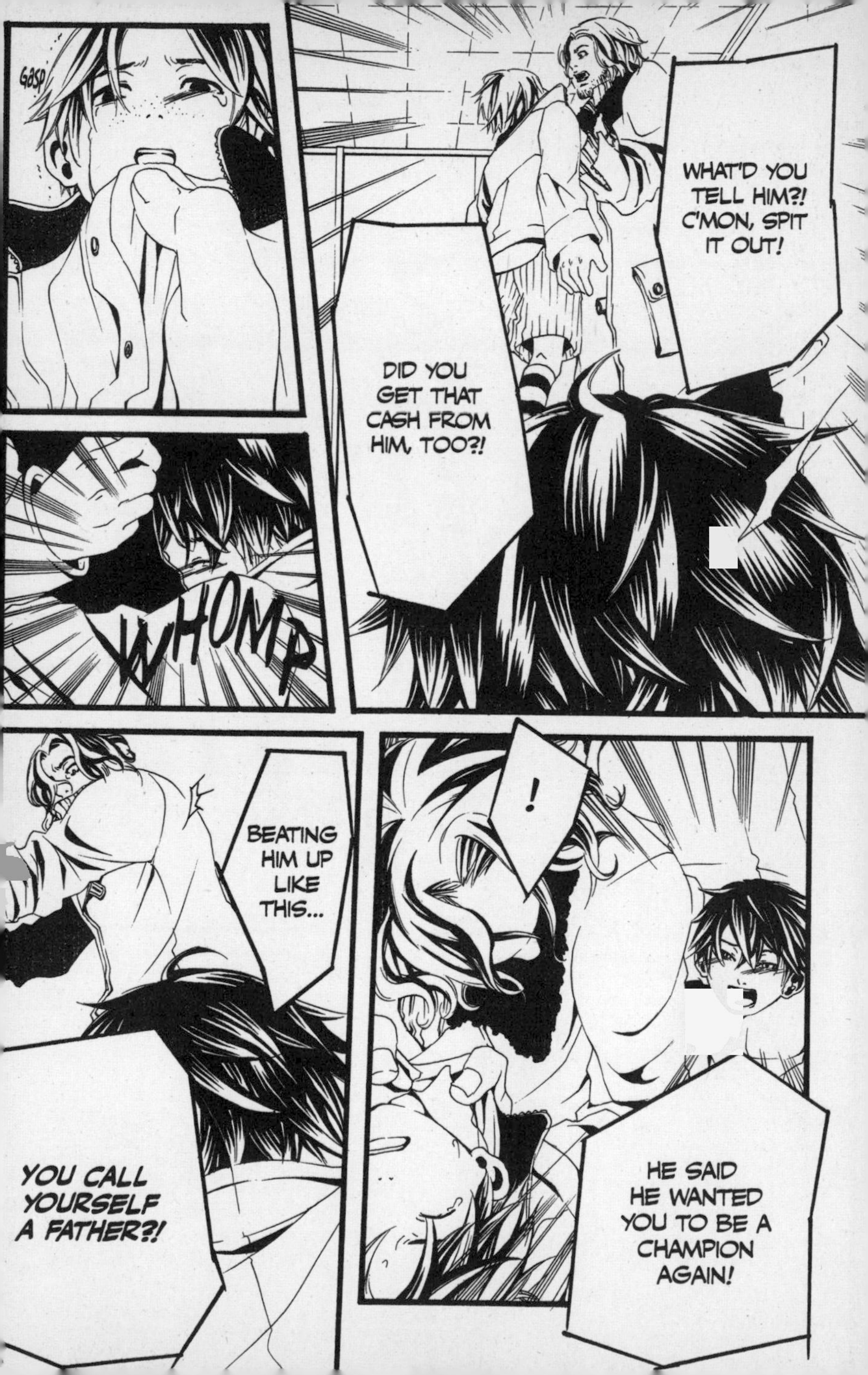
WHAT'D YOU TELL HIM?! C'MON, SPIT IT OUT!
DID YOU GET THAT CASH FROM HIM, TOO?!
GASP
WHOMP
!
HE SAID HE WANTED YOU TO BE A CHAMPION AGAIN!
BEATING HIM UP LIKE THIS...
YOU CALL YOURSELF A FATHER?!

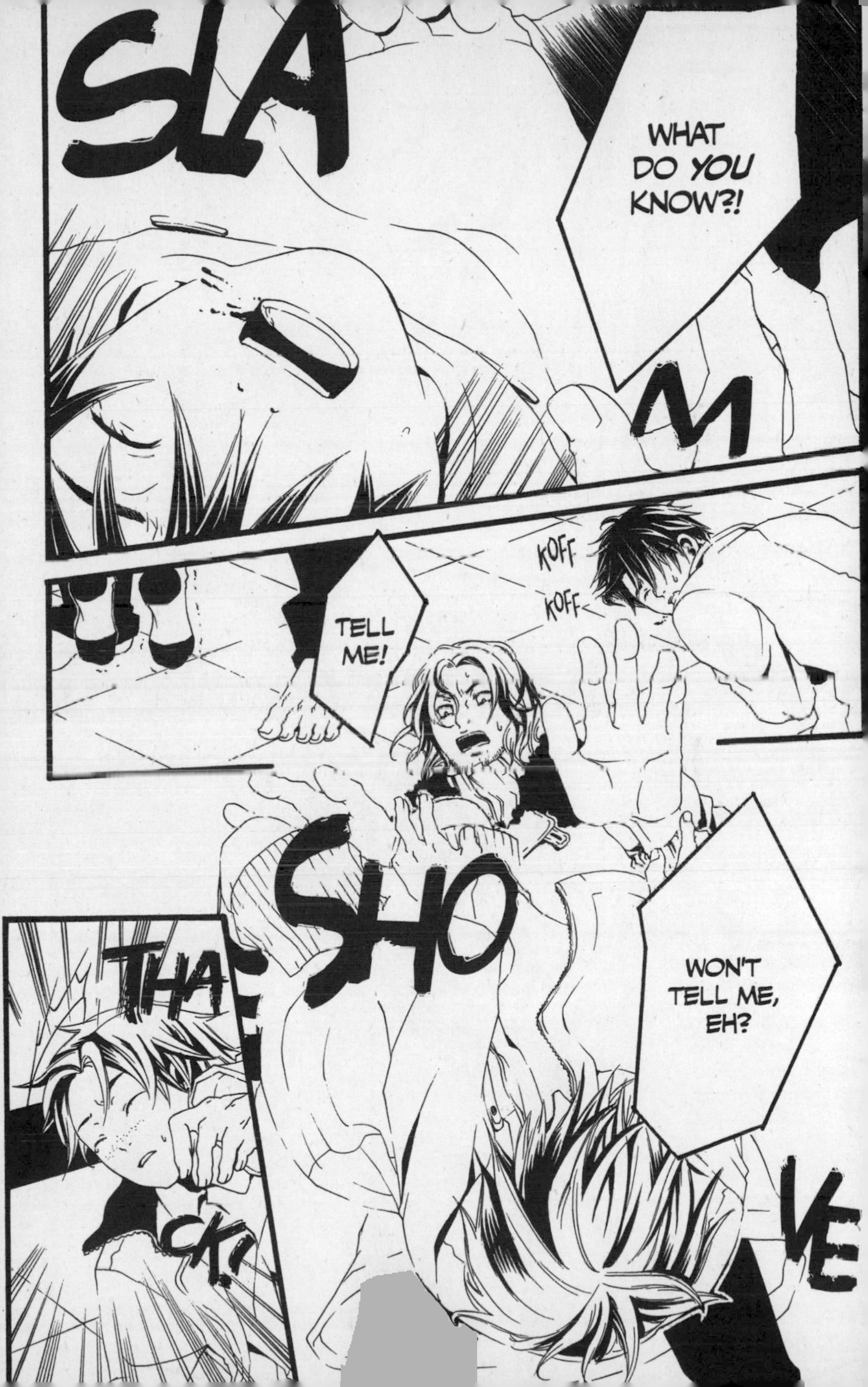
WHAT DO YOU KNOW?!
SLA
M
KOFF
KOFF
TELL ME!
WON'T TELL ME, EH?
SHO
VE
THA
CK!

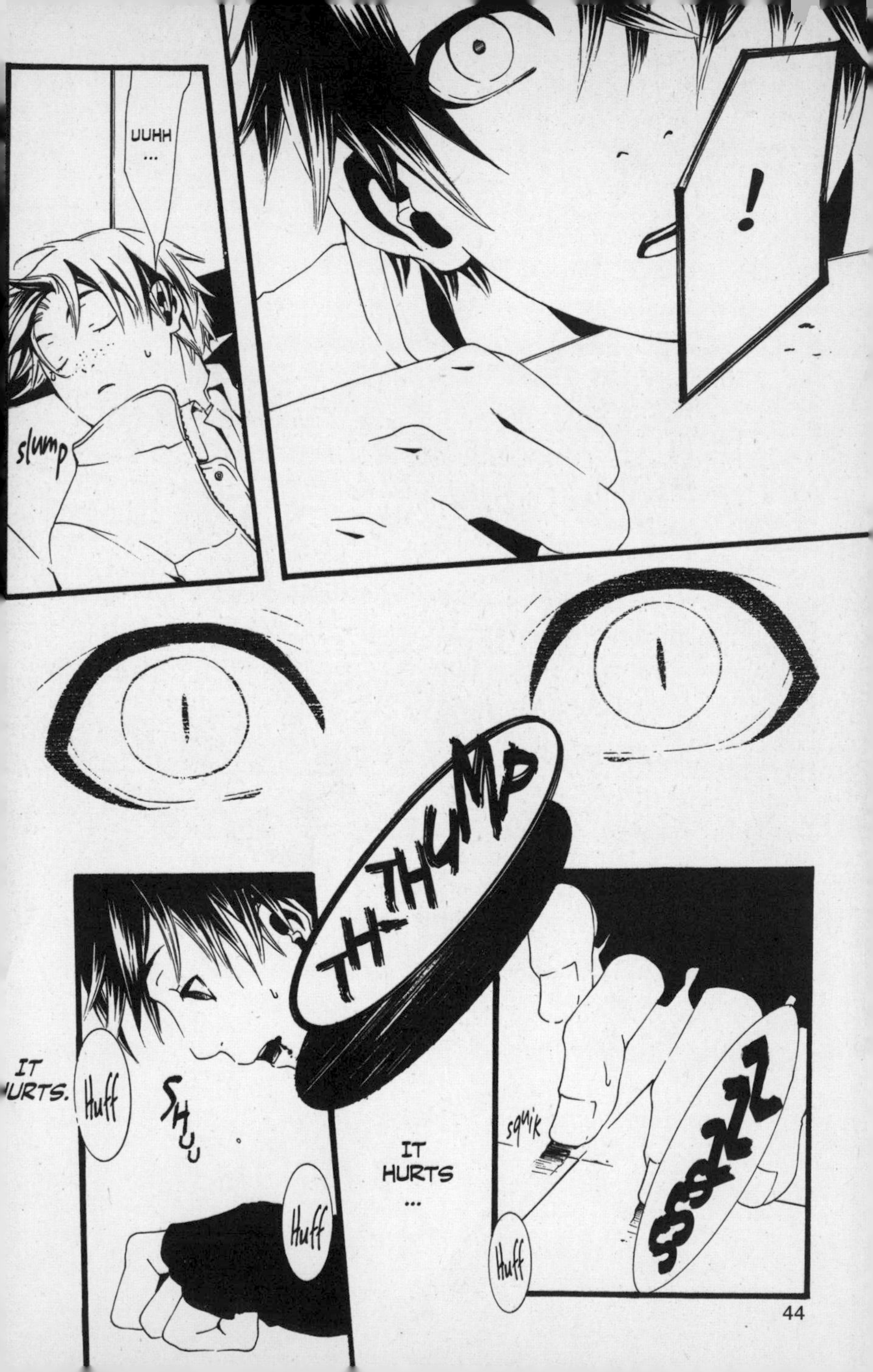
!
UUHH ...
slump
THTHUMP
squik
SSKZZ
Huff
IT HURTS ...
Huff
SHUU
IT HURTS.
Huff

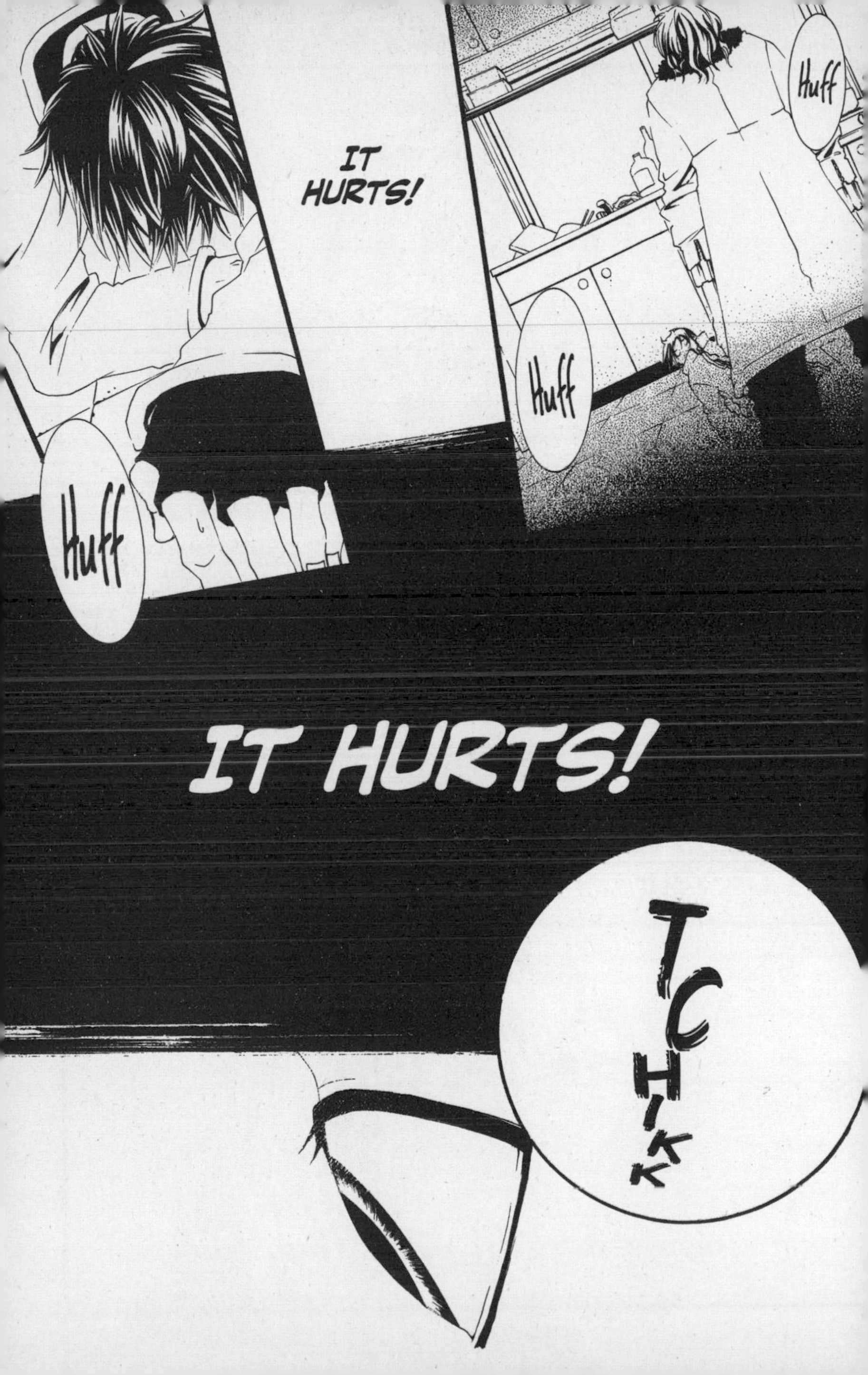
Huff
Huff
IT HURTS!
Huff
IT HURTS!
TCHIKK

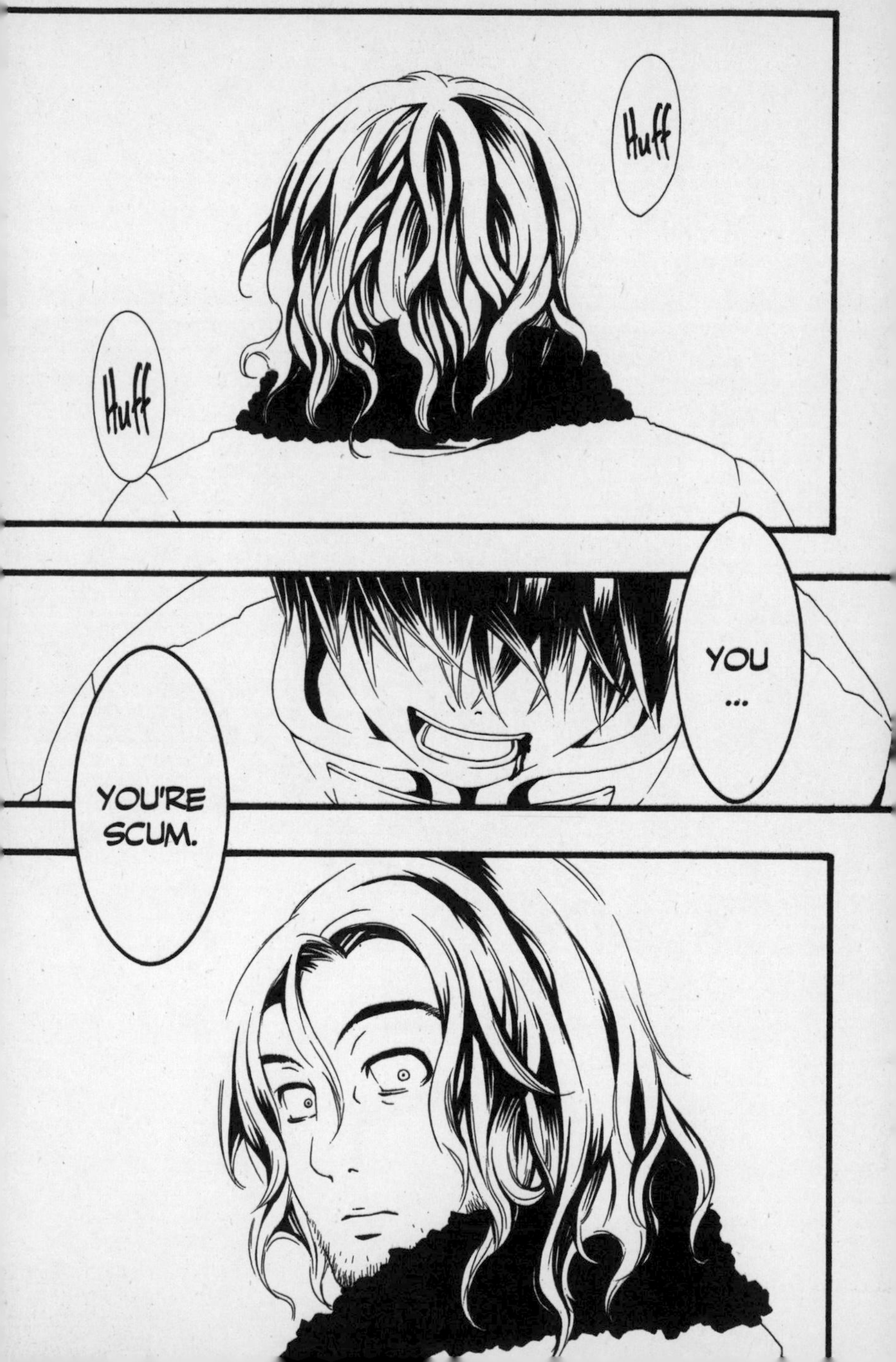
Huff
Huff
YOU ...
YOU'RE SCUM.

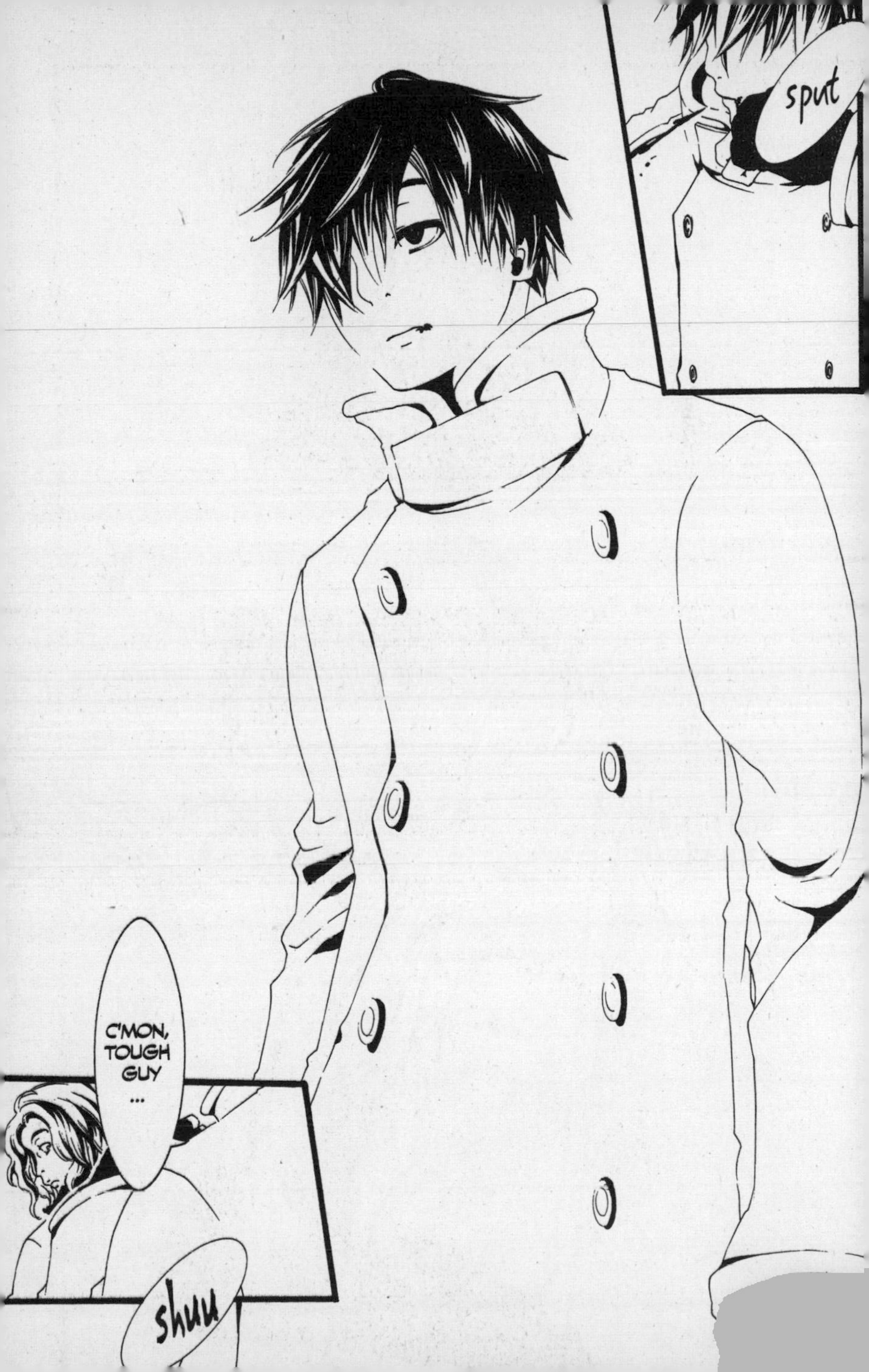
sput
C'MON, TOUGH GUY ...
shuu

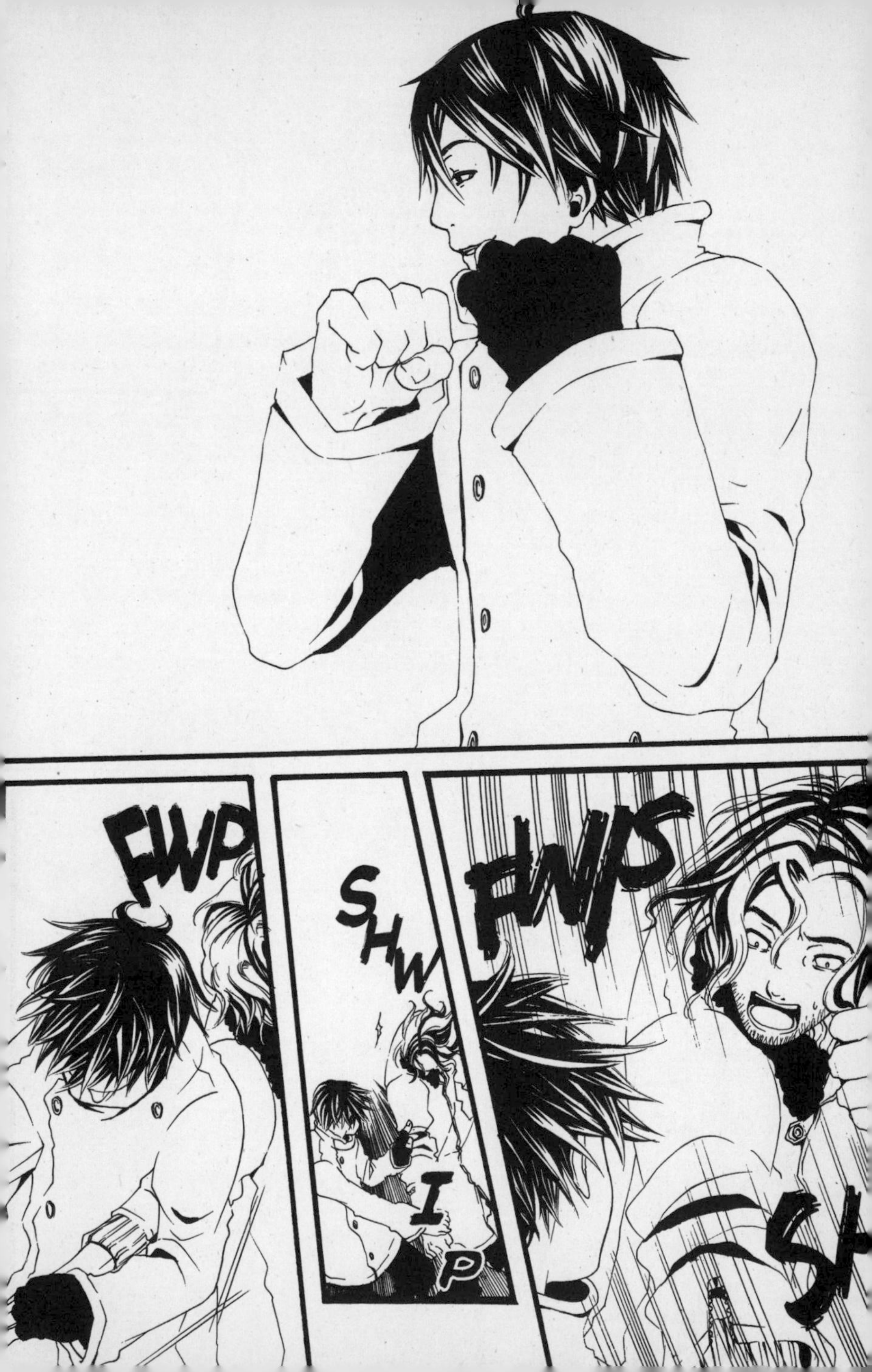
FWPS
SH
SHW
IP
FWP

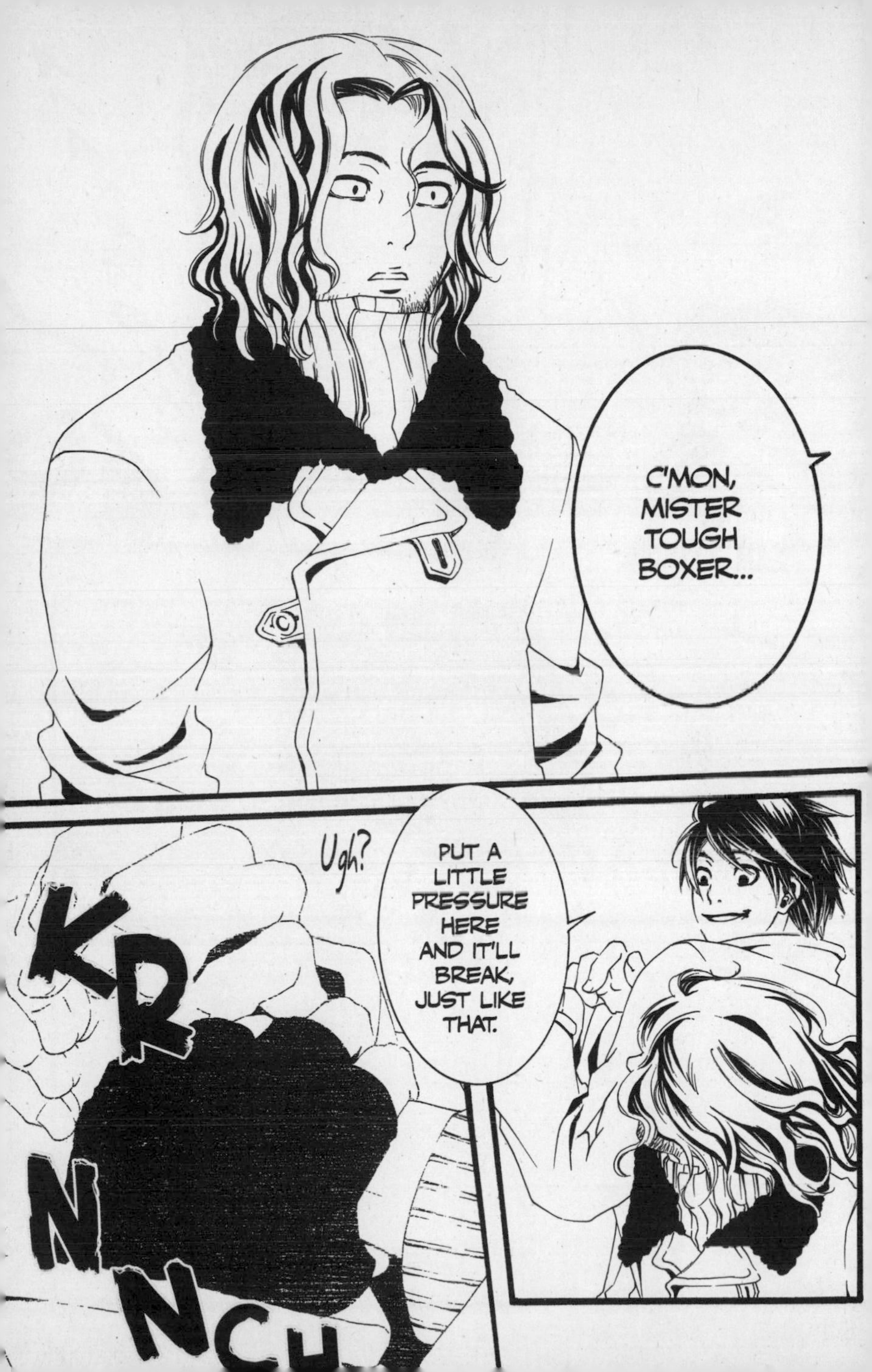
C'MON, MISTER TOUGH BOXER...
PUT A LITTLE PRESSURE HERE AND IT'LL BREAK, JUST LIKE THAT.
Ugh?
KRNNCH

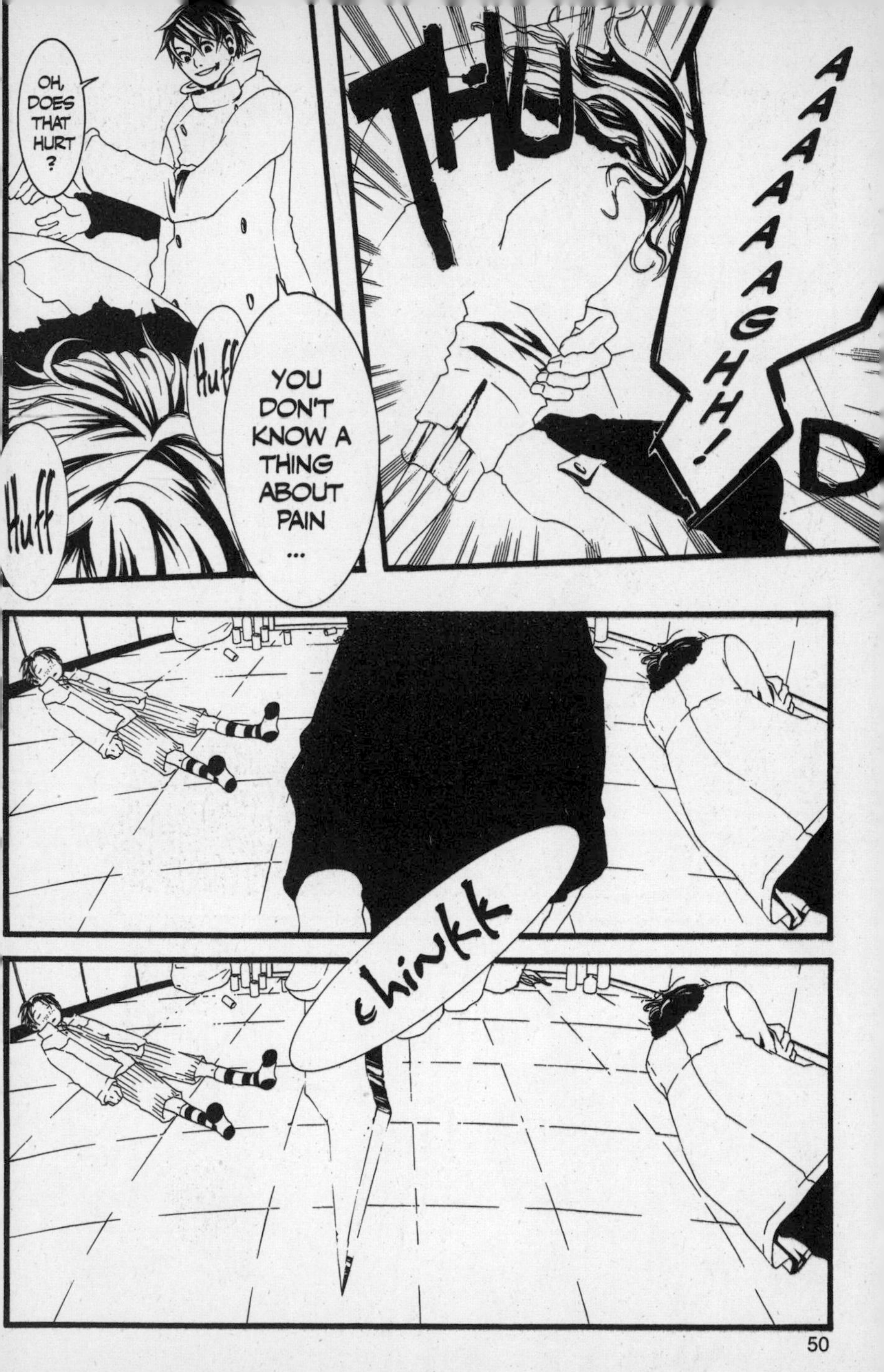
THU-
D
AAAAAAGHH!
OH, DOES THAT HURT?
Huff
Huff
YOU DON'T KNOW A THING ABOUT PAIN...
chinkk

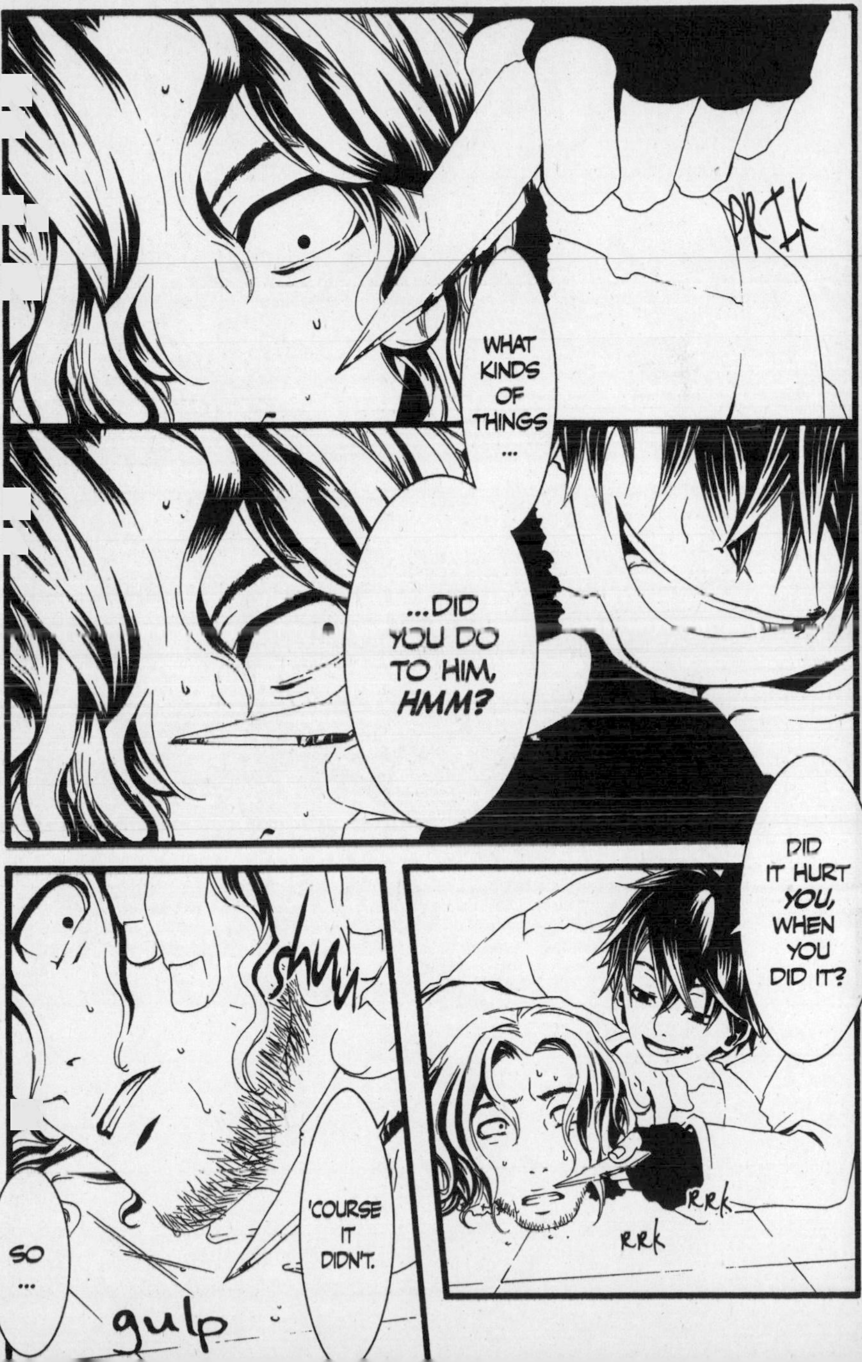
PRIK
WHAT KINDS OF THINGS ...
...DID YOU DO TO HIM, *HMM?*
DID IT HURT *YOU*, WHEN YOU DID IT?
RRK
RRK
'COURSE IT DIDN'T.
shuu
SO ...
gulp

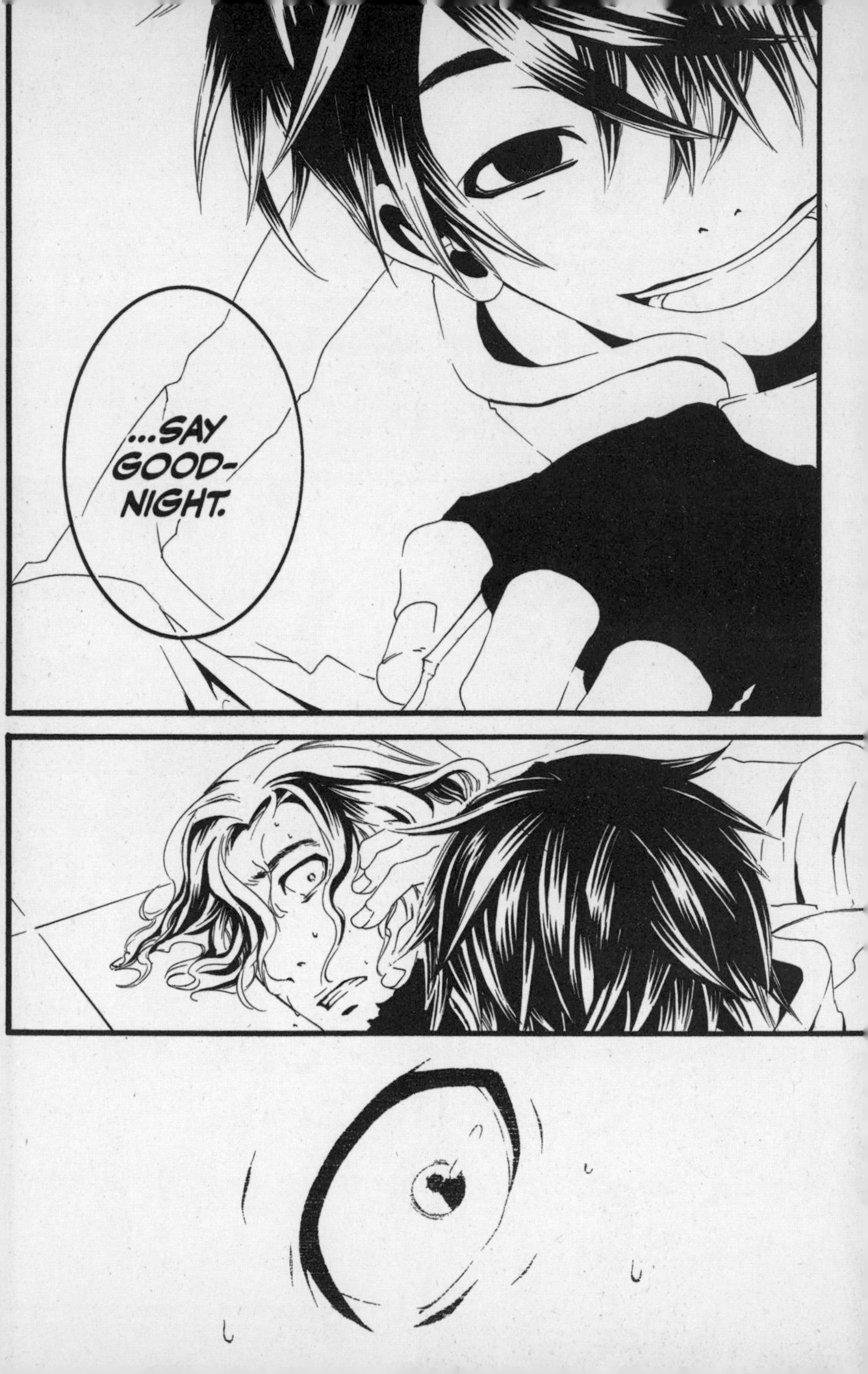
...SAY GOOD-NIGHT.

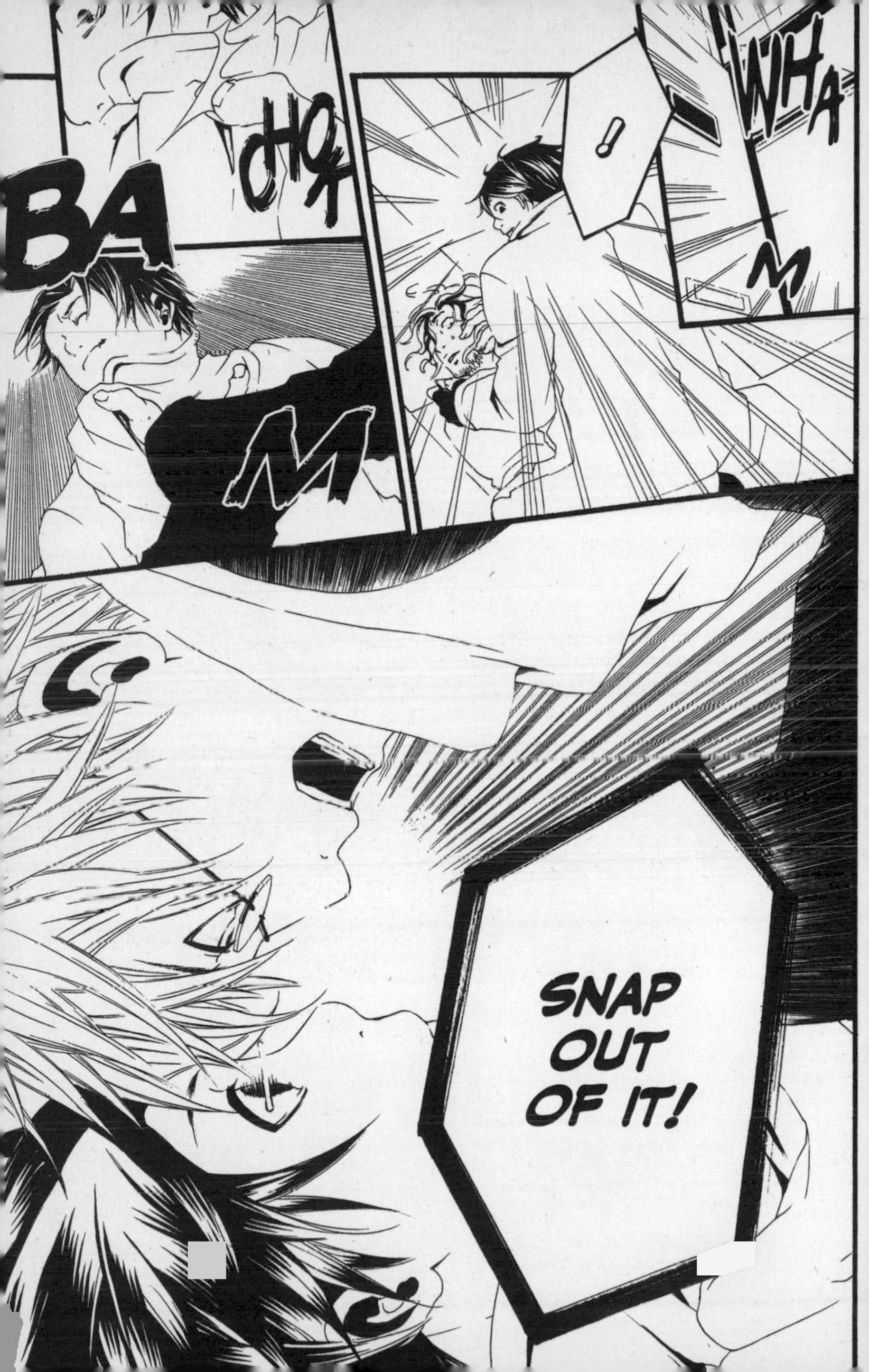
WHAM
!
CHOK
BAM
SNAP OUT OF IT!

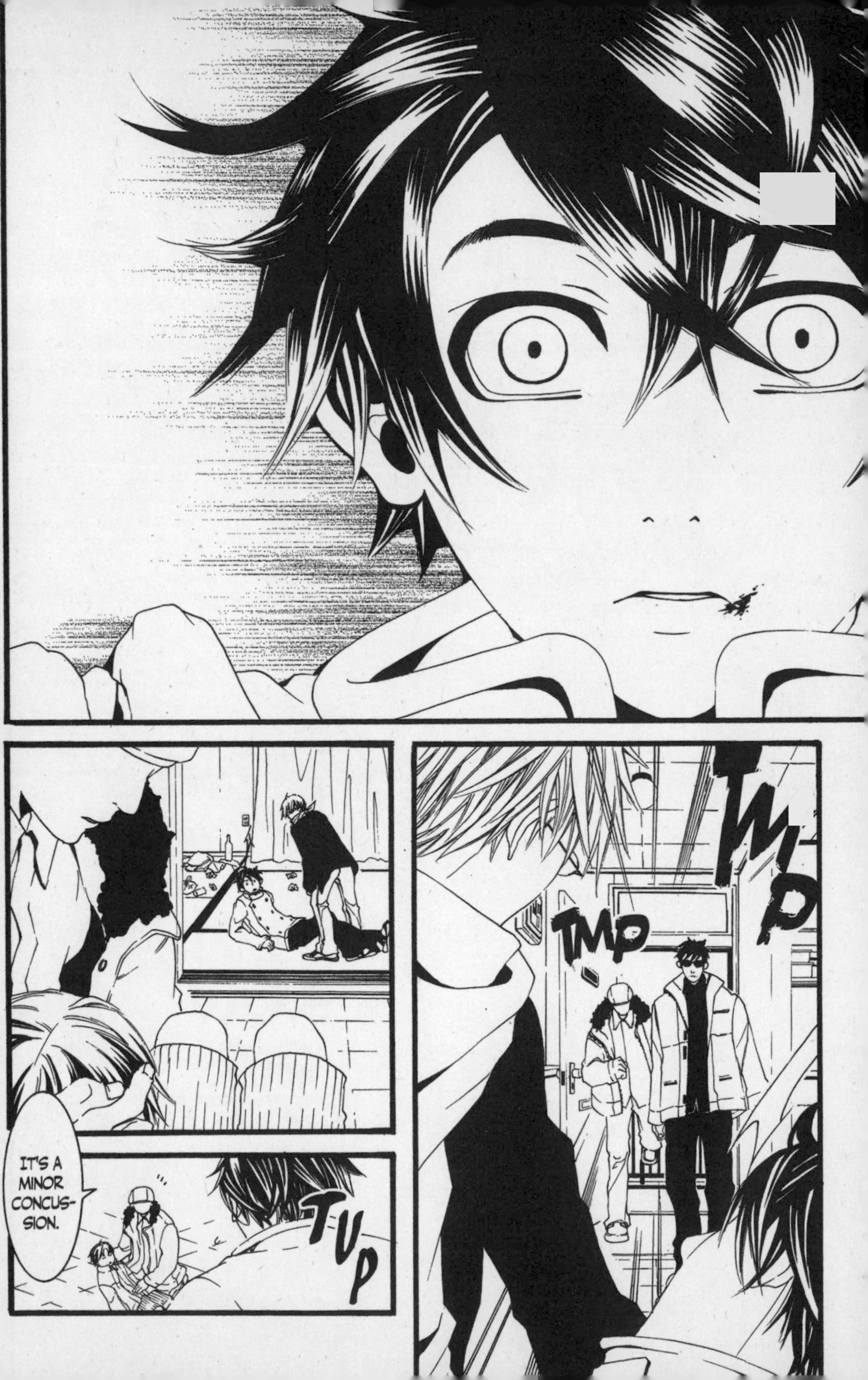
TMP
TMP
IT'S A MINOR CONCUSSION.
TUP

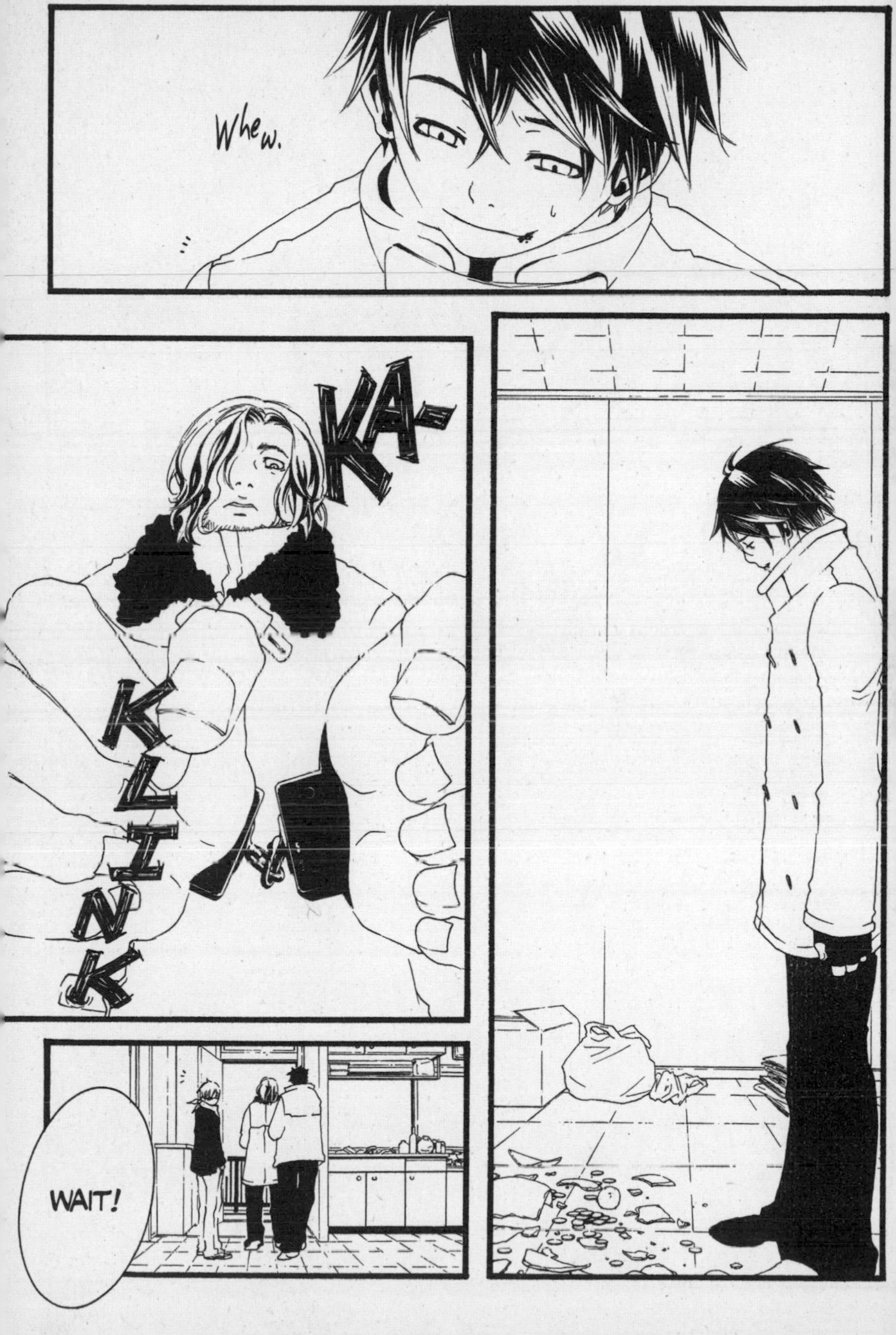
Whew.
...
KA-
KLINK
WAIT!

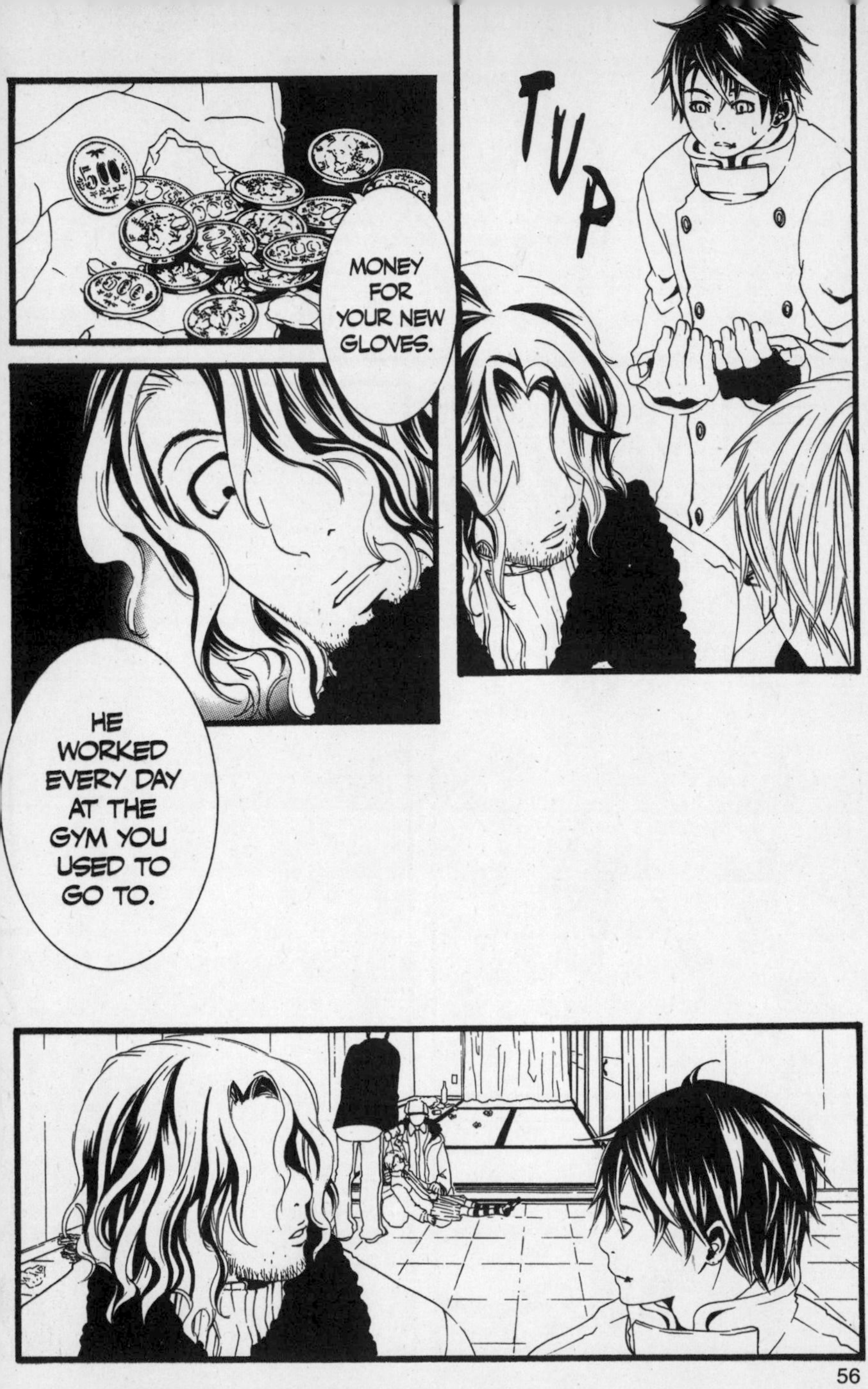
TUP
MONEY FOR YOUR NEW GLOVES.
HE WORKED EVERY DAY AT THE GYM YOU USED TO GO TO.

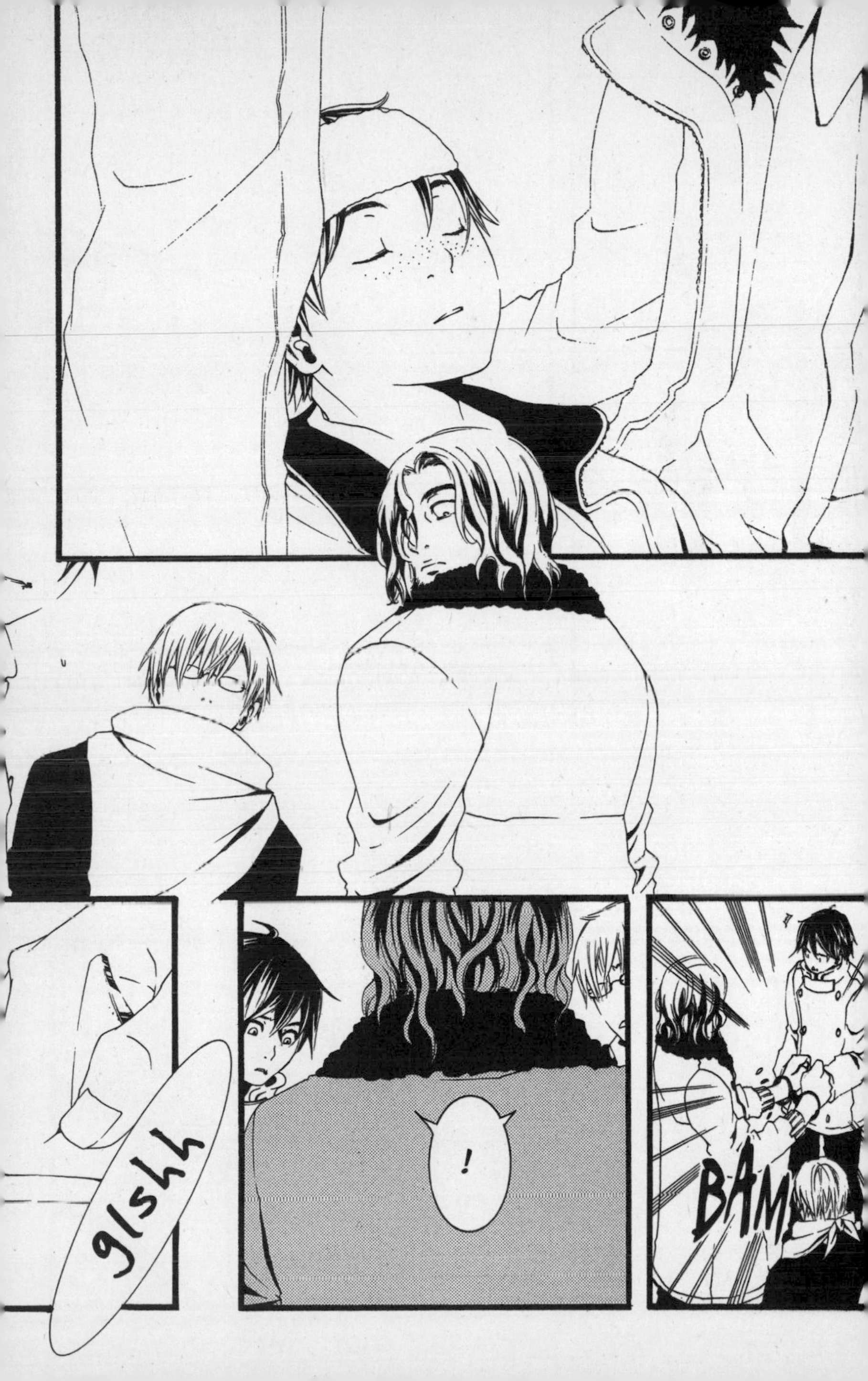
BAM
!
glshh

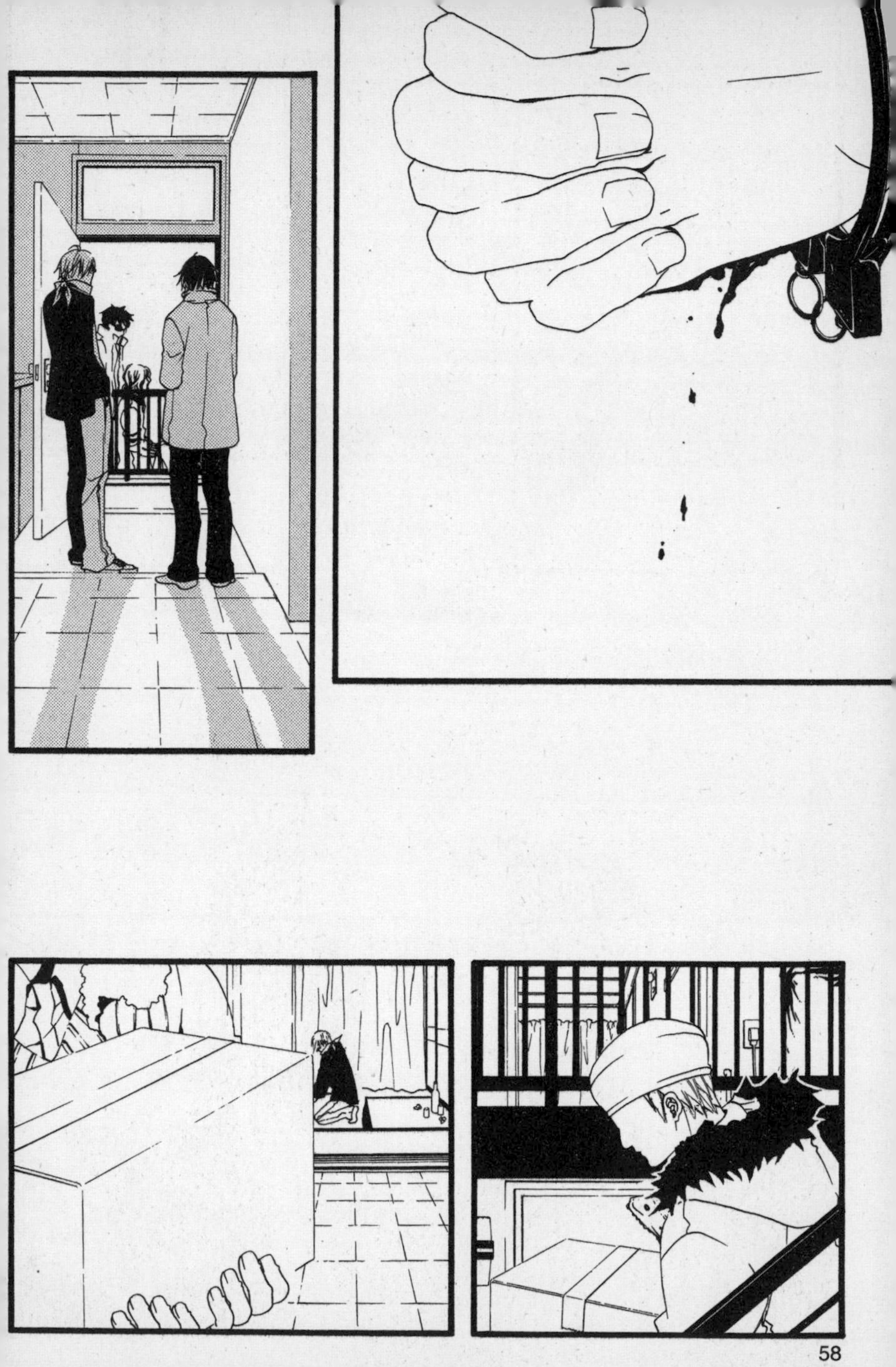

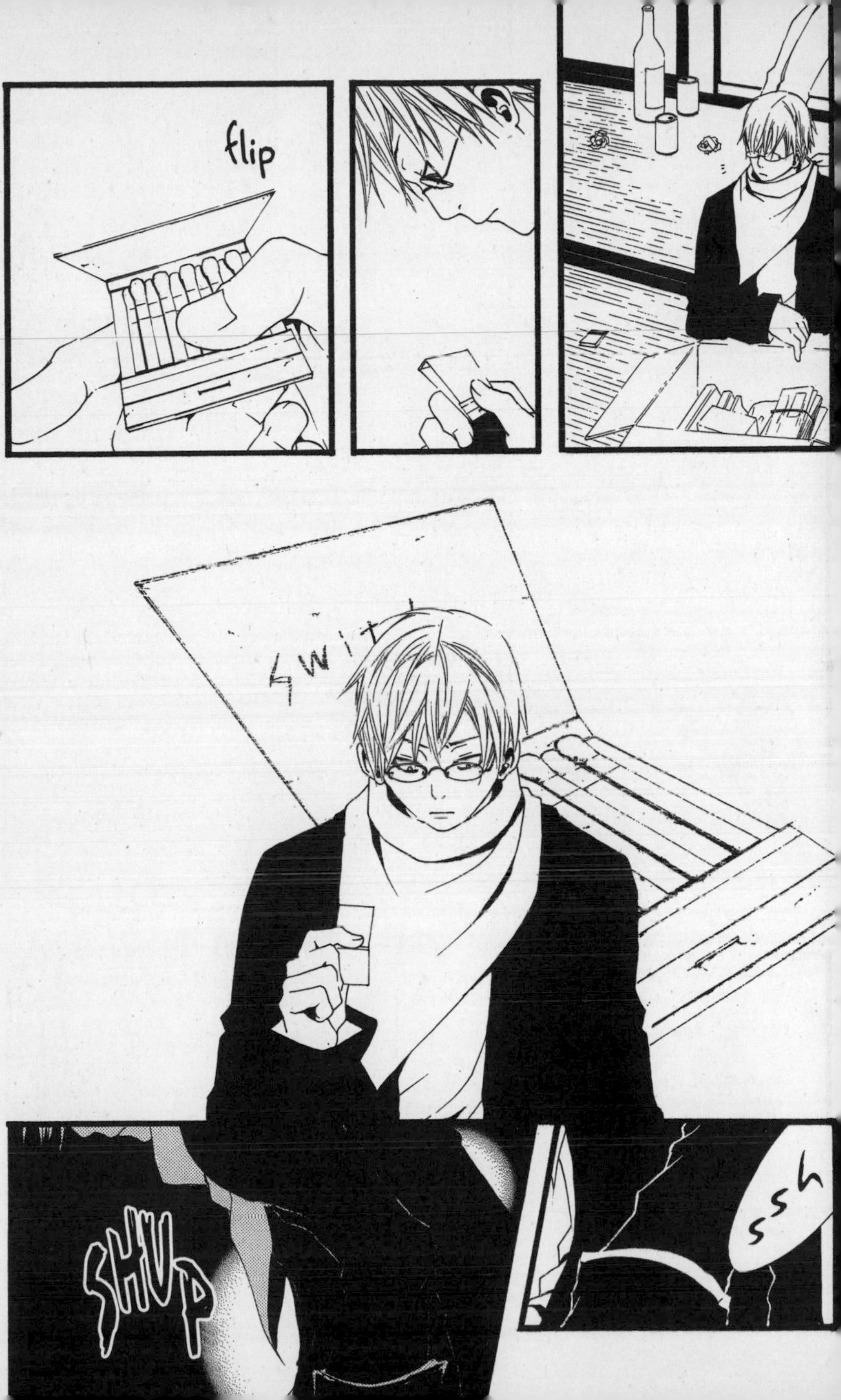
flip
ssh
SHUP

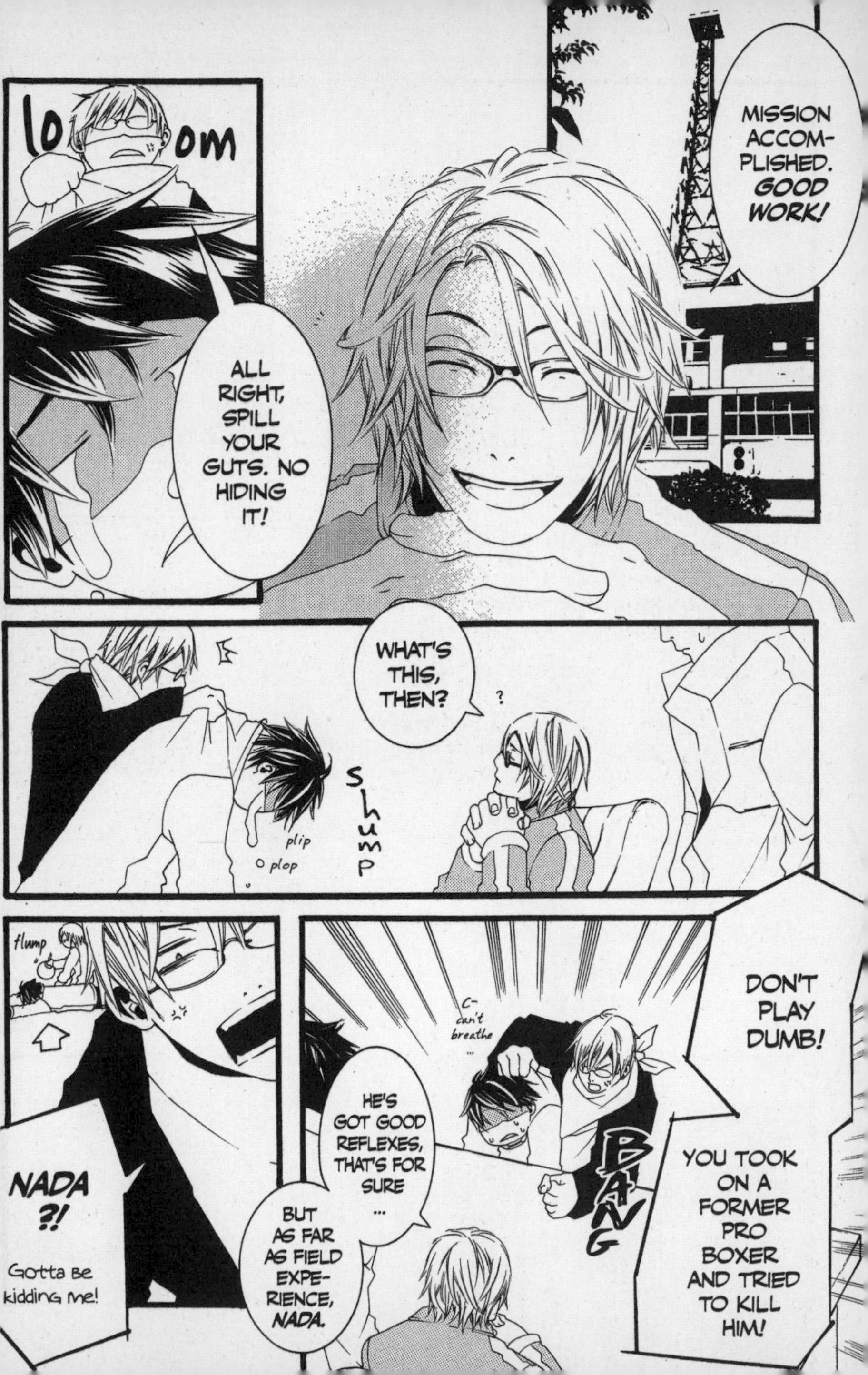
MISSION ACCOMPLISHED. GOOD WORK!
lo om
ALL RIGHT, SPILL YOUR GUTS. NO HIDING IT!
WHAT'S THIS, THEN?
?
shump
plip
plop
DON'T PLAY DUMB!
YOU TOOK ON A FORMER PRO BOXER AND TRIED TO KILL HIM!
BANG
C-can't breathe ...
HE'S GOT GOOD REFLEXES, THAT'S FOR SURE ...
BUT AS FAR AS FIELD EXPERIENCE, NADA.
flump
NADA ?!
Gotta be kidding me!

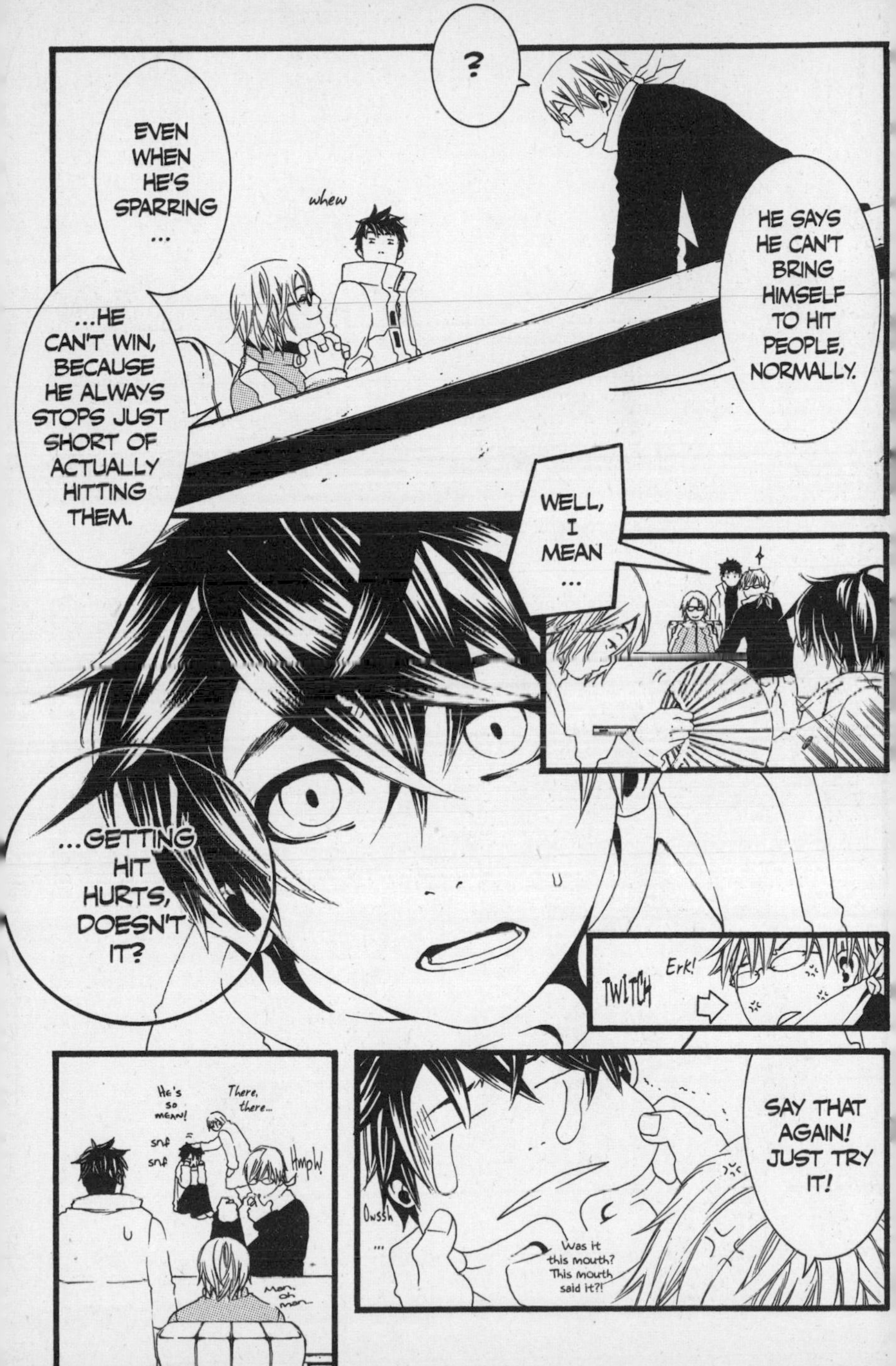
?
HE SAYS HE CAN'T BRING HIMSELF TO HIT PEOPLE, NORMALLY.
EVEN WHEN HE'S SPARRING...
whew
...HE CAN'T WIN, BECAUSE HE ALWAYS STOPS JUST SHORT OF ACTUALLY HITTING THEM.
WELL, I MEAN...
...GETTING HIT HURTS, DOESN'T IT?
Erk!
TWITCH
SAY THAT AGAIN! JUST TRY IT!
Was it this mouth? This mouth said it?!
Owssh...
There, there...
He's so mean!
snf
snf
Hmph!
Man, oh man...

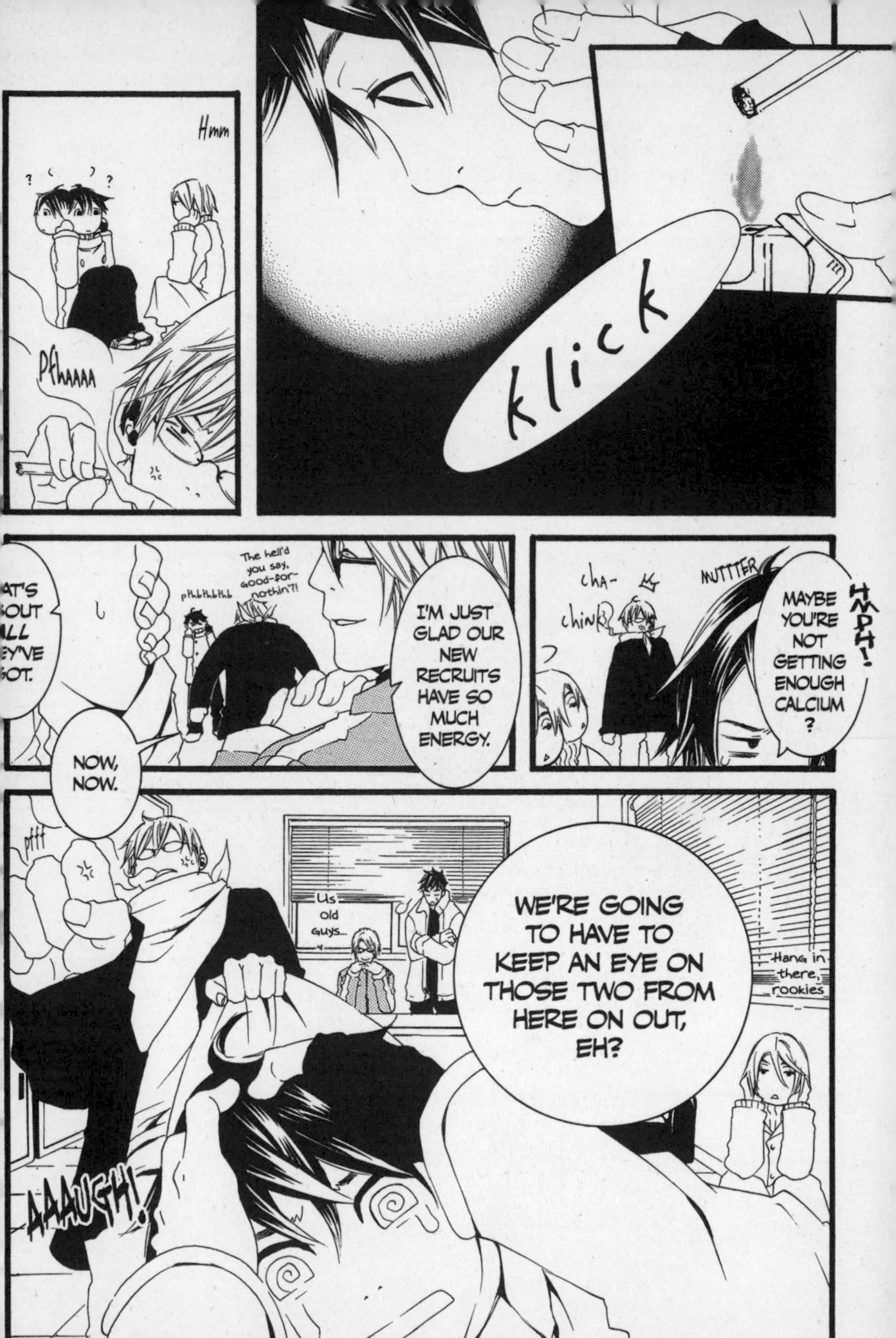
klick
Hmm
Pfhaaaa
cha-chink
MUTTTER
MAYBE YOU'RE NOT GETTING ENOUGH CALCIUM?
HMPH!
I'M JUST GLAD OUR NEW RECRUITS HAVE SO MUCH ENERGY.
The hell'd you say, good-for-nothin'?!
pthbthbthb
AT'S OUT LL EY'VE OT.
NOW, NOW.
WE'RE GOING TO HAVE TO KEEP AN EYE ON THOSE TWO FROM HERE ON OUT, EH?
Hang in there, rookies...
Us old guys...
pfff
AAAUCH!

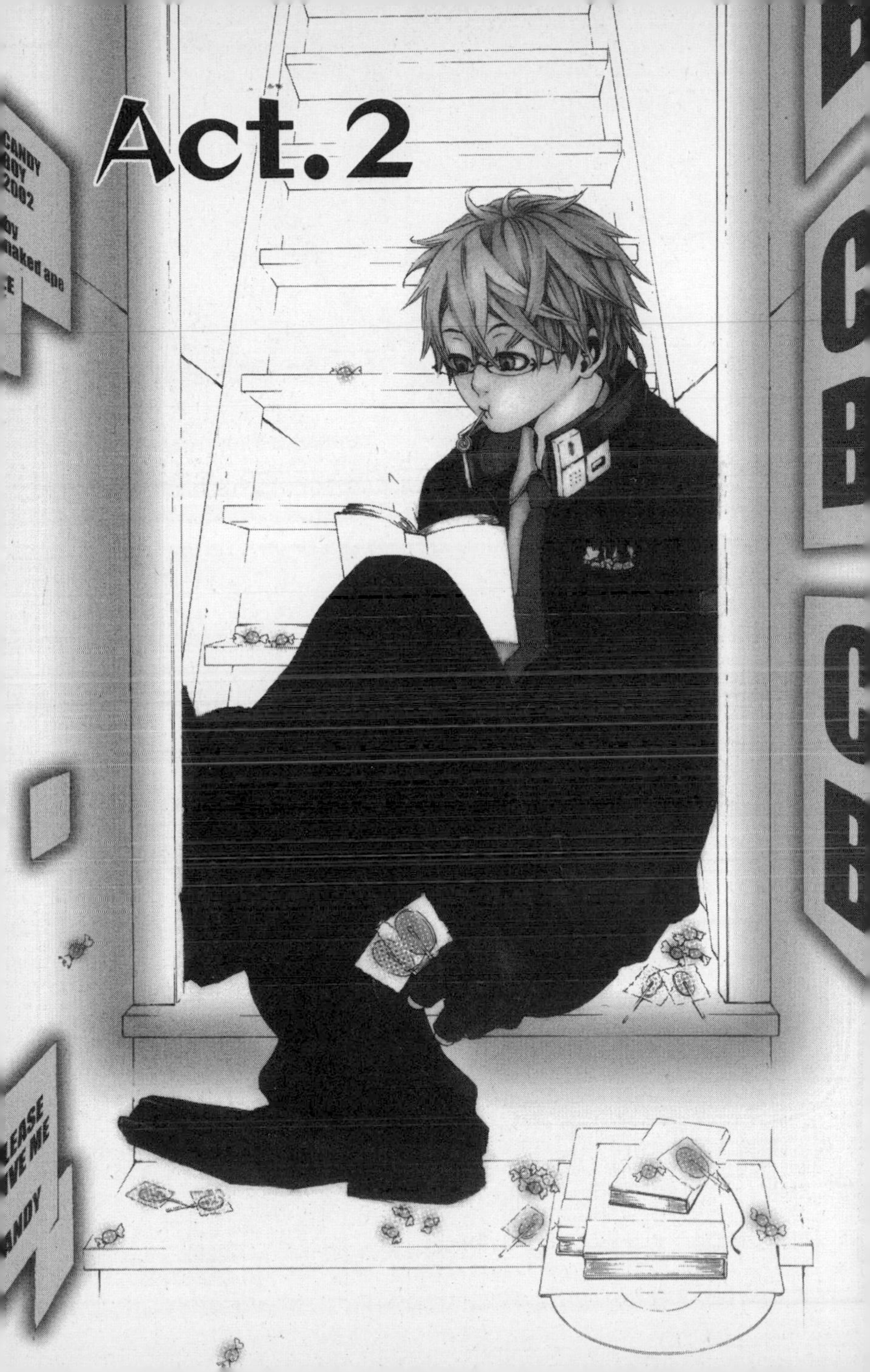
Act.2
CANDY
2002
naked ape

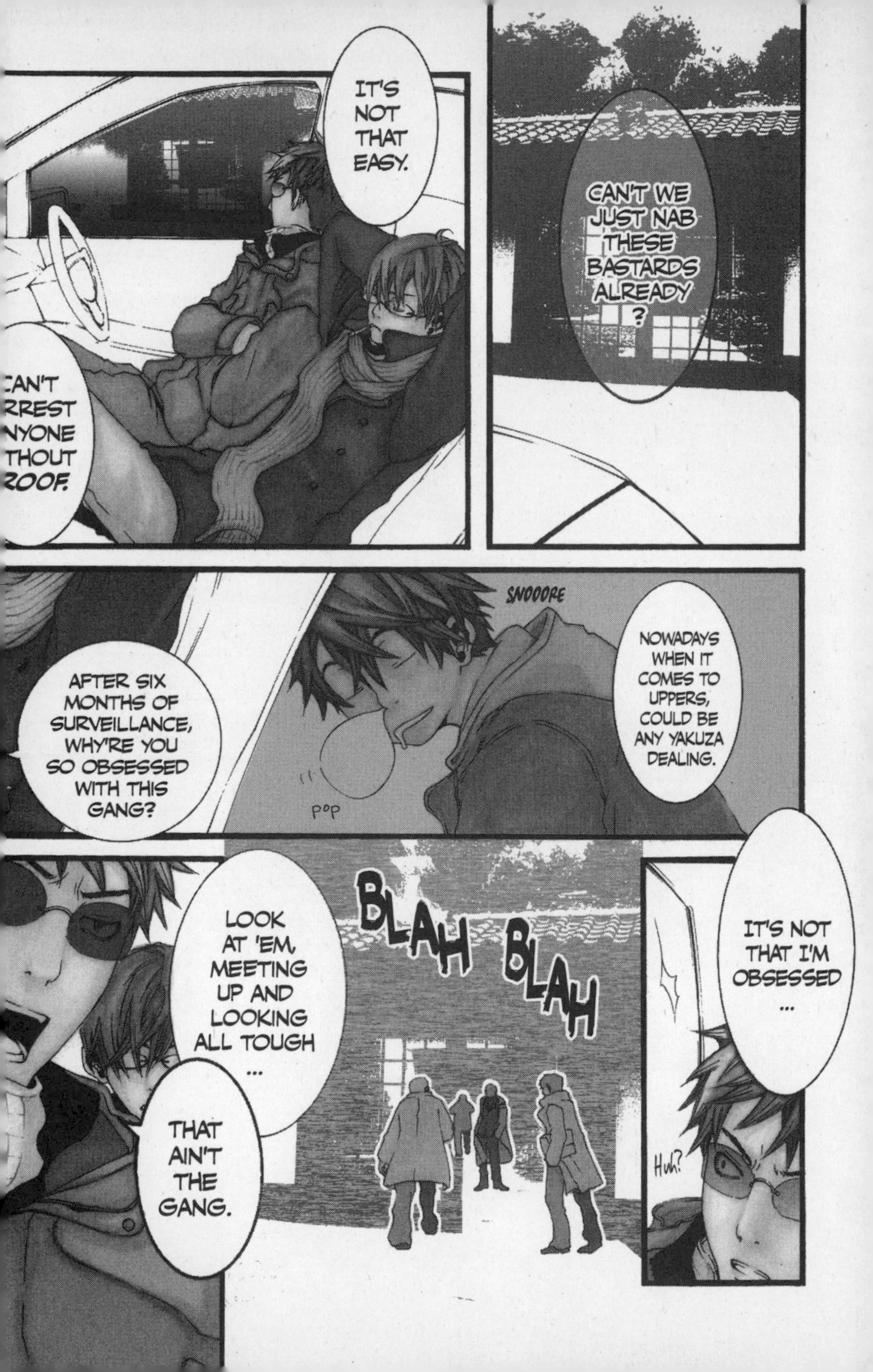
CAN'T WE JUST NAB THESE BASTARDS ALREADY?
IT'S NOT THAT EASY.
CAN'T ARREST ANYONE WITHOUT PROOF.
SNOOORE
NOWADAYS WHEN IT COMES TO UPPERS, COULD BE ANY YAKUZA DEALING.
AFTER SIX MONTHS OF SURVEILLANCE, WHY'RE YOU SO OBSESSED WITH THIS GANG?
POP
IT'S NOT THAT I'M OBSESSED...
HUH?
BLAH BLAH
LOOK AT 'EM, MEETING UP AND LOOKING ALL TOUGH...
THAT AIN'T THE GANG.

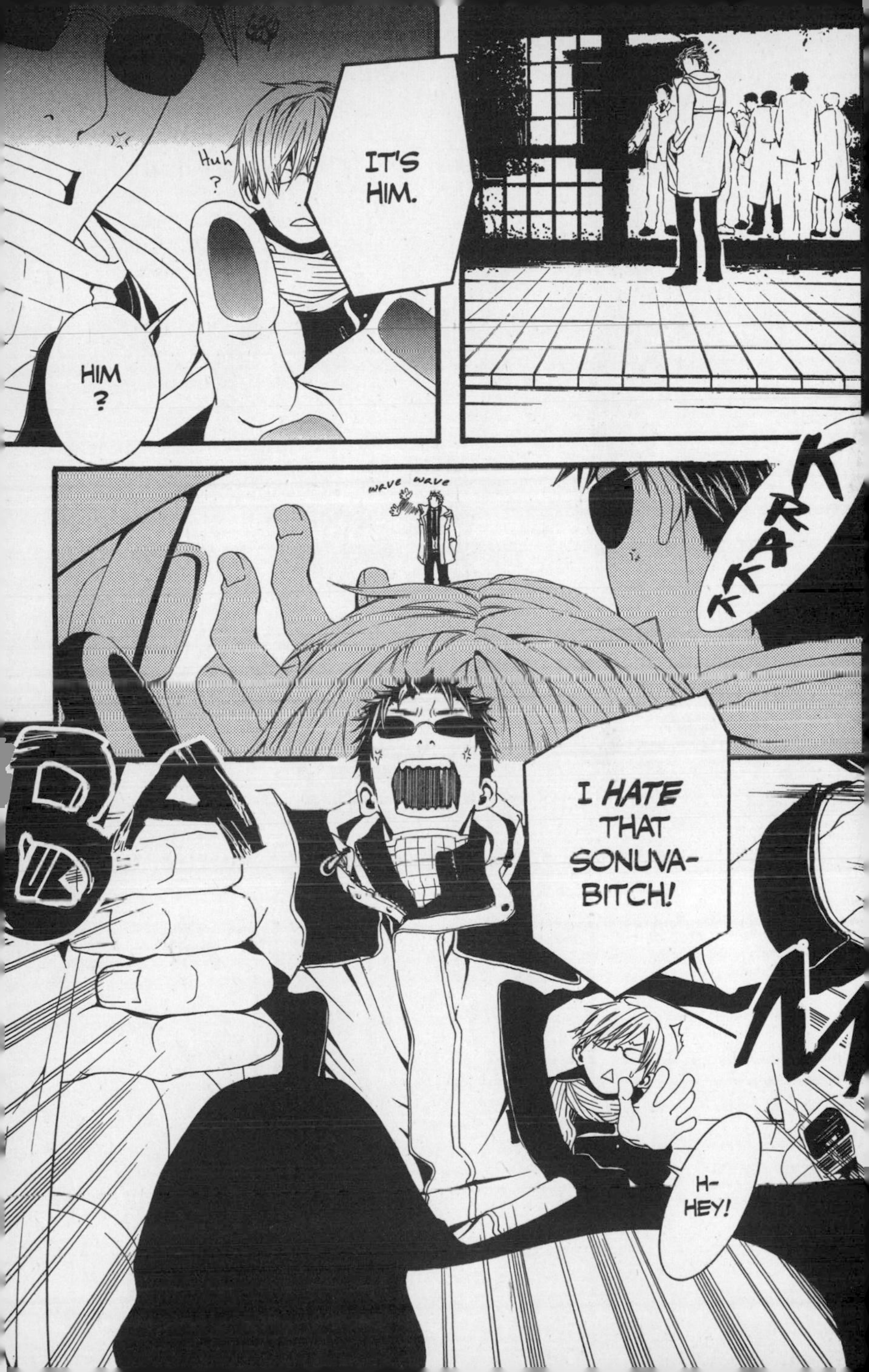
IT'S HIM.
Huh ?
HIM ?
KRAKK
wave wave
I HATE THAT SONUVA-BITCH!
H-HEY!
BAM

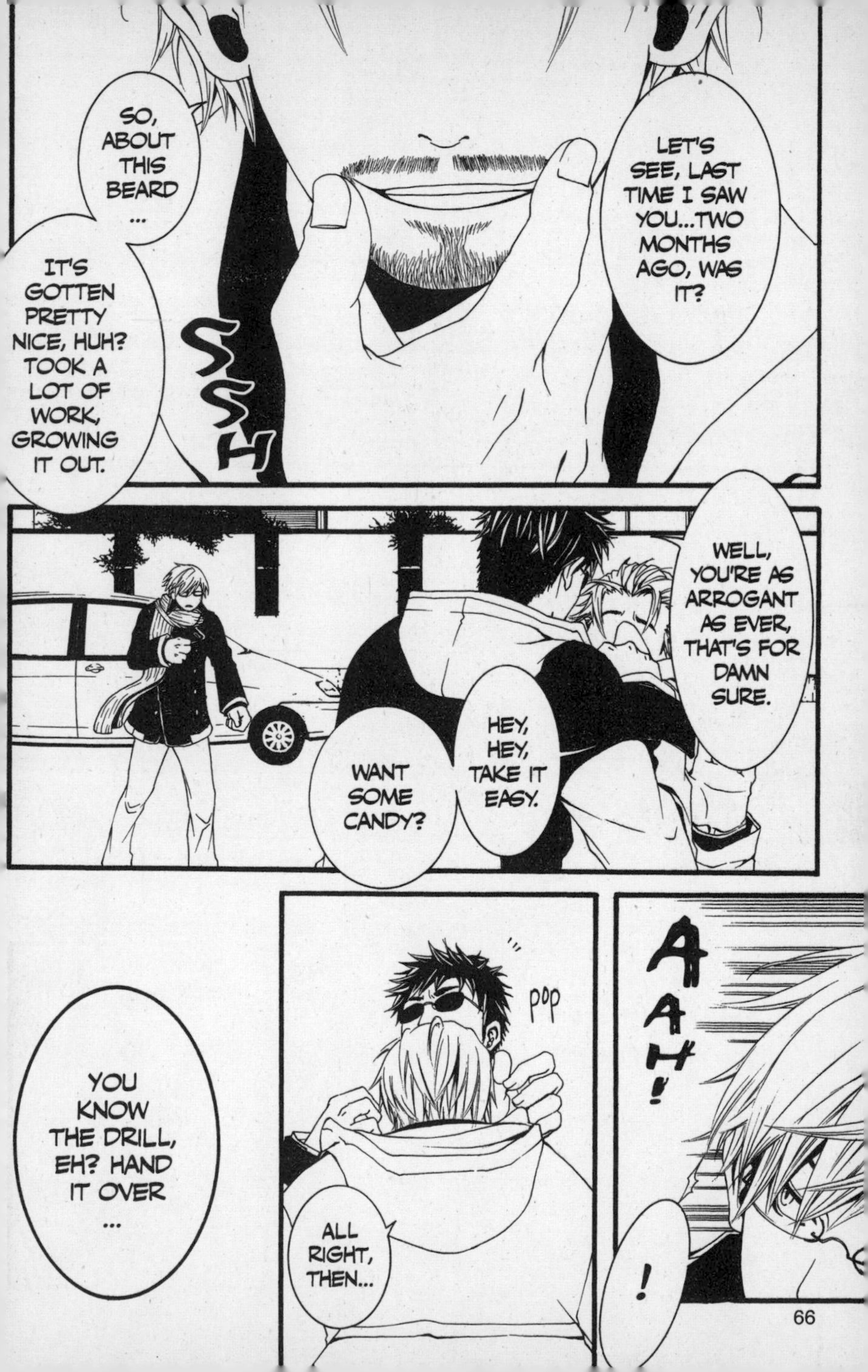
LET'S SEE, LAST TIME I SAW YOU...TWO MONTHS AGO, WAS IT?
SO, ABOUT THIS BEARD ...
IT'S GOTTEN PRETTY NICE, HUH? TOOK A LOT OF WORK, GROWING IT OUT.
SSH
WELL, YOU'RE AS ARROGANT AS EVER, THAT'S FOR DAMN SURE.
HEY, HEY, TAKE IT EASY.
WANT SOME CANDY?
AAAH!
!
pop
ALL RIGHT, THEN...
YOU KNOW THE DRILL, EH? HAND IT OVER ...

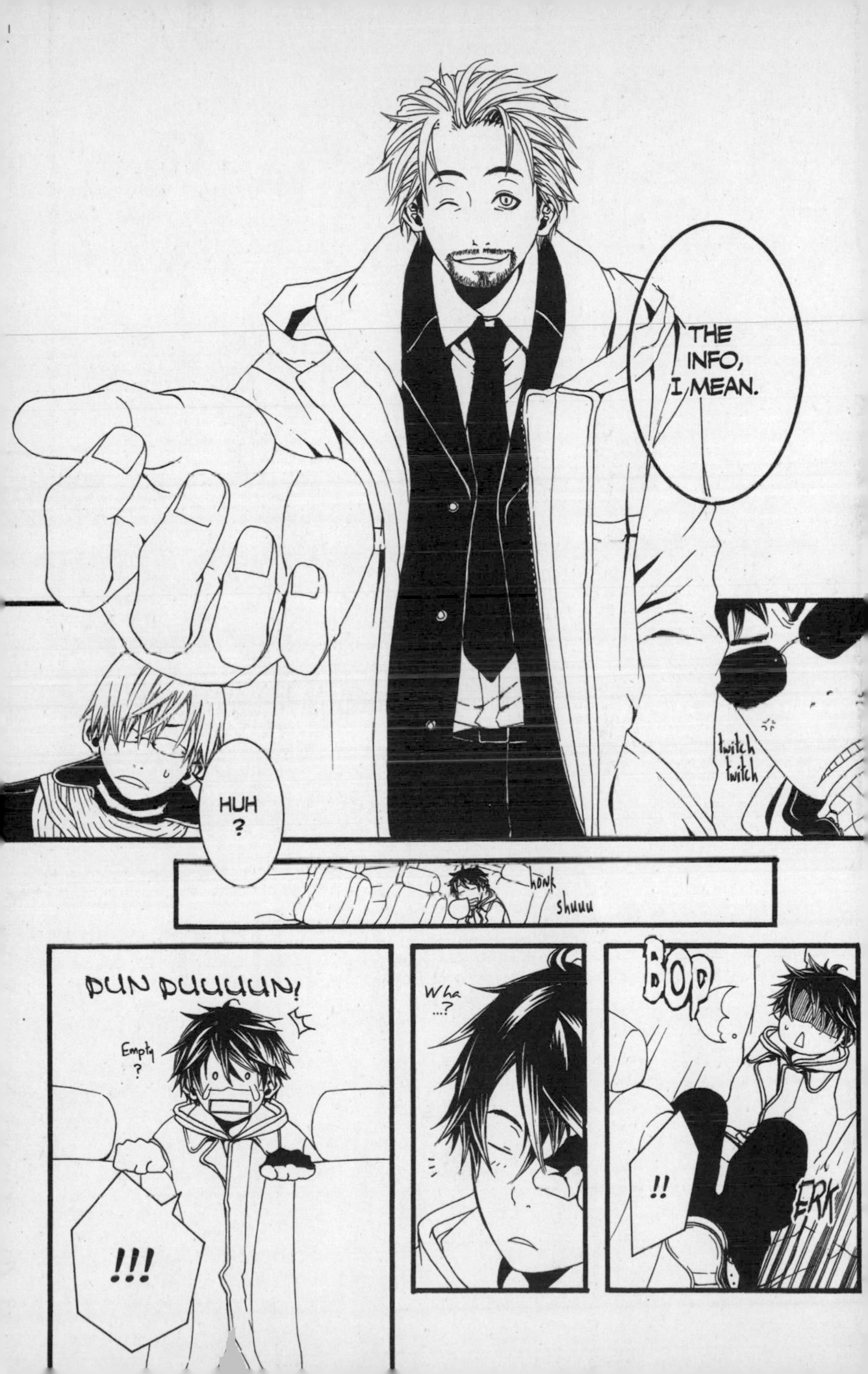
THE INFO, I MEAN.
twitch twitch
HUH ?
honk
shuuu
BOP
!!
ERK
Wha ...?
DUN DUUUUN!
Empty ?
!!!

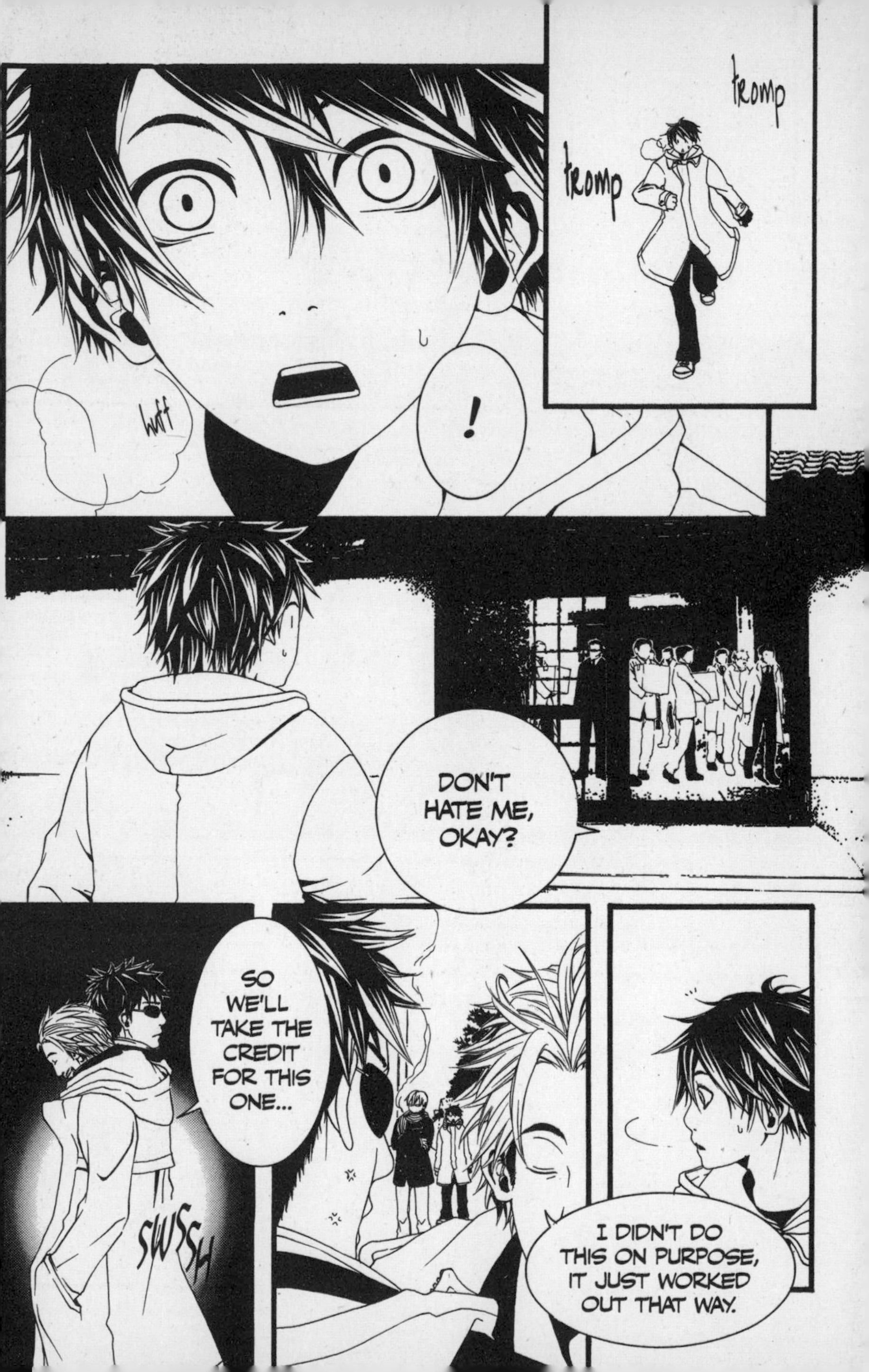
tromp
tromp
wff
!
DON'T HATE ME, OKAY?
I DIDN'T DO THIS ON PURPOSE, IT JUST WORKED OUT THAT WAY.
SO WE'LL TAKE THE CREDIT FOR THIS ONE...
SWSSH

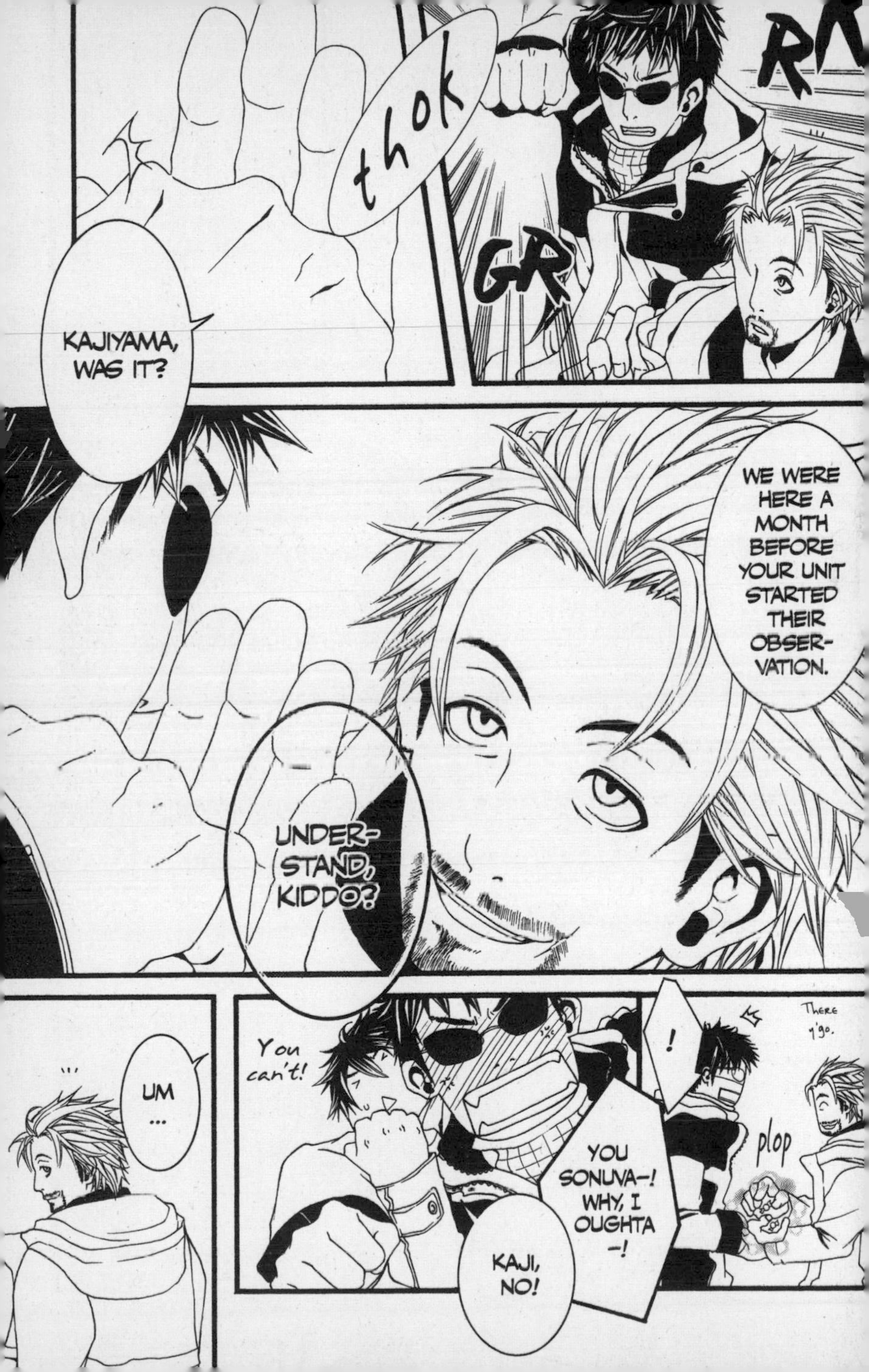
RA
GR
thok
WE WERE HERE A MONTH BEFORE YOUR UNIT STARTED THEIR OBSER-VATION.
KAJIYAMA, WAS IT?
UNDER-STAND, KIDDO?
There y'go.
!
plop
You can't!
YOU SONUVA—! WHY, I OUGHTA—!
KAJI, NO!
UM ...

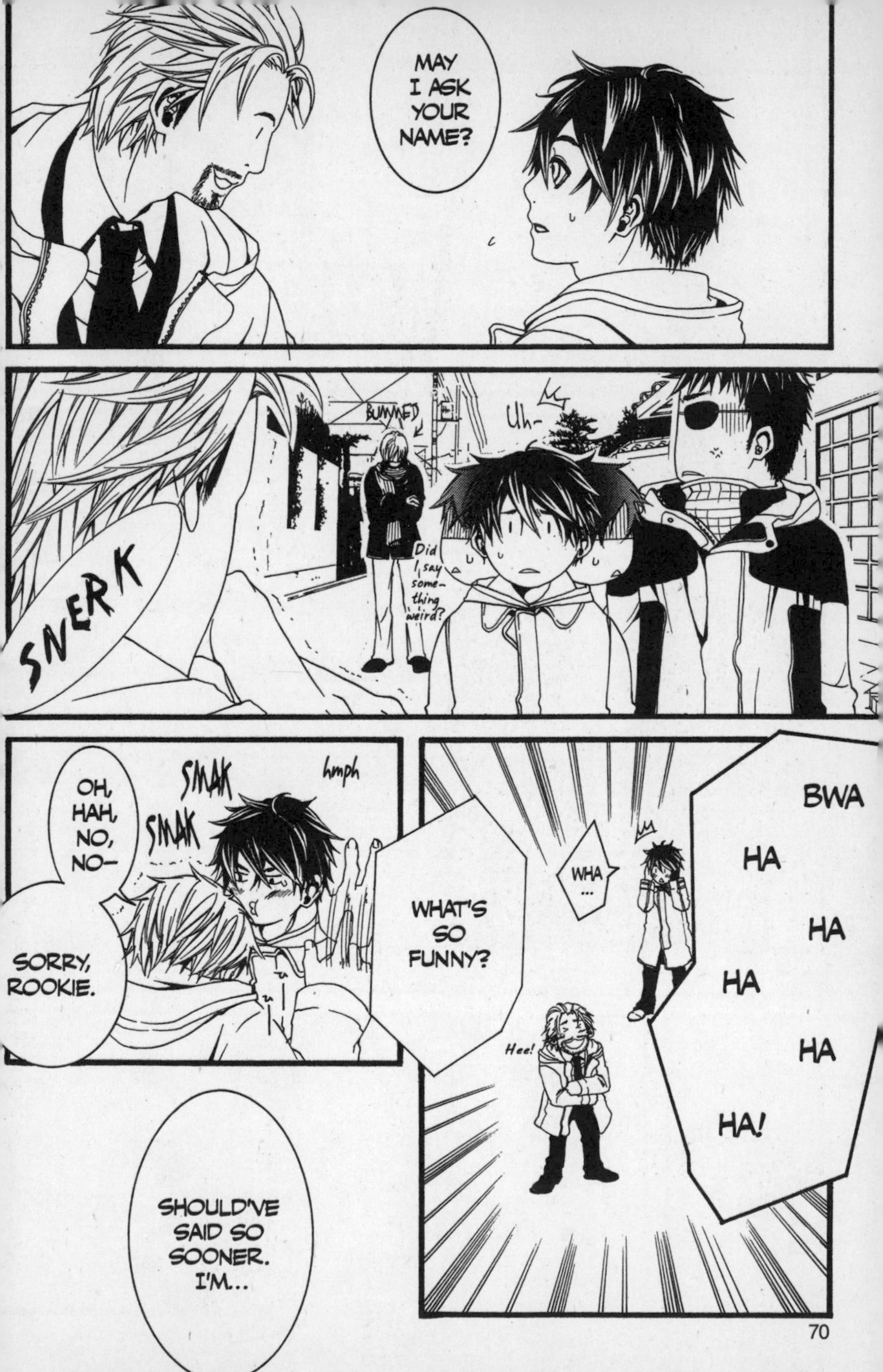
MAY I ASK YOUR NAME?
Uh-
BUMMED
Did I say something weird?
SNERK
BWA HA HA HA HA HA!
WHA...
Hee!
WHAT'S SO FUNNY?
hmph
SMAK SMAK
OH, HAH, NO, NO-
SORRY, ROOKIE.
SHOULD'VE SAID SO SOONER. I'M...

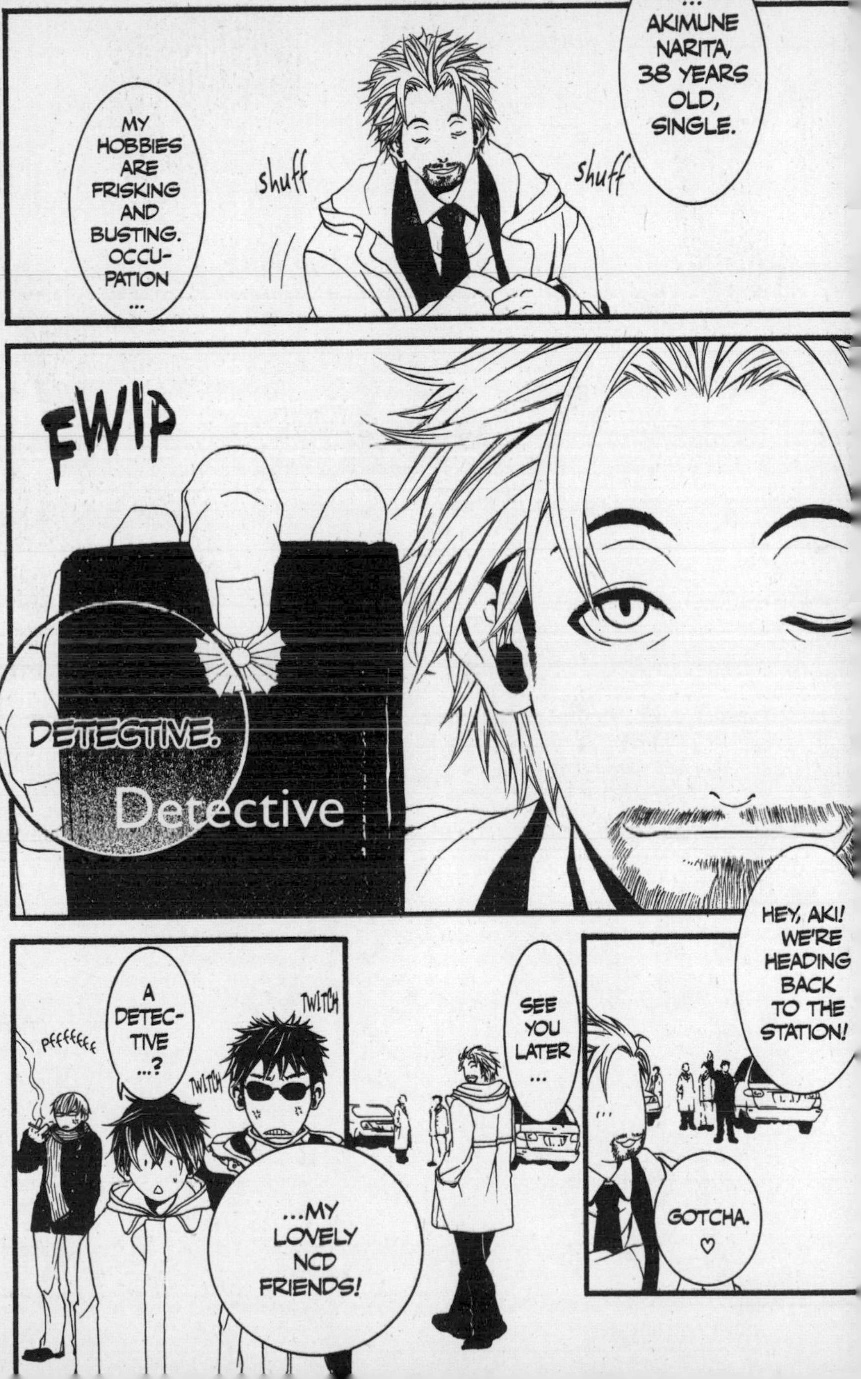
...
AKIMUNE NARITA, 38 YEARS OLD, SINGLE.
shuff
shuff
MY HOBBIES ARE FRISKING AND BUSTING. OCCUPATION ...
FWIP
DETECTIVE.
Detective
HEY, AKI! WE'RE HEADING BACK TO THE STATION!
...
GOTCHA. ♡
SEE YOU LATER ...
TWITCH
A DETEC-TIVE ...?
TWITCH
pffffffff
...MY LOVELY NCD FRIENDS!

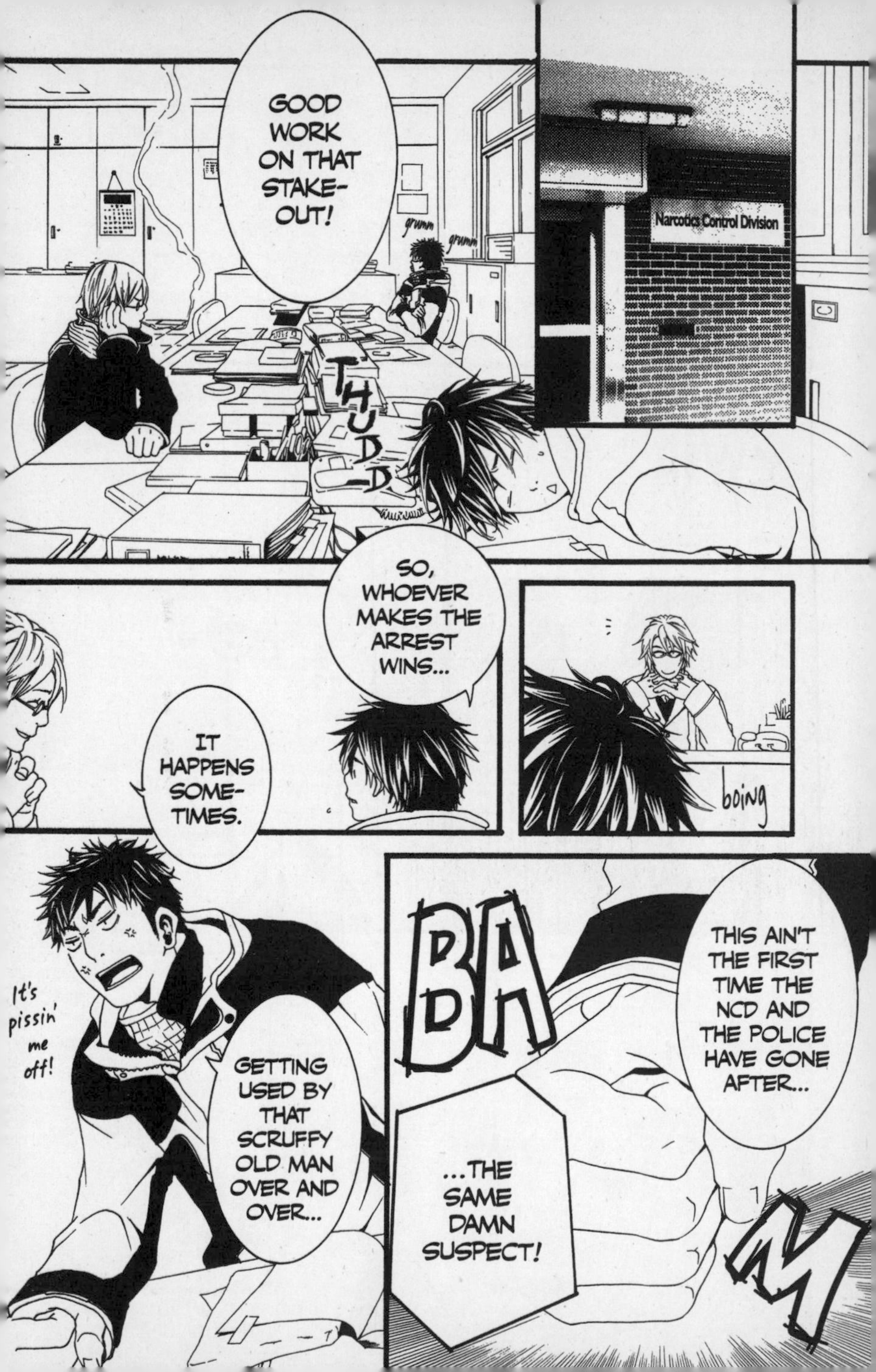
Narcotics Control Division
GOOD WORK ON THAT STAKE-OUT!
grumm grumm
THUD
boing
SO, WHOEVER MAKES THE ARREST WINS...
IT HAPPENS SOME-TIMES.
BAM
THIS AIN'T THE FIRST TIME THE NCD AND THE POLICE HAVE GONE AFTER...
...THE SAME DAMN SUSPECT!
GETTING USED BY THAT SCRUFFY OLD MAN OVER AND OVER...
It's pissin' me off!

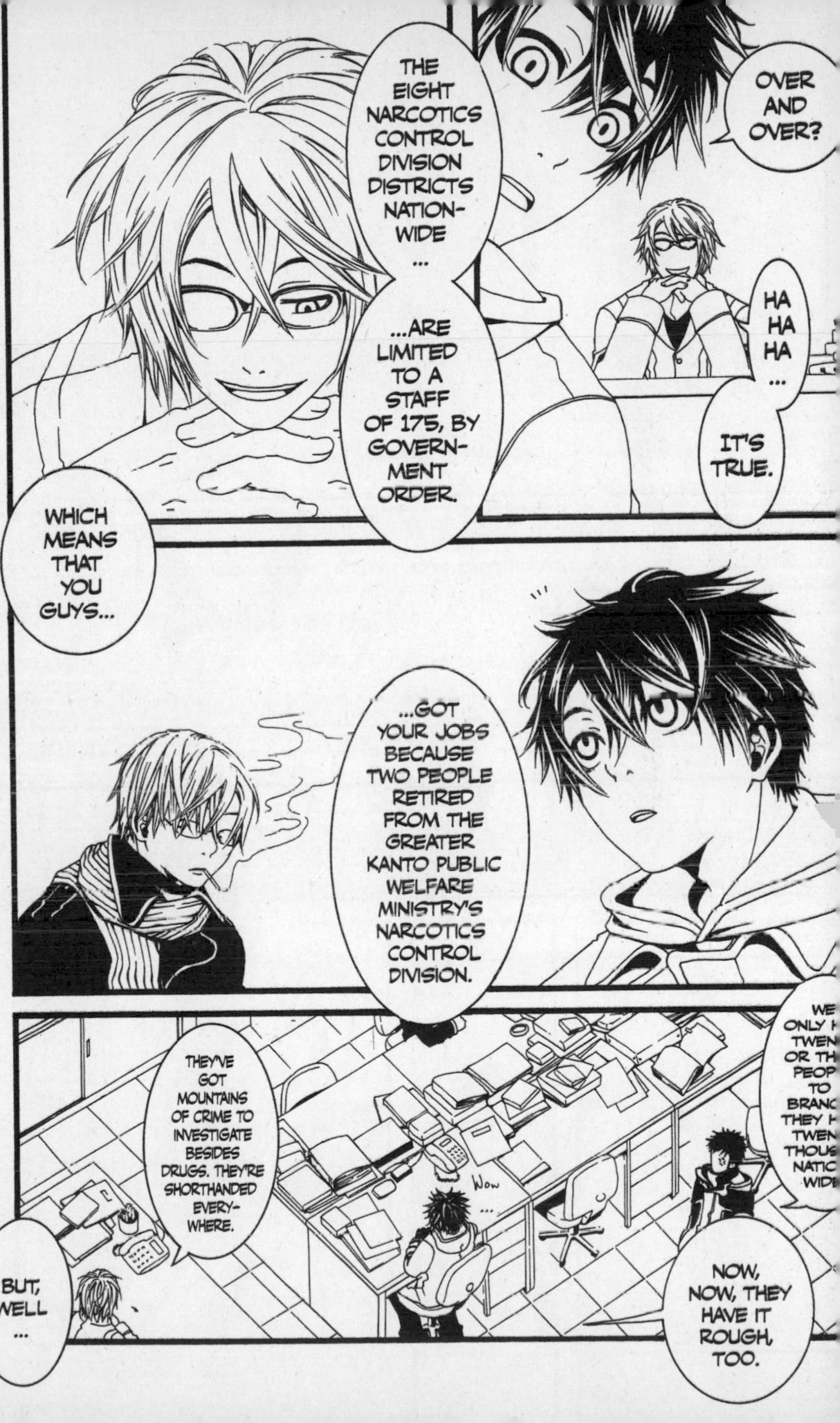
OVER AND OVER?
HA HA HA...
IT'S TRUE.
THE EIGHT NARCOTICS CONTROL DIVISION DISTRICTS NATION-WIDE...
...ARE LIMITED TO A STAFF OF 175, BY GOVERN-MENT ORDER.
WHICH MEANS THAT YOU GUYS...
...GOT YOUR JOBS BECAUSE TWO PEOPLE RETIRED FROM THE GREATER KANTO PUBLIC WELFARE MINISTRY'S NARCOTICS CONTROL DIVISION.
WE ONLY H TWEN OR TH PEOP TO BRANC THEY H TWEN THOUS NATIC WIDI
NOW, NOW, THEY HAVE IT ROUGH, TOO.
WOW...
THEY'VE GOT MOUNTAINS OF CRIME TO INVESTIGATE BESIDES DRUGS. THEY'RE SHORTHANDED EVERY-WHERE.
BUT, WELL...

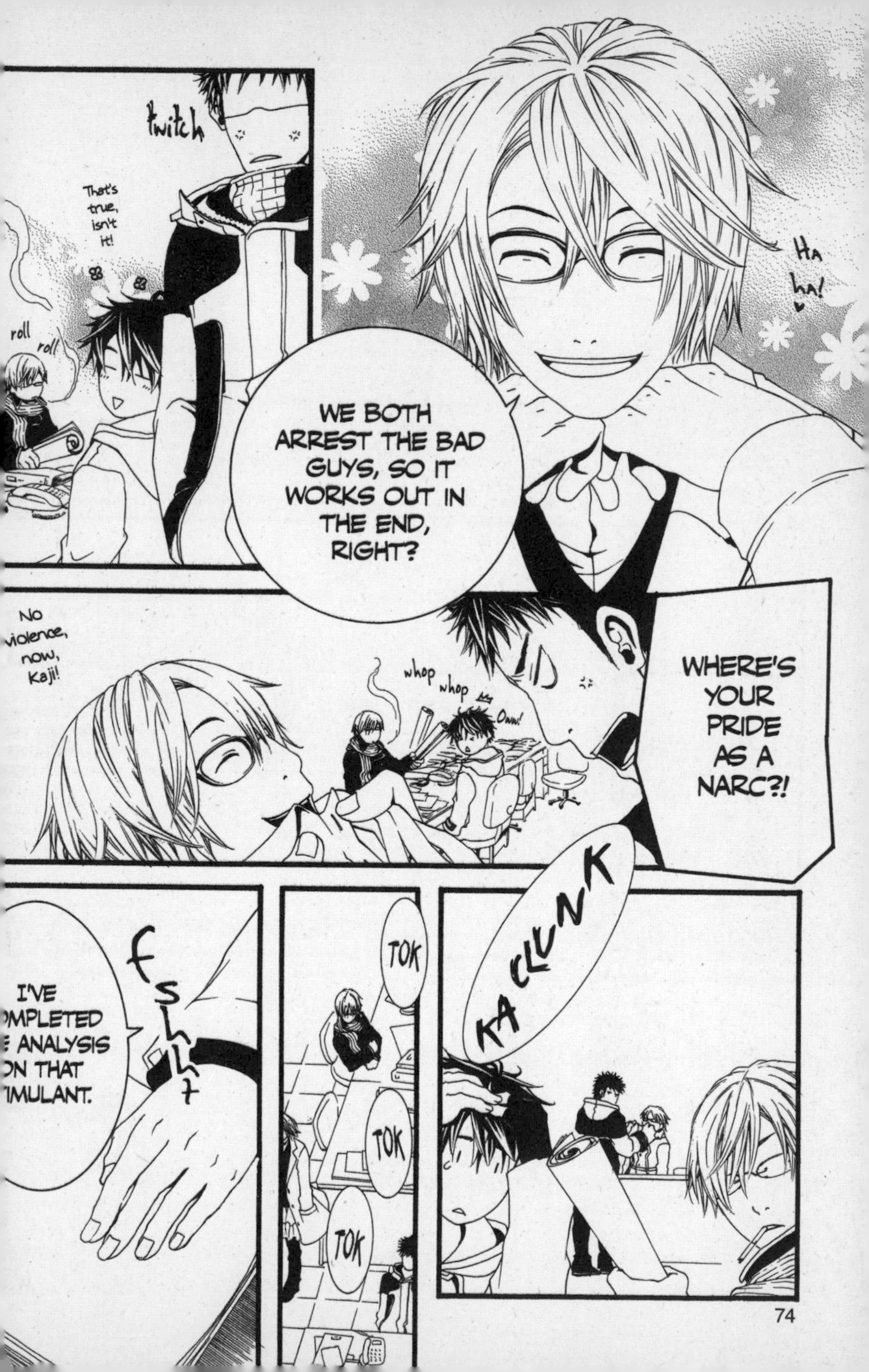
Ha ha!
WE BOTH ARREST THE BAD GUYS, SO IT WORKS OUT IN THE END, RIGHT?
twitch
That's true, isn't it!
roll
roll
WHERE'S YOUR PRIDE AS A NARC?!
whop
whop
Oww!
No violence, now, Kaji!
KA CLUNK
TOK
TOK
TOK
fshht
I'VE MPLETED ANALYSIS ON THAT TIMULANT.

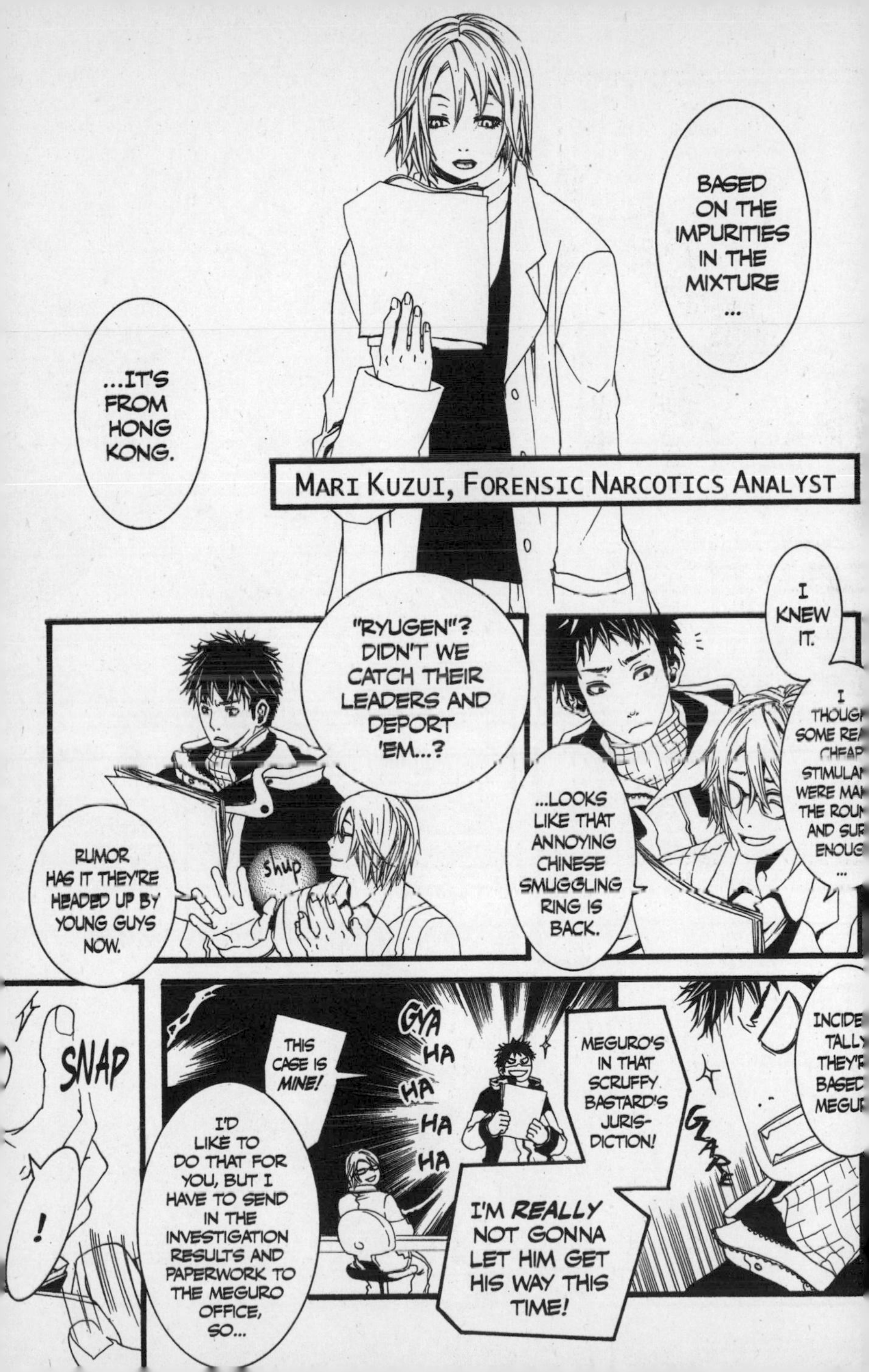
BASED ON THE IMPURITIES IN THE MIXTURE ...
...IT'S FROM HONG KONG.
MARI KUZUI, FORENSIC NARCOTICS ANALYST
I KNEW IT.
I THOUG SOME RE CHEAP STIMULA WERE MA THE ROU AND SU ENOUG ...
...LOOKS LIKE THAT ANNOYING CHINESE SMUGGLING RING IS BACK.
"RYUGEN"? DIDN'T WE CATCH THEIR LEADERS AND DEPORT 'EM...?
shup
RUMOR HAS IT THEY'RE HEADED UP BY YOUNG GUYS NOW.
INCIDE TALLY THEY'R BASED MEGUR
GLARE
MEGURO'S IN THAT SCRUFFY BASTARD'S JURIS-DICTION!
I'M *REALLY* NOT GONNA LET HIM GET HIS WAY THIS TIME!
GYA HA HA HA HA
THIS CASE IS *MINE!*
I'D LIKE TO DO THAT FOR YOU, BUT I HAVE TO SEND IN THE INVESTIGATION RESULTS AND PAPERWORK TO THE MEGURO OFFICE, SO...
SNAP
!

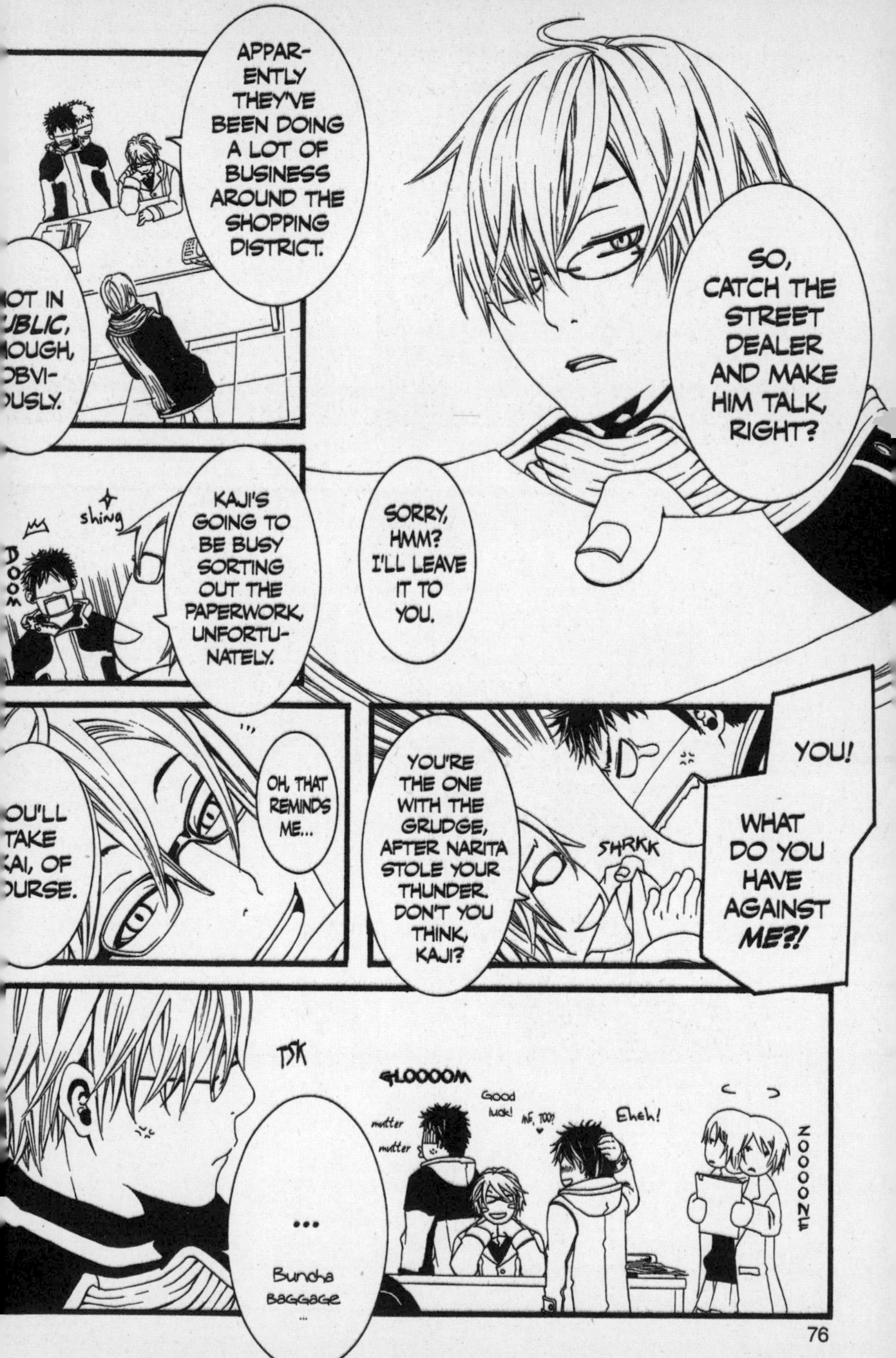
SO, CATCH THE STREET DEALER AND MAKE HIM TALK, RIGHT?
SORRY, HMM? I'LL LEAVE IT TO YOU.
APPAR-ENTLY THEY'VE BEEN DOING A LOT OF BUSINESS AROUND THE SHOPPING DISTRICT.
OT IN UBLIC, HOUGH, OBVI-OUSLY.
KAJI'S GOING TO BE BUSY SORTING OUT THE PAPERWORK, UNFORTU-NATELY.
shing
DOOM
YOU!
WHAT DO YOU HAVE AGAINST *ME?!*
SHRKK
YOU'RE THE ONE WITH THE GRUDGE, AFTER NARITA STOLE YOUR THUNDER. DON'T YOU THINK, KAJI?
OH, THAT REMINDS ME...
OU'LL TAKE AI, OF OURSE.
ZOOOOONE
Eheh!
ME, TOO?
Good luck!
mutter mutter
GLOOOOM
TSK
...
Buncha Baggage ...

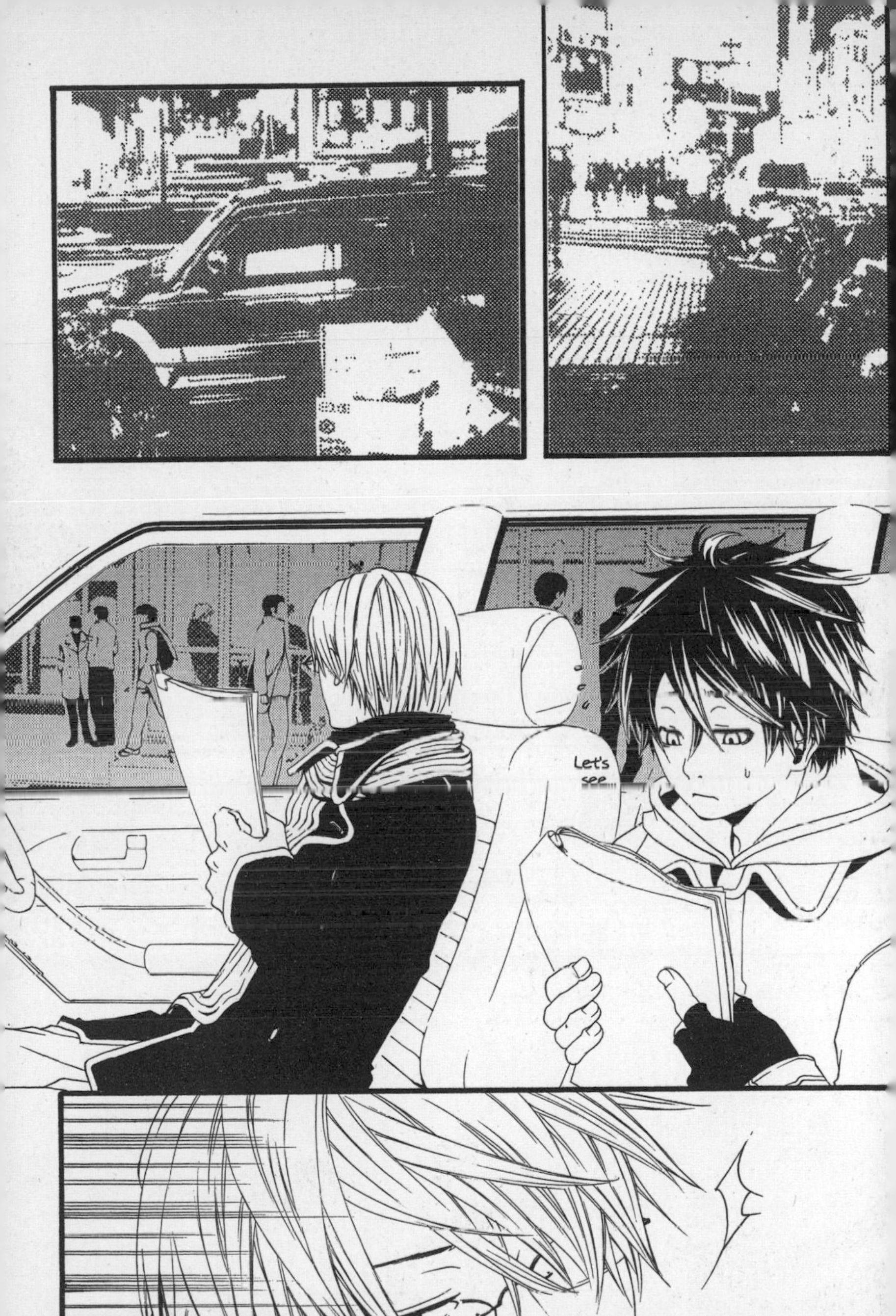
Let's see...

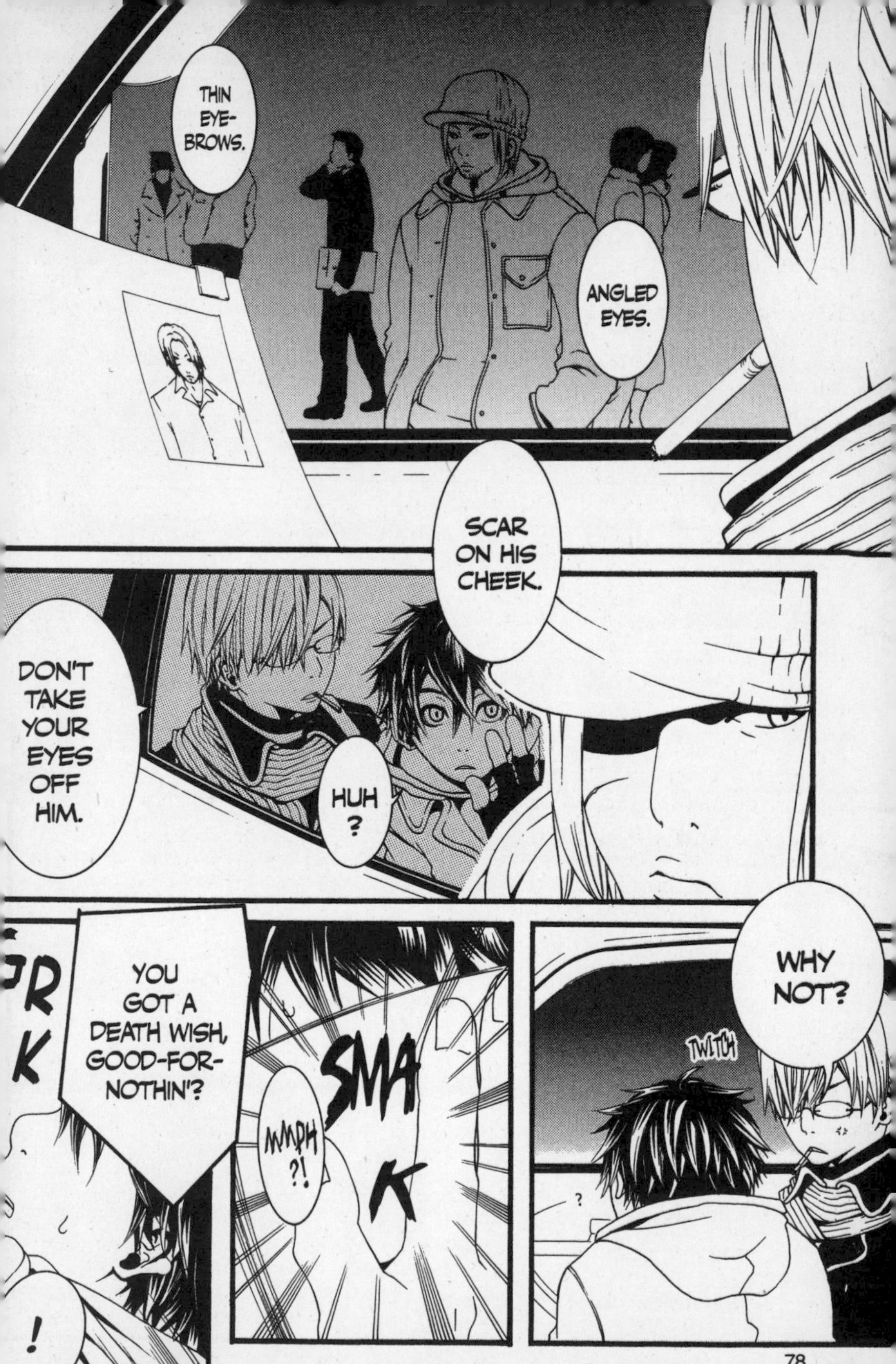
THIN EYE-BROWS.
ANGLED EYES.
SCAR ON HIS CHEEK.
HUH ?
DON'T TAKE YOUR EYES OFF HIM.
WHY NOT?
TWITCH
?
SMAK
MMPH ?!
YOU GOT A DEATH WISH, GOOD-FOR-NOTHIN'?
GRK
!

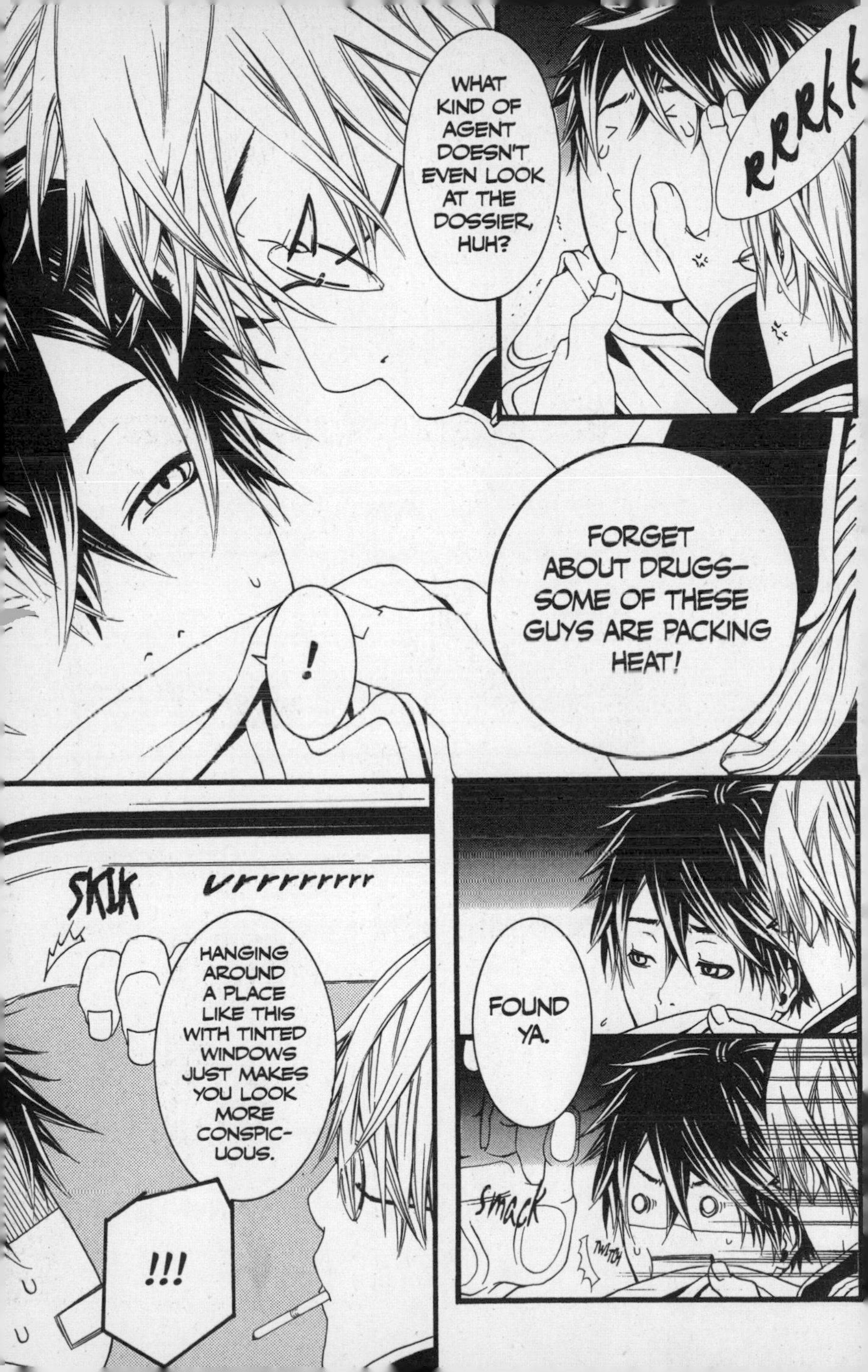
WHAT KIND OF AGENT DOESN'T EVEN LOOK AT THE DOSSIER, HUH?
RRRKK
!
FORGET ABOUT DRUGS- SOME OF THESE GUYS ARE PACKING HEAT!
FOUND YA.
SMACK
TWITCH
SKIK
VRRRRRRRR
HANGING AROUND A PLACE LIKE THIS WITH TINTED WINDOWS JUST MAKES YOU LOOK MORE CONSPIC-UOUS.
!!!

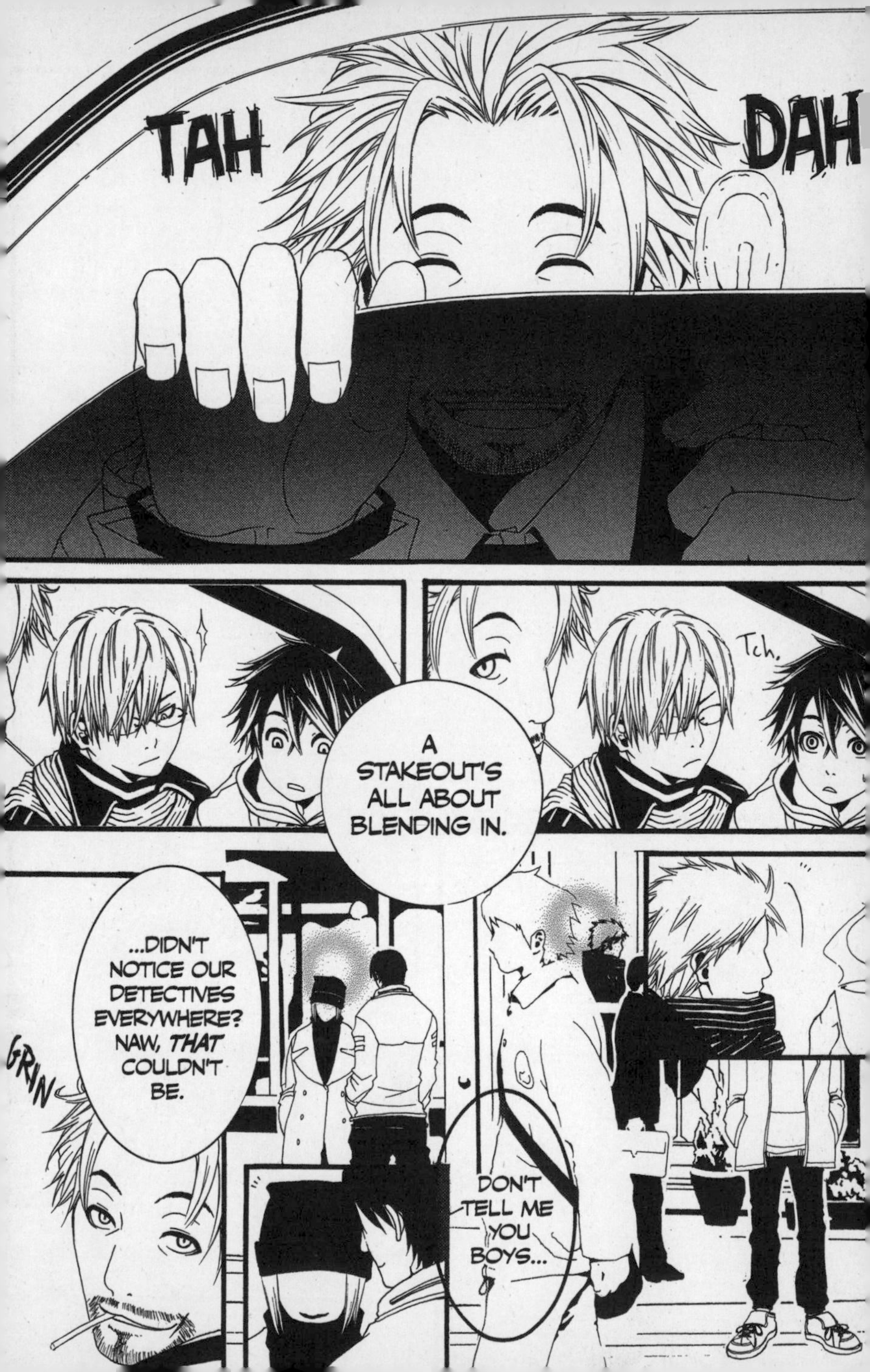
DAH
TAH
Tch.
A STAKEOUT'S ALL ABOUT BLENDING IN.
DON'T TELL ME YOU BOYS...
...DIDN'T NOTICE OUR DETECTIVES EVERYWHERE? NAW, *THAT* COULDN'T BE.
GRIN

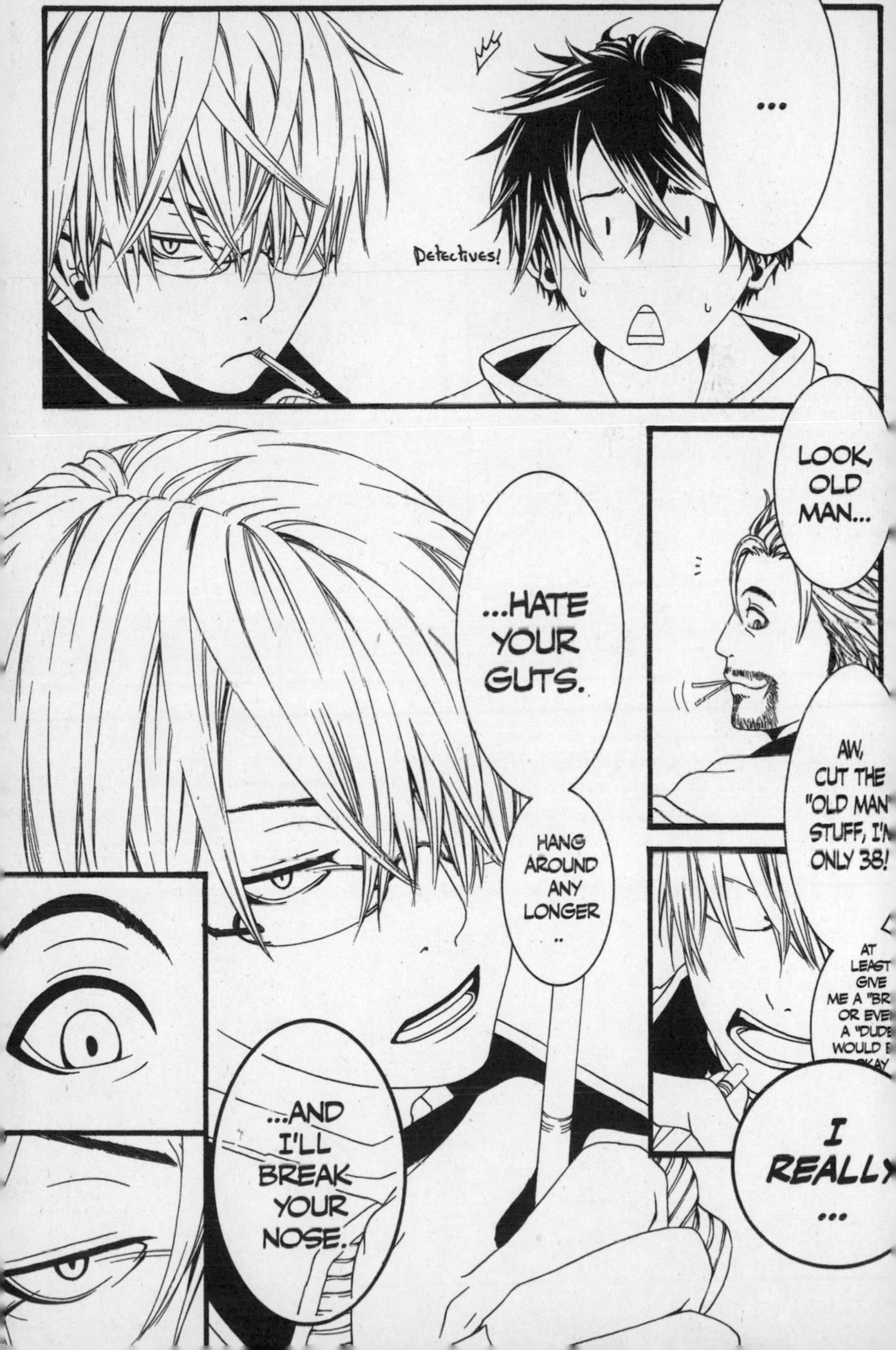
...
Detectives!
LOOK, OLD MAN...
AW, CUT THE "OLD MAN STUFF, I'M ONLY 38!
AT LEAST GIVE ME A "BR OR EVE A "DUDE WOULD B OKAY
I REALLY ...
...HATE YOUR GUTS.
HANG AROUND ANY LONGER...
...AND I'LL BREAK YOUR NOSE..

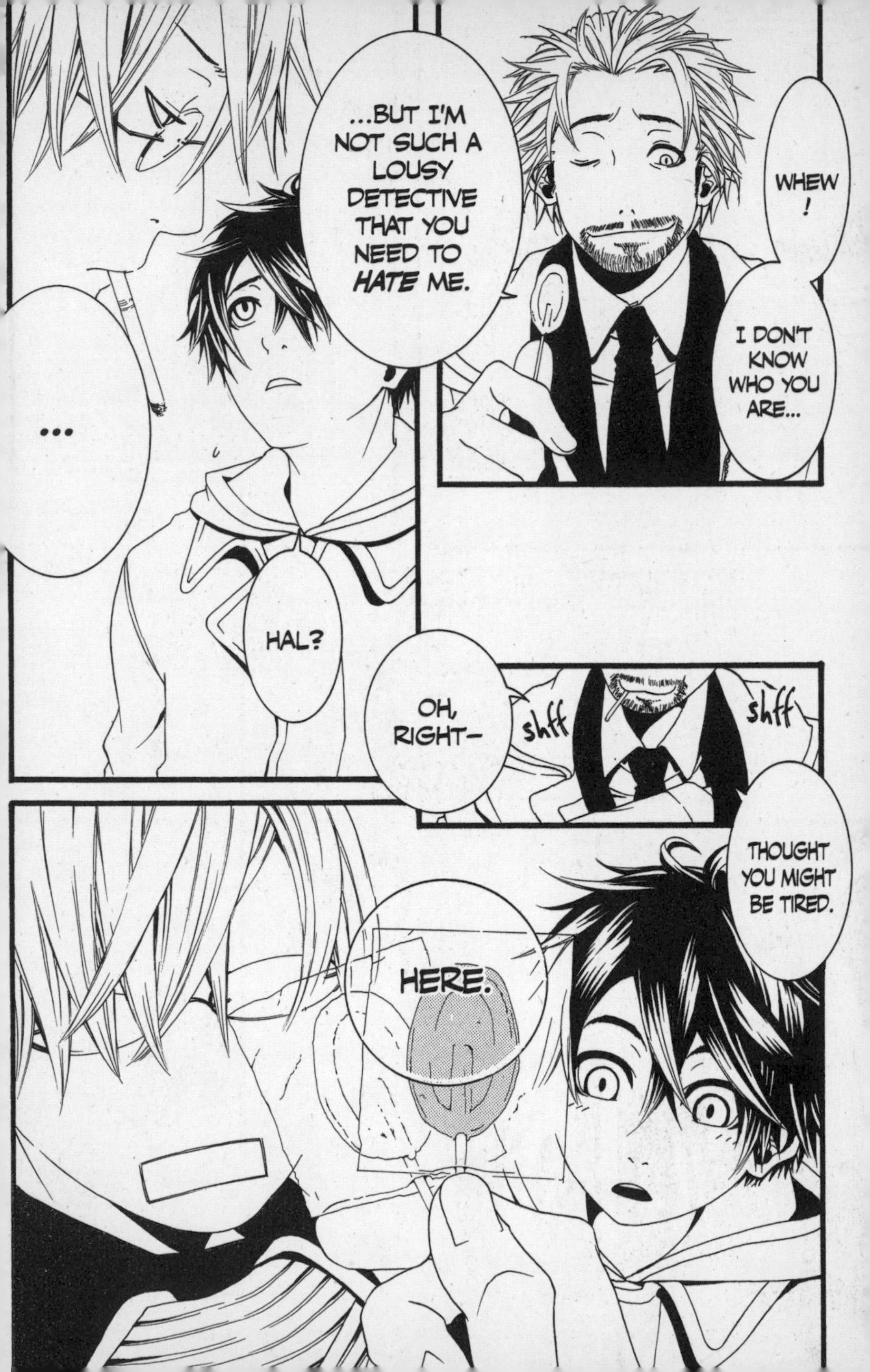
WHEW!
I DON'T KNOW WHO YOU ARE...
...BUT I'M NOT SUCH A LOUSY DETECTIVE THAT YOU NEED TO *HATE* ME.
...
HAL?
OH, RIGHT-
shff
shff
THOUGHT YOU MIGHT BE TIRED.
HERE.

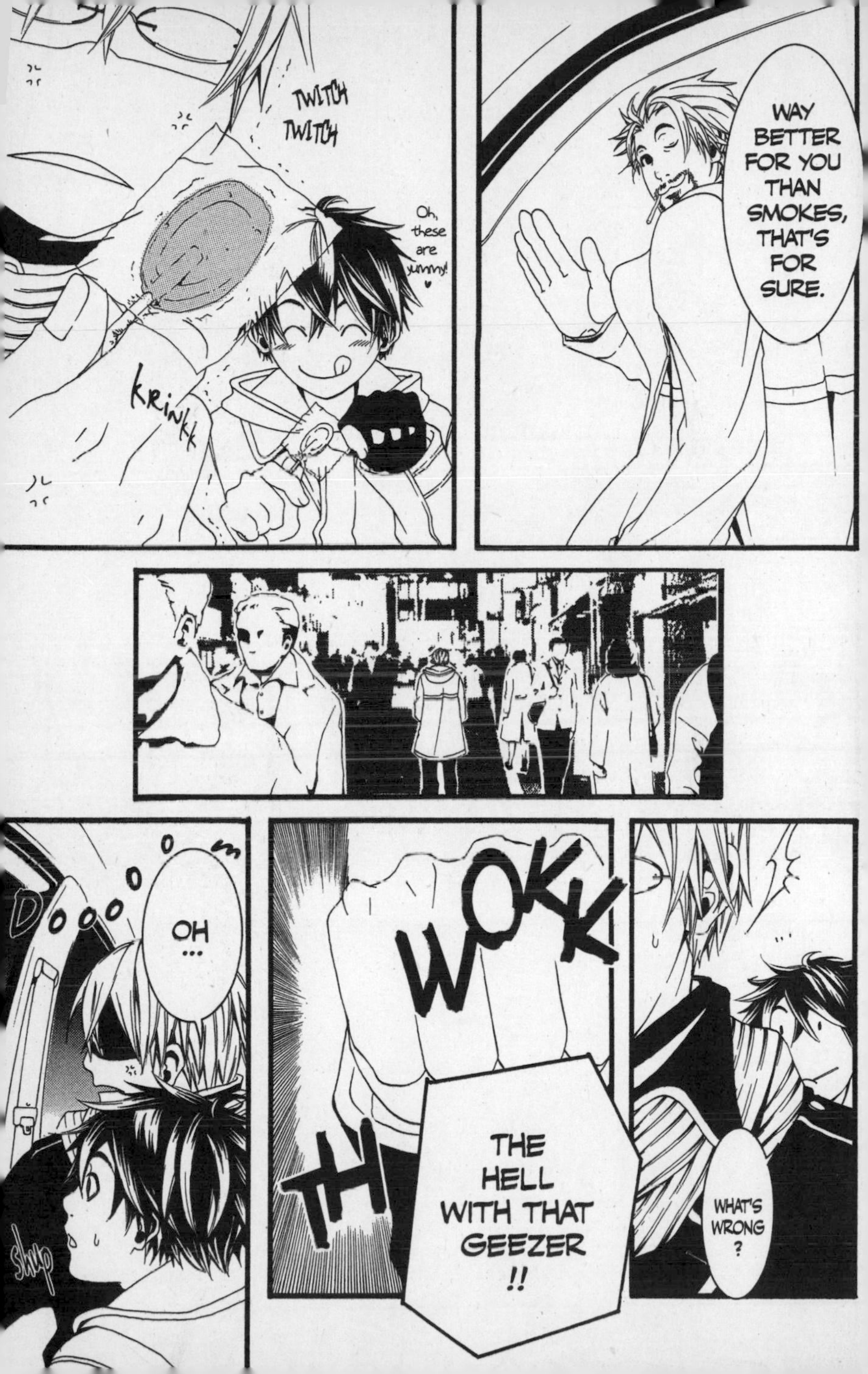
WAY BETTER FOR YOU THAN SMOKES, THAT'S FOR SURE.
TWITCH TWITCH
Oh, these are yummy! ♥
KRINKK
...
WHAT'S WRONG ?
WOKK
TH
THE HELL WITH THAT GEEZER !!
OH ...

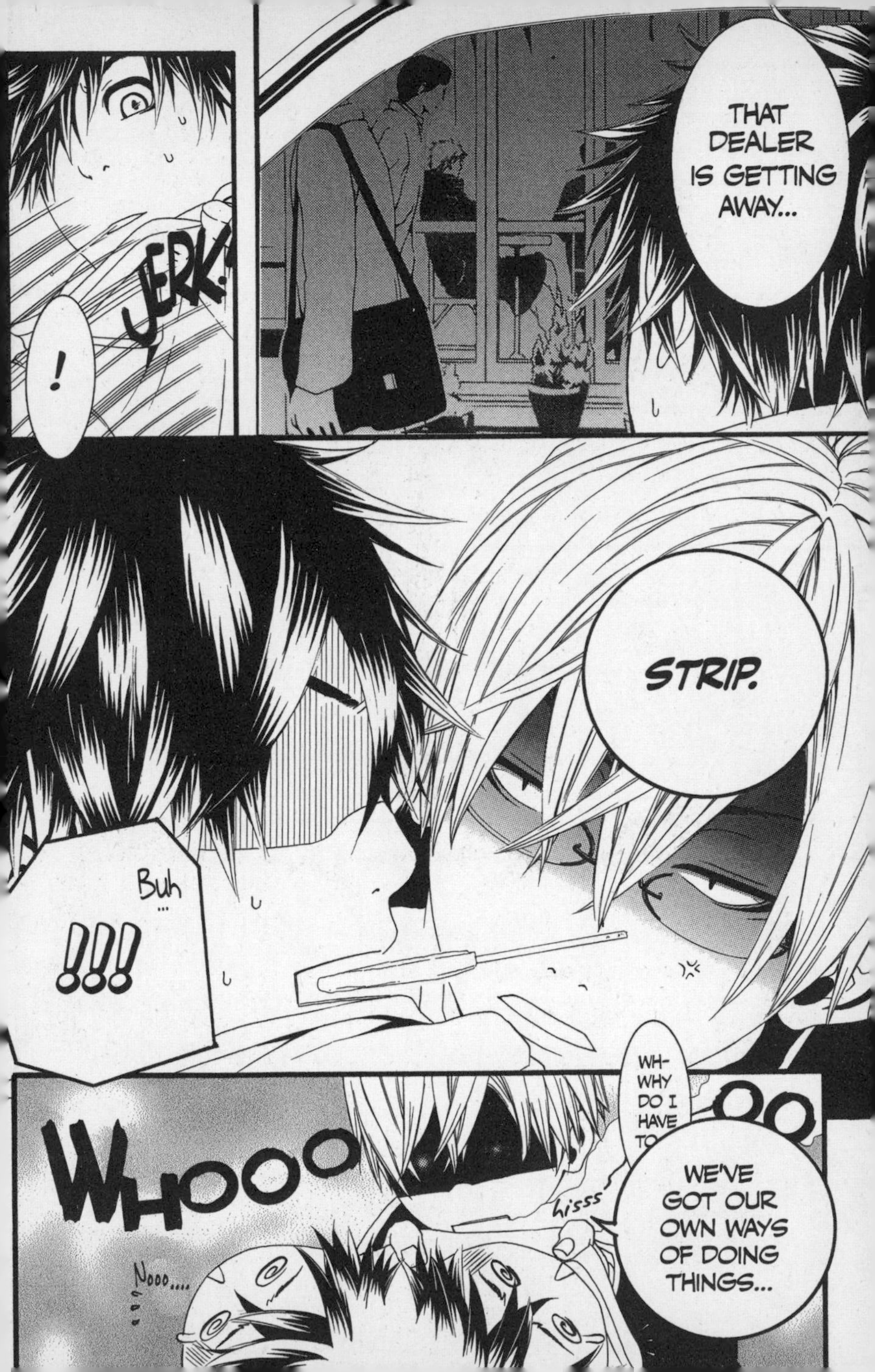
THAT DEALER IS GETTING AWAY...
JERK!
!
STRIP.
Buh...
!!!
WH-WHY DO I HAVE TO
WE'VE GOT OUR OWN WAYS OF DOING THINGS...
hisss
WHOOOOO
Nooo....

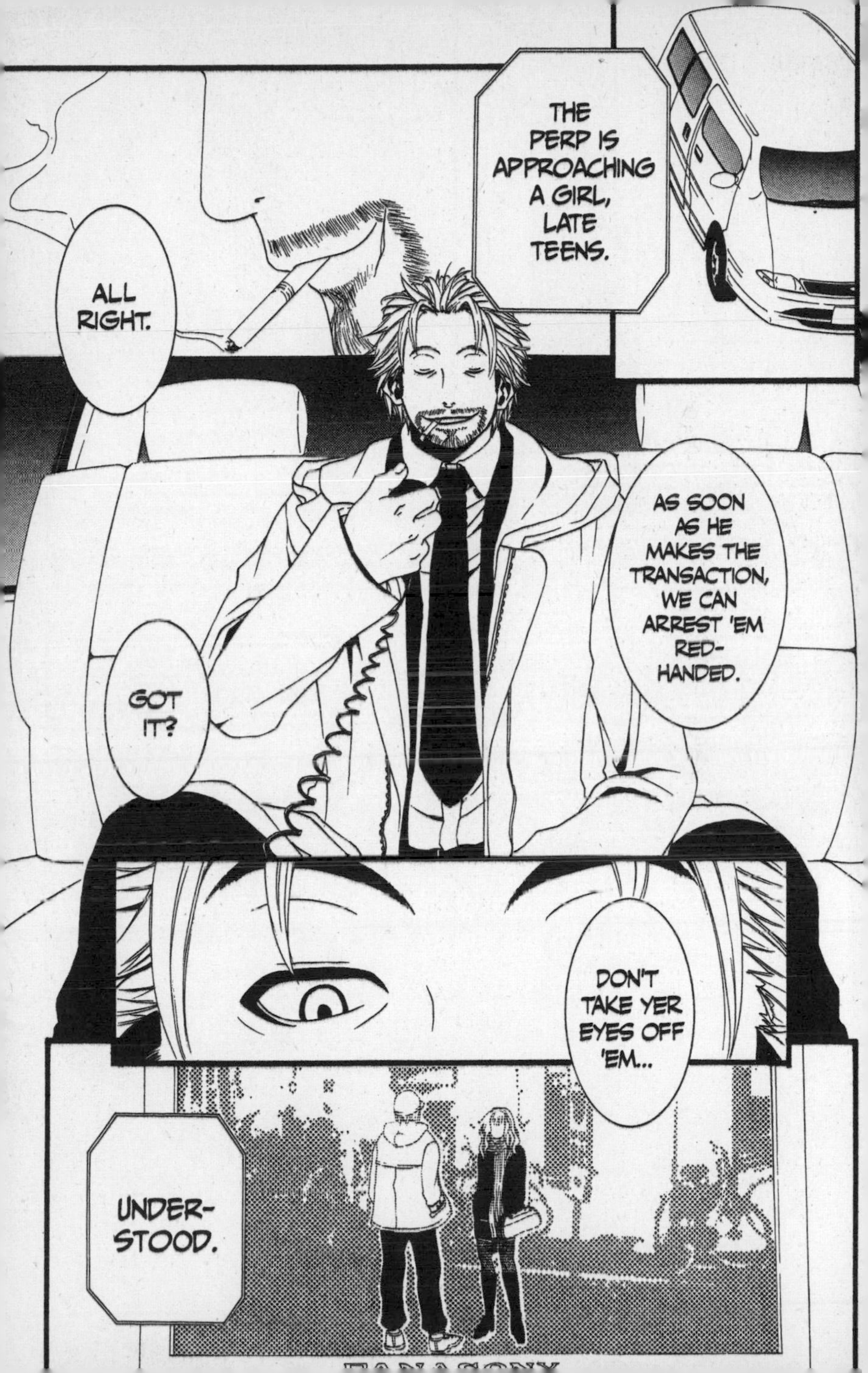
THE PERP IS APPROACHING A GIRL, LATE TEENS.
ALL RIGHT.
AS SOON AS HE MAKES THE TRANSACTION, WE CAN ARREST 'EM RED-HANDED.
GOT IT?
DON'T TAKE YER EYES OFF 'EM...
UNDER-STOOD.

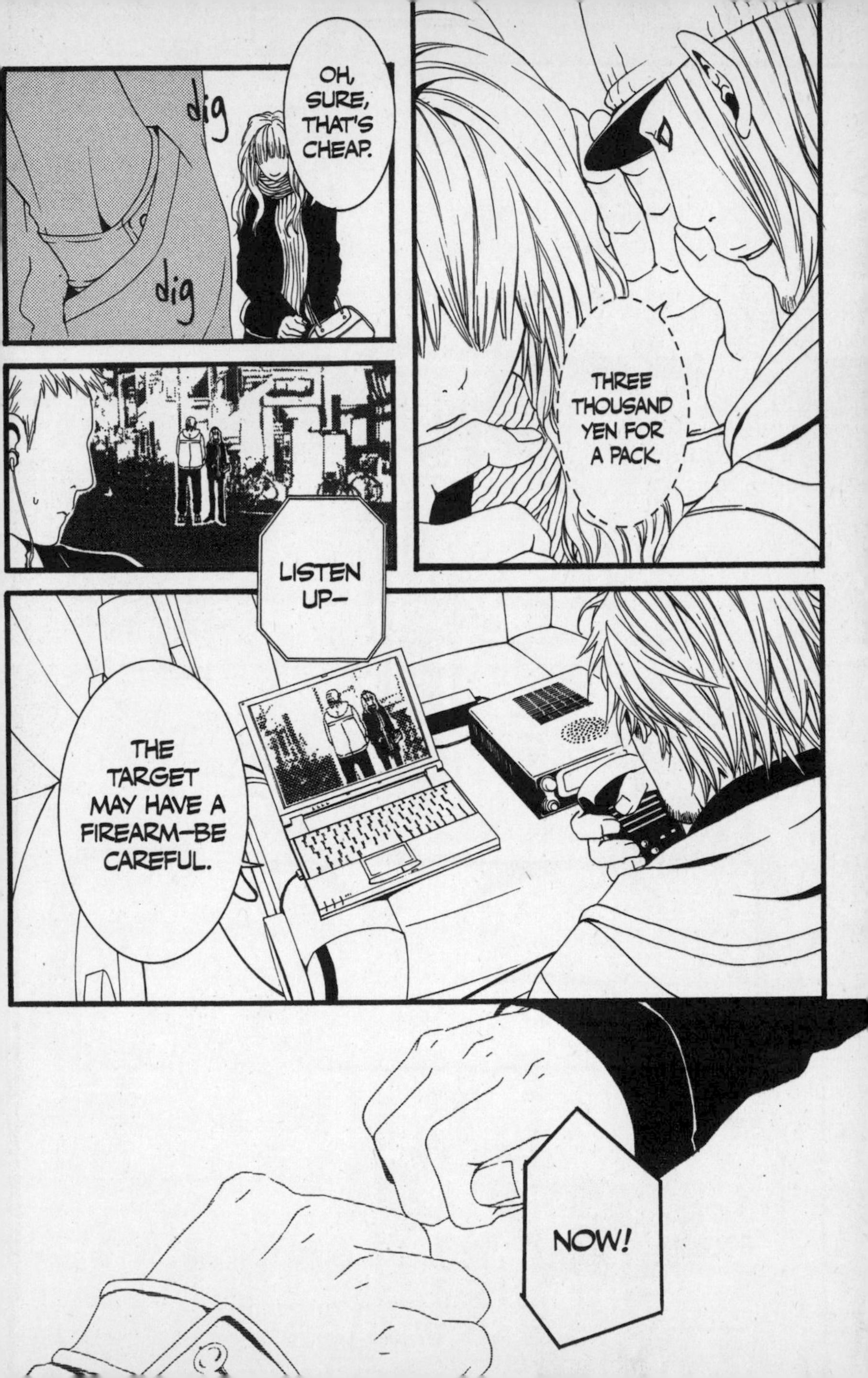
THREE THOUSAND YEN FOR A PACK.
OH, SURE, THAT'S CHEAP.
dig
dig
LISTEN UP—
THE TARGET MAY HAVE A FIREARM—BE CAREFUL.
NOW!

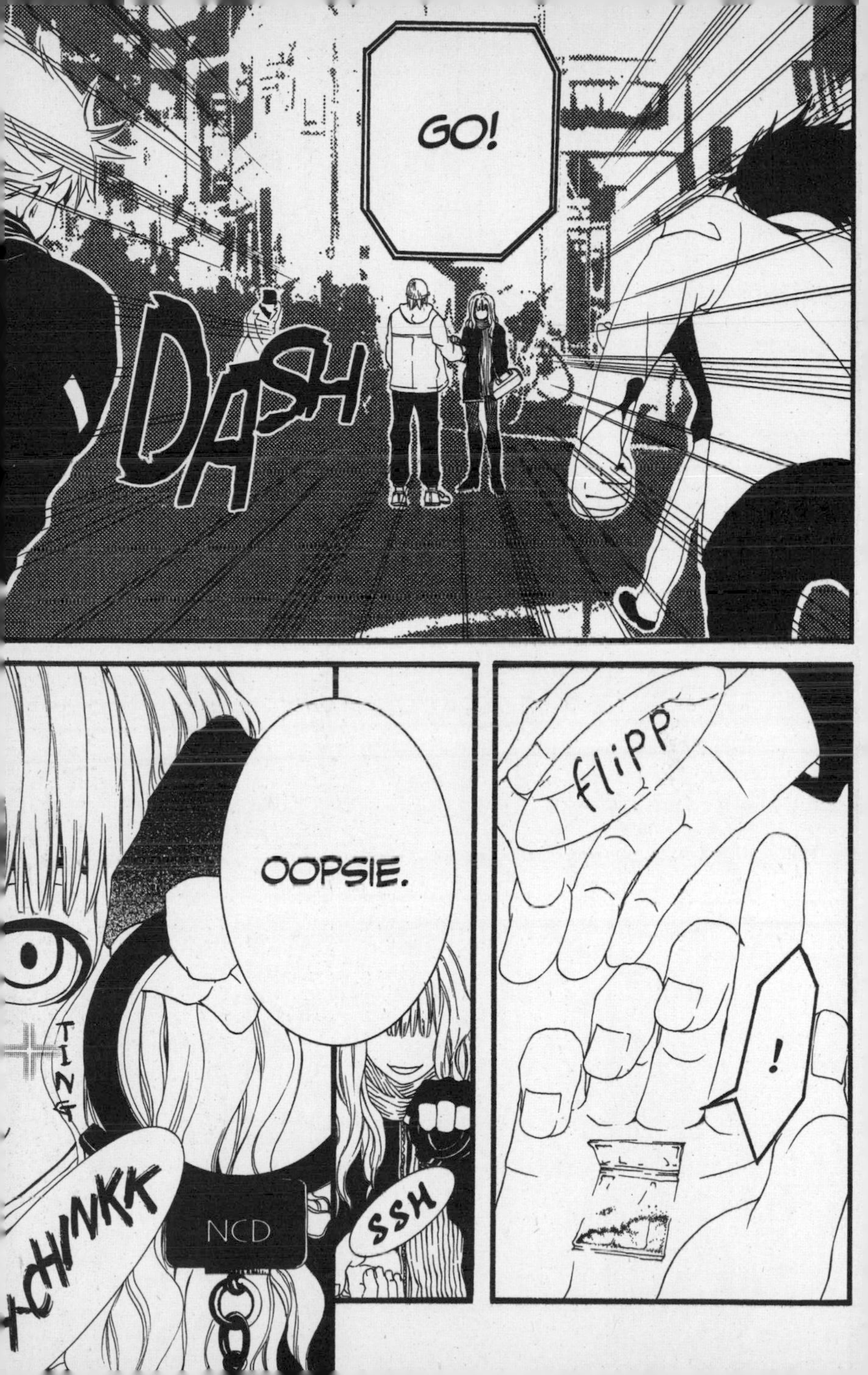
GO!
DASH
flipp
!
OOPSIE.
TING
CHINKK
NCD
SSH

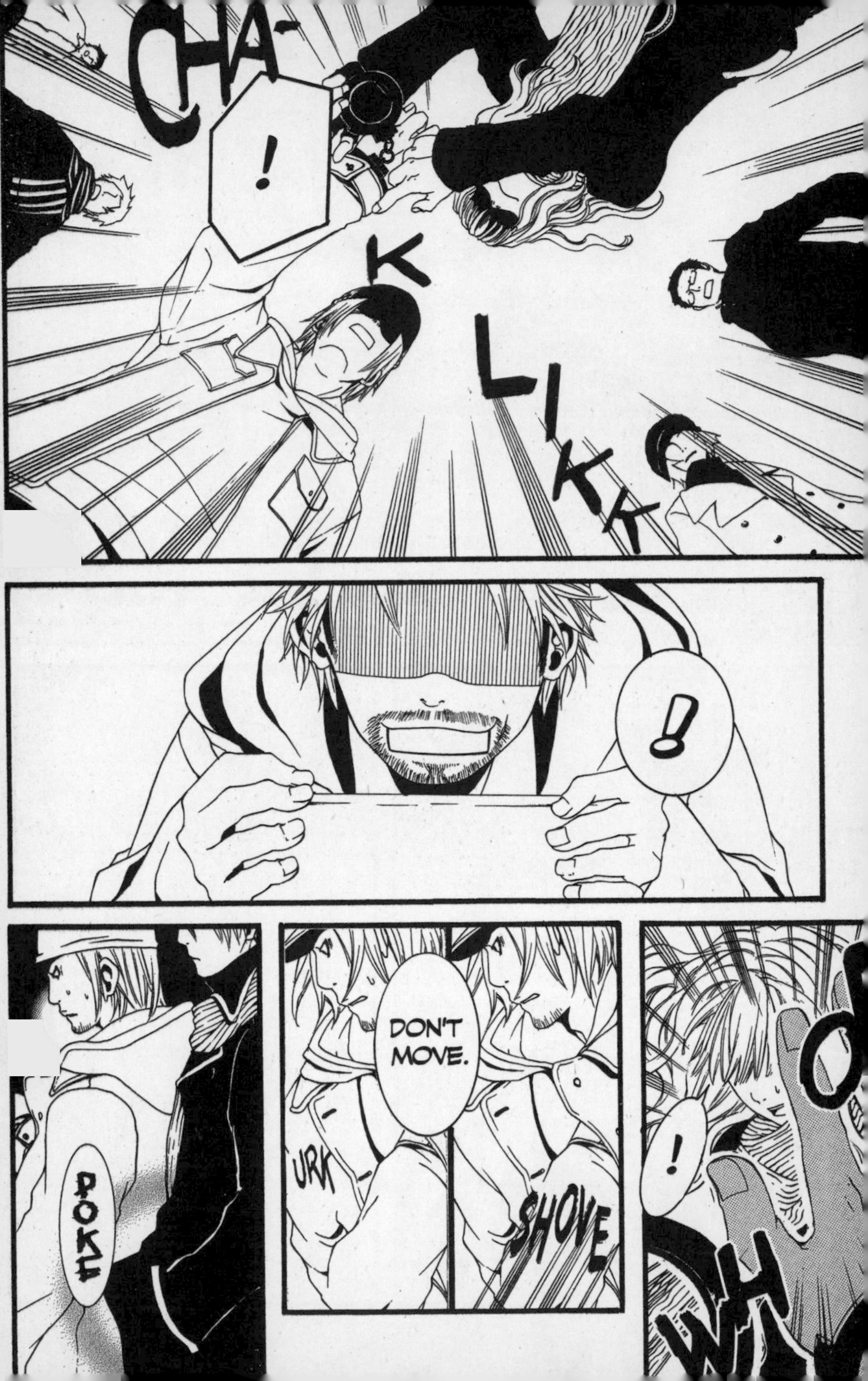

CHA-K
!
LIKKK
!
!
DON'T MOVE.
SHOVE
URK
POKE

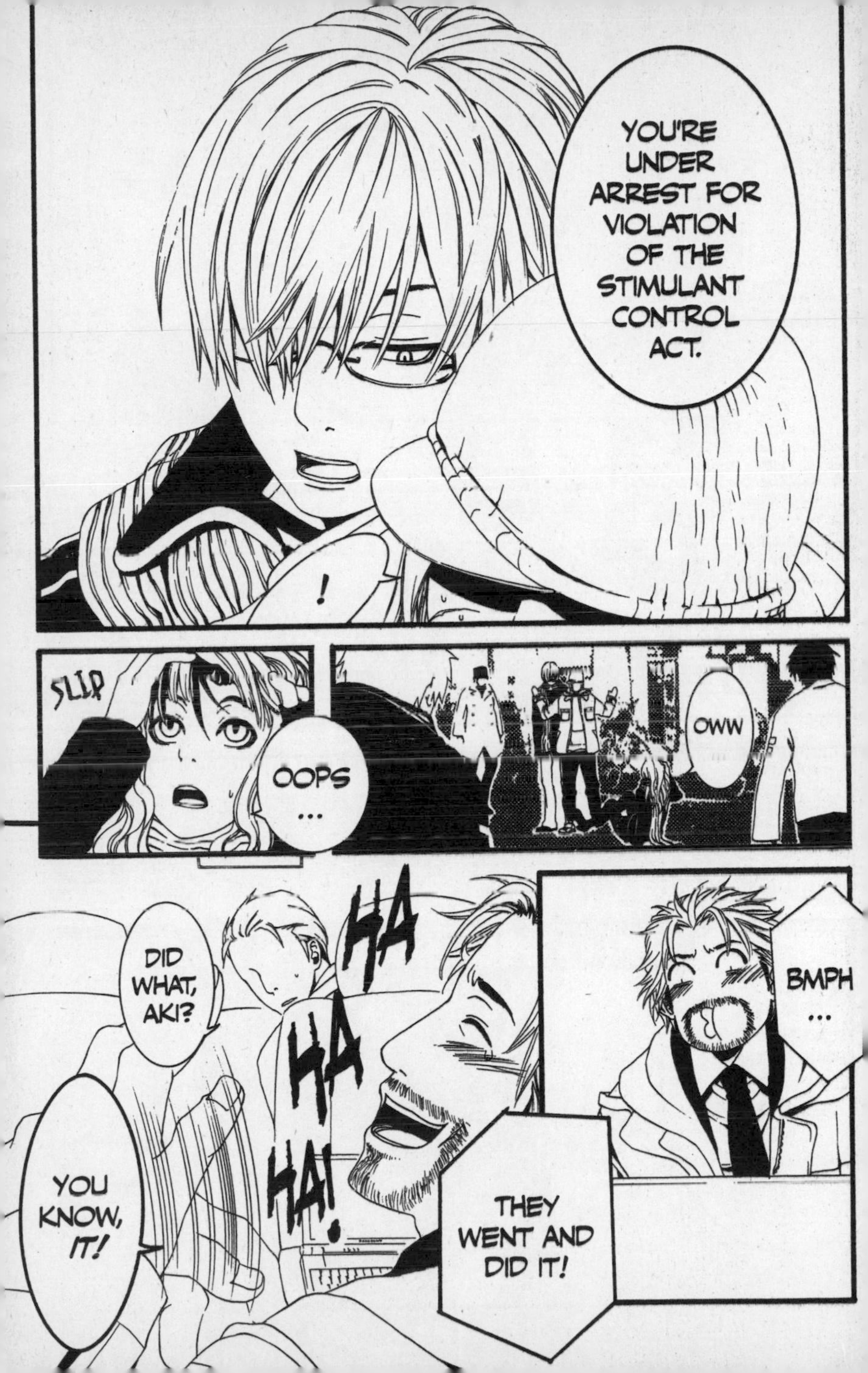
YOU'RE UNDER ARREST FOR VIOLATION OF THE STIMULANT CONTROL ACT.
!
OWW
SLIP
OOPS ...
BMPH ...
HA HA HA!
THEY WENT AND DID IT!
DID WHAT, AKI?
YOU KNOW, IT!

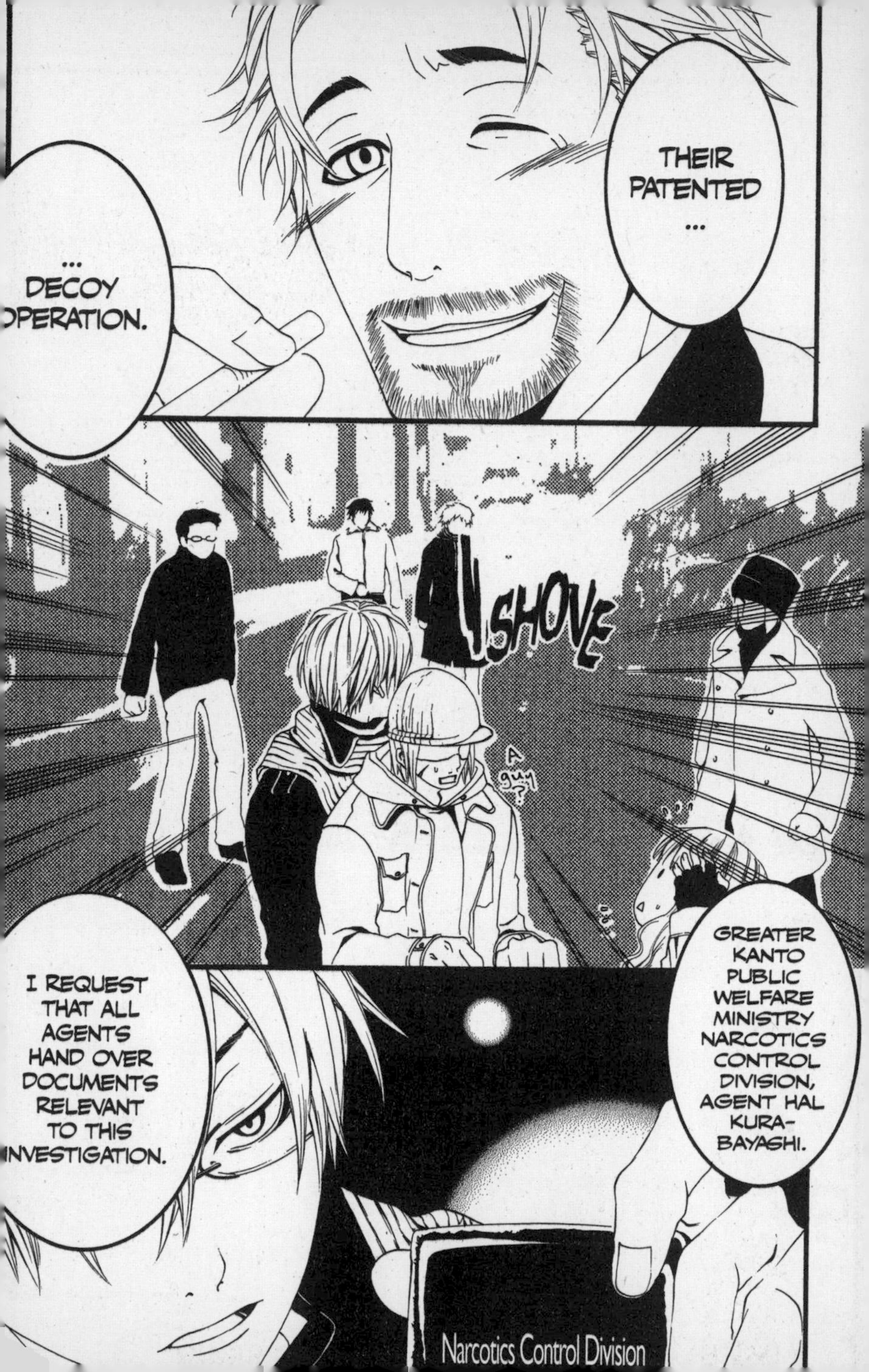
THEIR PATENTED ...
... DECOY OPERATION.
SHOVE
A guy?
GREATER KANTO PUBLIC WELFARE MINISTRY NARCOTICS CONTROL DIVISION, AGENT HAL KURA-BAYASHI.
I REQUEST THAT ALL AGENTS HAND OVER DOCUMENTS RELEVANT TO THIS INVESTIGATION.
Narcotics Control Division

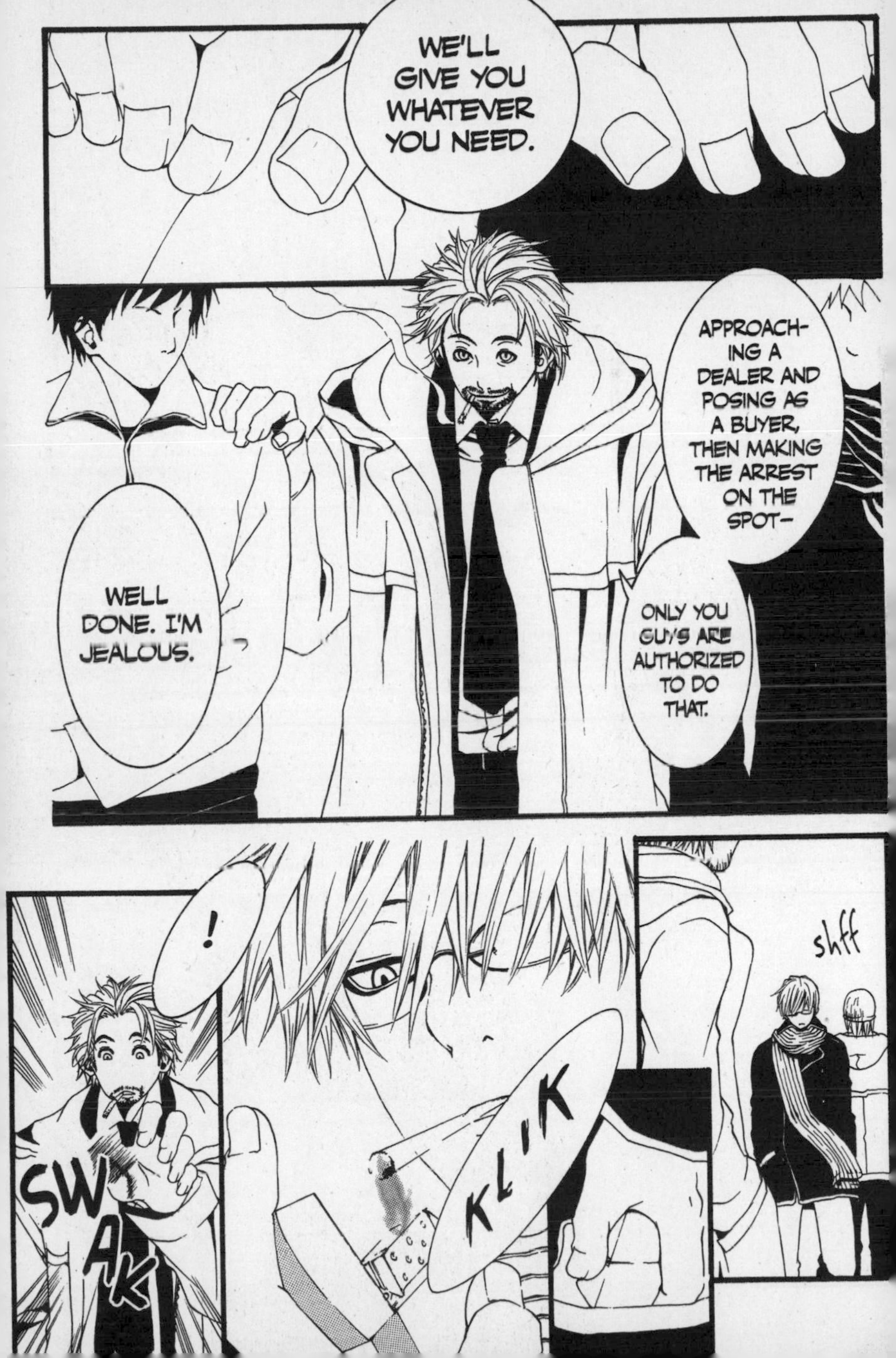
WE'LL GIVE YOU WHATEVER YOU NEED.
APPROACHING A DEALER AND POSING AS A BUYER, THEN MAKING THE ARREST ON THE SPOT-
ONLY YOU GUY'S ARE AUTHORIZED TO DO THAT.
WELL DONE. I'M JEALOUS.
shff
!
KLIK
SWAK

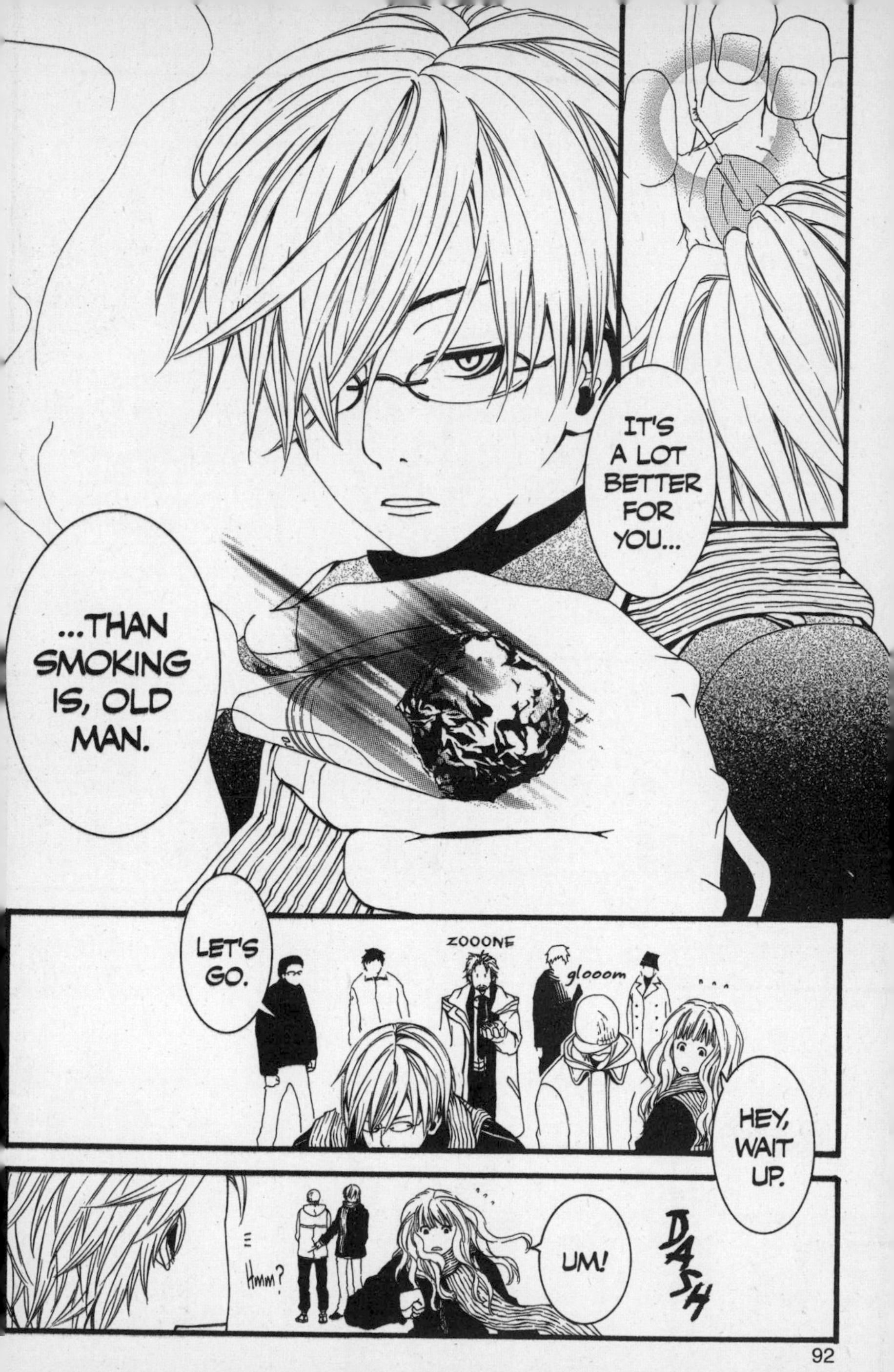
IT'S A LOT BETTER FOR YOU...
...THAN SMOKING IS, OLD MAN.
...
glooom
ZOOONE
LET'S GO.
HEY, WAIT UP.
DASH
UM!
...
Hmm?

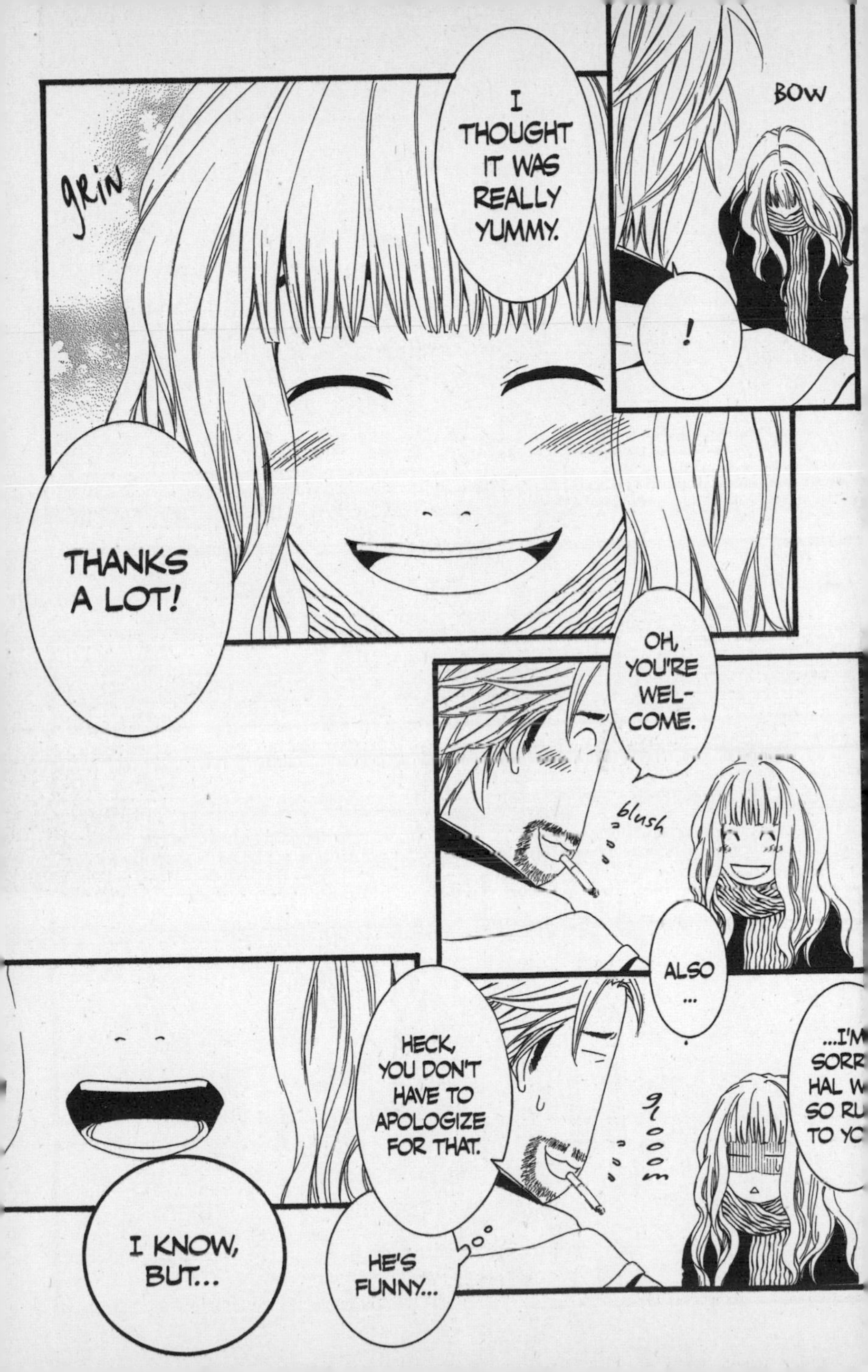
BOW
!
GRIN
I THOUGHT IT WAS REALLY YUMMY.
THANKS A LOT!
OH, YOU'RE WEL-COME.
BLUSH
ALSO...
...I'M SORR HAL W SO RU TO YO
GLOOM
HECK, YOU DON'T HAVE TO APOLOGIZE FOR THAT.
I KNOW, BUT...
HE'S FUNNY...

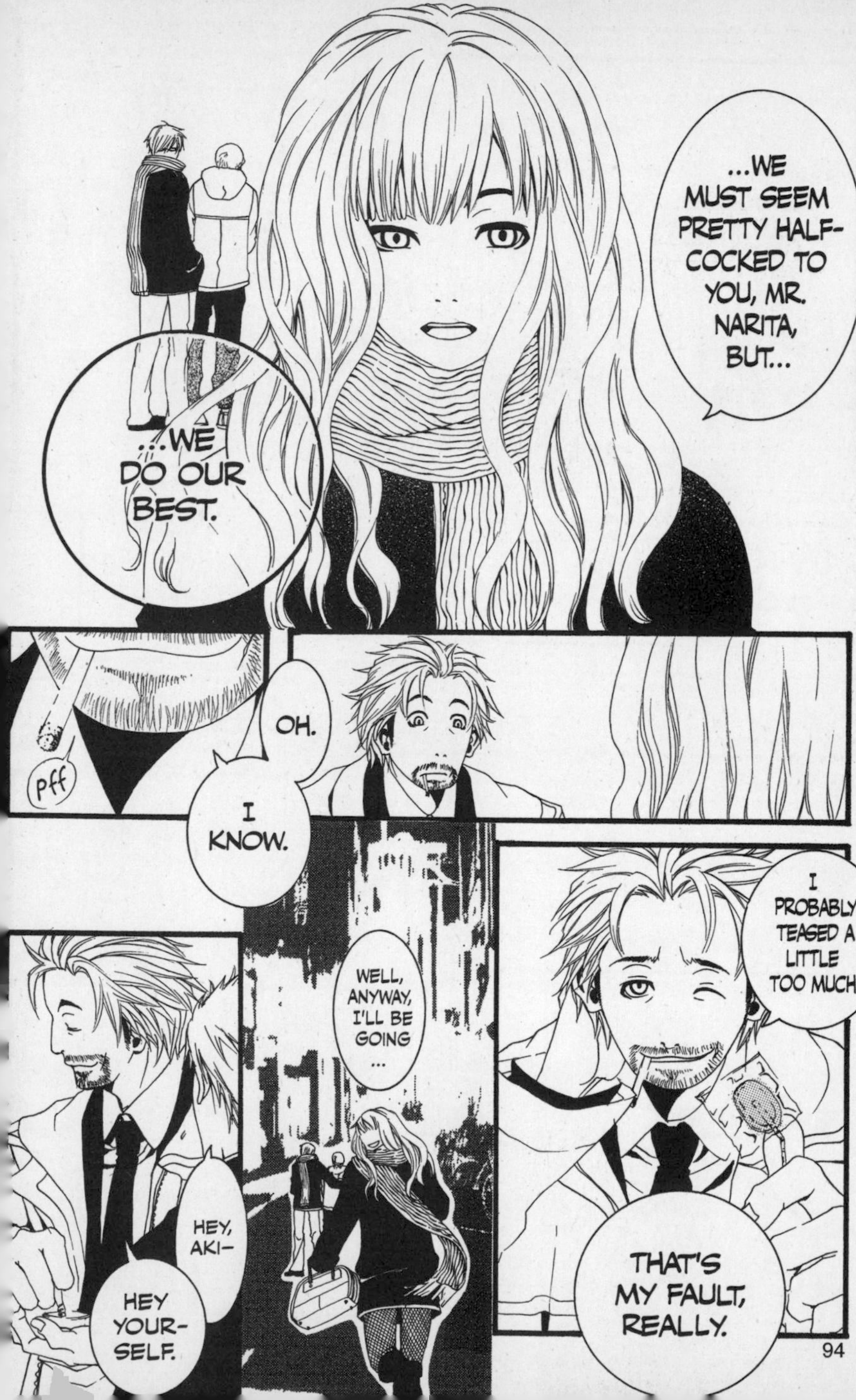
...WE MUST SEEM PRETTY HALF-COCKED TO YOU, MR. NARITA, BUT...
...WE DO OUR BEST.
OH.
I KNOW.
pff
I PROBABLY TEASED A LITTLE TOO MUCH.
THAT'S MY FAULT, REALLY.
WELL, ANYWAY, I'LL BE GOING ...
HEY, AKI-
HEY YOURSELF.

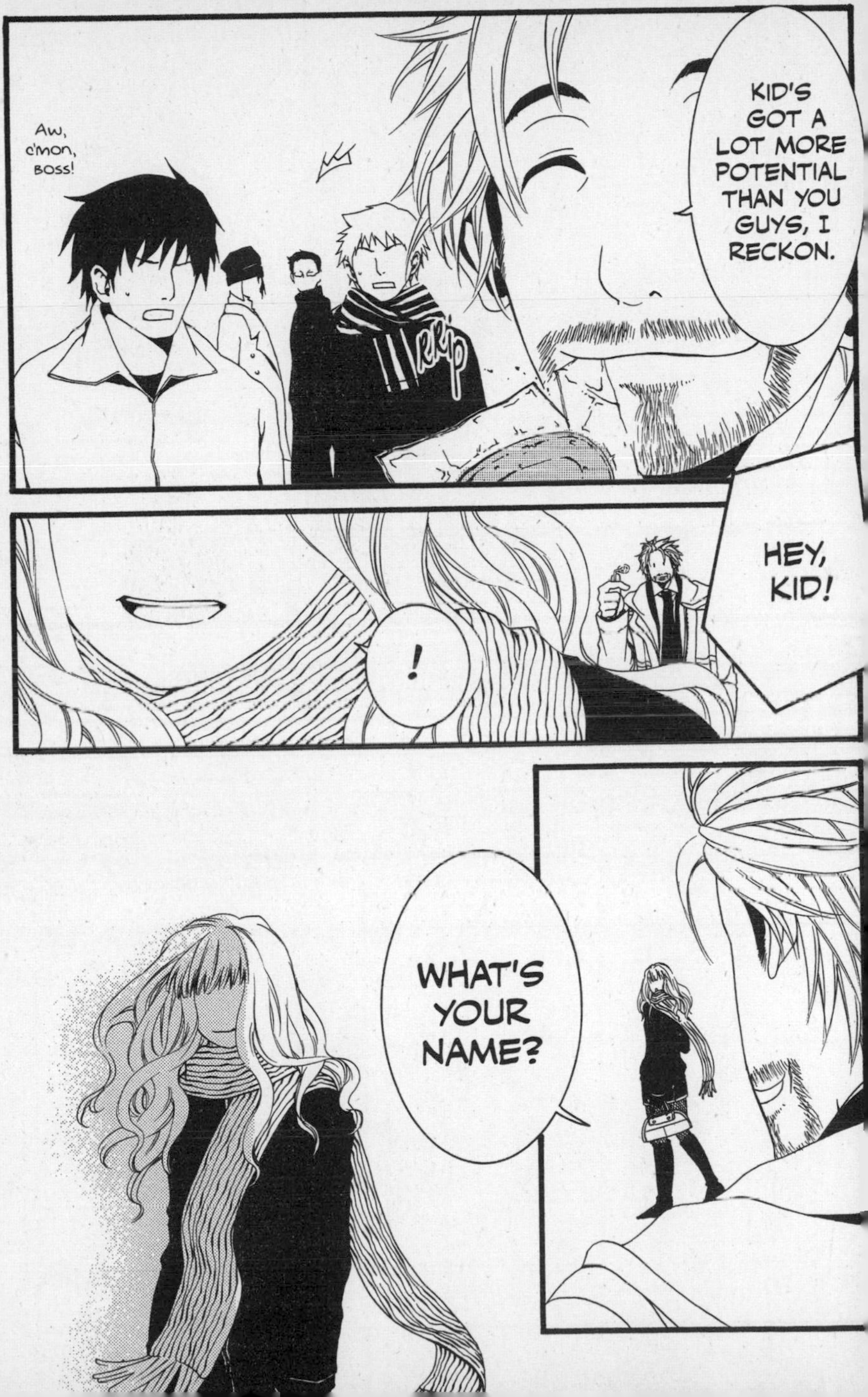
KID'S GOT A LOT MORE POTENTIAL THAN YOU GUYS, I RECKON.
Aw, c'mon, boss!
HEY, KID!
!
WHAT'S YOUR NAME?

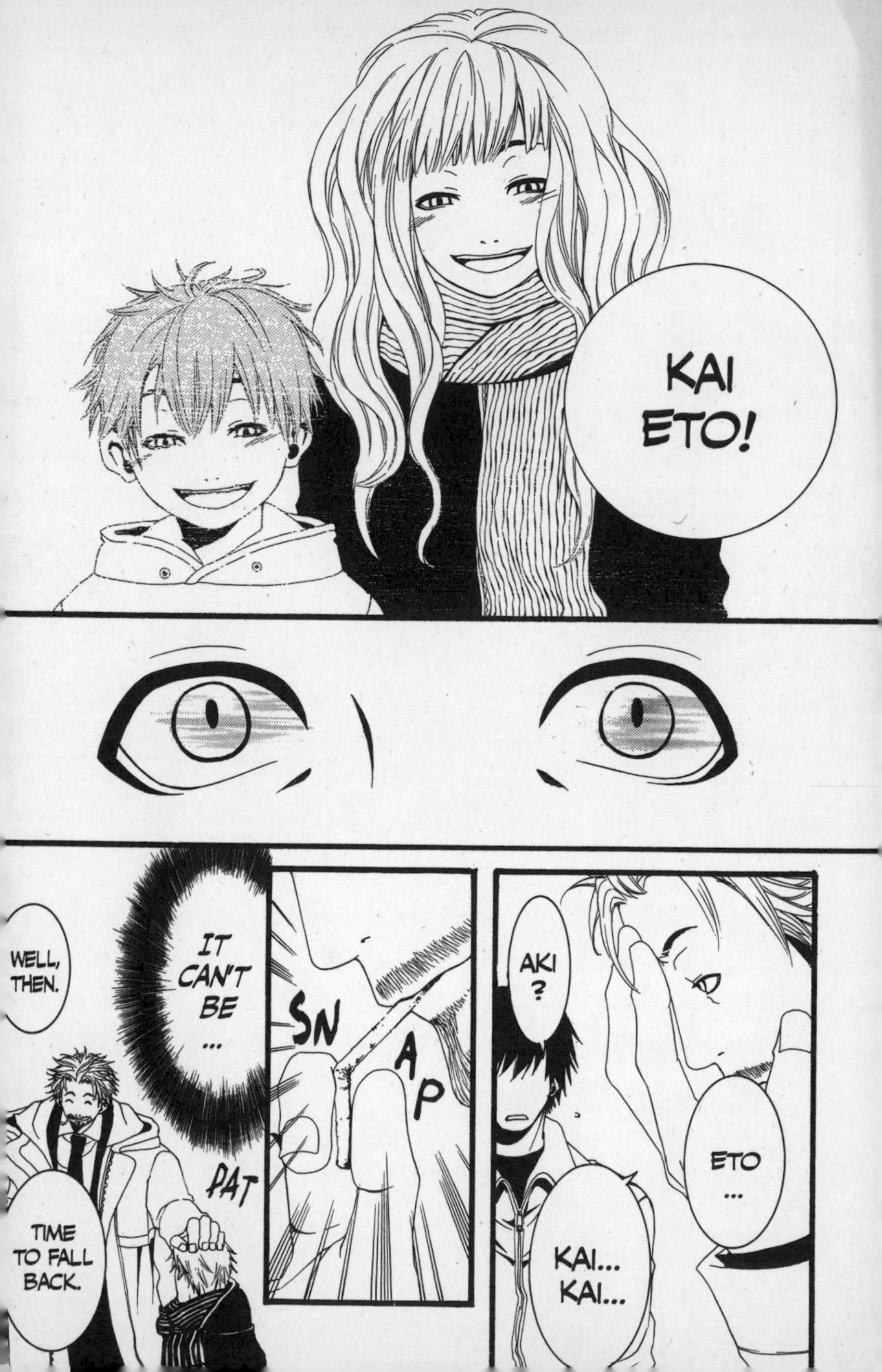
KAI ETO!
AKI?
ETO ...
KAI... KAI...
SNAP
IT CAN'T BE ...
WELL, THEN.
PAT
TIME TO FALL BACK.

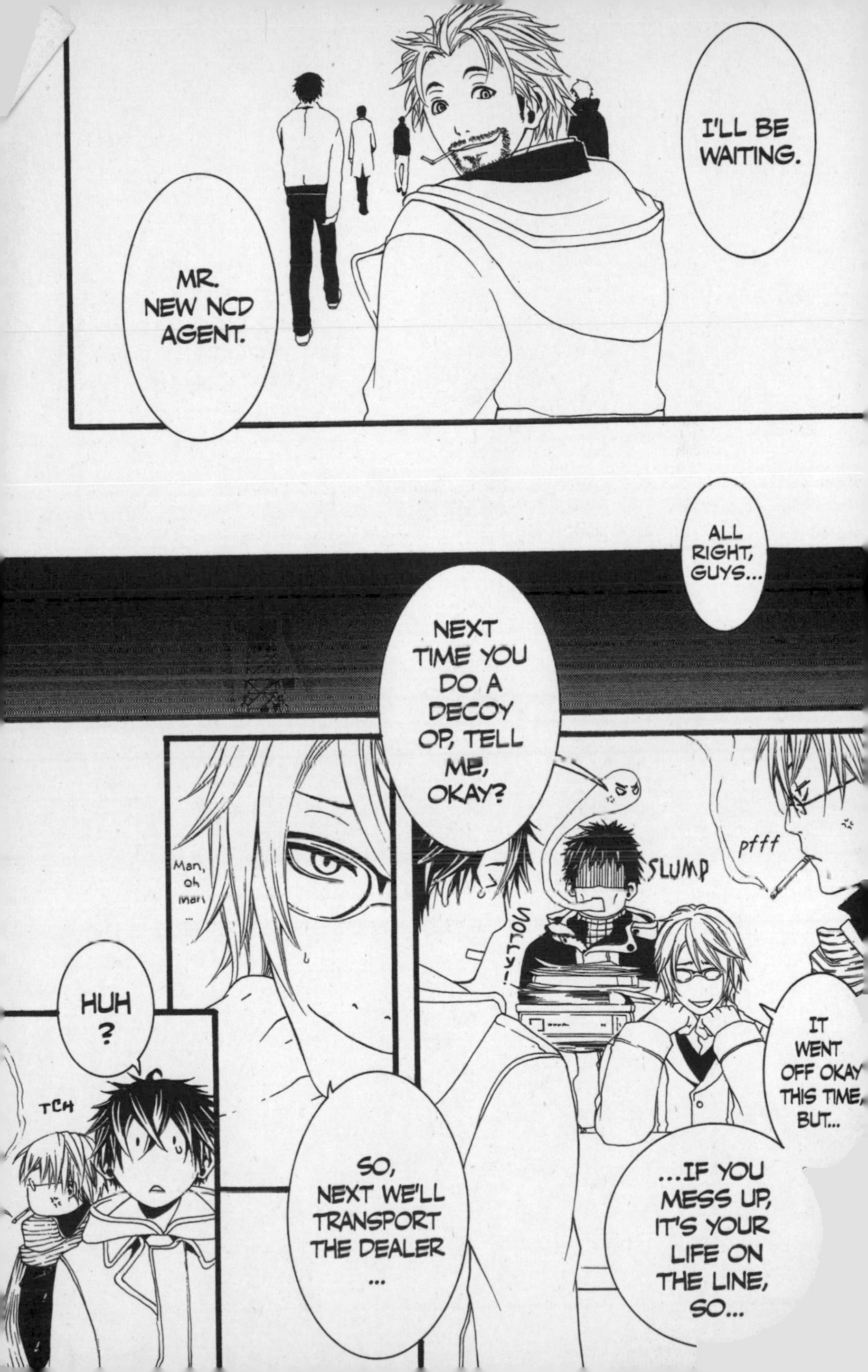
I'LL BE WAITING.
MR. NEW NCD AGENT.
ALL RIGHT, GUYS...
pfff
NEXT TIME YOU DO A DECOY OP, TELL ME, OKAY?
SLUMP
Sorry!
IT WENT OFF OKAY THIS TIME, BUT...
...IF YOU MESS UP, IT'S YOUR LIFE ON THE LINE, SO...
Man, oh man ...
SO, NEXT WE'LL TRANSPORT THE DEALER ...
HUH?
TCH

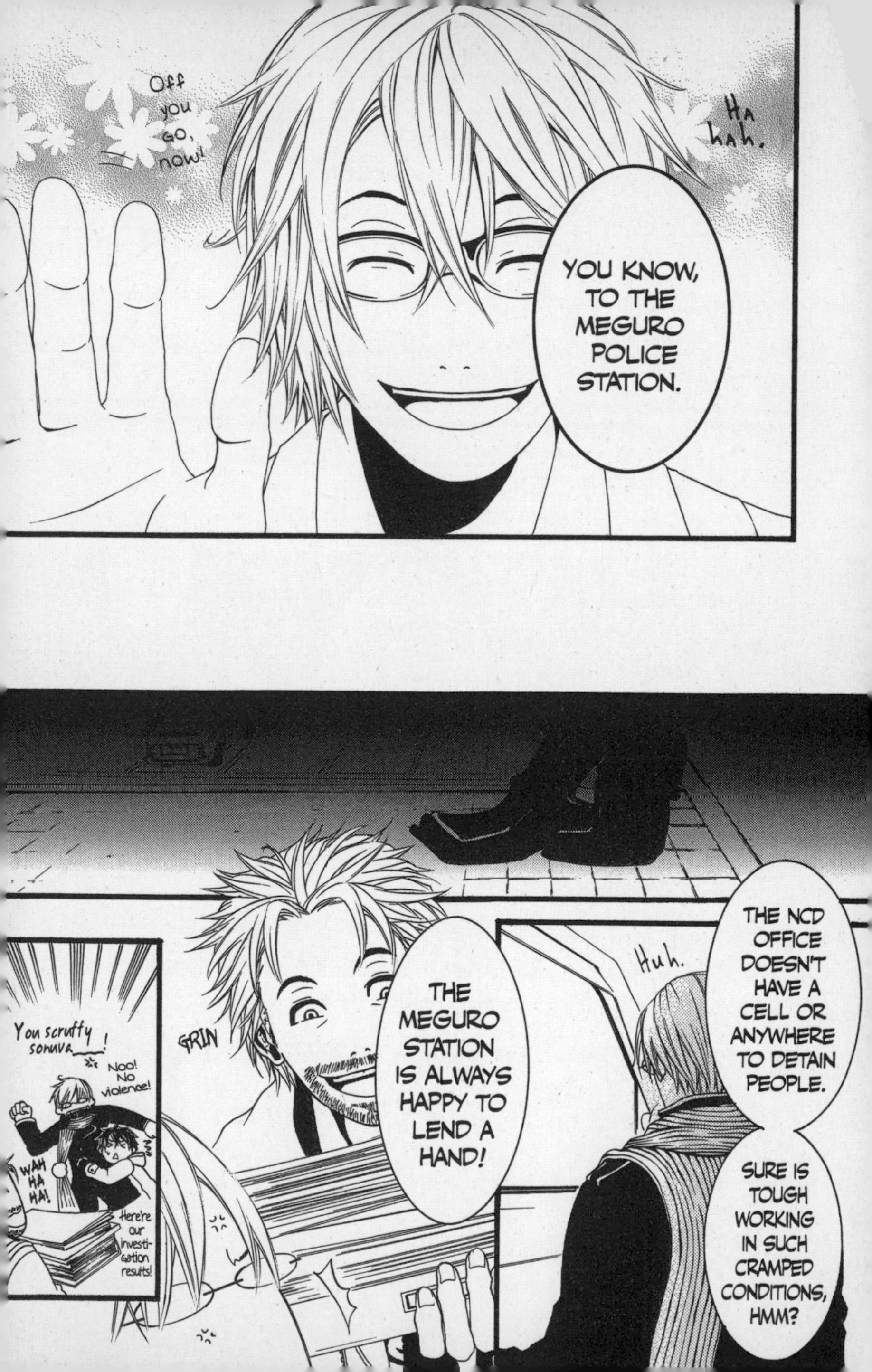
Ha hah.
YOU KNOW, TO THE MEGURO POLICE STATION.
Off you go, now!
THE NCD OFFICE DOESN'T HAVE A CELL OR ANYWHERE TO DETAIN PEOPLE.
SURE IS TOUGH WORKING IN SUCH CRAMPED CONDITIONS, HMM?
Huh.
THE MEGURO STATION IS ALWAYS HAPPY TO LEND A HAND!
GRIN
You scruffy sonuva___!
Noo! No violence!
WAH HA HA!
Here're our investi-gation results!

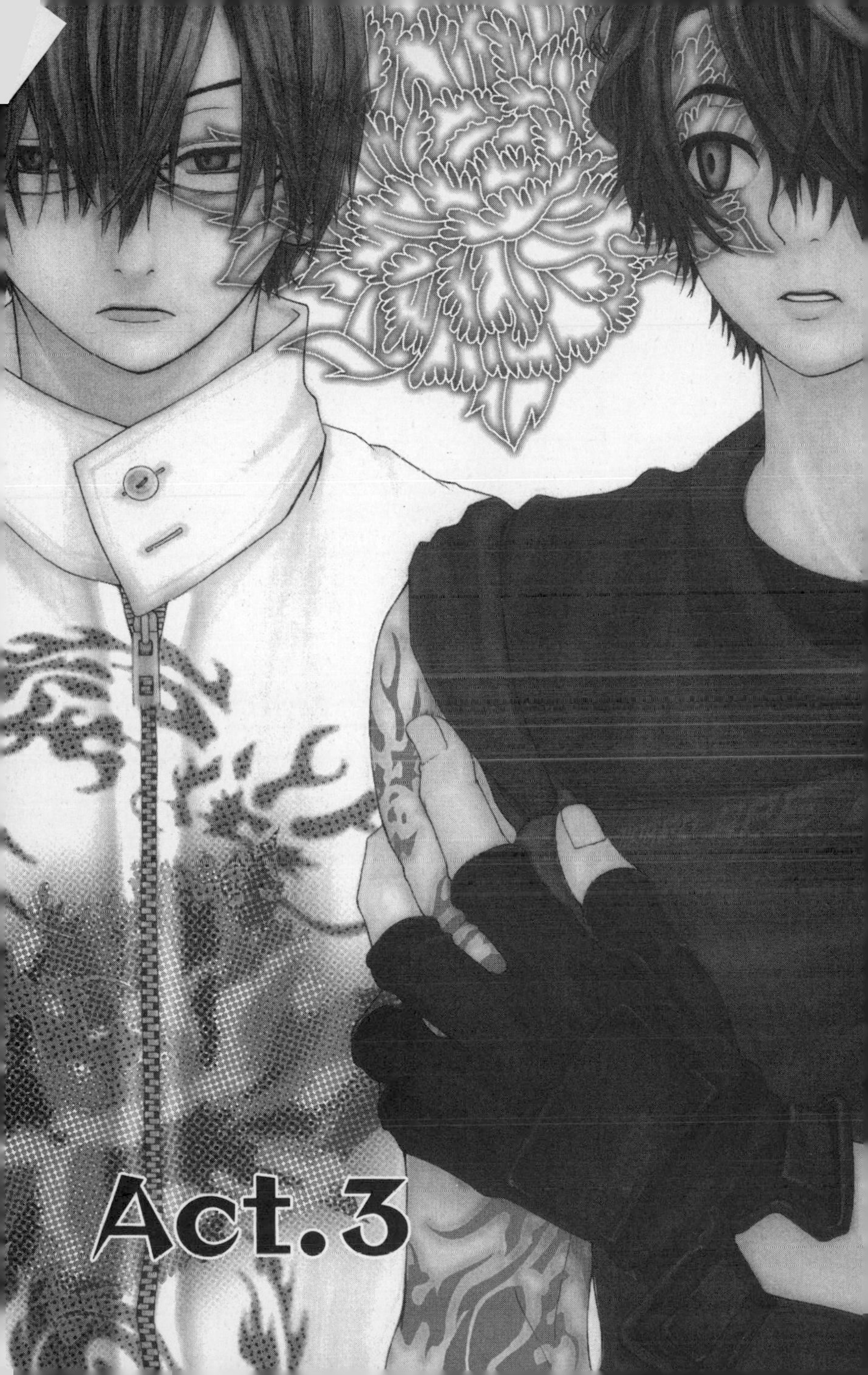
Act. 3

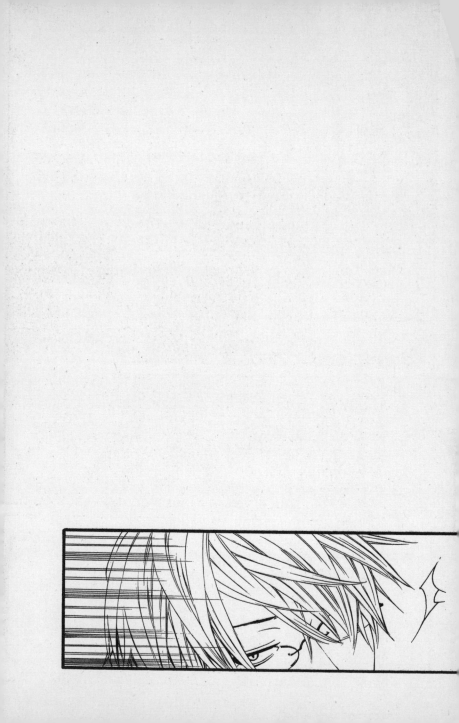

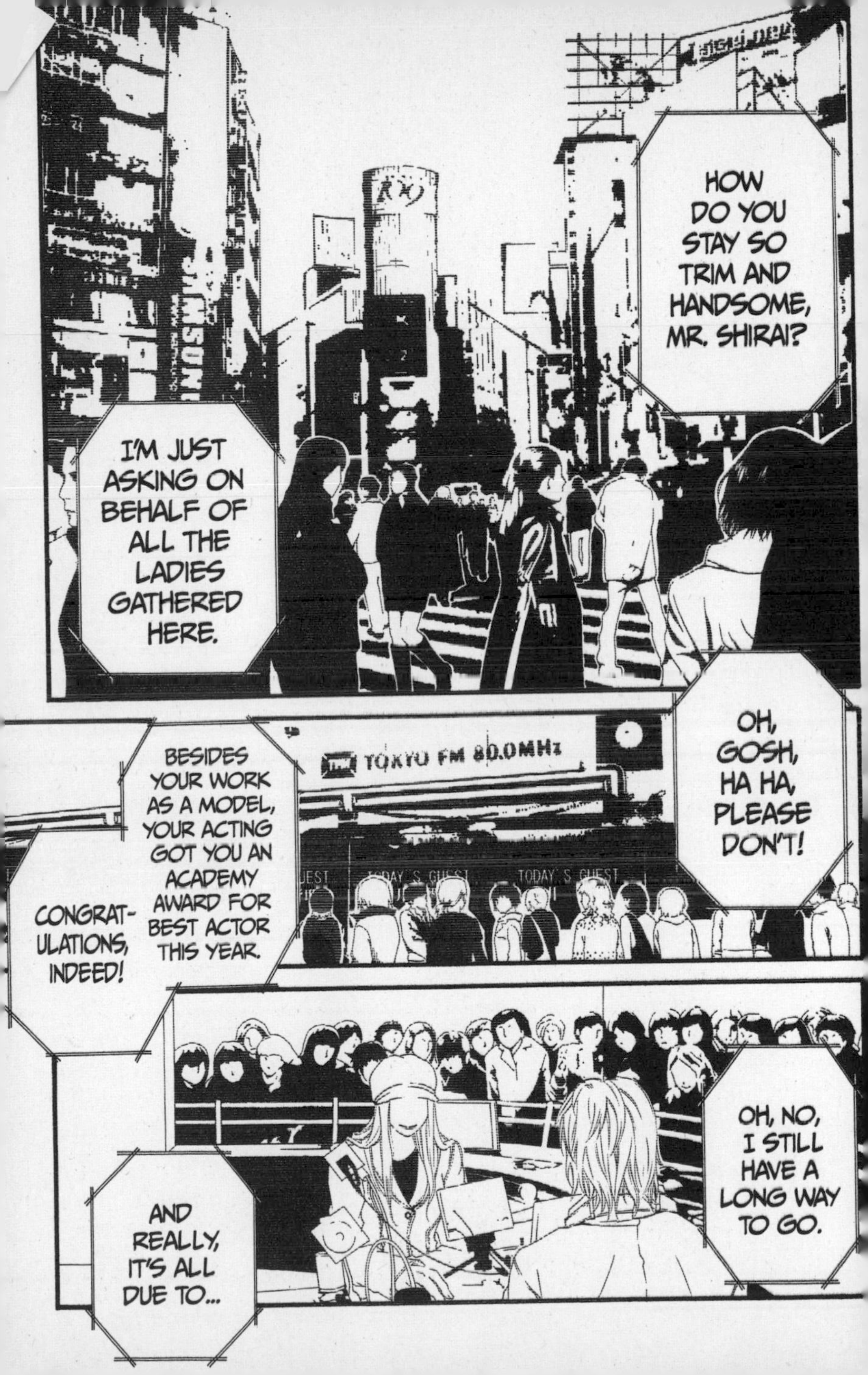
HOW DO YOU STAY SO TRIM AND HANDSOME, MR. SHIRAI?
I'M JUST ASKING ON BEHALF OF ALL THE LADIES GATHERED HERE.
OH, GOSH, HA HA, PLEASE DON'T!
TOKYO FM 80.0MHz
BESIDES YOUR WORK AS A MODEL, YOUR ACTING GOT YOU AN ACADEMY AWARD FOR BEST ACTOR THIS YEAR.
CONGRAT-ULATIONS, INDEED!
OH, NO, I STILL HAVE A LONG WAY TO GO.
AND REALLY, IT'S ALL DUE TO...

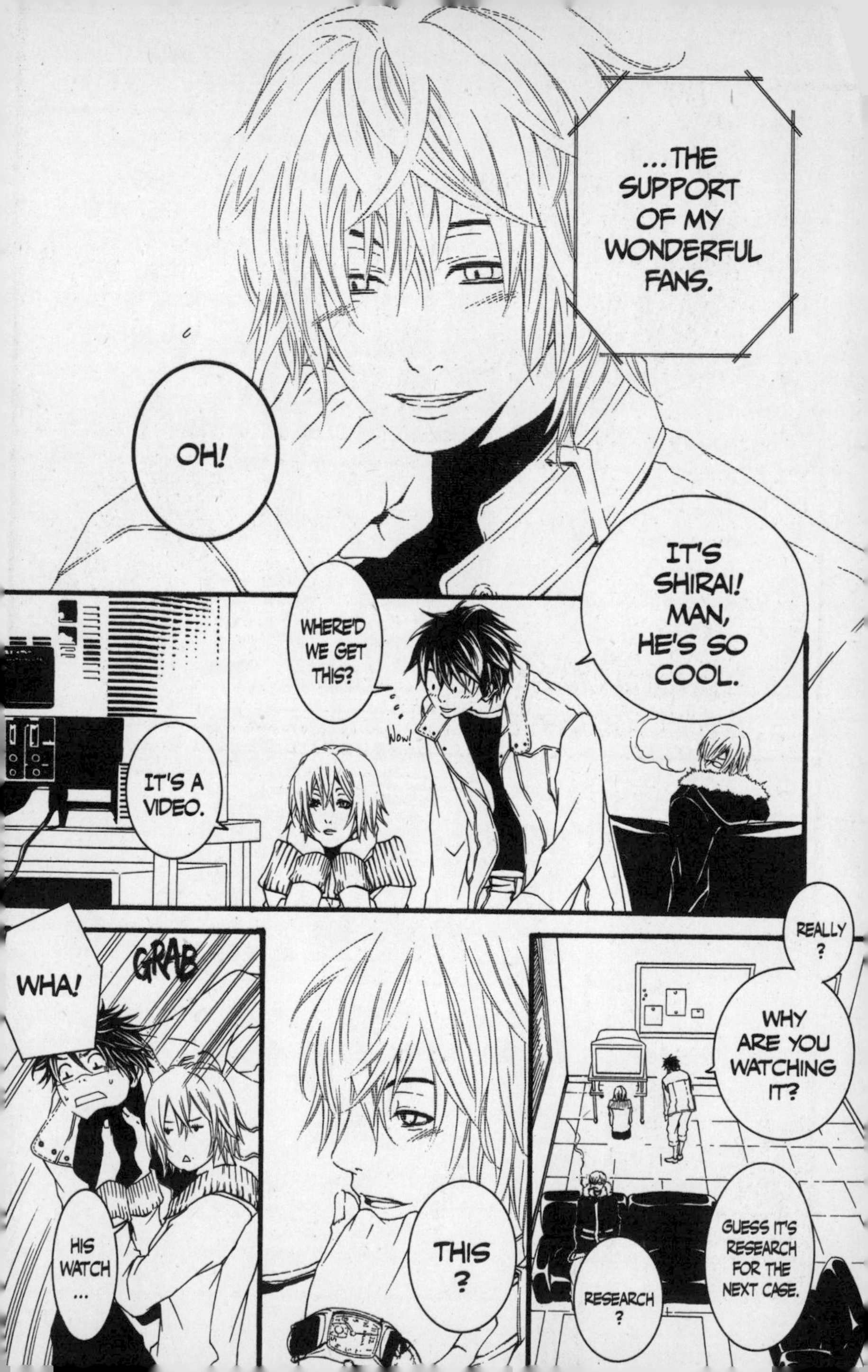
...THE SUPPORT OF MY WONDERFUL FANS.
OH!
IT'S SHIRAI! MAN, HE'S SO COOL.
WHERE'D WE GET THIS?
WOW!
IT'S A VIDEO.
REALLY?
WHY ARE YOU WATCHING IT?
GUESS IT'S RESEARCH FOR THE NEXT CASE.
RESEARCH?
THIS?
GRAB
WHA!
HIS WATCH...

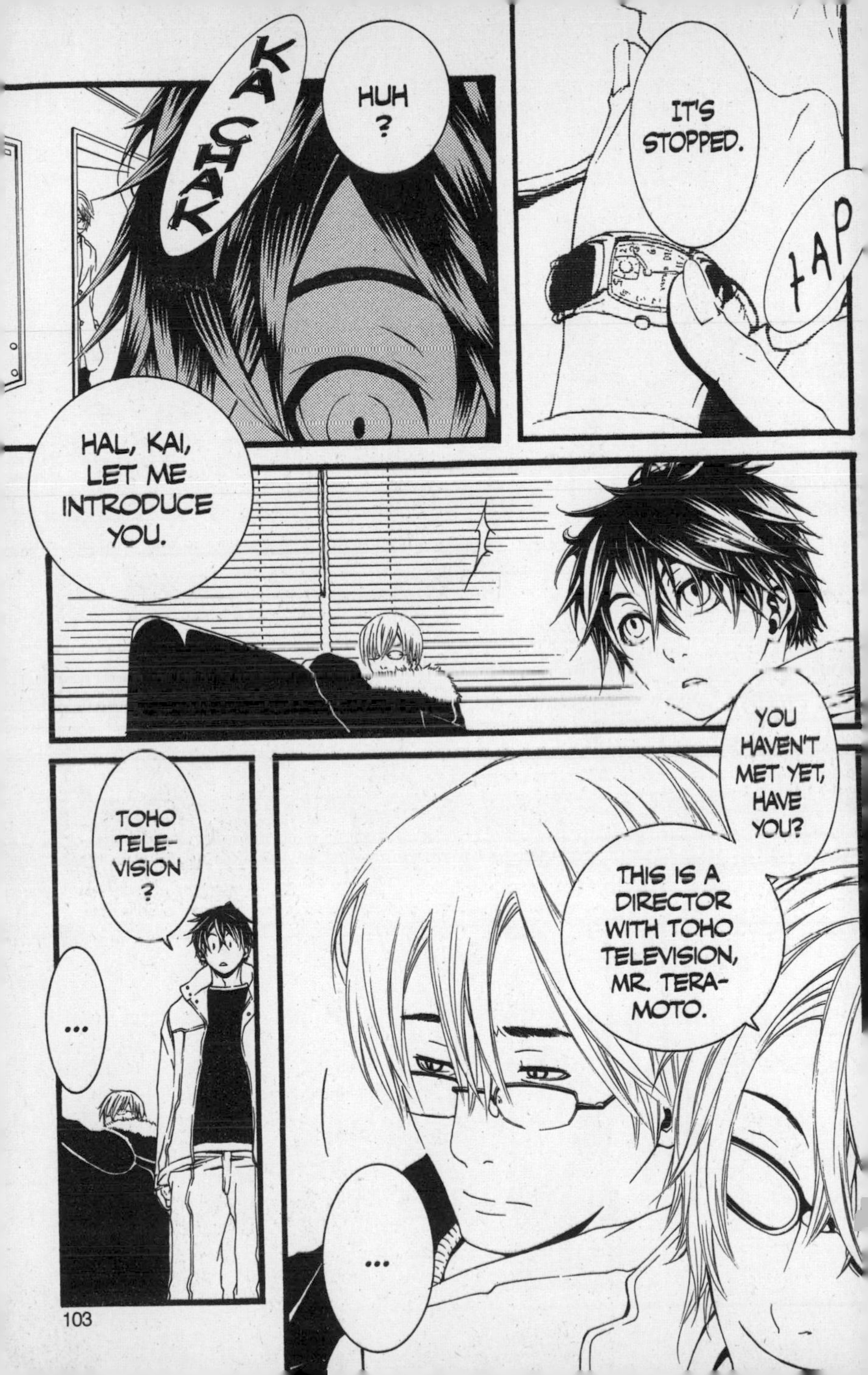
IT'S STOPPED.
TAP
HUH ?
KA CHAK
HAL, KAI, LET ME INTRODUCE YOU.
YOU HAVEN'T MET YET, HAVE YOU?
THIS IS A DIRECTOR WITH TOHO TELEVISION, MR. TERA-MOTO.
...
TOHO TELE-VISION ?
...

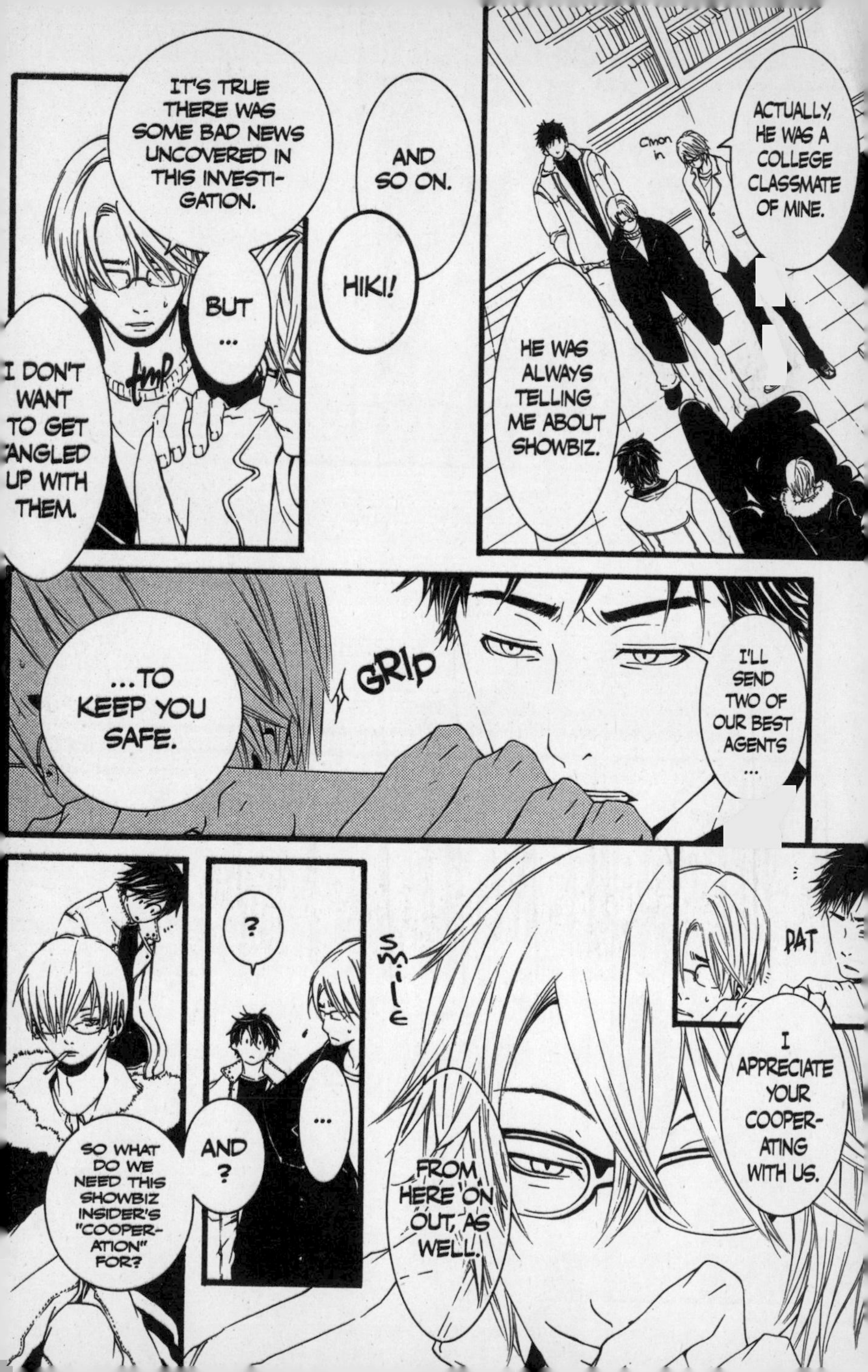
C'mon in
ACTUALLY, HE WAS A COLLEGE CLASSMATE OF MINE.
HE WAS ALWAYS TELLING ME ABOUT SHOWBIZ.
AND SO ON.
HIKI!
IT'S TRUE THERE WAS SOME BAD NEWS UNCOVERED IN THIS INVESTIGATION.
BUT ...
I DON'T WANT TO GET ANGLED UP WITH THEM.
I'LL SEND TWO OF OUR BEST AGENTS ...
GRIP
...TO KEEP YOU SAFE.
PAT
I APPRECIATE YOUR COOPERATING WITH US.
FROM HERE ON OUT, AS WELL.
SMILE
?
...
AND ?
...
SO WHAT DO WE NEED THIS SHOWBIZ INSIDER'S "COOPERATION" FOR?

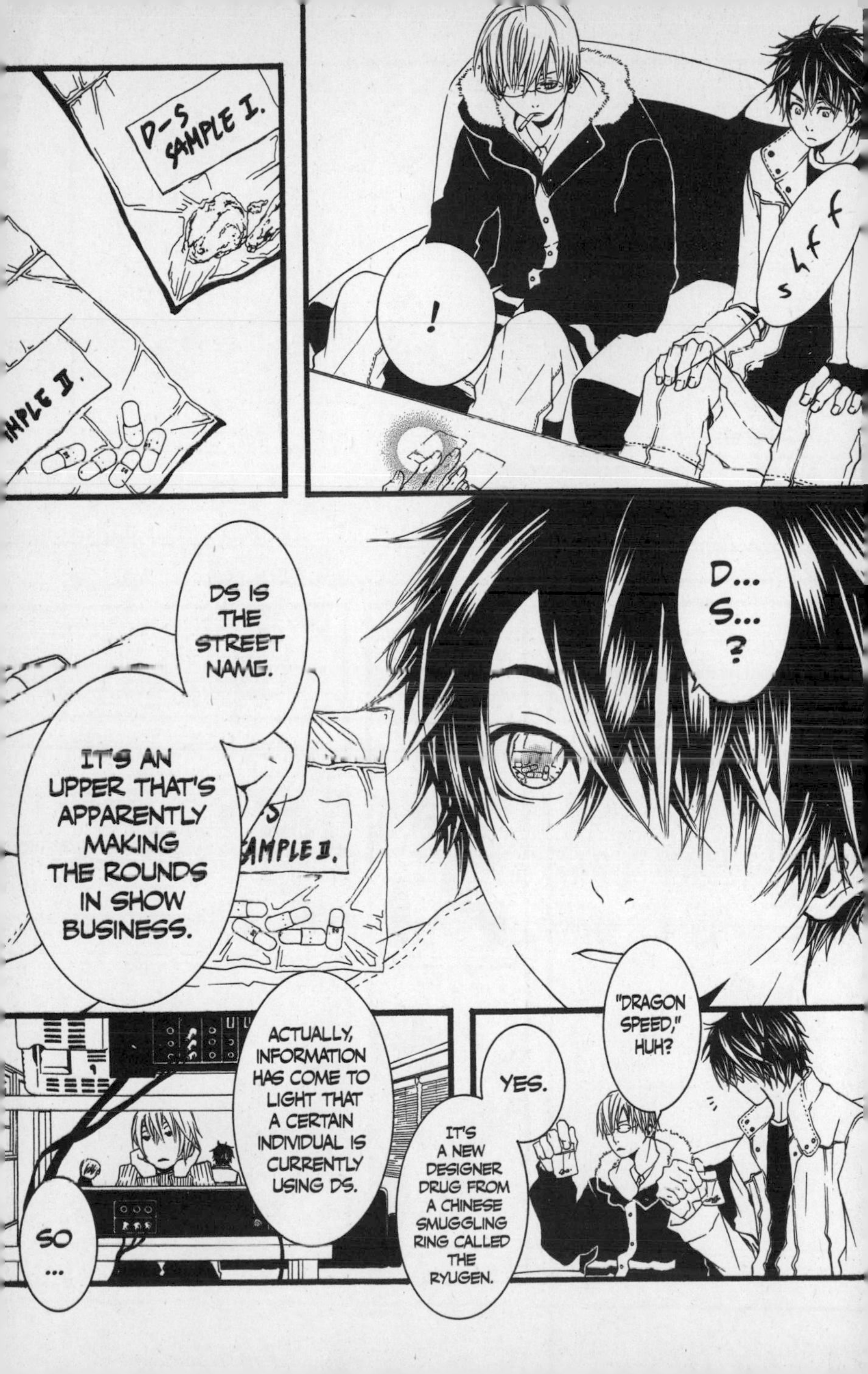
shff
!
D-S SAMPLE I.
D... S...?
DS IS THE STREET NAME.
IT'S AN UPPER THAT'S APPARENTLY MAKING THE ROUNDS IN SHOW BUSINESS.
"DRAGON SPEED," HUH?
YES.
IT'S A NEW DESIGNER DRUG FROM A CHINESE SMUGGLING RING CALLED THE RYUGEN.
ACTUALLY, INFORMATION HAS COME TO LIGHT THAT A CERTAIN INDIVIDUAL IS CURRENTLY USING DS.
SO ...

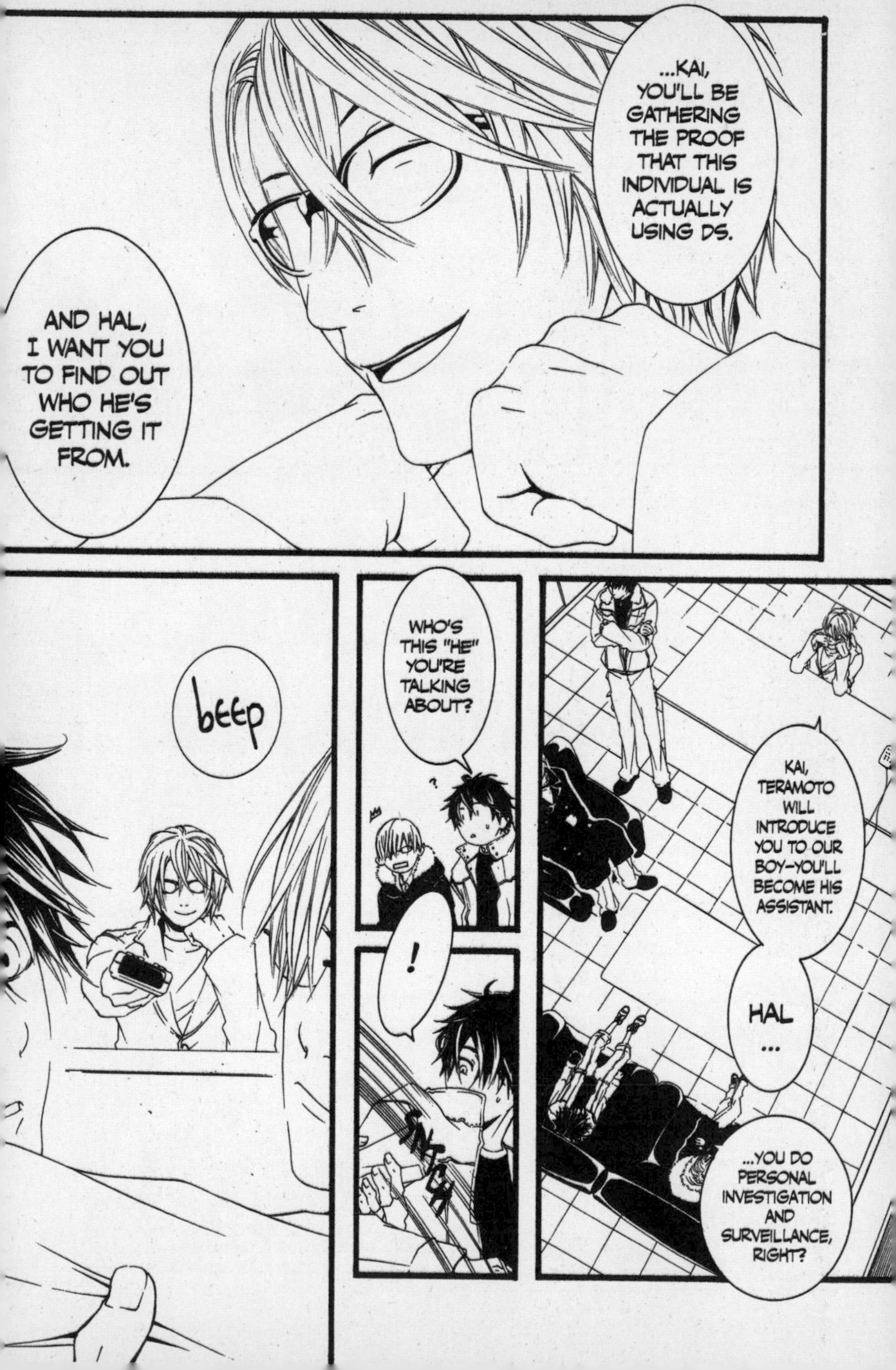
...KAI, YOU'LL BE GATHERING THE PROOF THAT THIS INDIVIDUAL IS ACTUALLY USING DS.
AND HAL, I WANT YOU TO FIND OUT WHO HE'S GETTING IT FROM.
KAI, TERAMOTO WILL INTRODUCE YOU TO OUR BOY—YOU'LL BECOME HIS ASSISTANT.
HAL...
...YOU DO PERSONAL INVESTIGATION AND SURVEILLANCE, RIGHT?
WHO'S THIS "HE" YOU'RE TALKING ABOUT?
!
SNATCH
beep

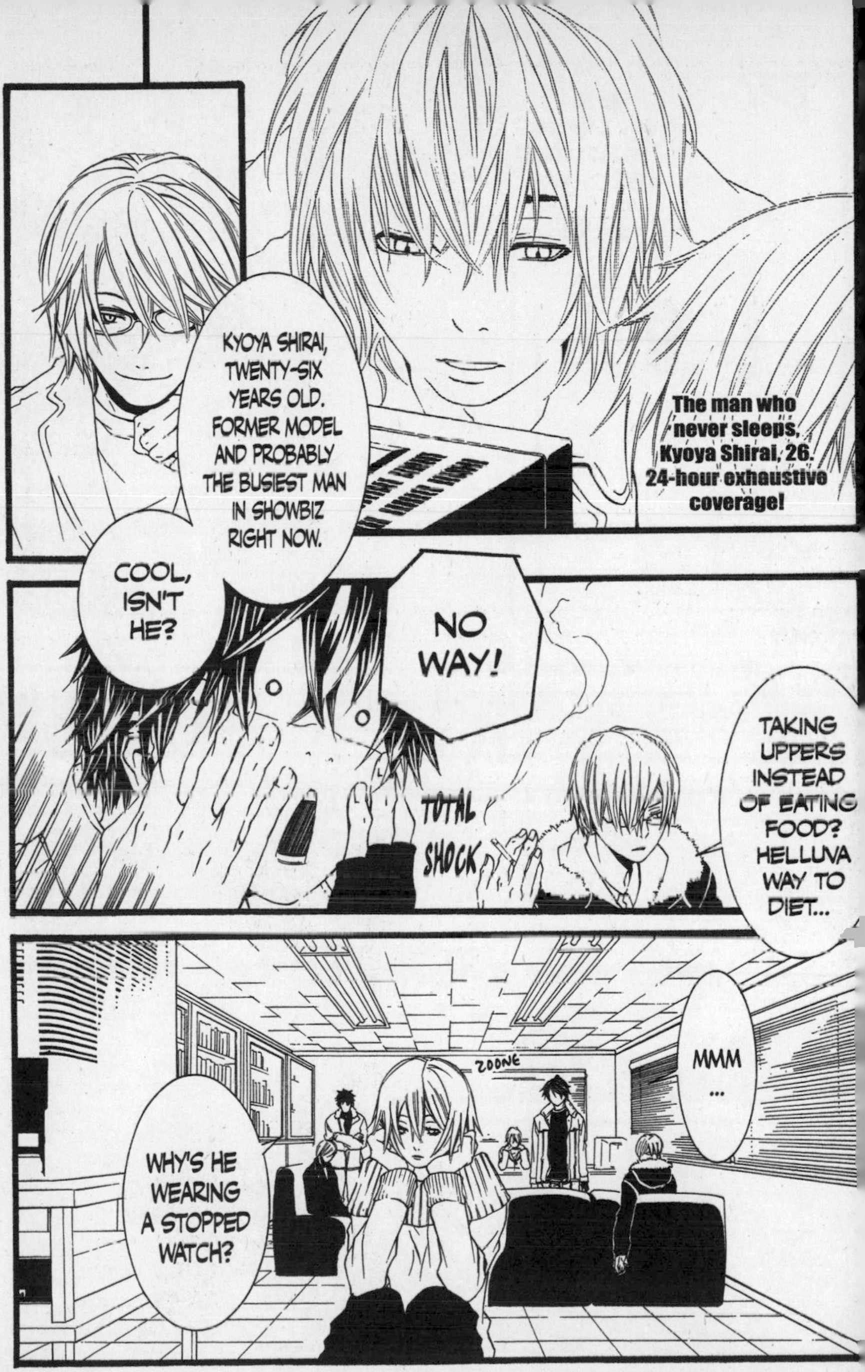
The man who never sleeps, Kyoya Shirai, 26. 24-hour exhaustive coverage!
KYOYA SHIRAI, TWENTY-SIX YEARS OLD. FORMER MODEL AND PROBABLY THE BUSIEST MAN IN SHOWBIZ RIGHT NOW.
COOL, ISN'T HE?
NO WAY!
TOTAL SHOCK
TAKING UPPERS INSTEAD OF EATING FOOD? HELLUVA WAY TO DIET...
MMM...
ZOONE
WHY'S HE WEARING A STOPPED WATCH?

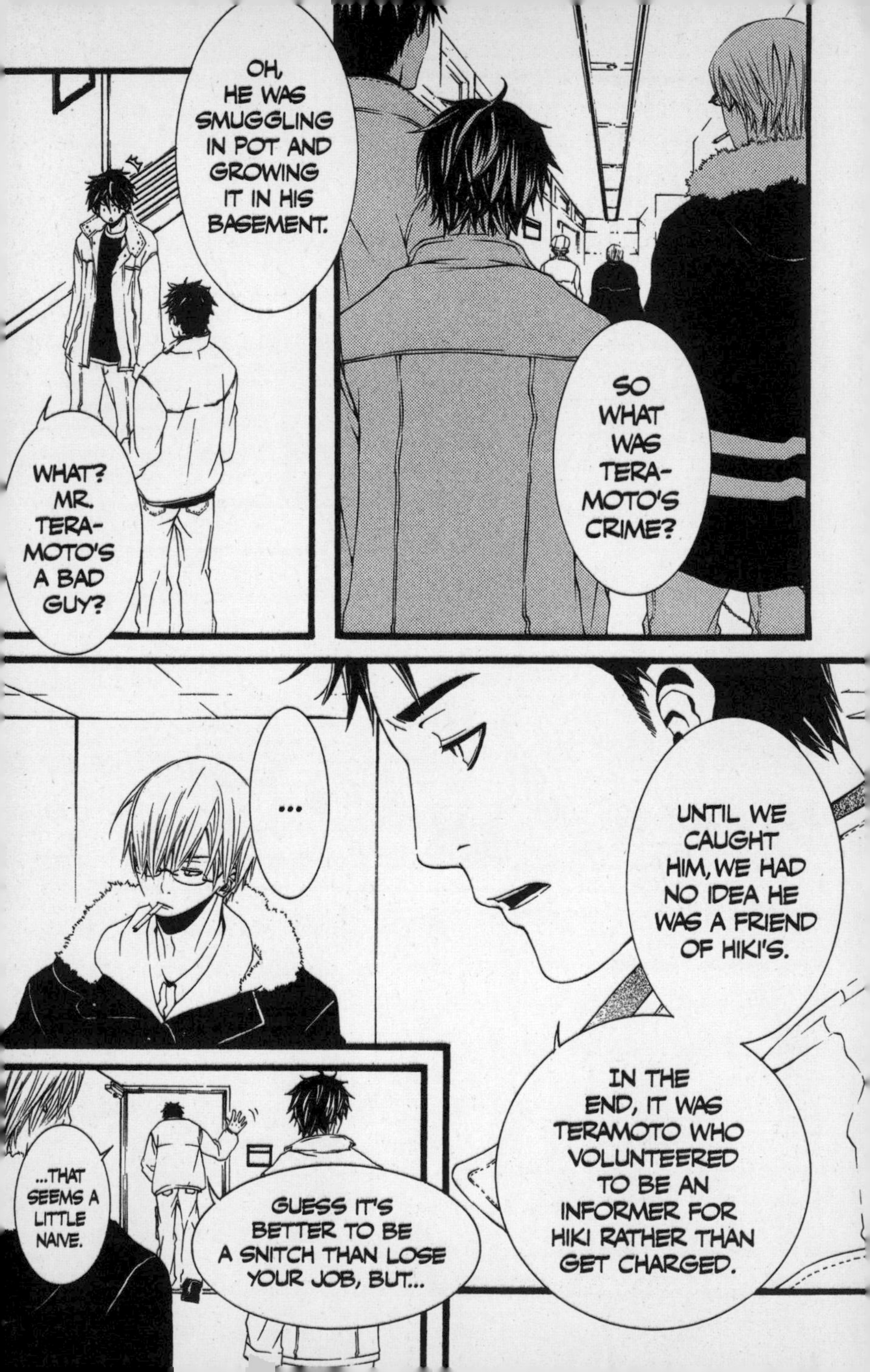
SO WHAT WAS TERA-MOTO'S CRIME?
OH, HE WAS SMUGGLING IN POT AND GROWING IT IN HIS BASEMENT.
WHAT? MR. TERA-MOTO'S A BAD GUY?
UNTIL WE CAUGHT HIM, WE HAD NO IDEA HE WAS A FRIEND OF HIKI'S.
IN THE END, IT WAS TERAMOTO WHO VOLUNTEERED TO BE AN INFORMER FOR HIKI RATHER THAN GET CHARGED.
...
GUESS IT'S BETTER TO BE A SNITCH THAN LOSE YOUR JOB, BUT...
...THAT SEEMS A LITTLE NAIVE.

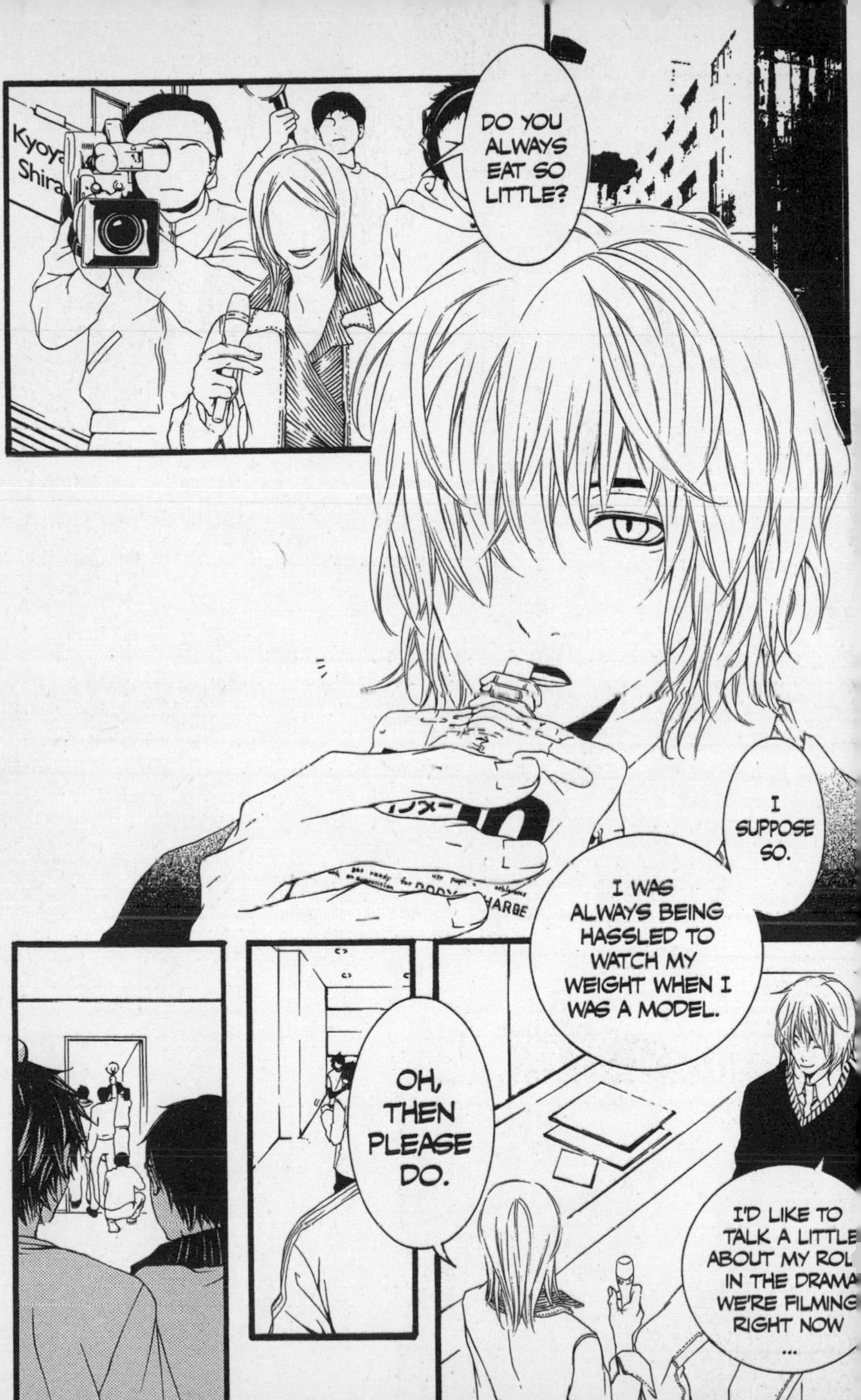
DO YOU ALWAYS EAT SO LITTLE?
I SUPPOSE SO.
I WAS ALWAYS BEING HASSLED TO WATCH MY WEIGHT WHEN I WAS A MODEL.
I'D LIKE TO TALK A LITTLE ABOUT MY ROL IN THE DRAMA WE'RE FILMING RIGHT NOW ...
OH, THEN PLEASE DO.

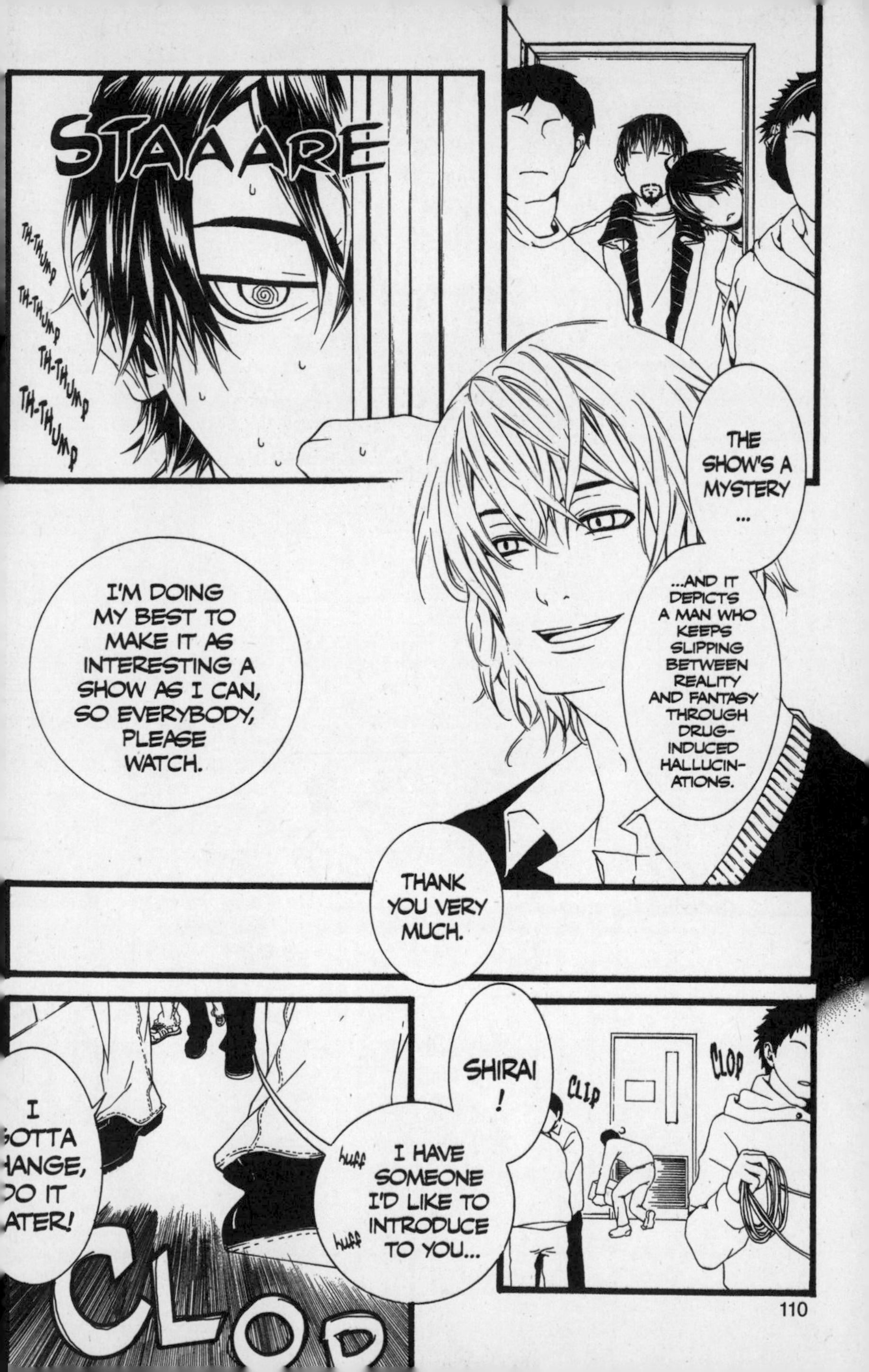
STAAARE
TH-THUMP TH-THUMP TH-THUMP TH-THUMP
THE SHOW'S A MYSTERY ...
...AND IT DEPICTS A MAN WHO KEEPS SLIPPING BETWEEN REALITY AND FANTASY THROUGH DRUG-INDUCED HALLUCIN-ATIONS.
I'M DOING MY BEST TO MAKE IT AS INTERESTING A SHOW AS I CAN, SO EVERYBODY, PLEASE WATCH.
THANK YOU VERY MUCH.
CLOP
CLIP
SHIRAI!
huff huff
I HAVE SOMEONE I'D LIKE TO INTRODUCE TO YOU...
I GOTTA HANGE, DO IT ATER!
CLOD

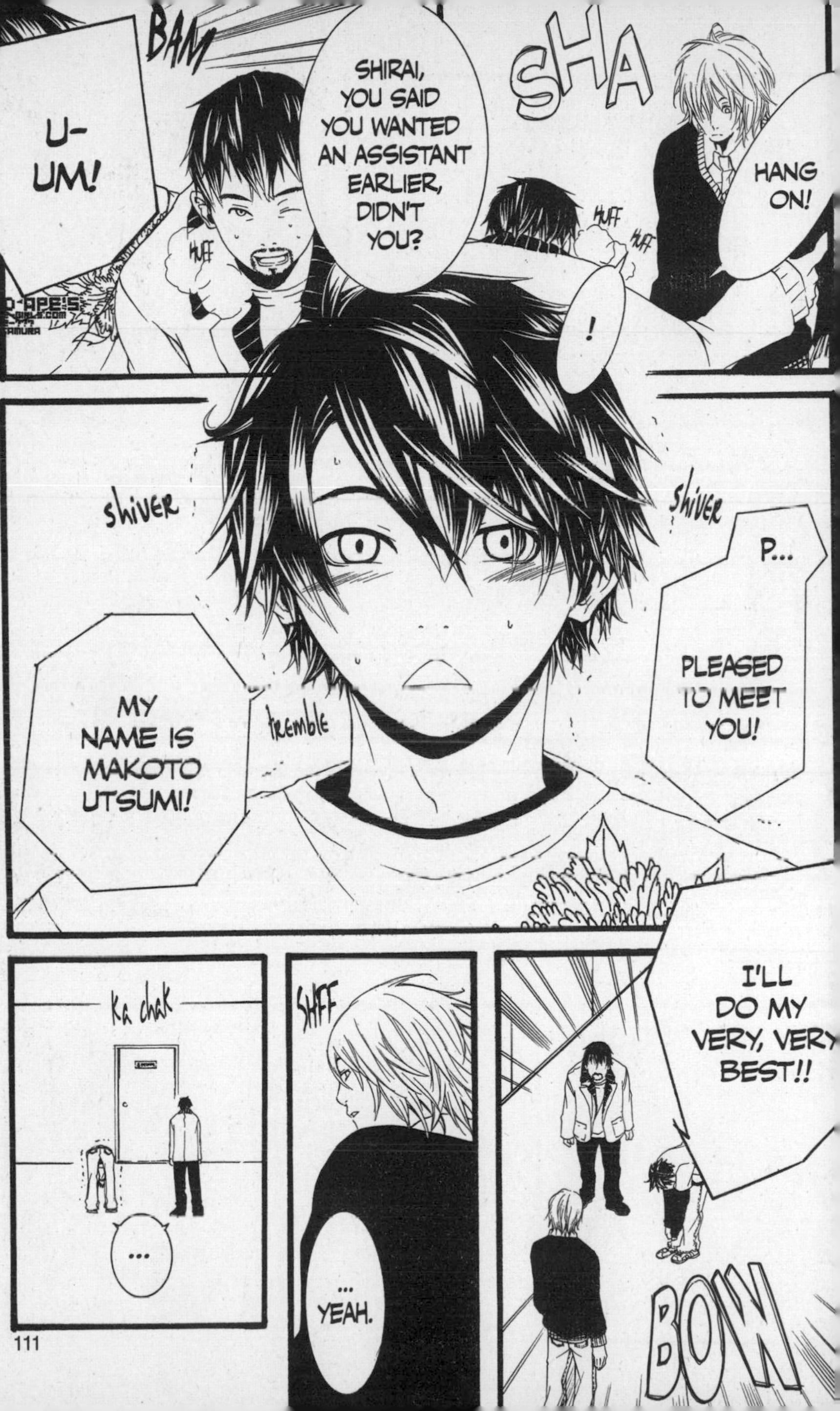
SHA
HANG ON!
HUFF
HUFF
!
SHIRAI, YOU SAID YOU WANTED AN ASSISTANT EARLIER, DIDN'T YOU?
BAM
U-UM!
HUFF
shiver
P...
PLEASED TO MEET YOU!
...
shiver
MY NAME IS MAKOTO UTSUMI!
tremble
I'LL DO MY VERY, VERY BEST!!
BOW
SHFF
... YEAH.
Ka chak
...

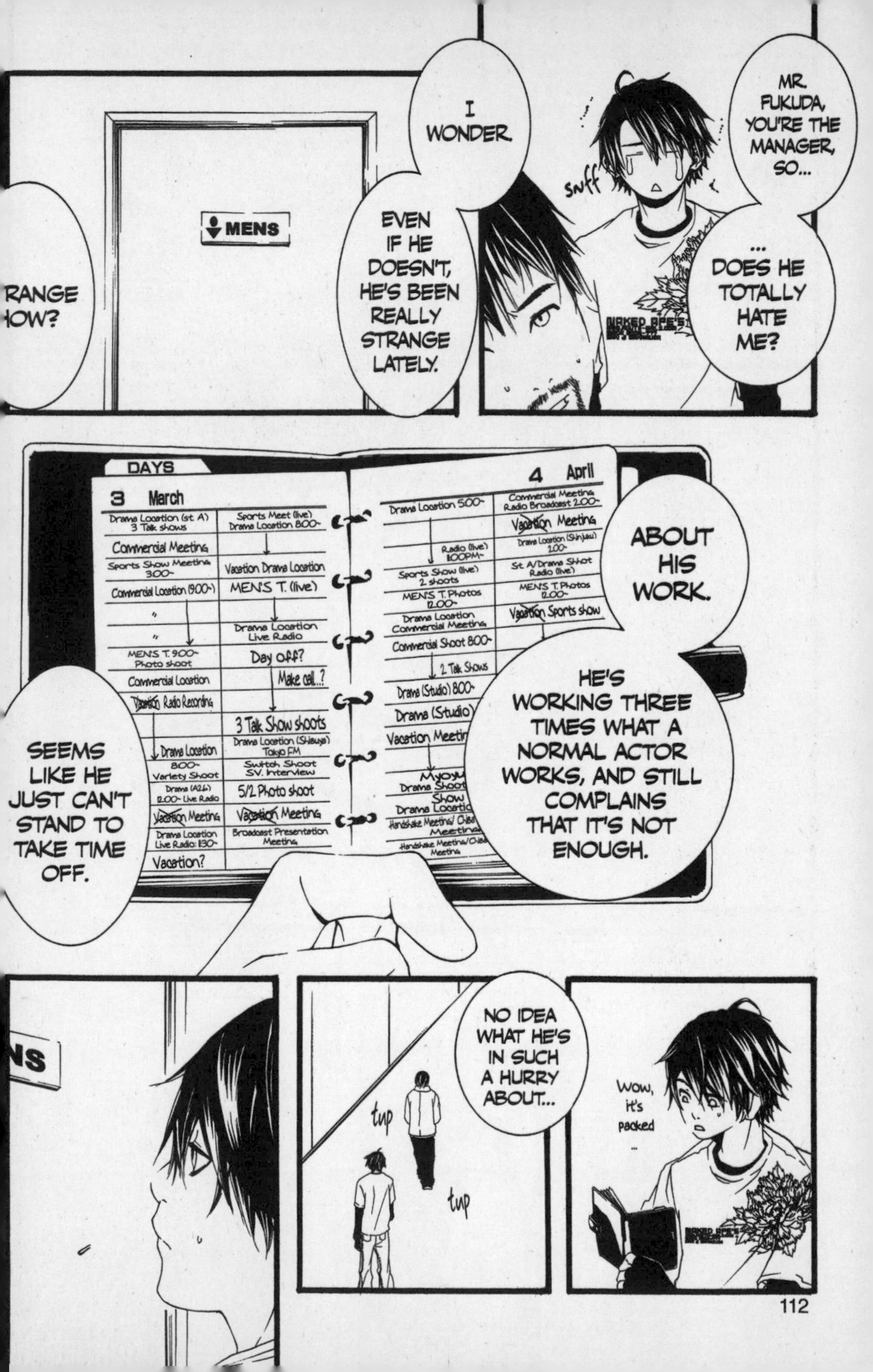
MR. FUKUDA, YOU'RE THE MANAGER, SO...
snff
... DOES HE TOTALLY HATE ME?
I WONDER.
EVEN IF HE DOESN'T, HE'S BEEN REALLY STRANGE LATELY.
RANGE
IOW?
MENS
DAYS
4 April
Commercial Meeting
Radio Broadcast 2:00~
Drama Location 5:00~
Vacation Meeting
Drama Location (Shinjuku) 2:00~
Radio (live) 11:00PM~
St. A/Drama Shoot
Radio (live)
Sports Show (live) 2 shoots
MEN'S T. Photos 12:00~
MEN'S T. Photos 12:00~
Vacation Sports show
Drama Location
Commercial Meeting
Commercial Shoot 8:00~
2 Talk Shows
Drama (Studio) 8:00~
Drama (Studio)
Vacation Meeting
3 March
Drama Location (st A)
3 Talk shows
Sports Meet (live)
Drama Location 8:00~
Commercial Meeting
Sports Show Meeting 3:00~
Vacation Drama Location
Commercial Location (9:00~)
MEN'S T. (live)
Drama Location
Live Radio
MEN'S T. 9:00~
Photo shoot
Day off?
Commercial Location
Make call...?
Vacation Radio Recording
3 Talk Show shoots
Drama Location
8:00~
Variety Shoot
Drama Location (Shibuya)
Tokyo FM
Switch Shoot
SV. Interview
5/2 Photo shoot
Vacation Meeting
Vacation Meeting
Broadcast Presentation Meeting
Vacation?
ABOUT HIS WORK.
HE'S WORKING THREE TIMES WHAT A NORMAL ACTOR WORKS, AND STILL COMPLAINS THAT IT'S NOT ENOUGH.
SEEMS LIKE HE JUST CAN'T STAND TO TAKE TIME OFF.
Wow, it's packed ...
NO IDEA WHAT HE'S IN SUCH A HURRY ABOUT...
tup
tup
NS

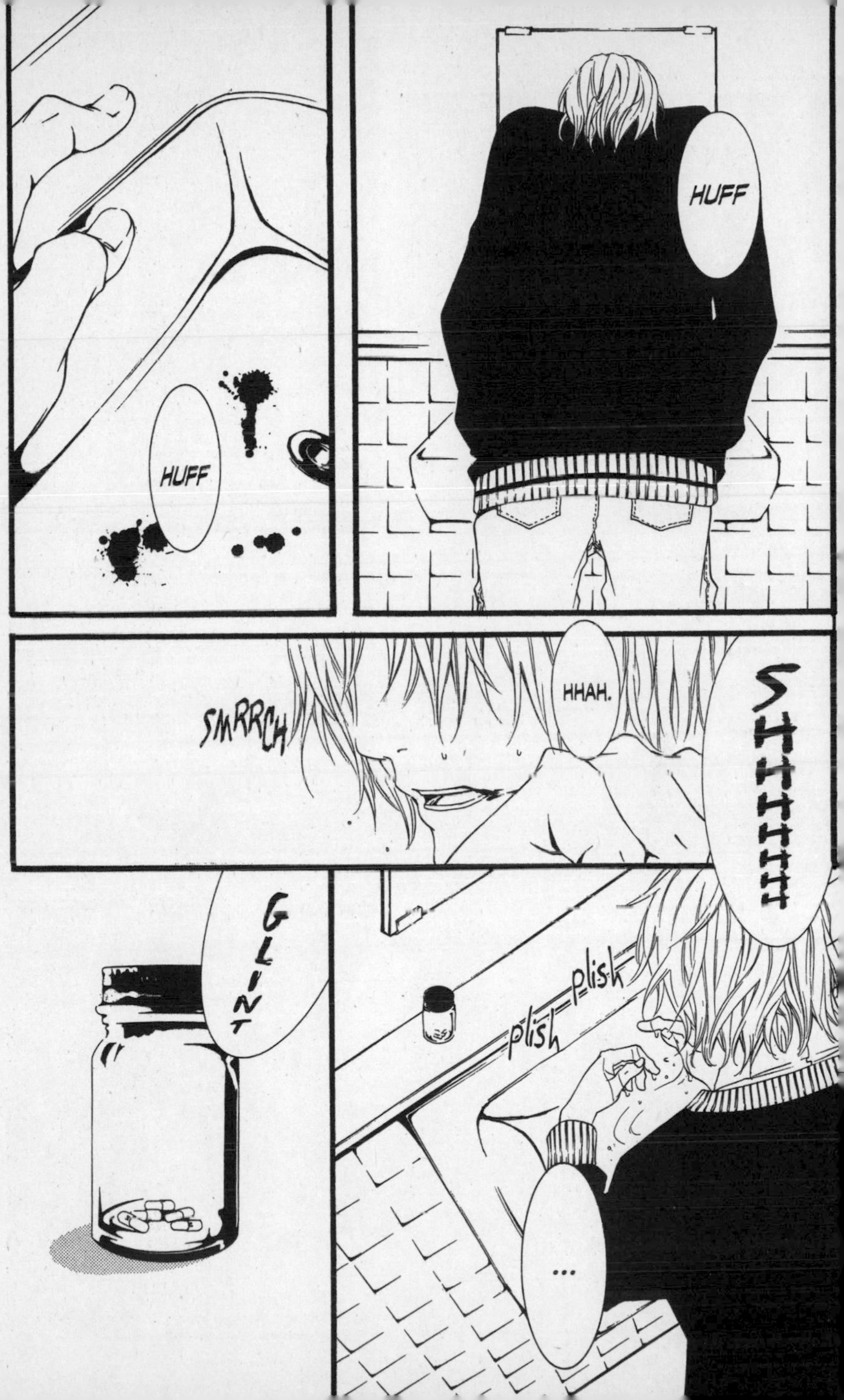
HUFF
HUFF
HHAH.
SMRRCH
SHHHHHH
plish
plish
...
GLINT

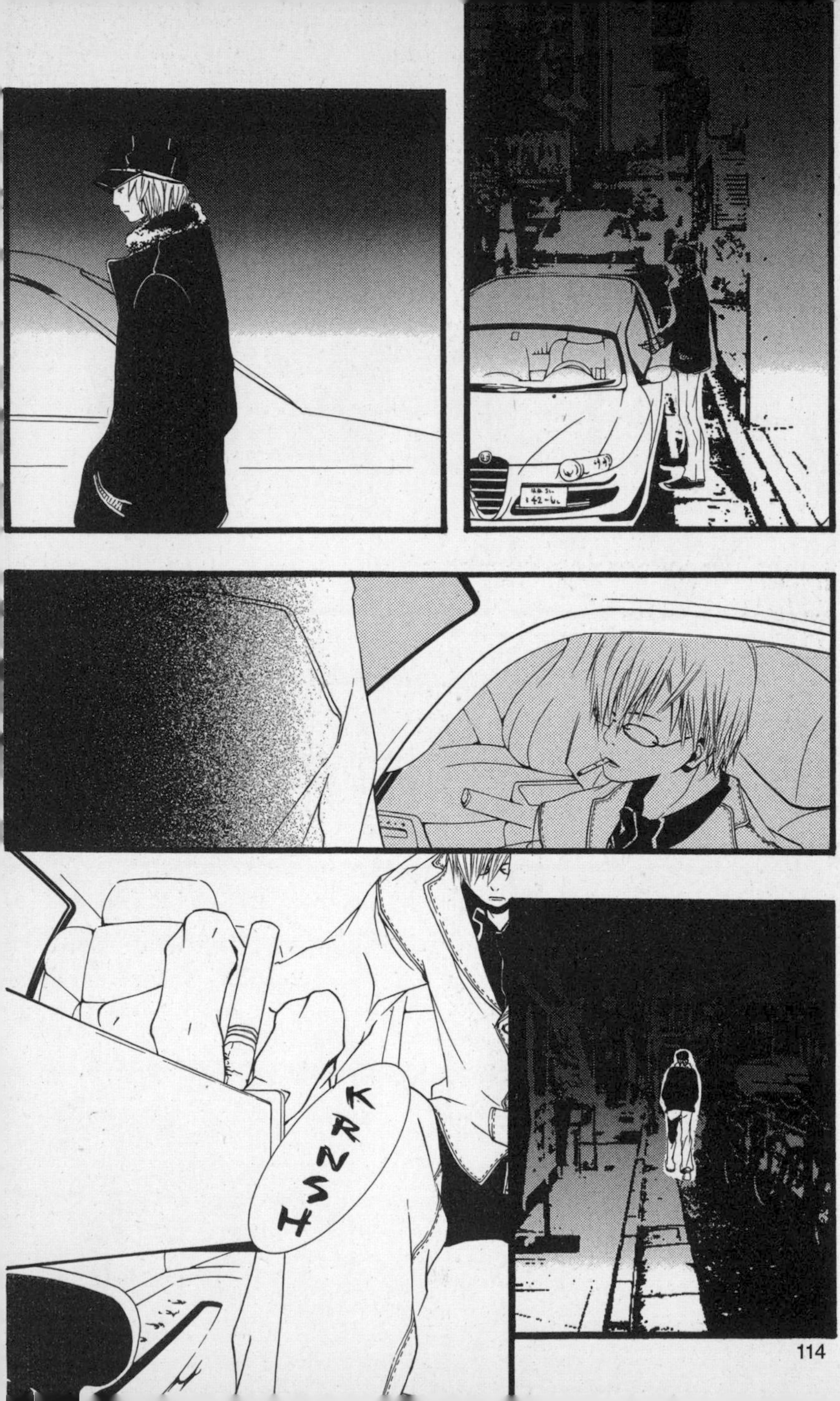
KRNSH

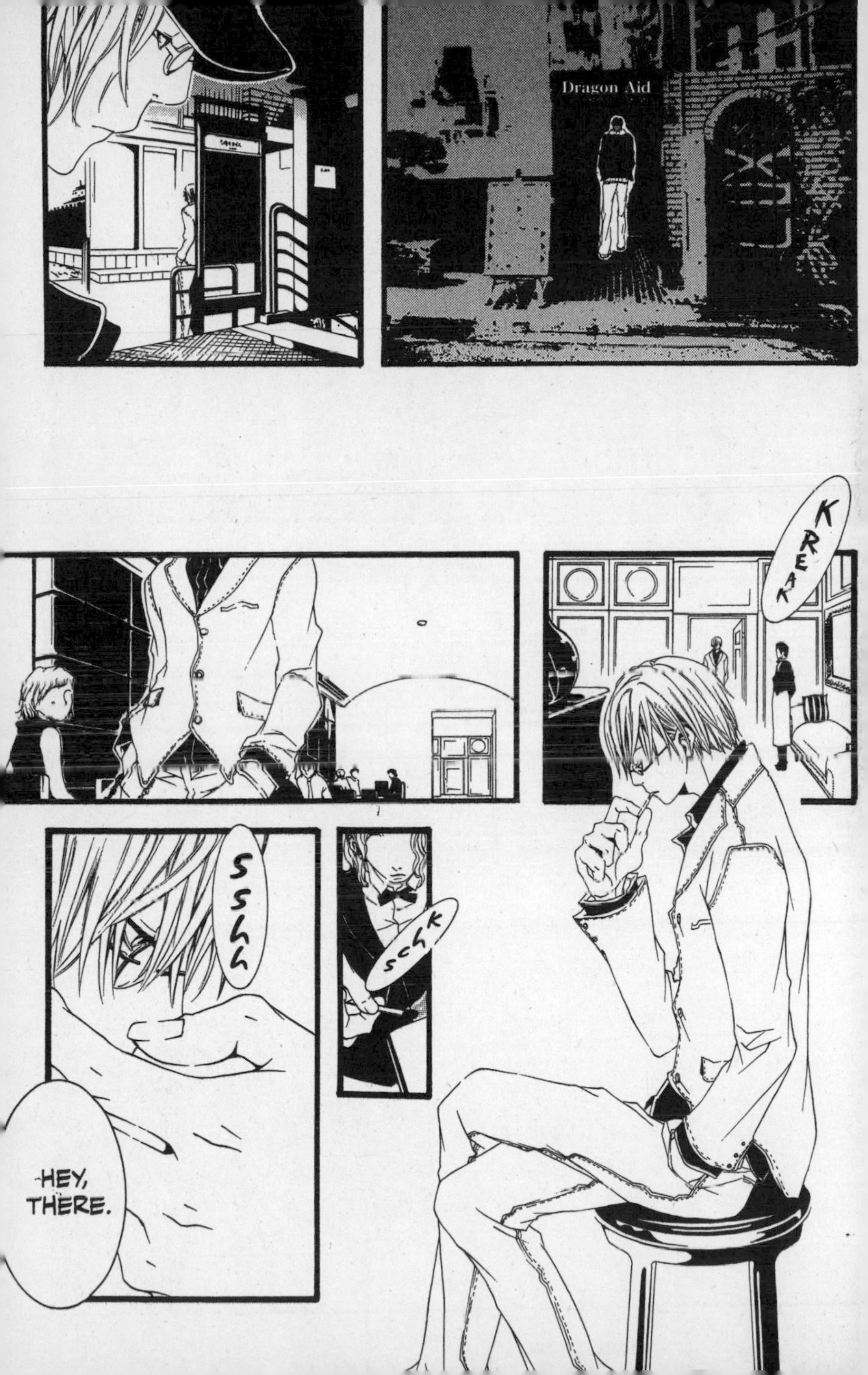
Dragon Aid
KREAK
SSHH
SCHK
HEY, THERE.

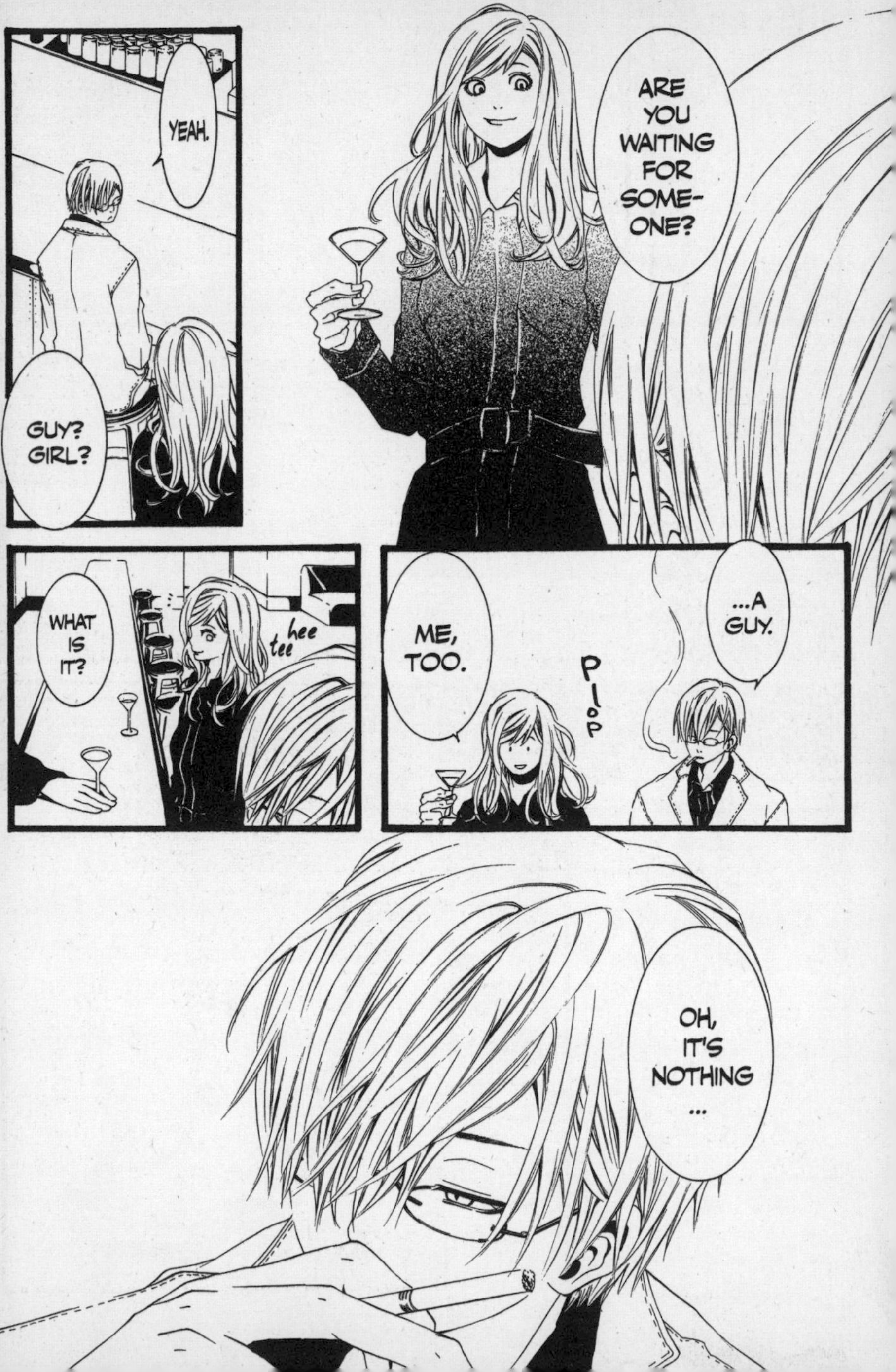
ARE YOU WAITING FOR SOME-ONE?
YEAH.
GUY? GIRL?
...A GUY.
Plop
ME, TOO.
tee hee
WHAT IS IT?
OH, IT'S NOTHING ...

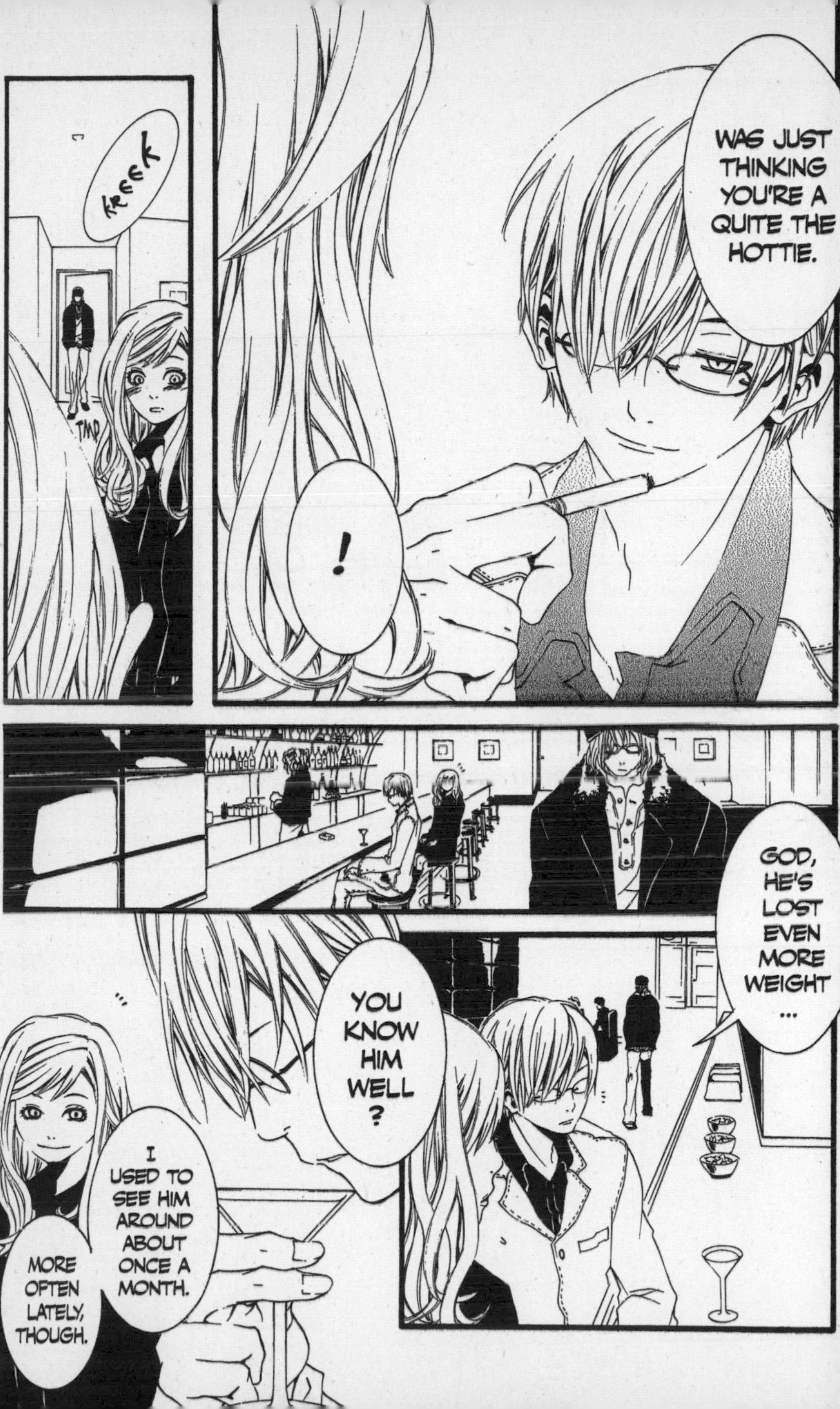
WAS JUST THINKING YOU'RE A QUITE THE HOTTIE.
!
kreek
TMP
GOD, HE'S LOST EVEN MORE WEIGHT ...
YOU KNOW HIM WELL ?
I USED TO SEE HIM AROUND ABOUT ONCE A MONTH.
MORE OFTEN LATELY, THOUGH.

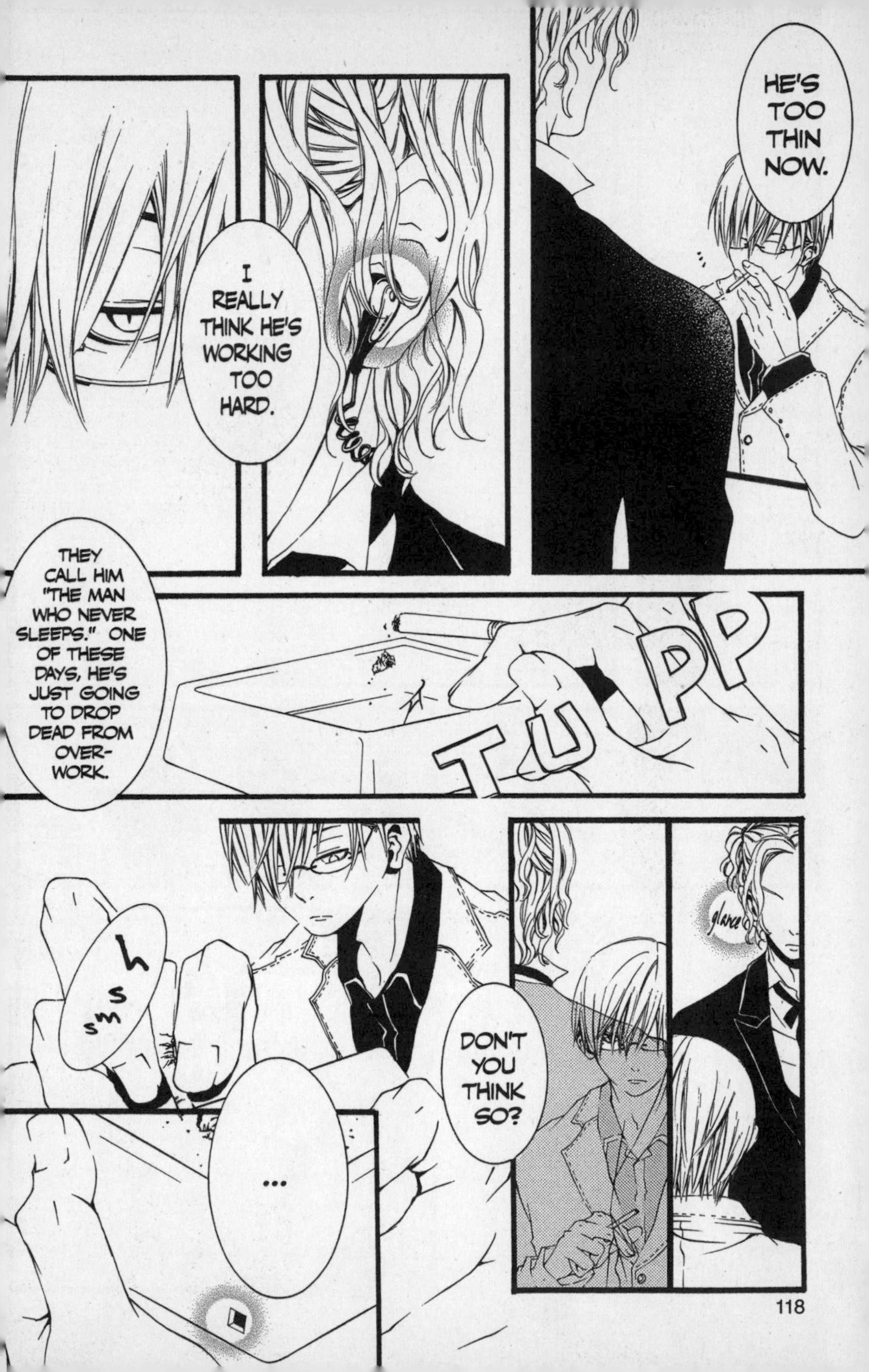
HE'S TOO THIN NOW.
I REALLY THINK HE'S WORKING TOO HARD.
THEY CALL HIM "THE MAN WHO NEVER SLEEPS." ONE OF THESE DAYS, HE'S JUST GOING TO DROP DEAD FROM OVER-WORK.
TUPP
glance
DON'T YOU THINK SO?
...

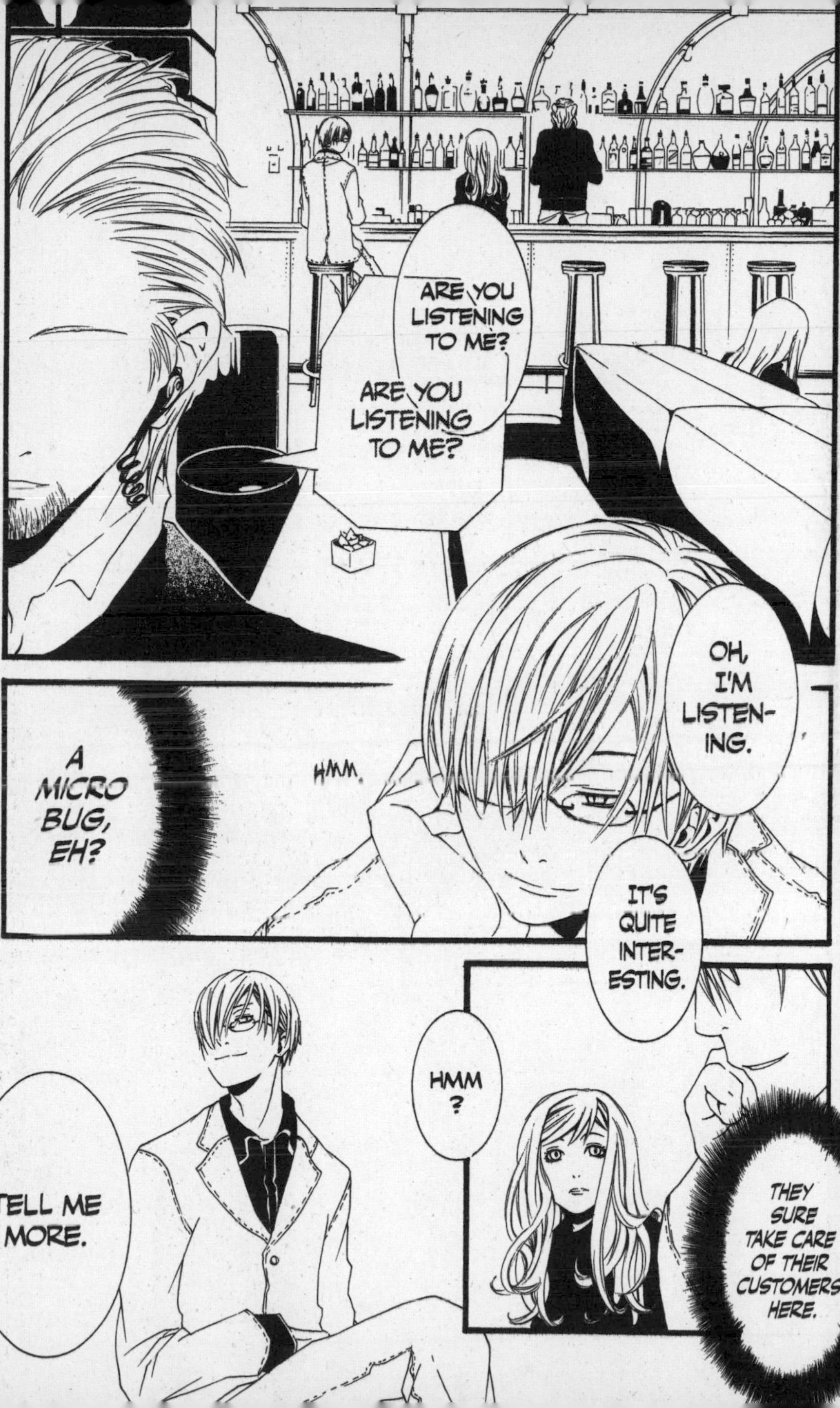
ARE YOU LISTENING TO ME?
ARE YOU LISTENING TO ME?
OH, I'M LISTEN-ING.
HMM.
A MICRO BUG, EH?
IT'S QUITE INTER-ESTING.
THEY SURE TAKE CARE OF THEIR CUSTOMERS HERE.
HMM?
TELL ME MORE.

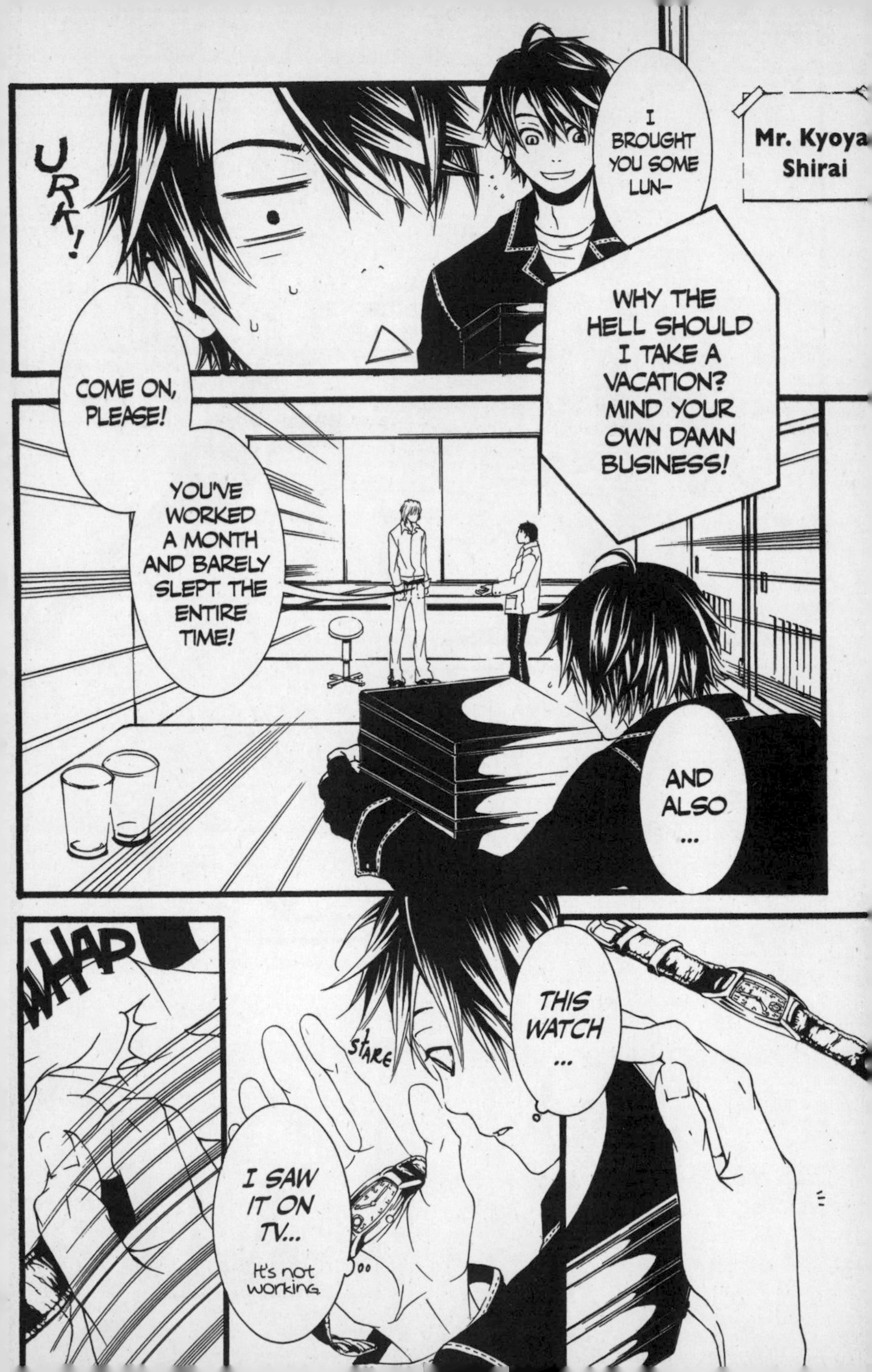
Mr. Kyoya Shirai
I BROUGHT YOU SOME LUN–
URK!
WHY THE HELL SHOULD I TAKE A VACATION? MIND YOUR OWN DAMN BUSINESS!
COME ON, PLEASE!
YOU'VE WORKED A MONTH AND BARELY SLEPT THE ENTIRE TIME!
AND ALSO ...
THIS WATCH ...
STARE
I SAW IT ON TV...
It's not working.
WHAP

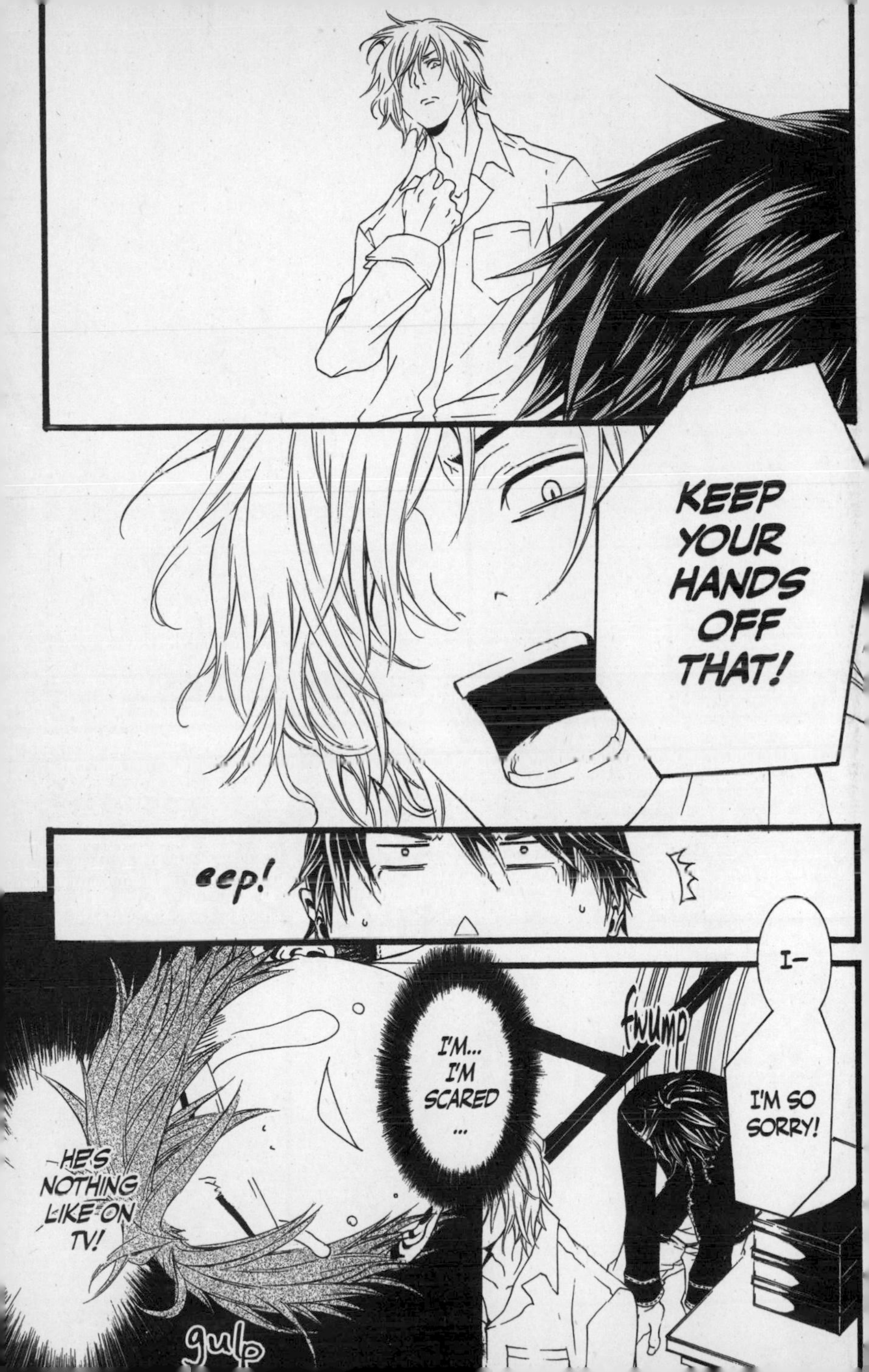
KEEP YOUR HANDS OFF THAT!
eep!
I-
I'M SO SORRY!
fwump
I'M... I'M SCARED ...
HE'S NOTHING LIKE ON TV!
gulp

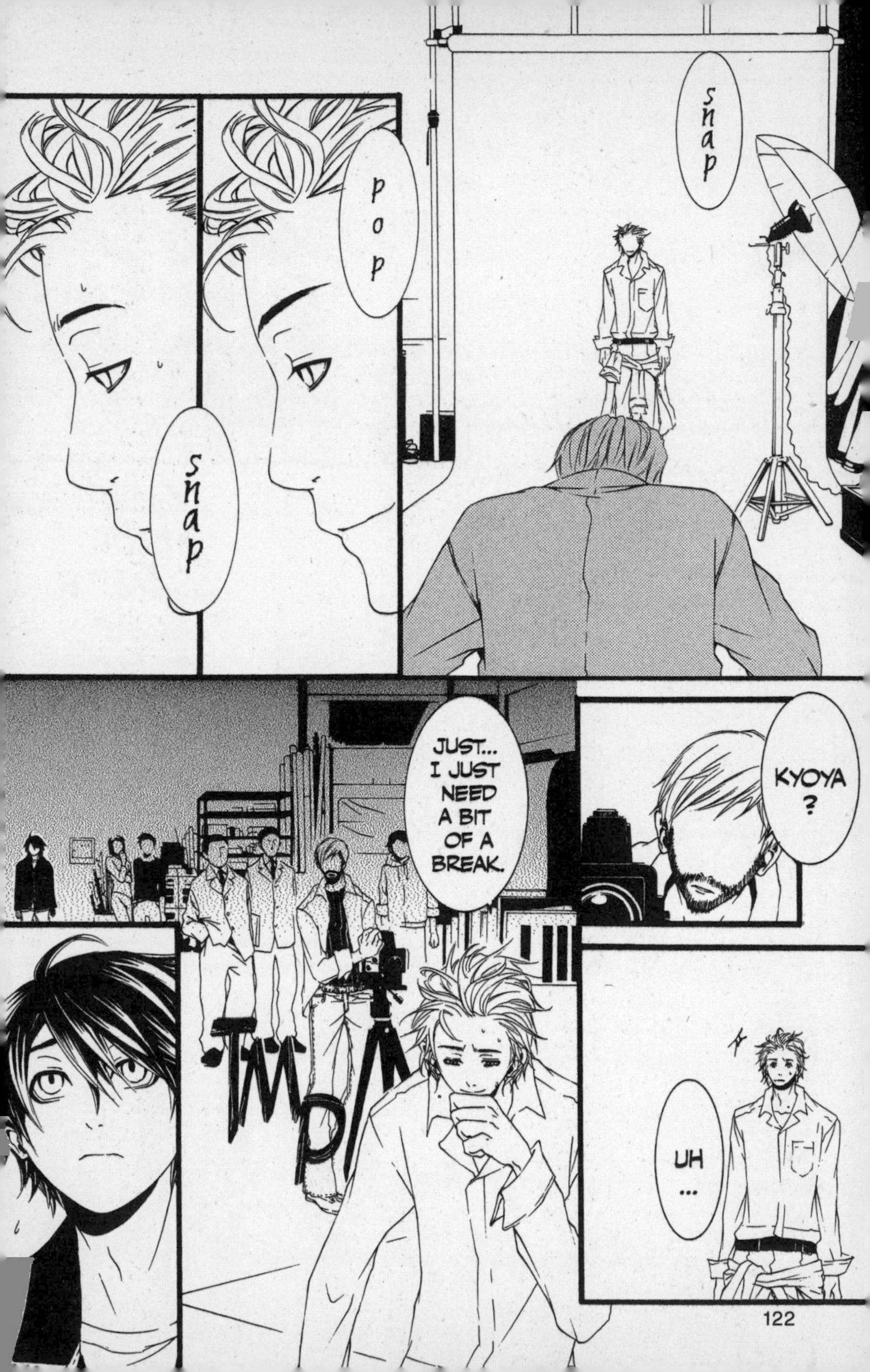
snap
pop
snap
KYOYA?
JUST... I JUST NEED A BIT OF A BREAK.
UH...
TMP

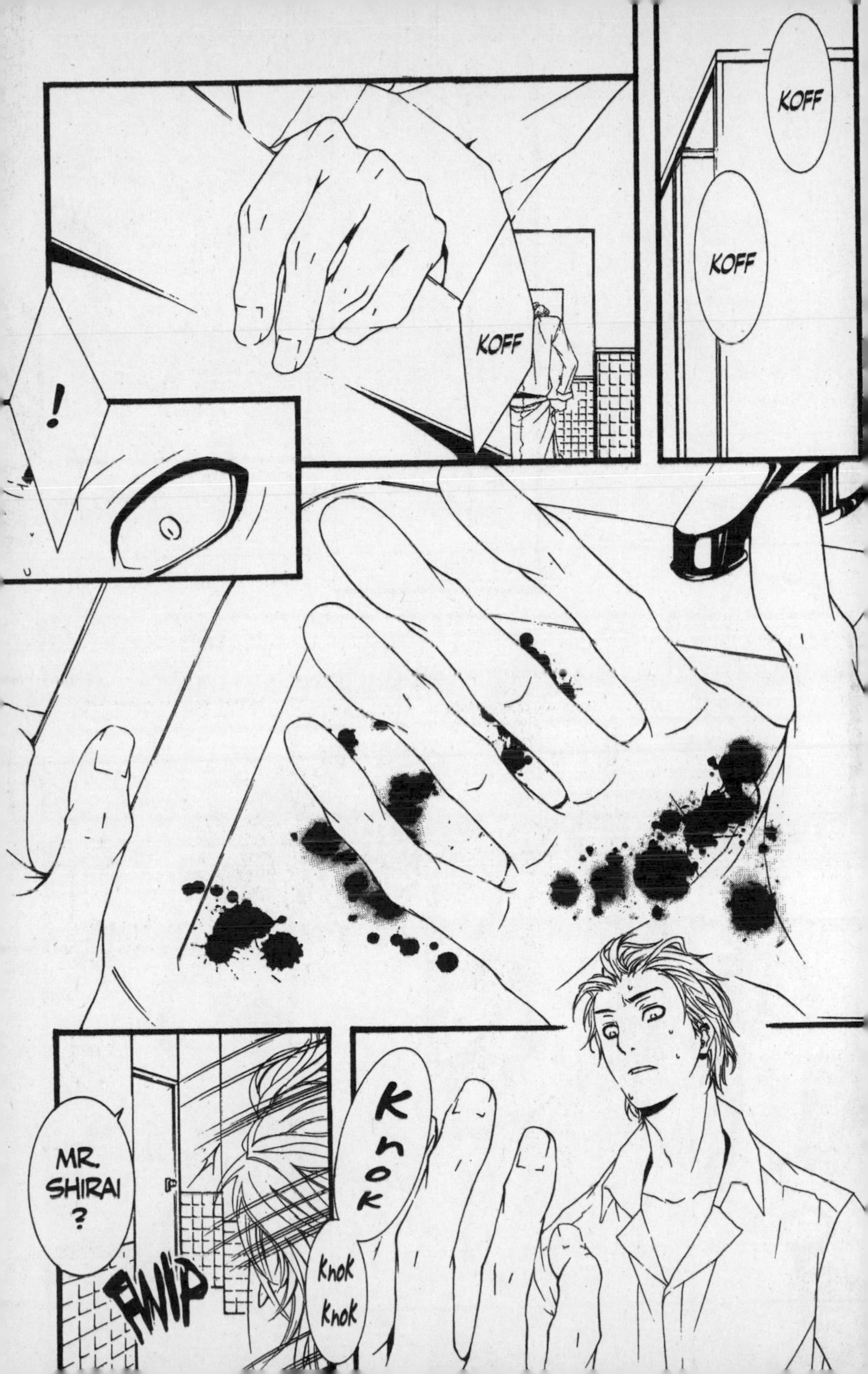
KOFF
KOFF
KOFF
!
Knok
Knok
Knok
MR. SHIRAI ?
FWIP

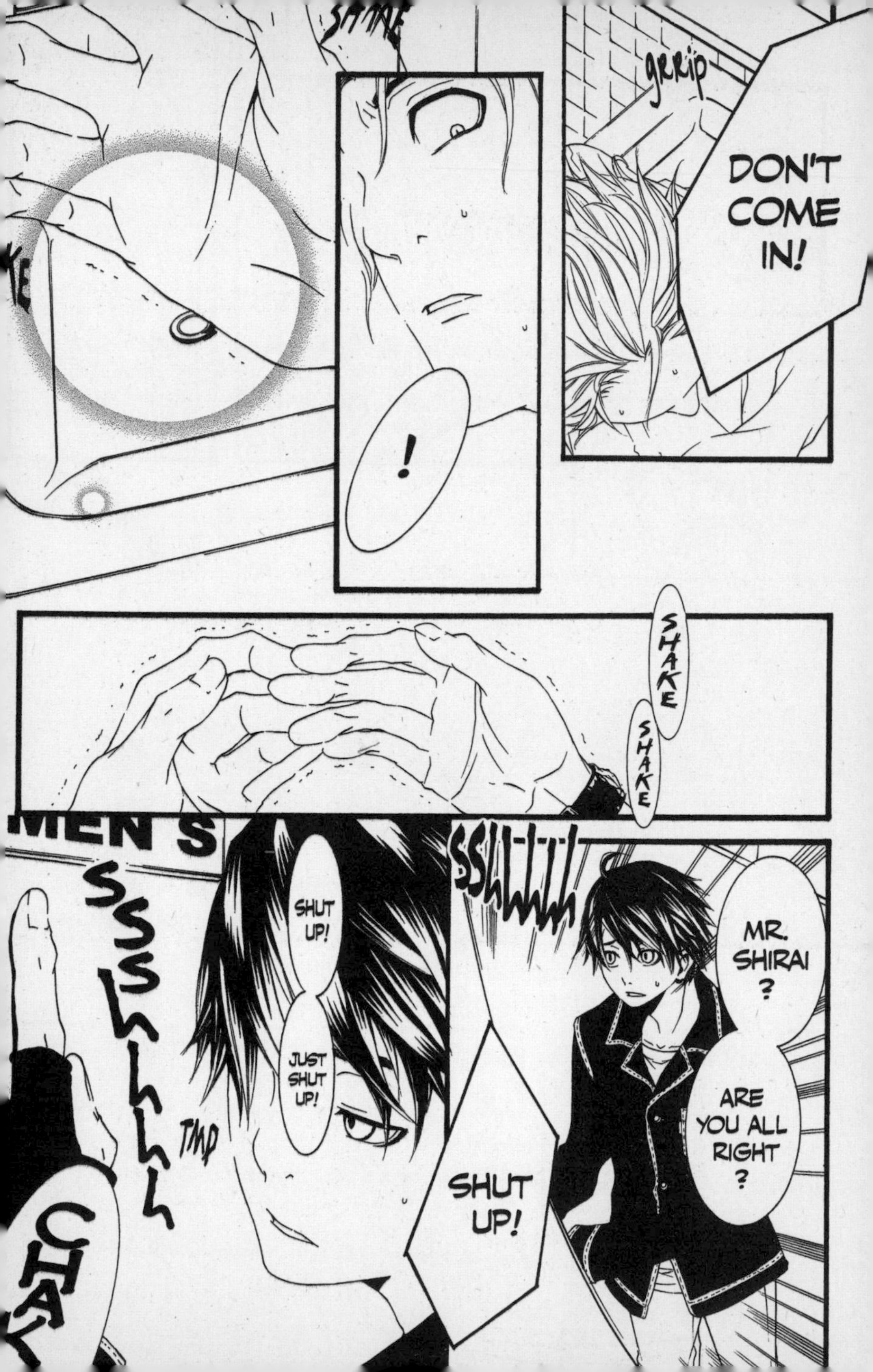
grrip
DON'T COME IN!
!
SHAKE
SHAKE
SShhhhh
MR. SHIRAI?
ARE YOU ALL RIGHT?
SHUT UP!
SHUT UP!
JUST SHUT UP!
TMP
MEN'S
SSShhhh
CHA

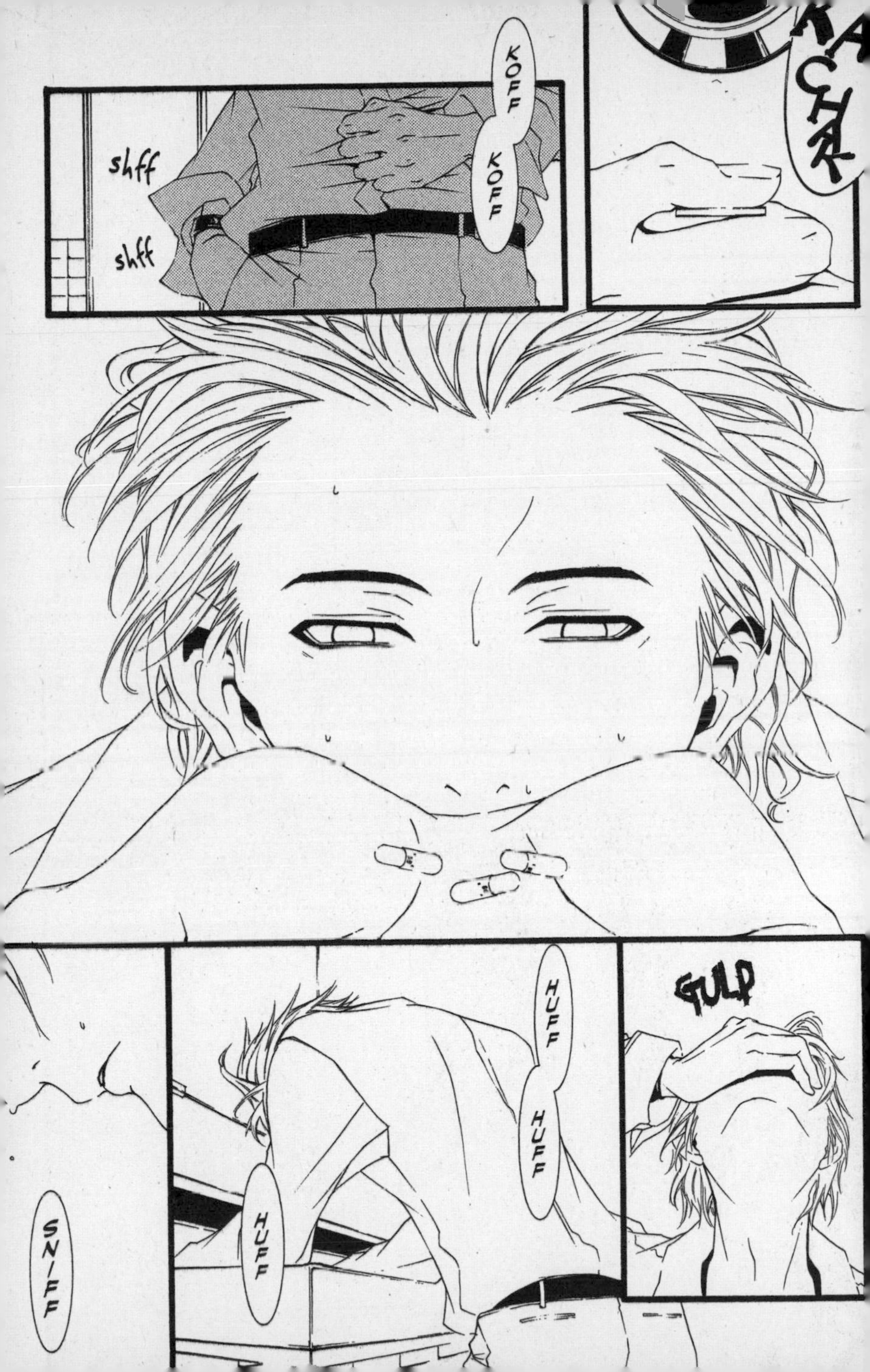
KACHAK
KOFF KOFF
shff
shff
GULP
HUFF HUFF
HUFF
SNIFF

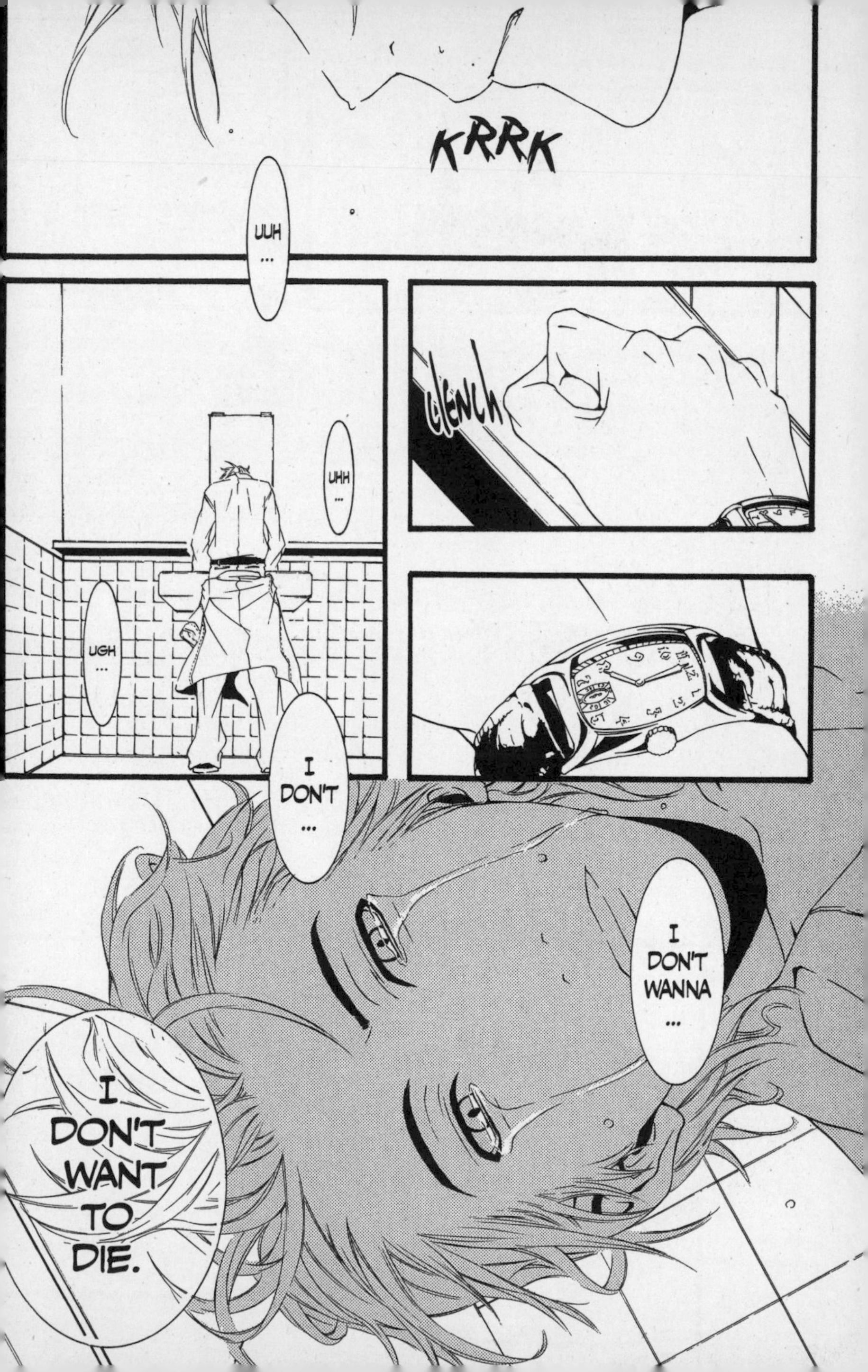
KRRK
UUH...
CLENCH
UHH...
UGH...
I DON'T...
I DON'T WANNA...
I DON'T WANT TO DIE.

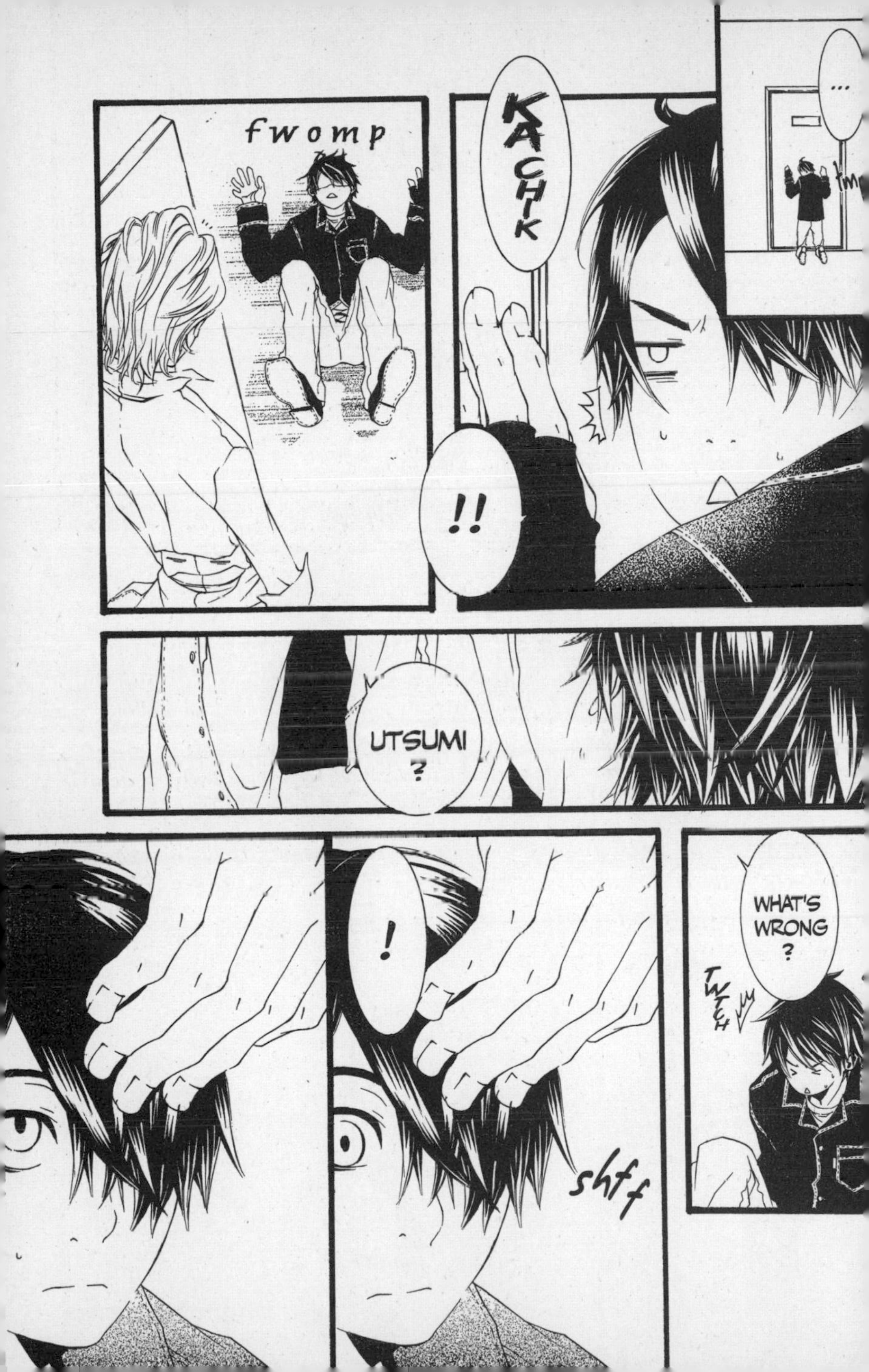
...
KACHIK
!!
fwomp
UTSUMI ?
WHAT'S WRONG ?
TWITCH
!
shff

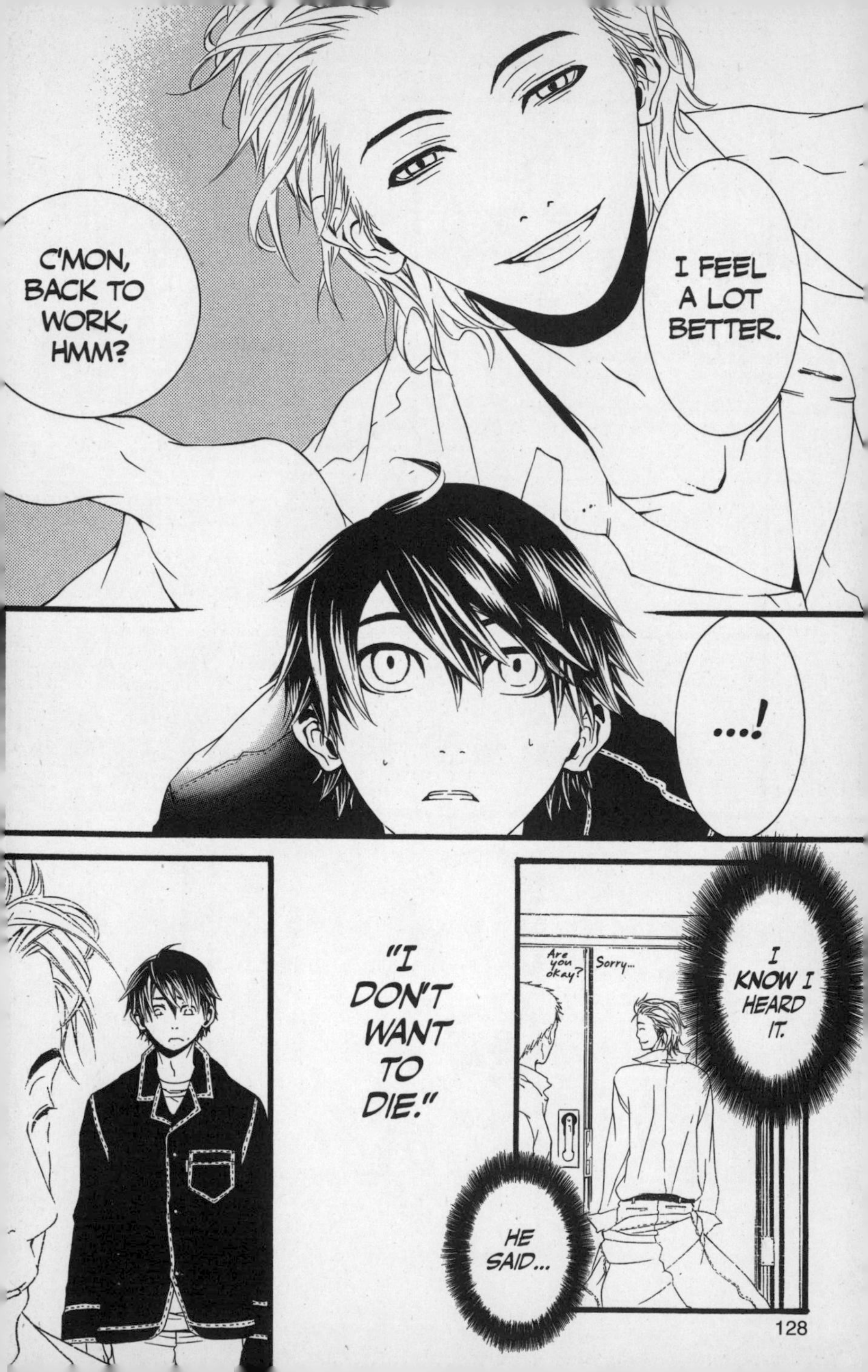
I FEEL A LOT BETTER.
C'MON, BACK TO WORK, HMM?
...!
I KNOW I HEARD IT.
Sorry...
Are you okay?
HE SAID...
"I DON'T WANT TO DIE."

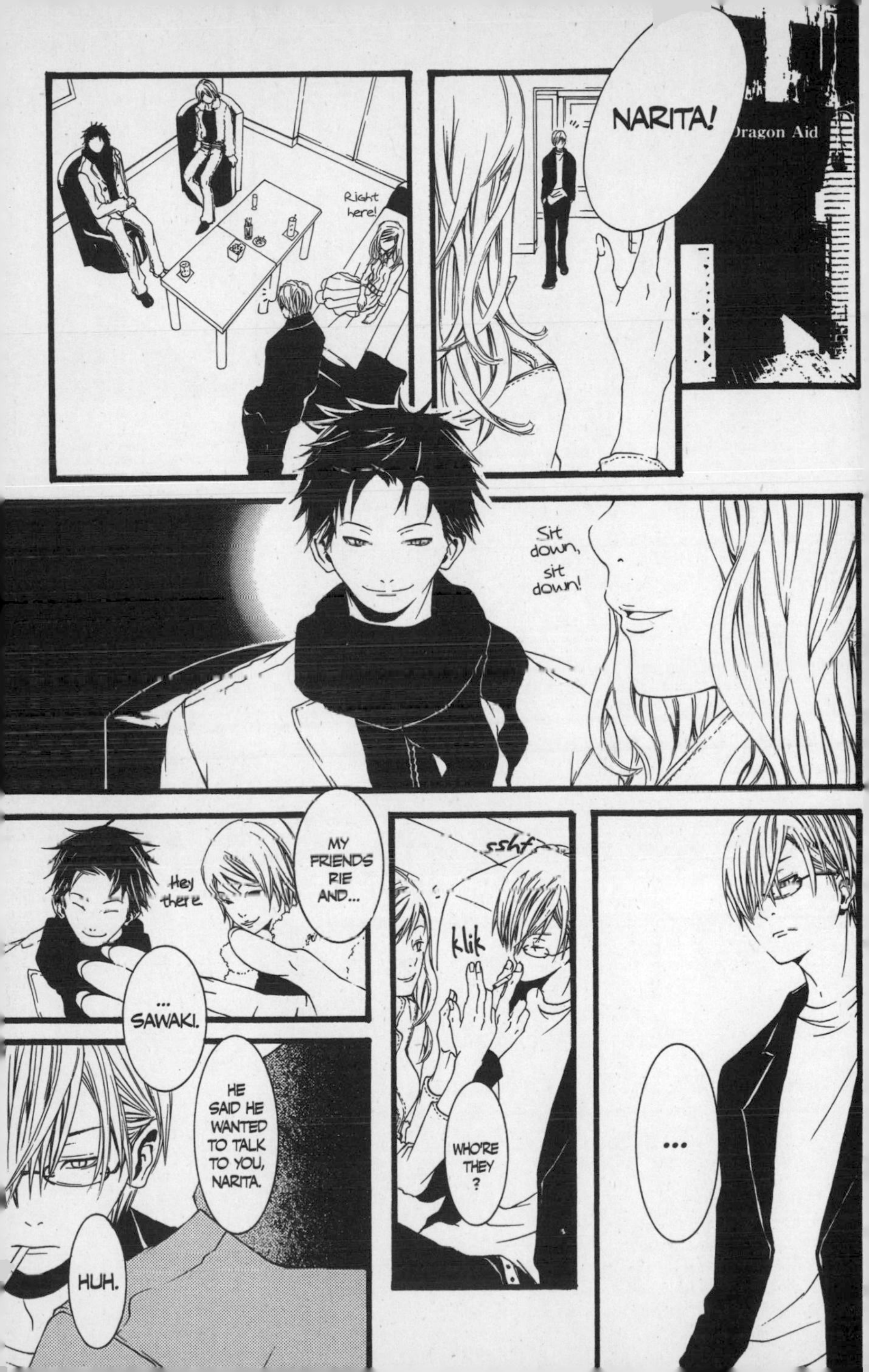
Dragon Aid
NARITA!
Right here!
Sit down, sit down!
...
sshf
klik
WHO'RE THEY?
MY FRIENDS RIE AND...
Hey there
...SAWAKI.
HE SAID HE WANTED TO TALK TO YOU, NARITA.
HUH.

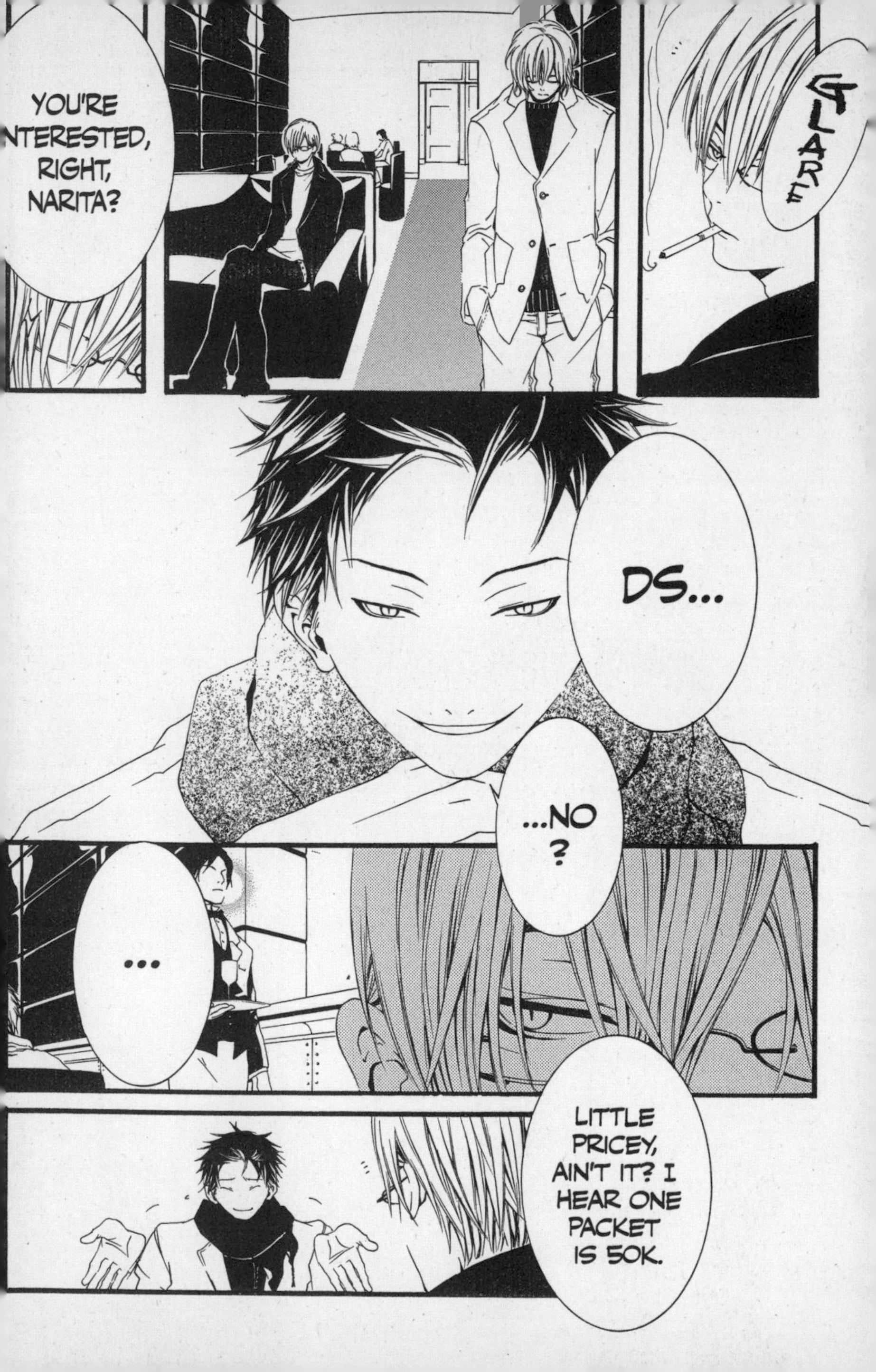
GLARE
YOU'RE NTERESTED, RIGHT, NARITA?
DS...
...NO?
...
LITTLE PRICEY, AIN'T IT? I HEAR ONE PACKET IS 50K.

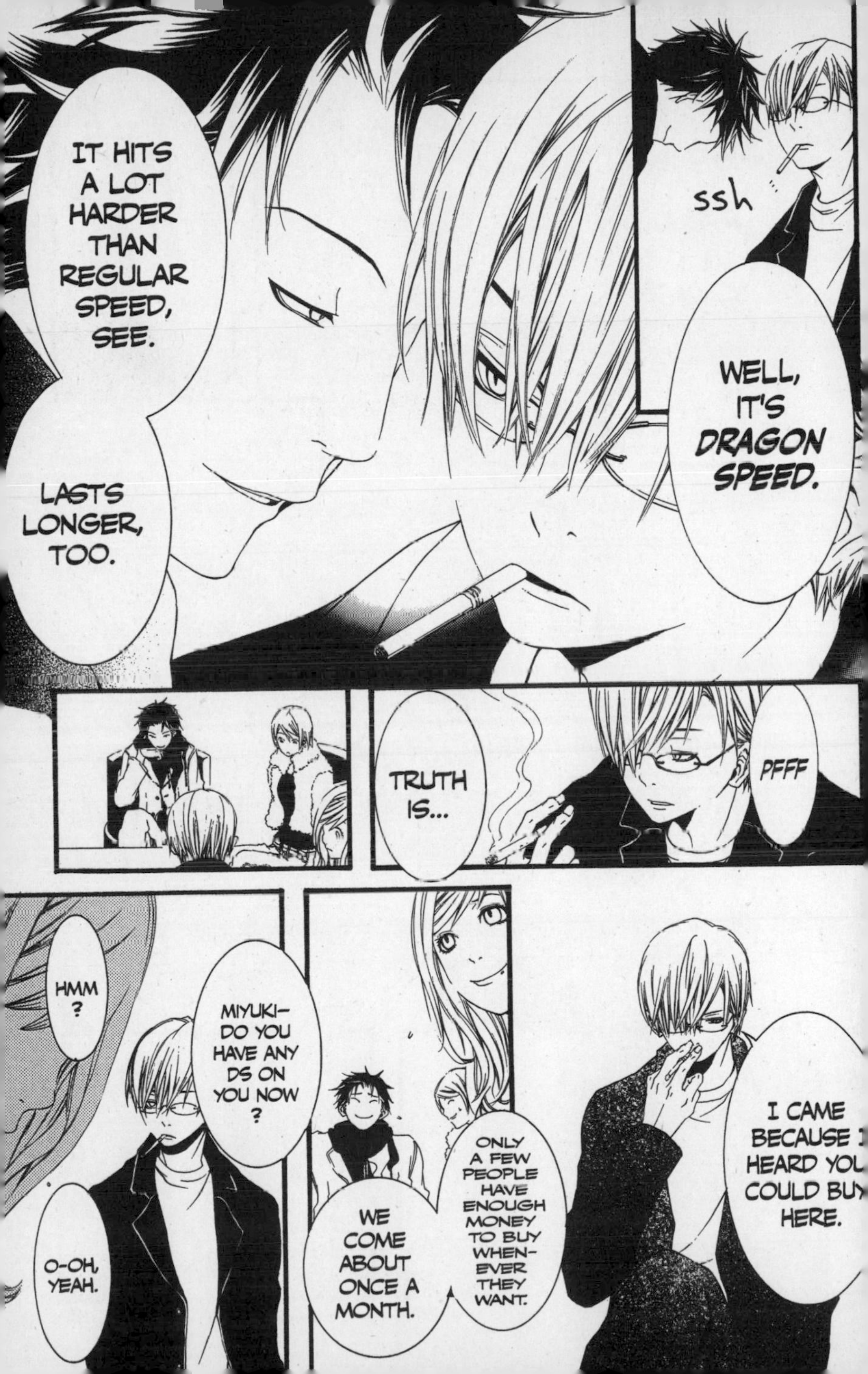
ssh
WELL, IT'S DRAGON SPEED.
IT HITS A LOT HARDER THAN REGULAR SPEED, SEE.
LASTS LONGER, TOO.
PFFF
TRUTH IS...
I CAME BECAUSE I HEARD YOU COULD BUY HERE.
ONLY A FEW PEOPLE HAVE ENOUGH MONEY TO BUY WHEN-EVER THEY WANT.
WE COME ABOUT ONCE A MONTH.
MIYUKI-DO YOU HAVE ANY DS ON YOU NOW?
HMM?
O-OH, YEAH.

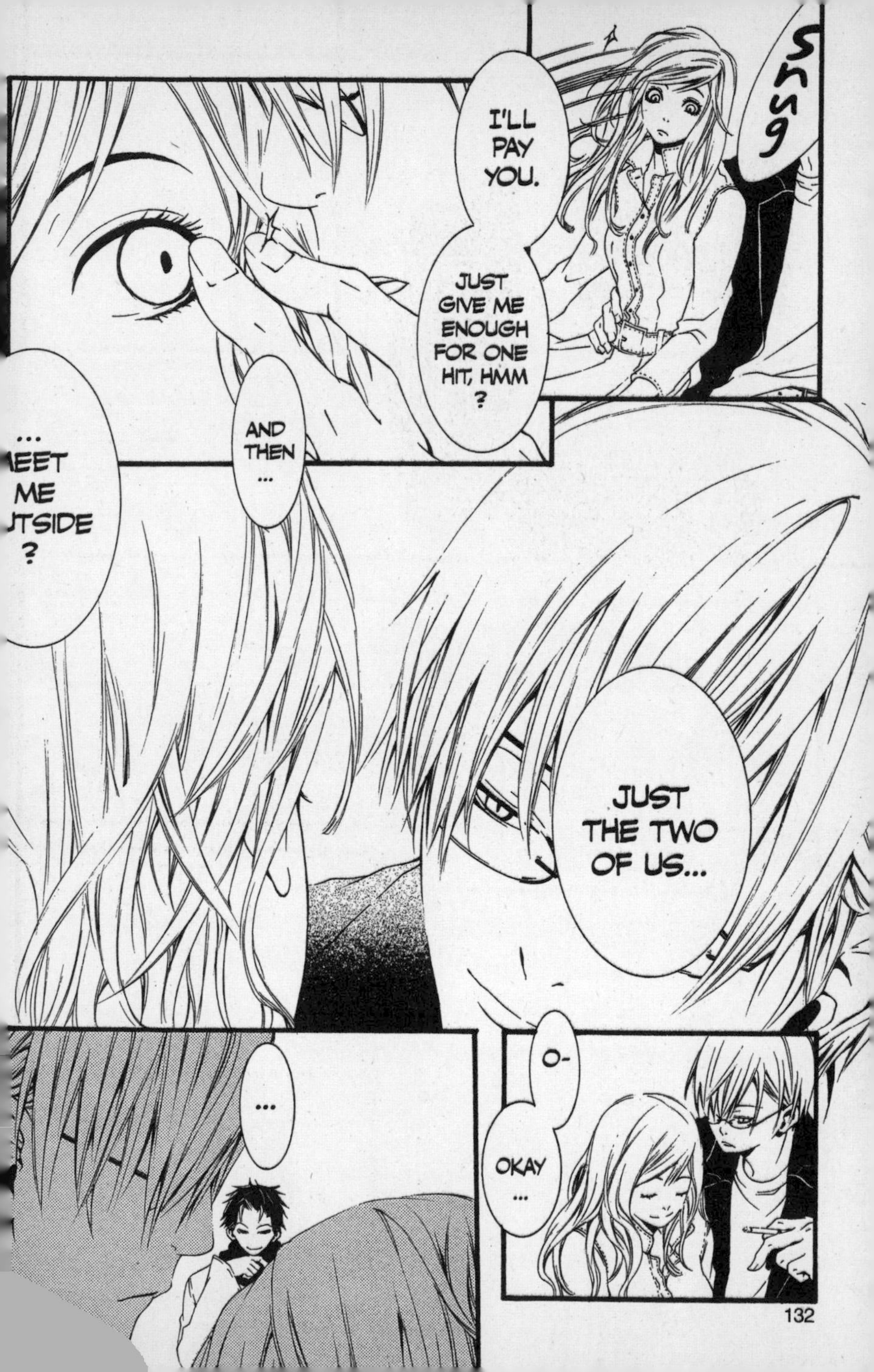
snug
I'LL PAY YOU.
JUST GIVE ME ENOUGH FOR ONE HIT, HMM?
AND THEN...
... EET ME TSIDE ?
JUST THE TWO OF US...
O-
OKAY...
...

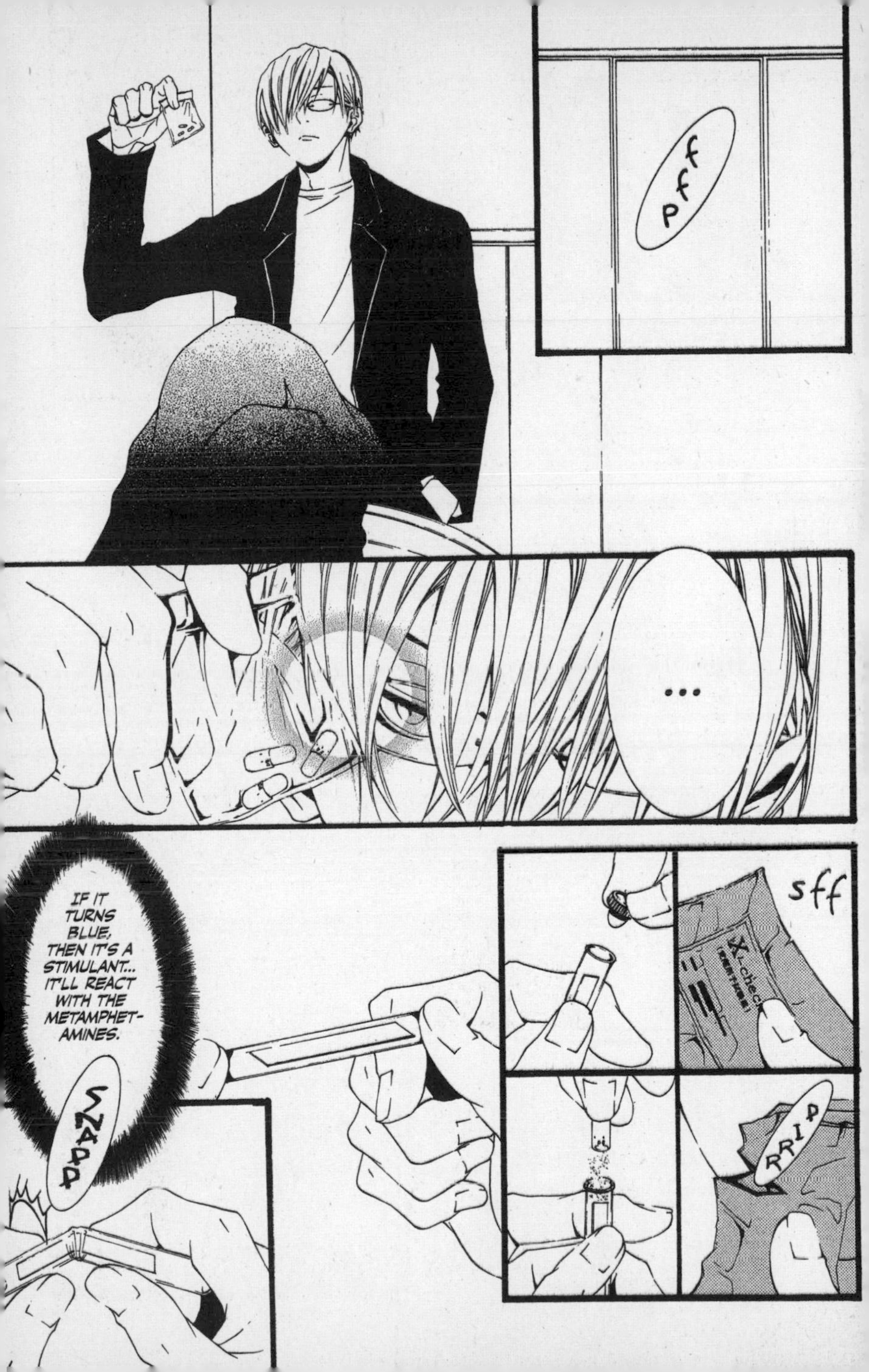
pff
...
sff
RRIP
IF IT TURNS BLUE, THEN IT'S A STIMULANT... IT'LL REACT WITH THE METAMPHET-AMINES.
SNAPP

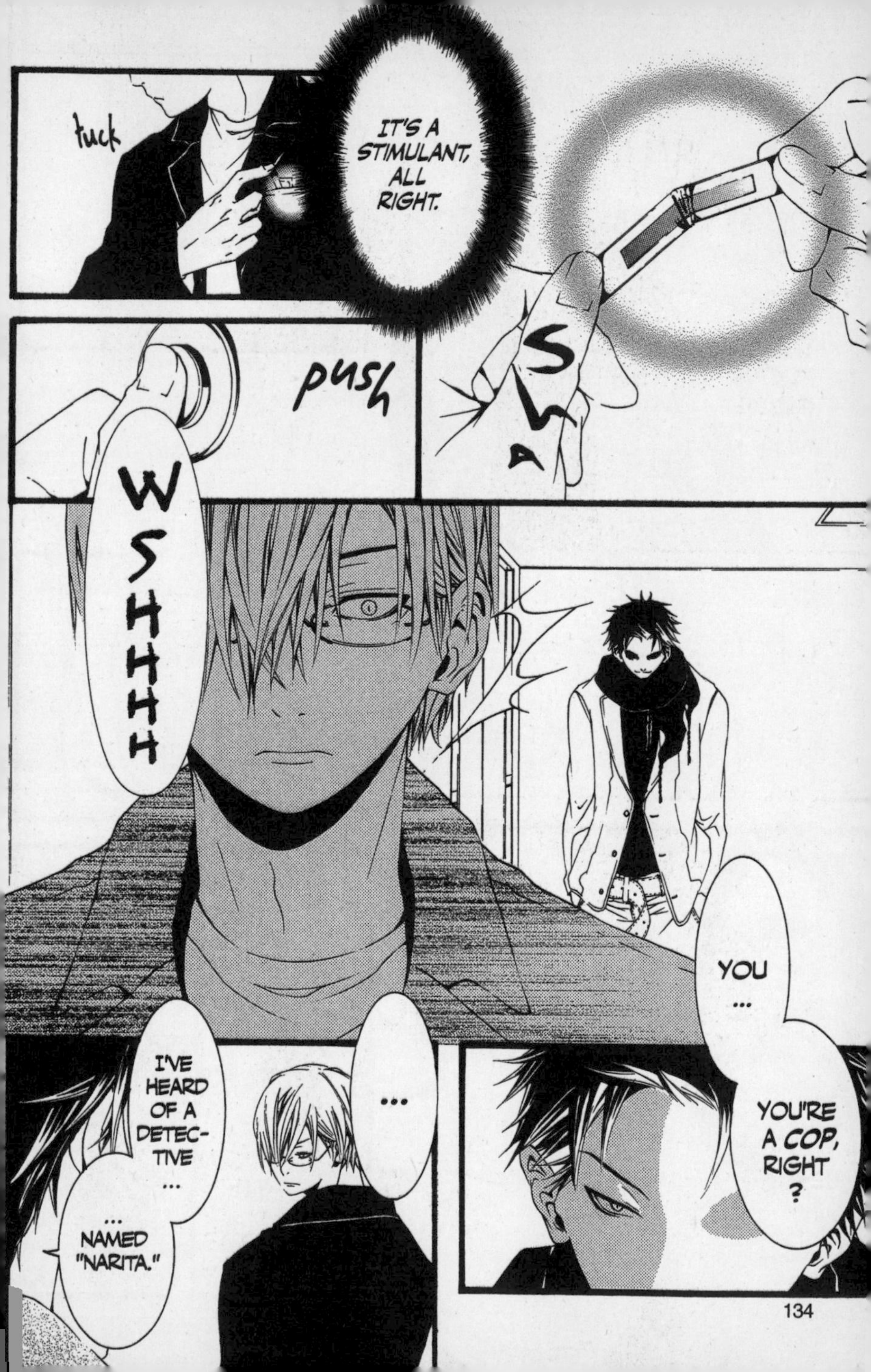
IT'S A STIMULANT, ALL RIGHT.
tuck
Sha
push
WSHHHH
YOU ...
YOU'RE A COP, RIGHT ?
...
I'VE HEARD OF A DETECTIVE ...
... NAMED "NARITA."

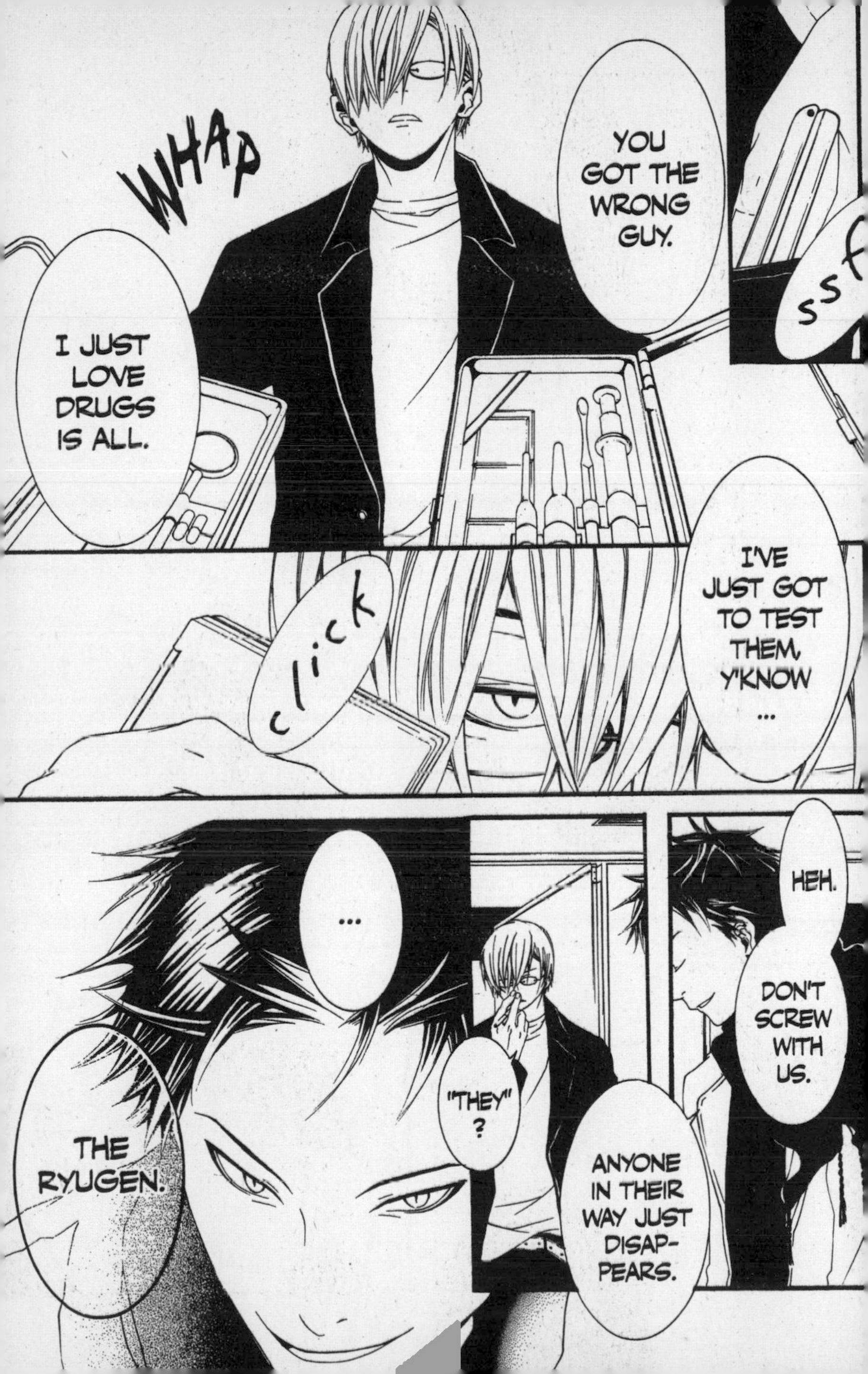
ssf
YOU GOT THE WRONG GUY.
WHAP
I JUST LOVE DRUGS IS ALL.
I'VE JUST GOT TO TEST THEM, Y'KNOW ...
click
HEH.
DON'T SCREW WITH US.
"THEY"?
...
THE RYUGEN.
ANYONE IN THEIR WAY JUST DISAP-PEARS.

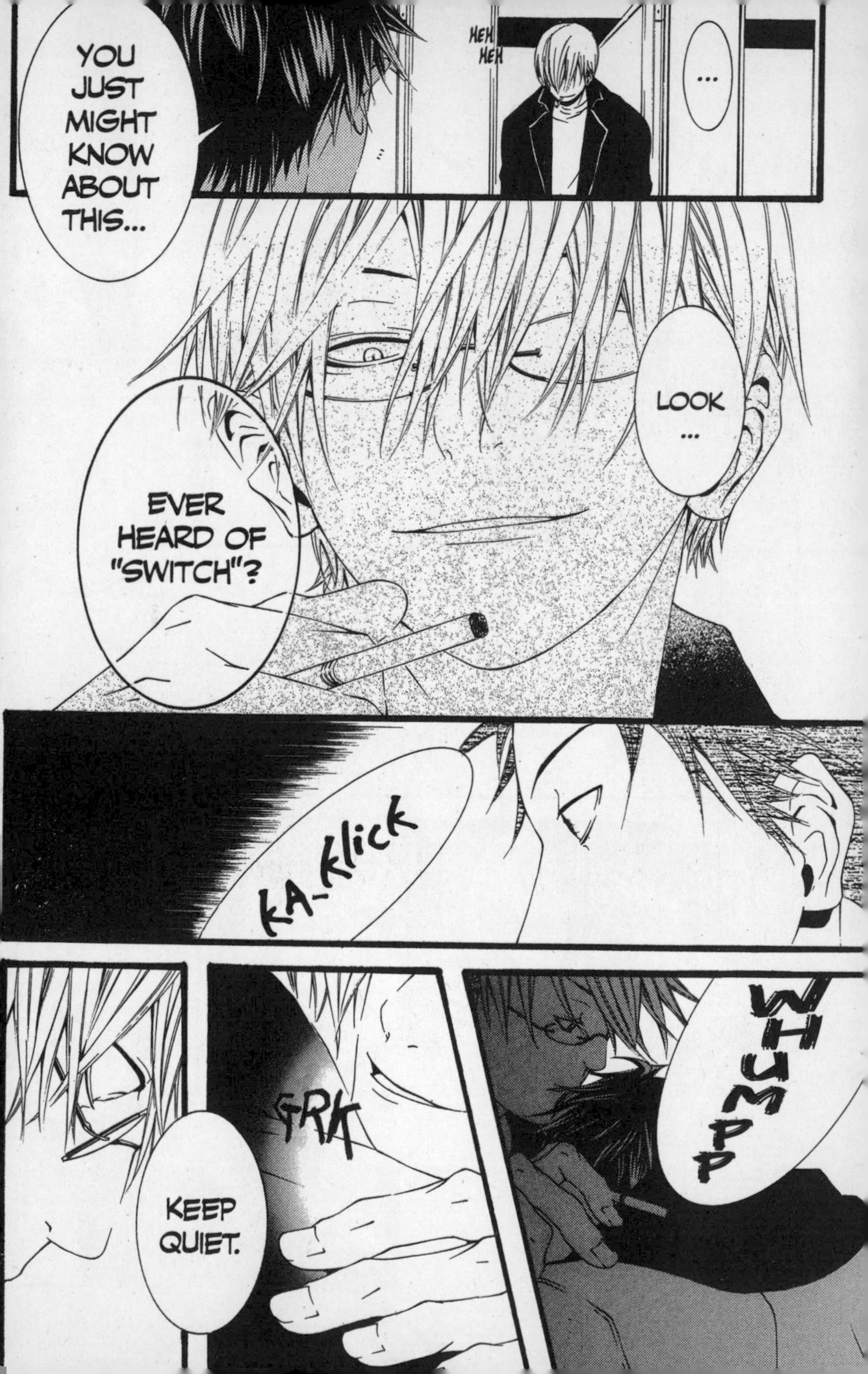
...
HEH HEH
YOU JUST MIGHT KNOW ABOUT THIS...
LOOK ...
EVER HEARD OF "SWITCH"?
KA-KLICK
WHUMPP
GRK
KEEP QUIET.

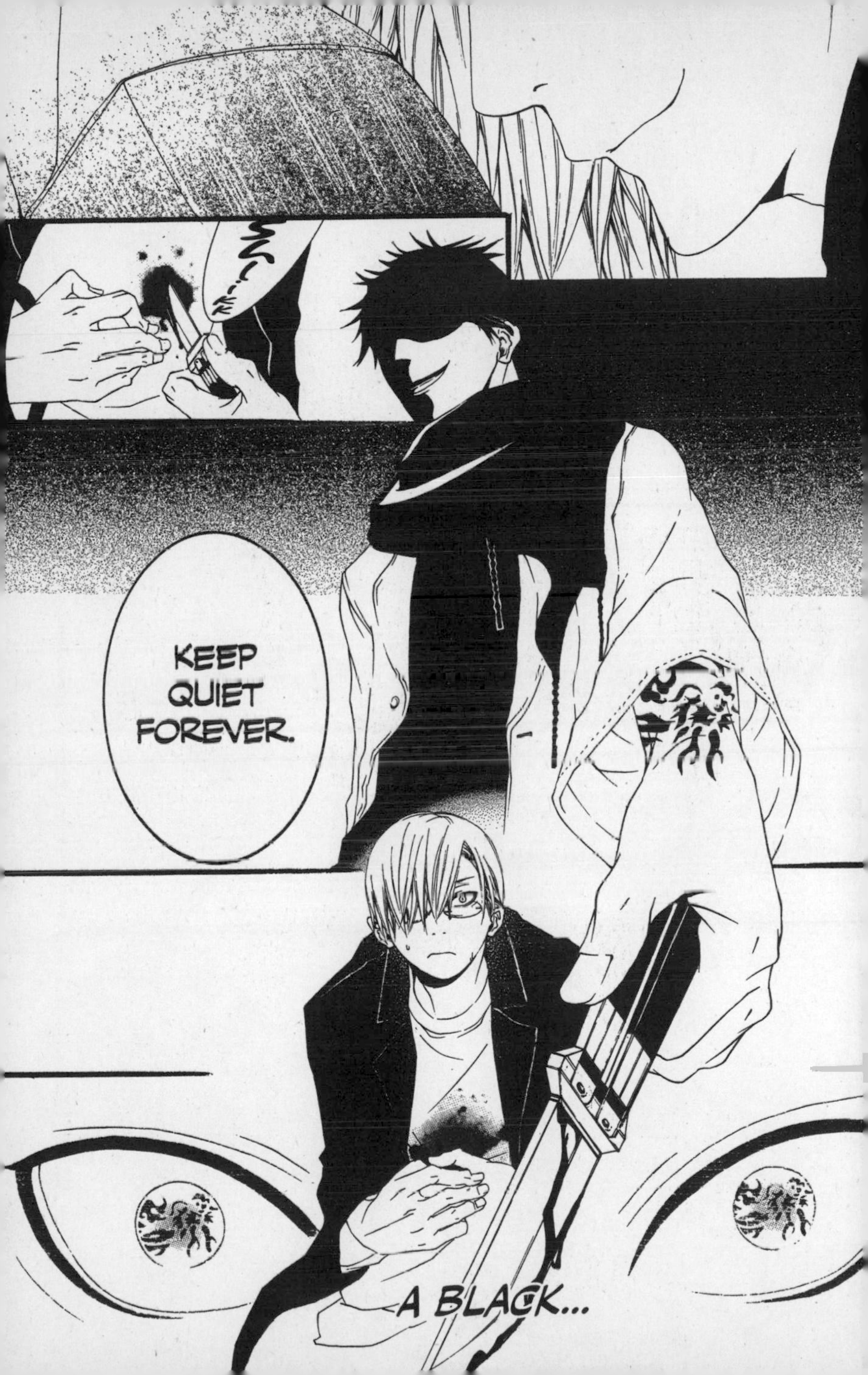
KEEP QUIET FOREVER.
A BLACK...

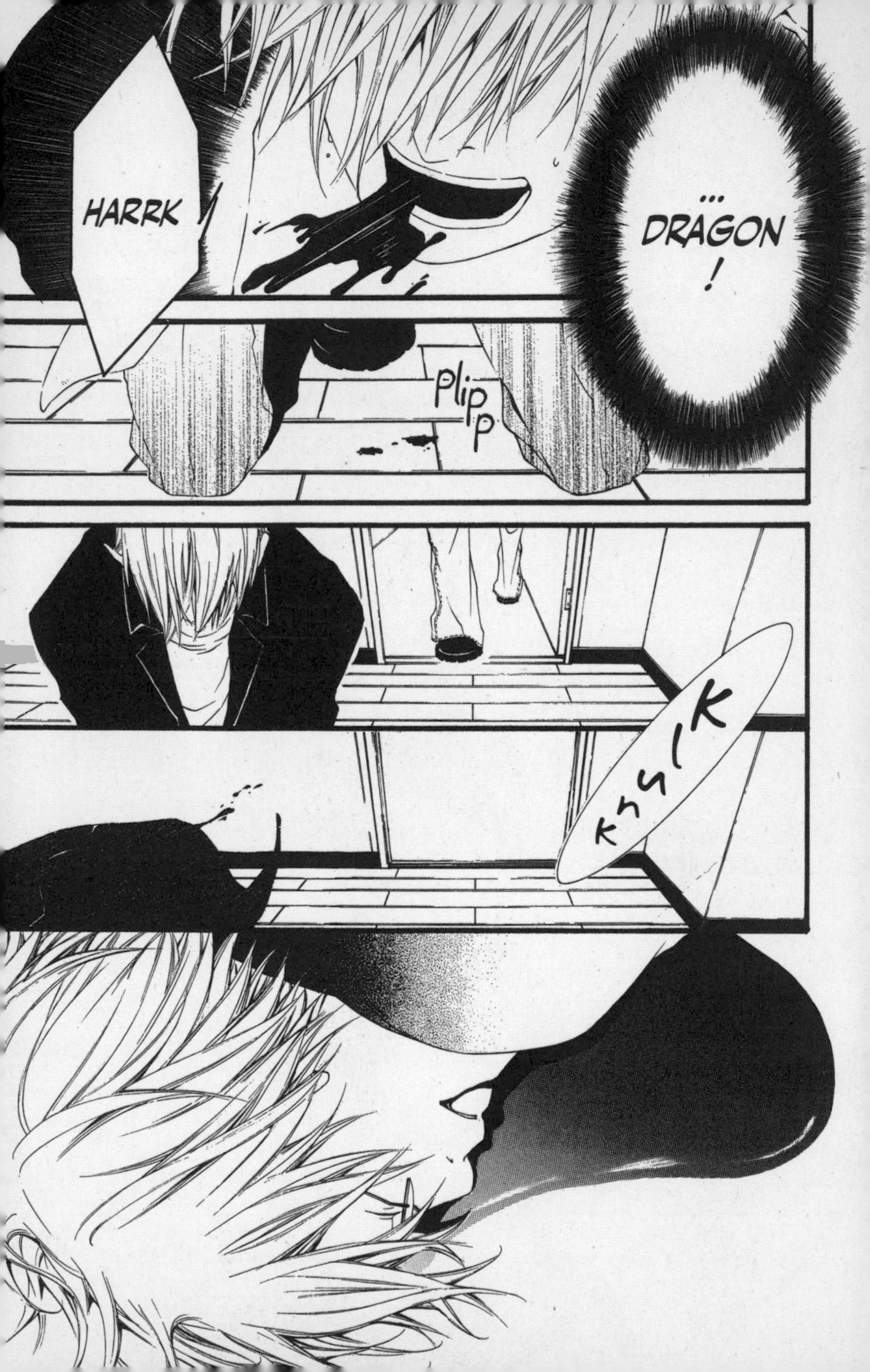

... DRAGON!
HARRK
plipp
knulk

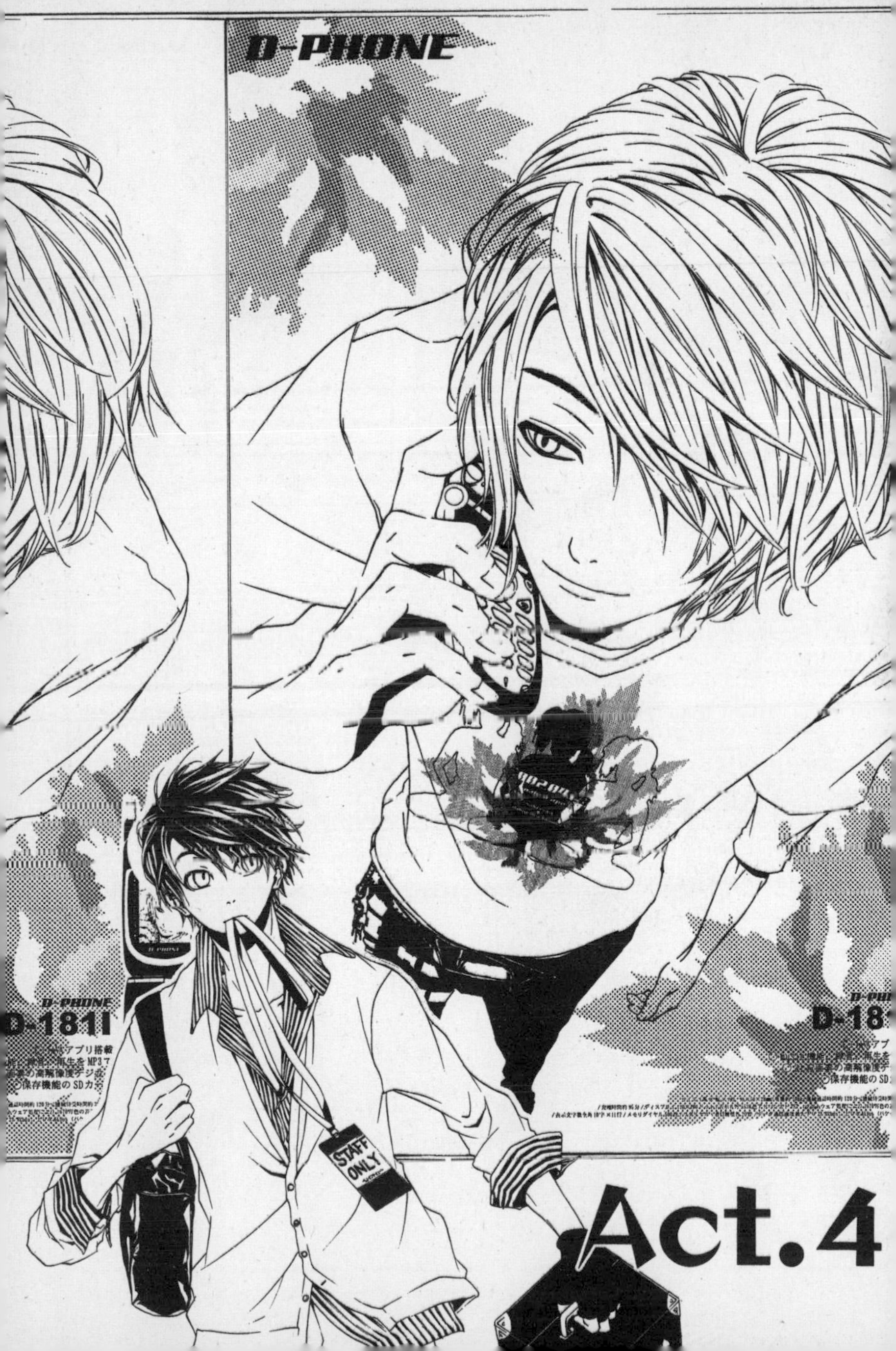
D-PHONE
D-PHONE
D-181I
STAFF ONLY
Act.4

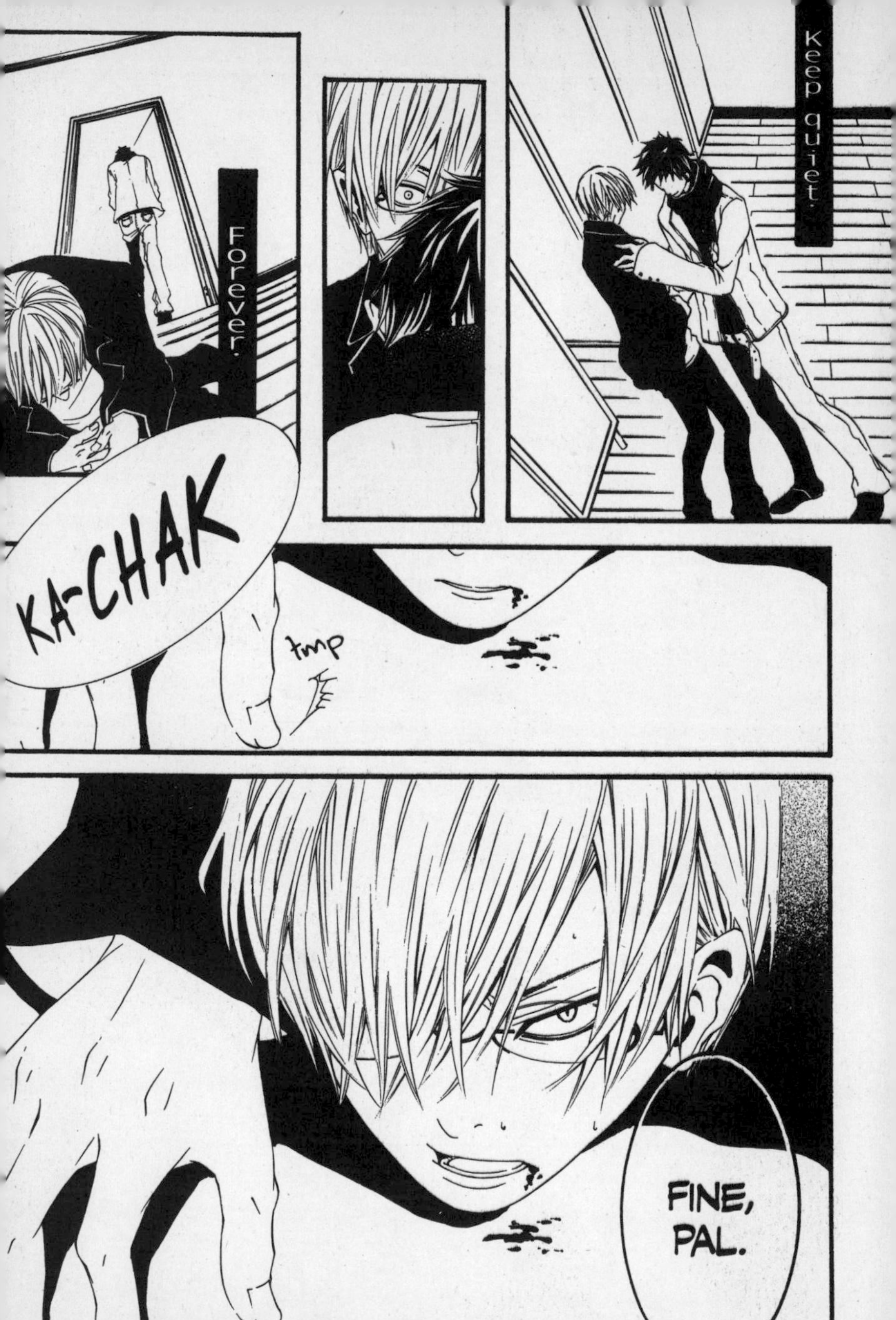
Keep quiet.
Forever.
KA-CHAK
tmp
FINE, PAL.

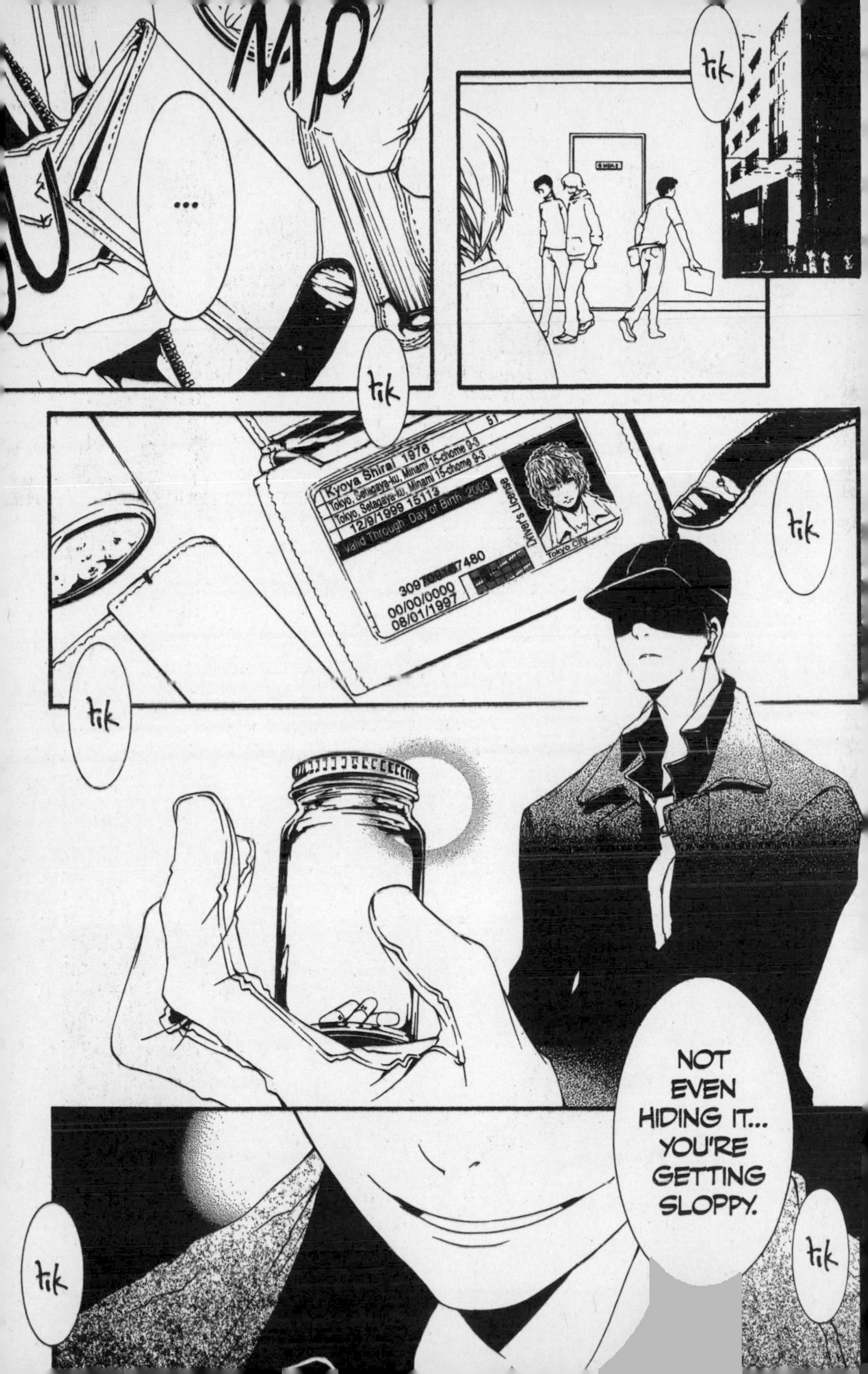
tik
...
MP
tik
tik
Kyoya Shirai 1978
Tokyo, Setagaya-ku, Minami 15-chome 9-3
Tokyo, Setagaya-ku, Minami 15-chome 9-3
12/9/1999 15113
Valid Through: Day of Birth, 2003
Driver's License
Tokyo City
00/00/0000
08/01/1997
tik
NOT EVEN HIDING IT... YOU'RE GETTING SLOPPY.
tik
tik

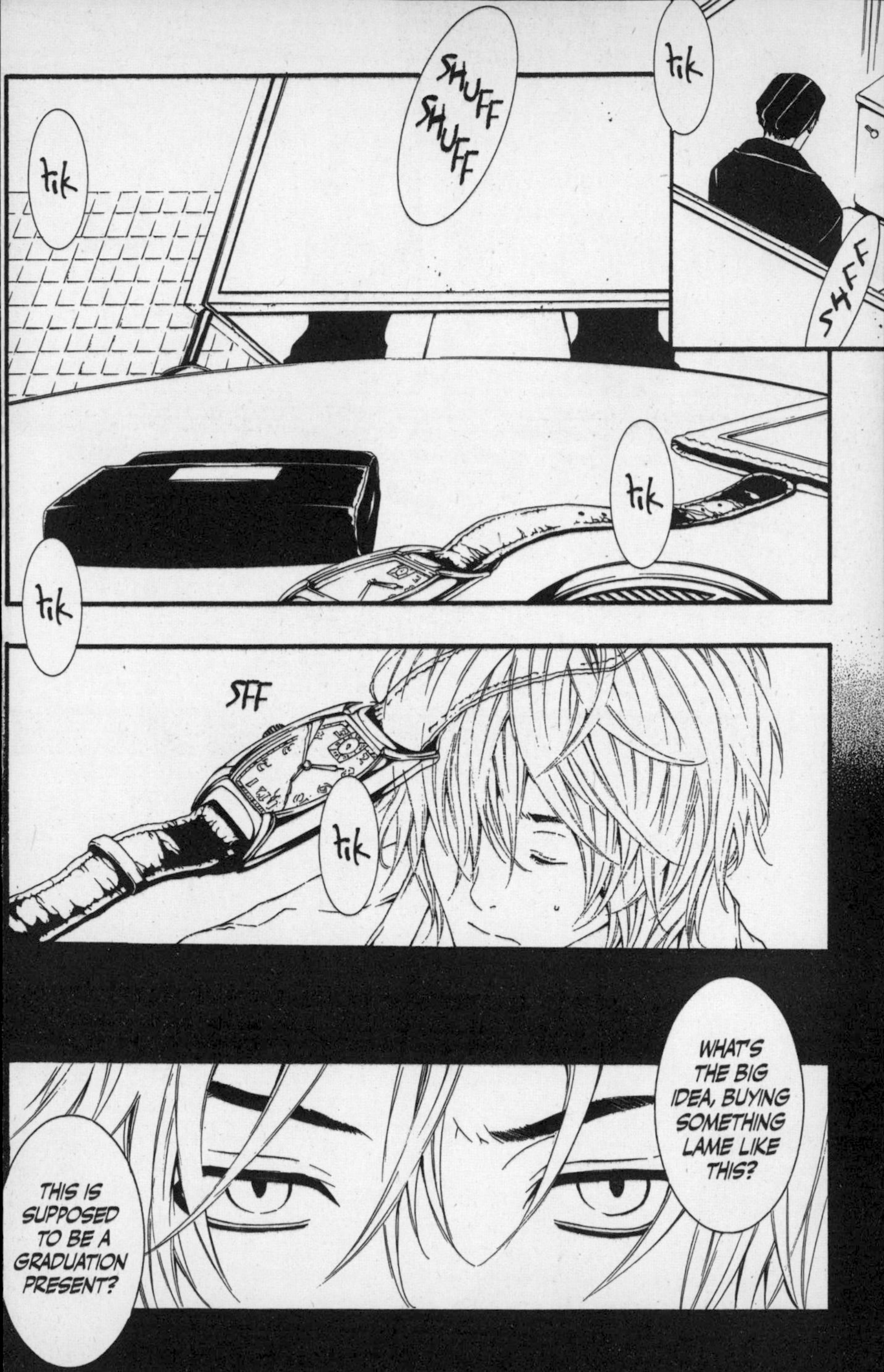
tik
SHFF
SHUFF SHUFF
tik
tik
tik
SFF
tik
WHAT'S THE BIG IDEA, BUYING SOMETHING LAME LIKE THIS?
THIS IS SUPPOSED TO BE A GRADUATION PRESENT?

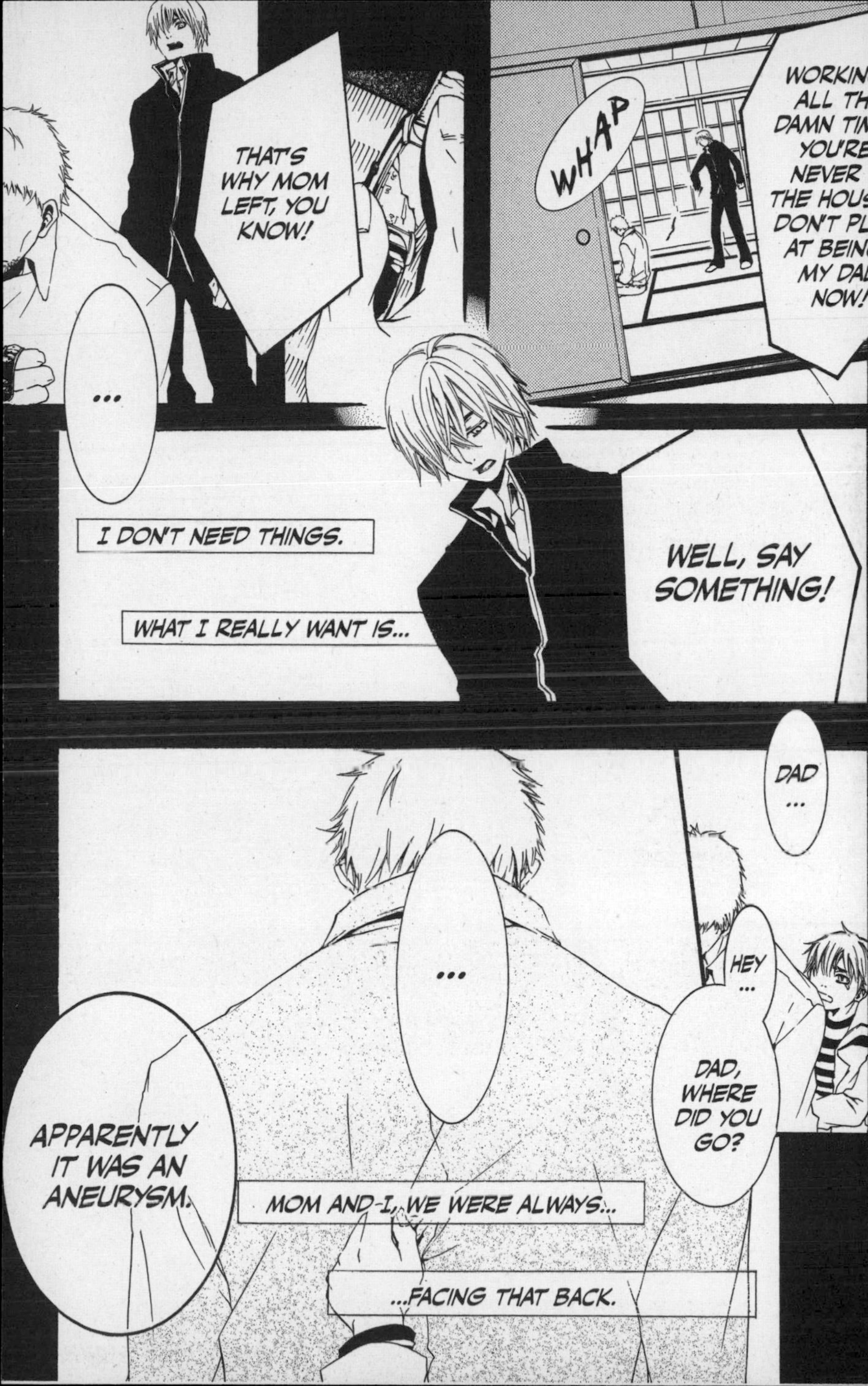
WORKIN ALL TH DAMN TIM YOU'RE NEVER THE HOUS DON'T PL AT BEIN MY DAD NOW!
WHAP
THAT'S WHY MOM LEFT, YOU KNOW!
...
WELL, SAY SOMETHING!
I DON'T NEED THINGS.
WHAT I REALLY WANT IS...
DAD ...
HEY ...
DAD, WHERE DID YOU GO?
...
APPARENTLY IT WAS AN ANEURYSM.
MOM AND I, WE WERE ALWAYS...
...FACING THAT BACK.

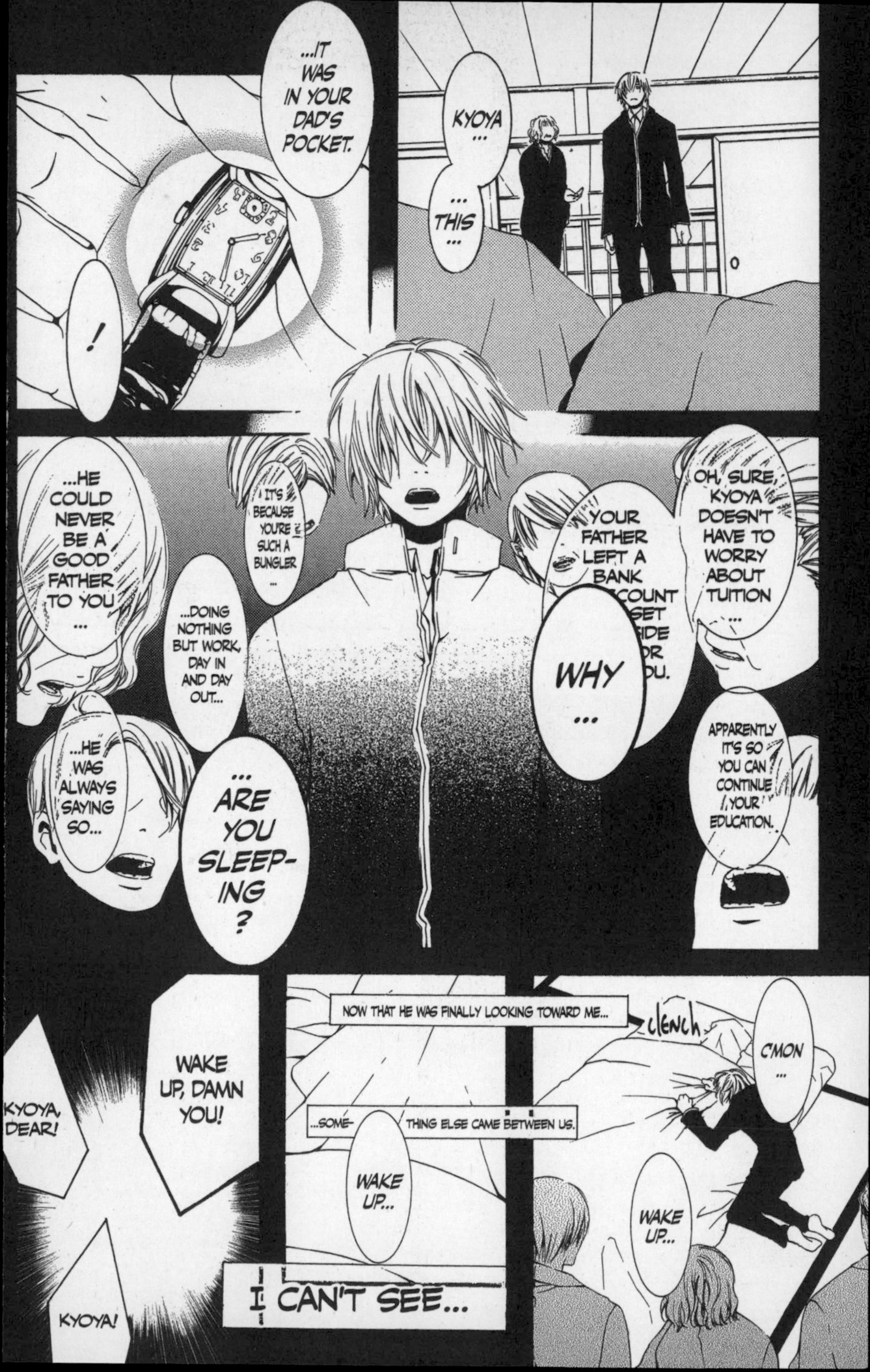
KYOYA...
...THIS...
...IT WAS IN YOUR DAD'S POCKET.
!
OH, SURE, KYOYA DOESN'T HAVE TO WORRY ABOUT TUITION...
YOUR FATHER LEFT A BANK
COUNT
SET
IDE
OR
OU.
APPARENTLY IT'S SO YOU CAN CONTINUE YOUR EDUCATION.
WHY...
IT'S BECAUSE YOU'RE SUCH A BUNGLER...
...DOING NOTHING BUT WORK, DAY IN AND DAY OUT...
...HE COULD NEVER BE A GOOD FATHER TO YOU...
...ARE YOU SLEEPING?
...HE WAS ALWAYS SAYING SO...
C'MON...
clench
WAKE UP...
NOW THAT HE WAS FINALLY LOOKING TOWARD ME...
...SOME-
THING ELSE CAME BETWEEN US.
WAKE UP...
I CAN'T SEE...
WAKE UP, DAMN YOU!
KYOYA, DEAR!
KYOYA!

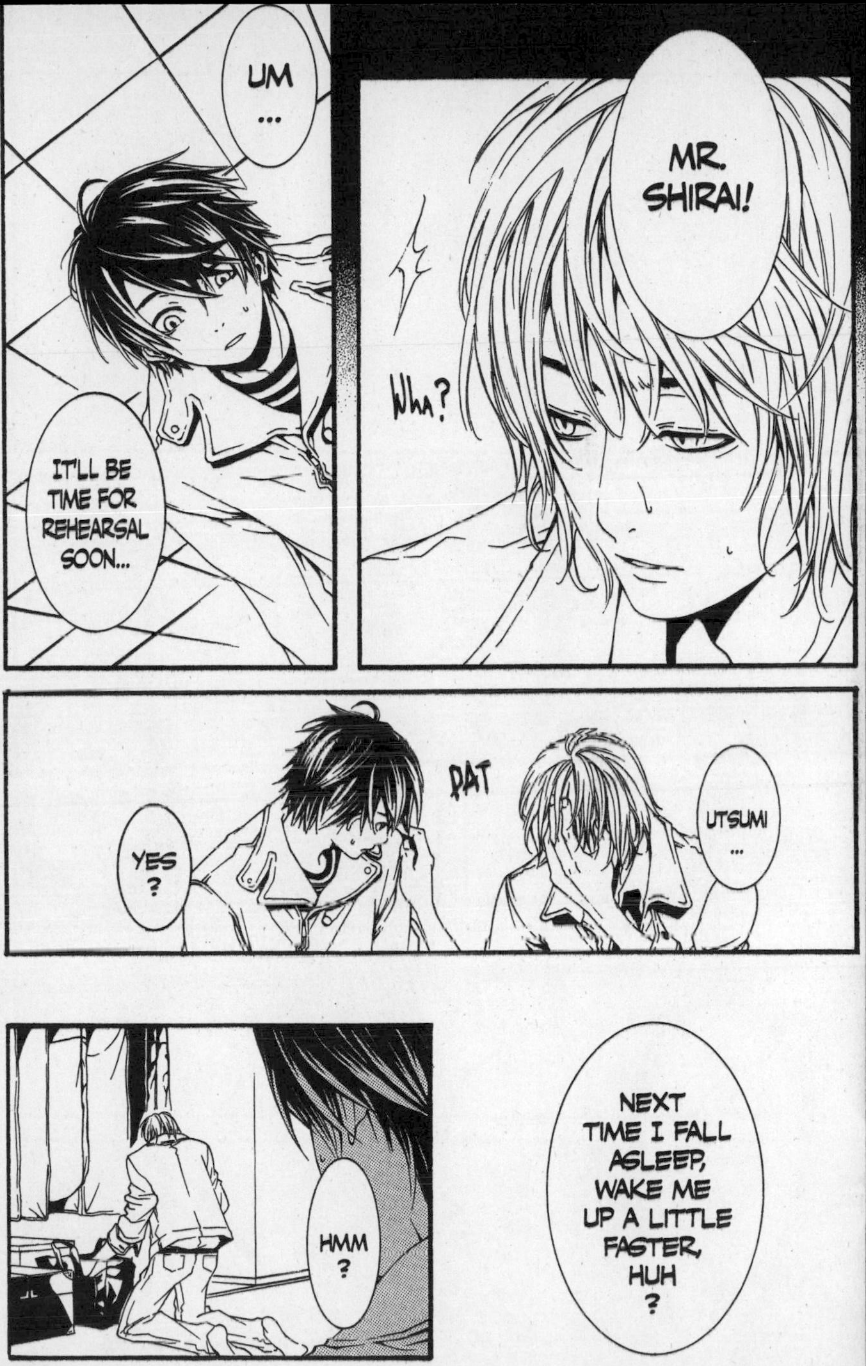
MR. SHIRAI!
Wha?
UM ...
IT'LL BE TIME FOR REHEARSAL SOON...
UTSUMI ...
PAT
YES ?
NEXT TIME I FALL ASLEEP, WAKE ME UP A LITTLE FASTER, HUH ?
HMM ?

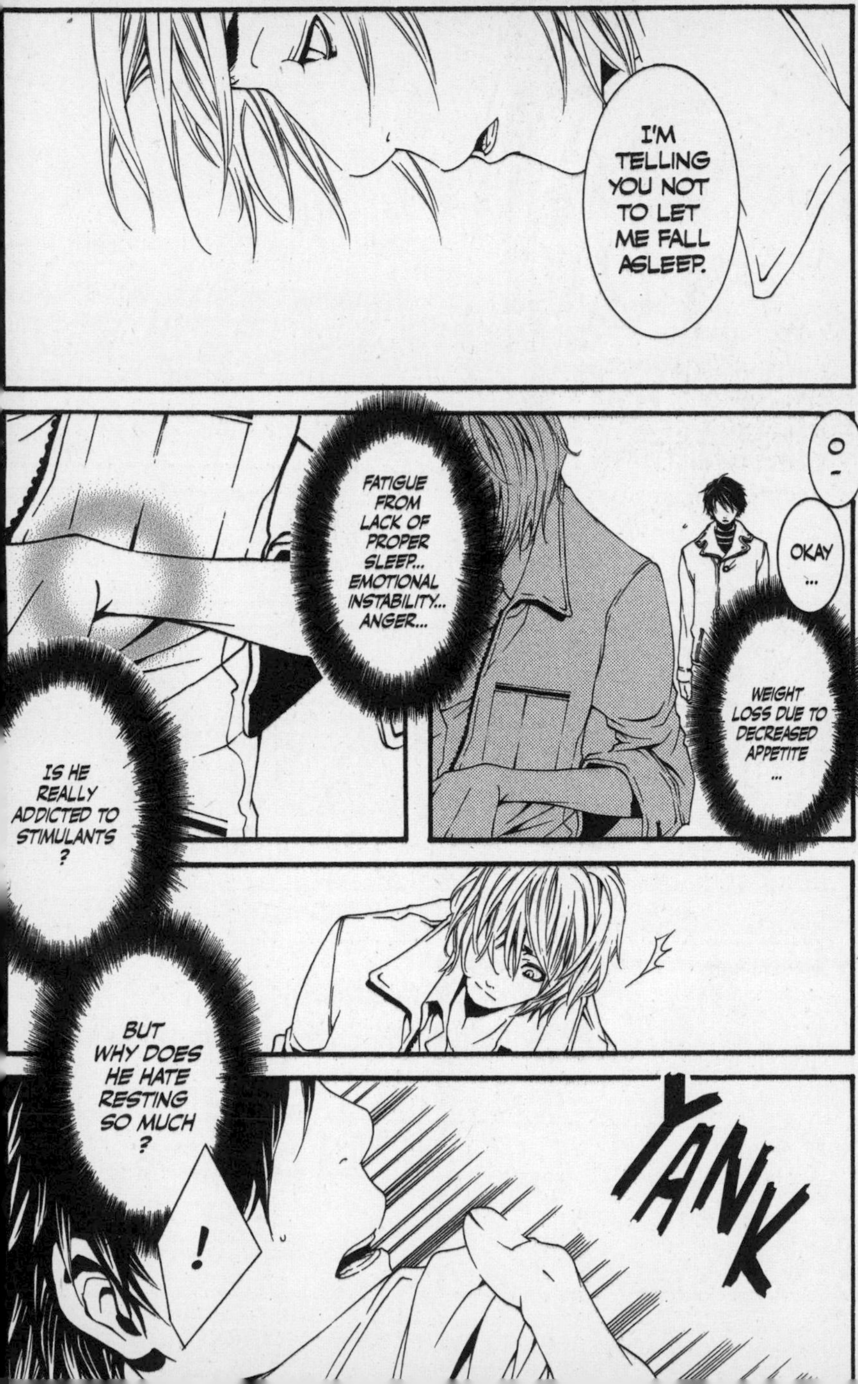
I'M TELLING YOU NOT TO LET ME FALL ASLEEP.
O-
OKAY...
WEIGHT LOSS DUE TO DECREASED APPETITE...
FATIGUE FROM LACK OF PROPER SLEEP... EMOTIONAL INSTABILITY... ANGER...
IS HE REALLY ADDICTED TO STIMULANTS?
BUT WHY DOES HE HATE RESTING SO MUCH?
YANK
!

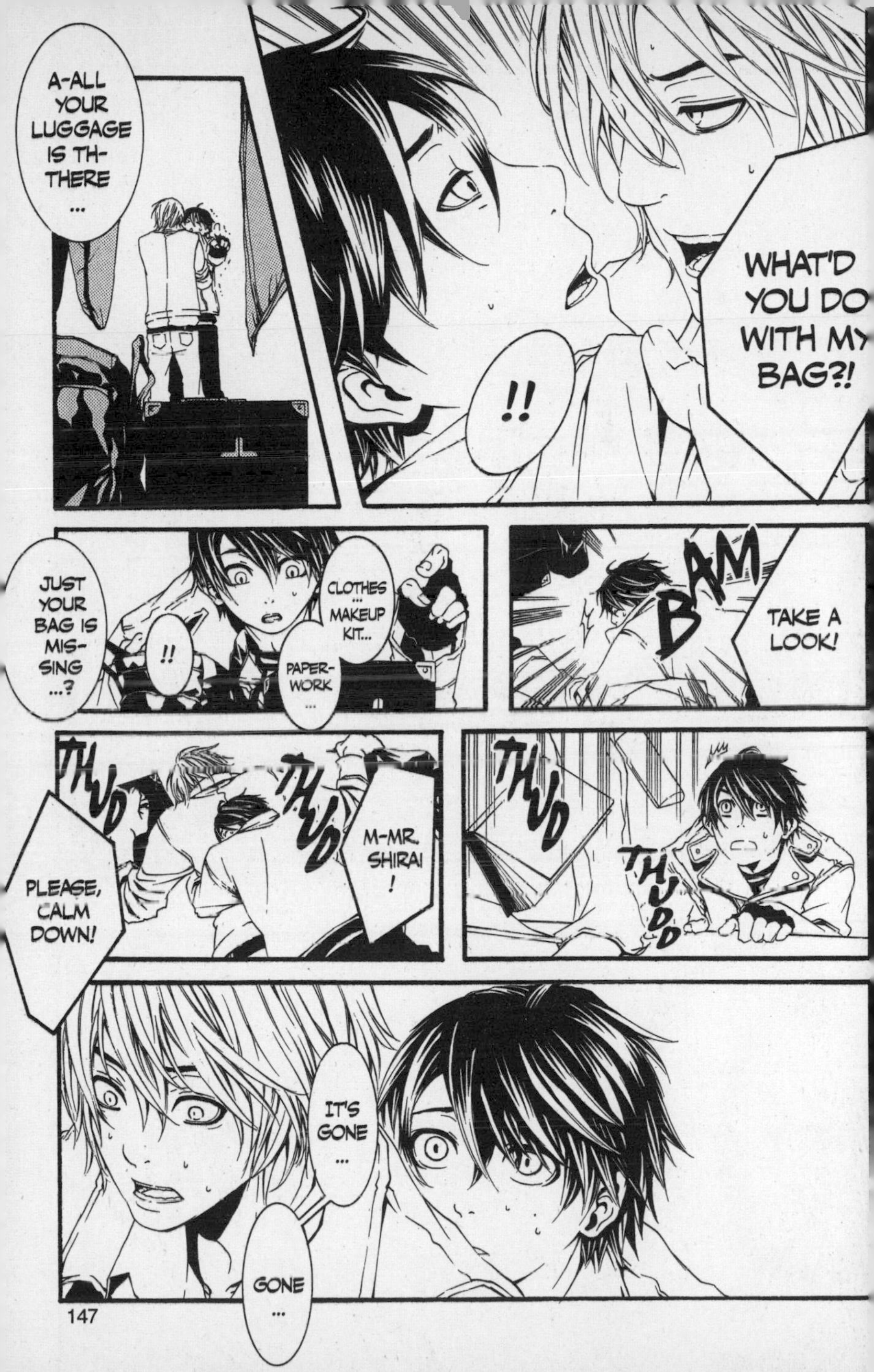
WHAT'D YOU DO WITH MY BAG?!
!!
A-ALL YOUR LUGGAGE IS TH-THERE ...
TAKE A LOOK!
BAM
CLOTHES ... MAKEUP KIT...
PAPER-WORK ...
!!
JUST YOUR BAG IS MIS-SING ...?
THUD
THUDD
M-MR. SHIRAI!
THUD
THUD
PLEASE, CALM DOWN!
IT'S GONE ...
GONE ...

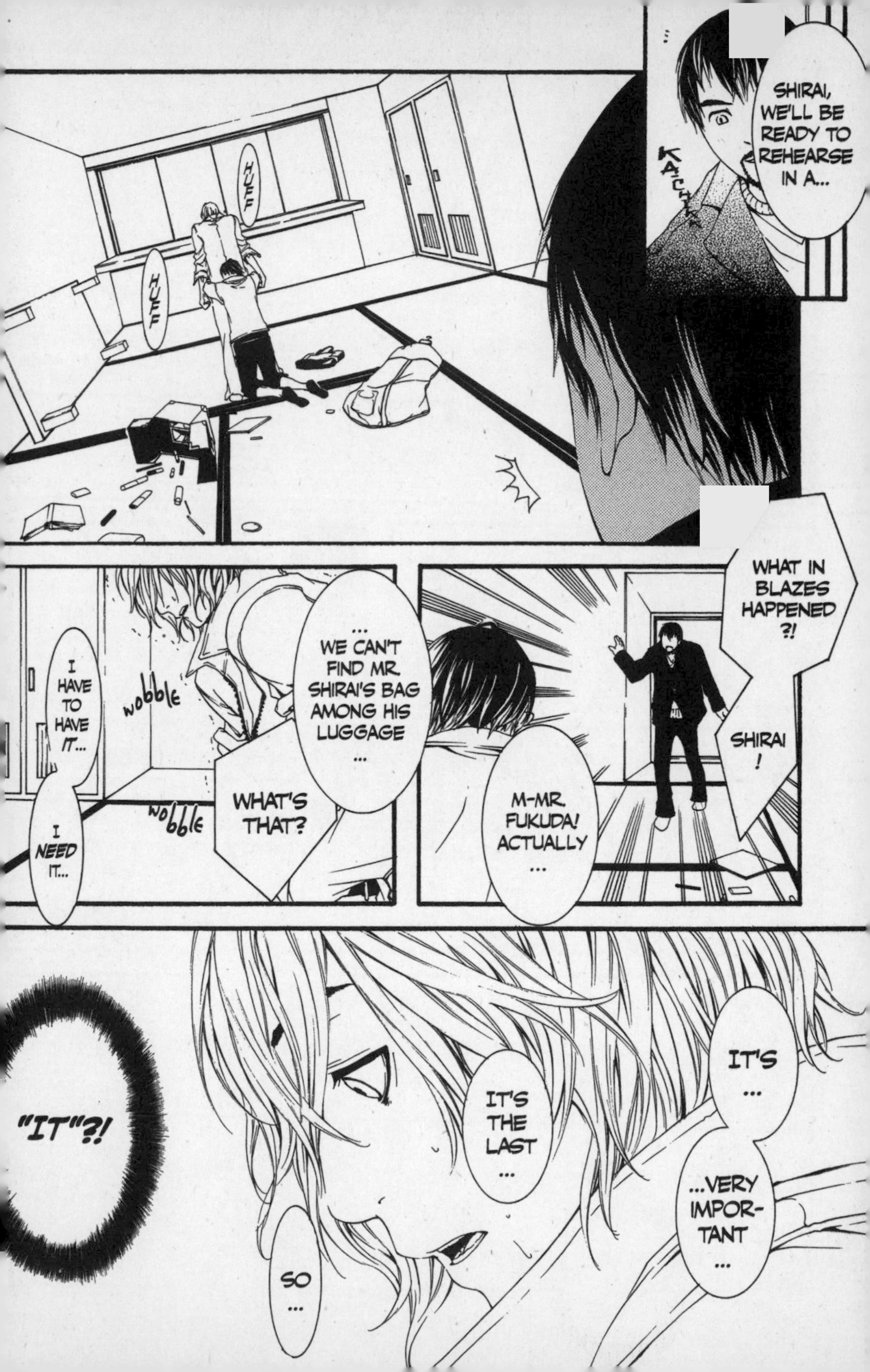
SHIRAI, WE'LL BE READY TO REHEARSE IN A...
HUFF
HUFF
WHAT IN BLAZES HAPPENED?!
SHIRAI!
M-MR. FUKUDA! ACTUALLY...
...WE CAN'T FIND MR. SHIRAI'S BAG AMONG HIS LUGGAGE...
WHAT'S THAT?
wobble
I HAVE TO HAVE IT...
wobble
I NEED IT...
IT'S...
...VERY IMPORTANT...
IT'S THE LAST...
SO...
"IT"?!

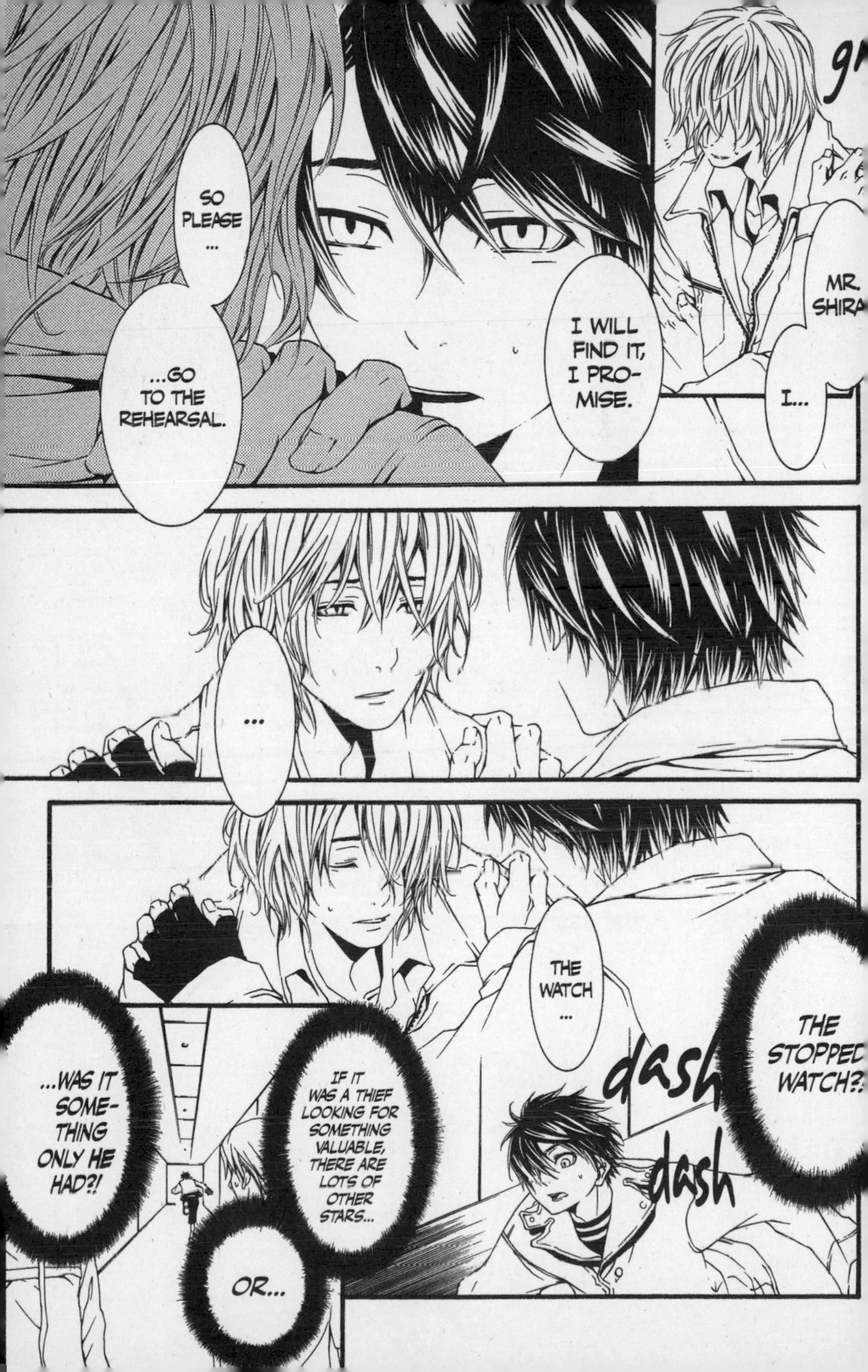
gr
MR. SHIRA
I...
I WILL FIND IT, I PRO-MISE.
SO PLEASE ...
...GO TO THE REHEARSAL.
...
THE WATCH ...
THE STOPPED WATCH?!
dash
dash
IF IT WAS A THIEF LOOKING FOR SOMETHING VALUABLE, THERE ARE LOTS OF OTHER STARS...
OR...
...WAS IT SOME-THING ONLY HE HAD?!

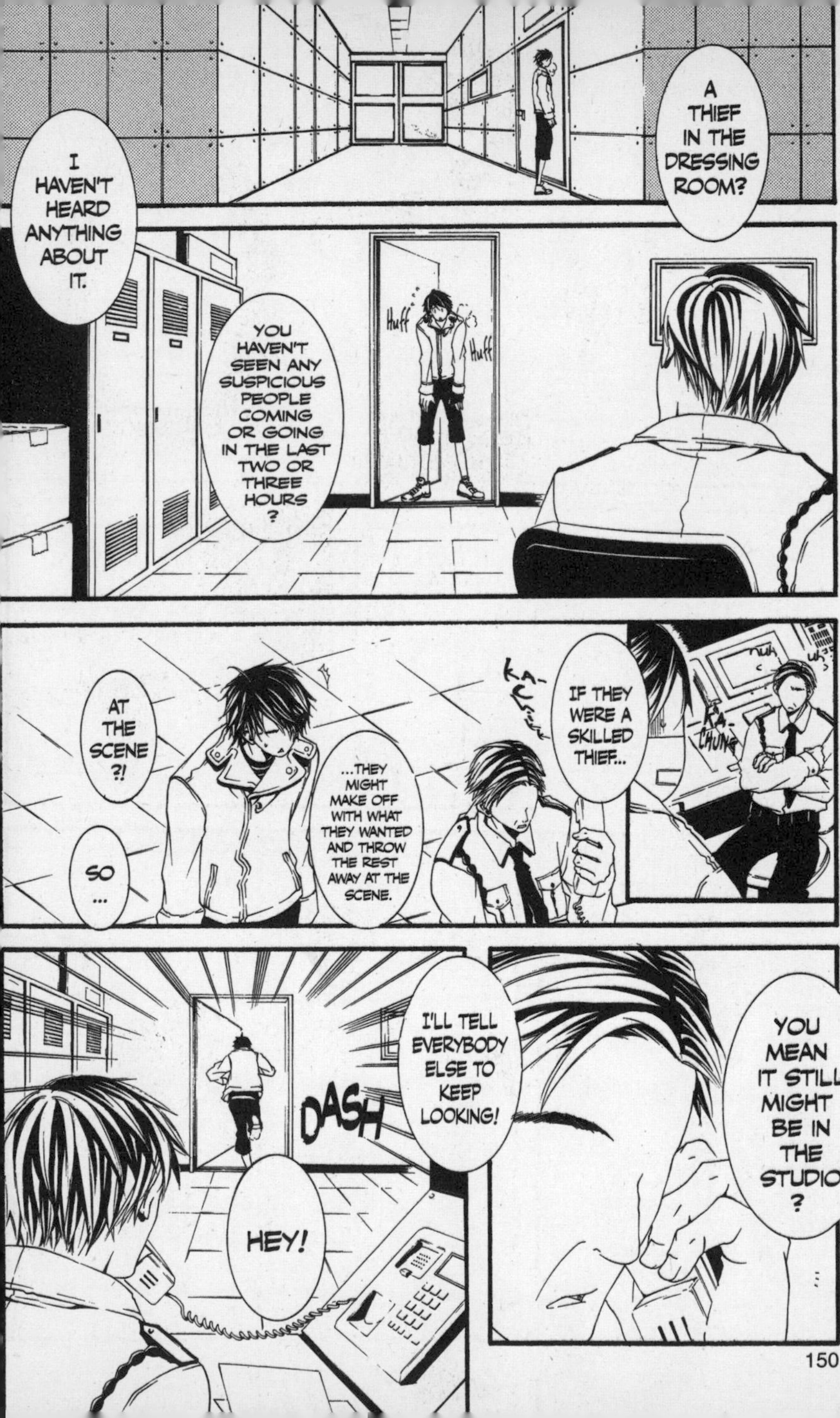
A THIEF IN THE DRESSING ROOM?
I HAVEN'T HEARD ANYTHING ABOUT IT.
Huff
Huff
YOU HAVEN'T SEEN ANY SUSPICIOUS PEOPLE COMING OR GOING IN THE LAST TWO OR THREE HOURS?
KA-CHUNG
IF THEY WERE A SKILLED THIEF...
KA-CHUNG
...THEY MIGHT MAKE OFF WITH WHAT THEY WANTED AND THROW THE REST AWAY AT THE SCENE.
AT THE SCENE?!
SO...
YOU MEAN IT STILL MIGHT BE IN THE STUDIO?
I'LL TELL EVERYBODY ELSE TO KEEP LOOKING!
DASH
HEY!

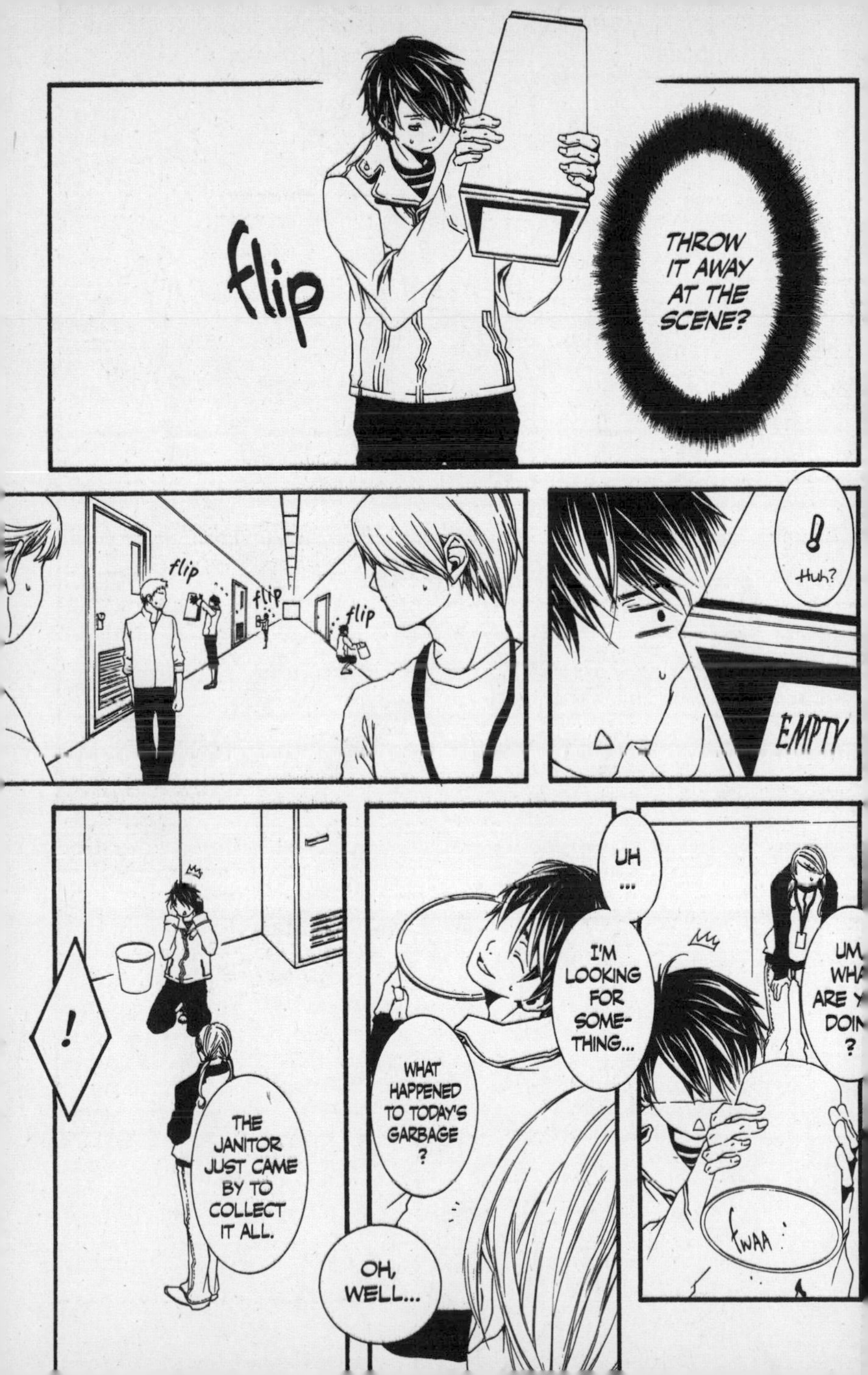
THROW IT AWAY AT THE SCENE?
flip
!
Huh?
EMPTY
flip
flip
flip
UM, WHA ARE Y DOIN ?
UH ...
I'M LOOKING FOR SOME-THING...
fwaa
WHAT HAPPENED TO TODAY'S GARBAGE ?
OH, WELL...
!
THE JANITOR JUST CAME BY TO COLLECT IT ALL.

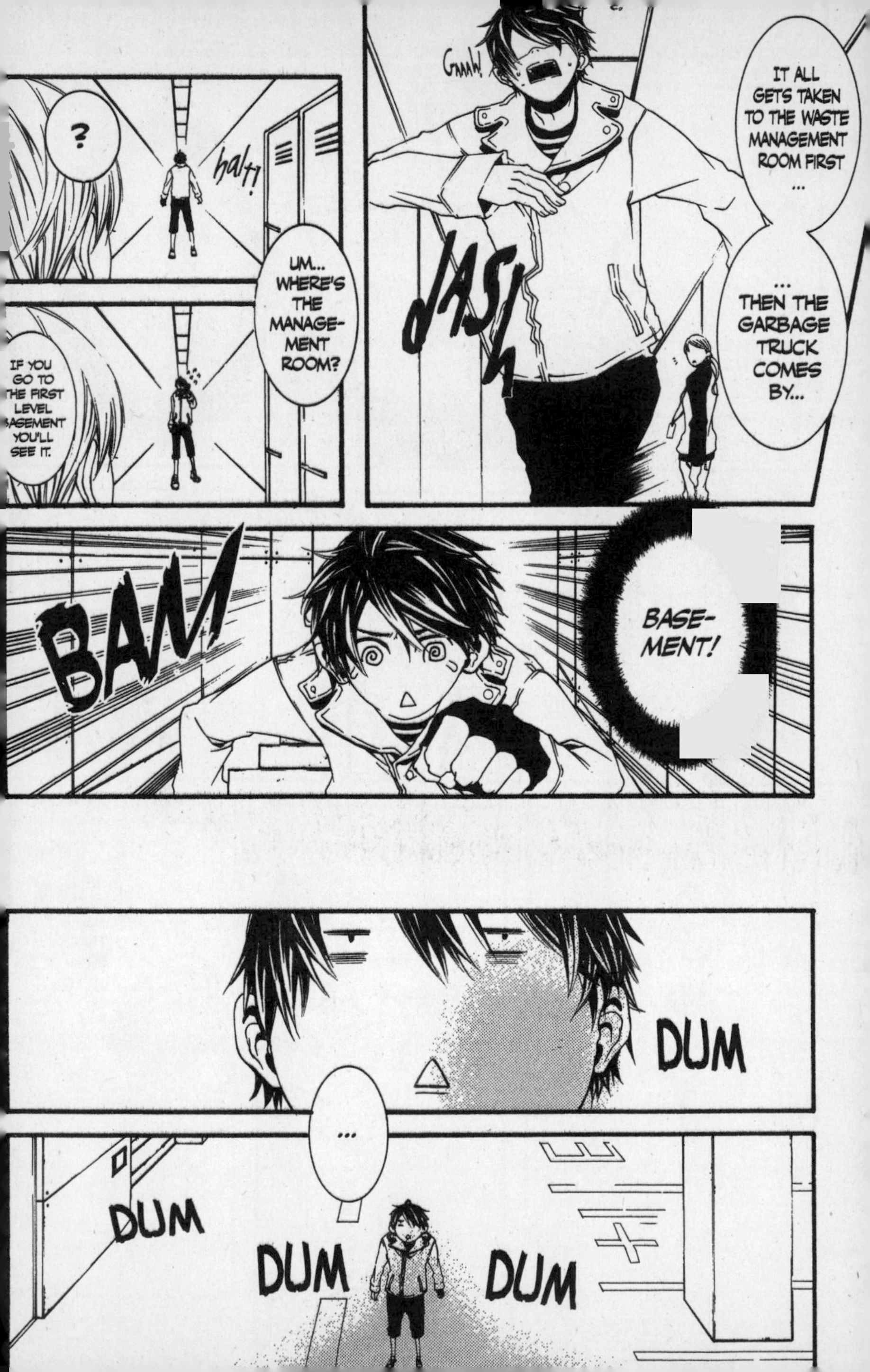

IT ALL GETS TAKEN TO THE WASTE MANAGEMENT ROOM FIRST ...
... THEN THE GARBAGE TRUCK COMES BY...
GAAAH!
DASH
halt!
?
UM... WHERE'S THE MANAGE-MENT ROOM?
IF YOU GO TO THE FIRST LEVEL BASEMENT YOU'LL SEE IT.
BASE-MENT!
BAM
DUM
...
DUM
DUM
DUM

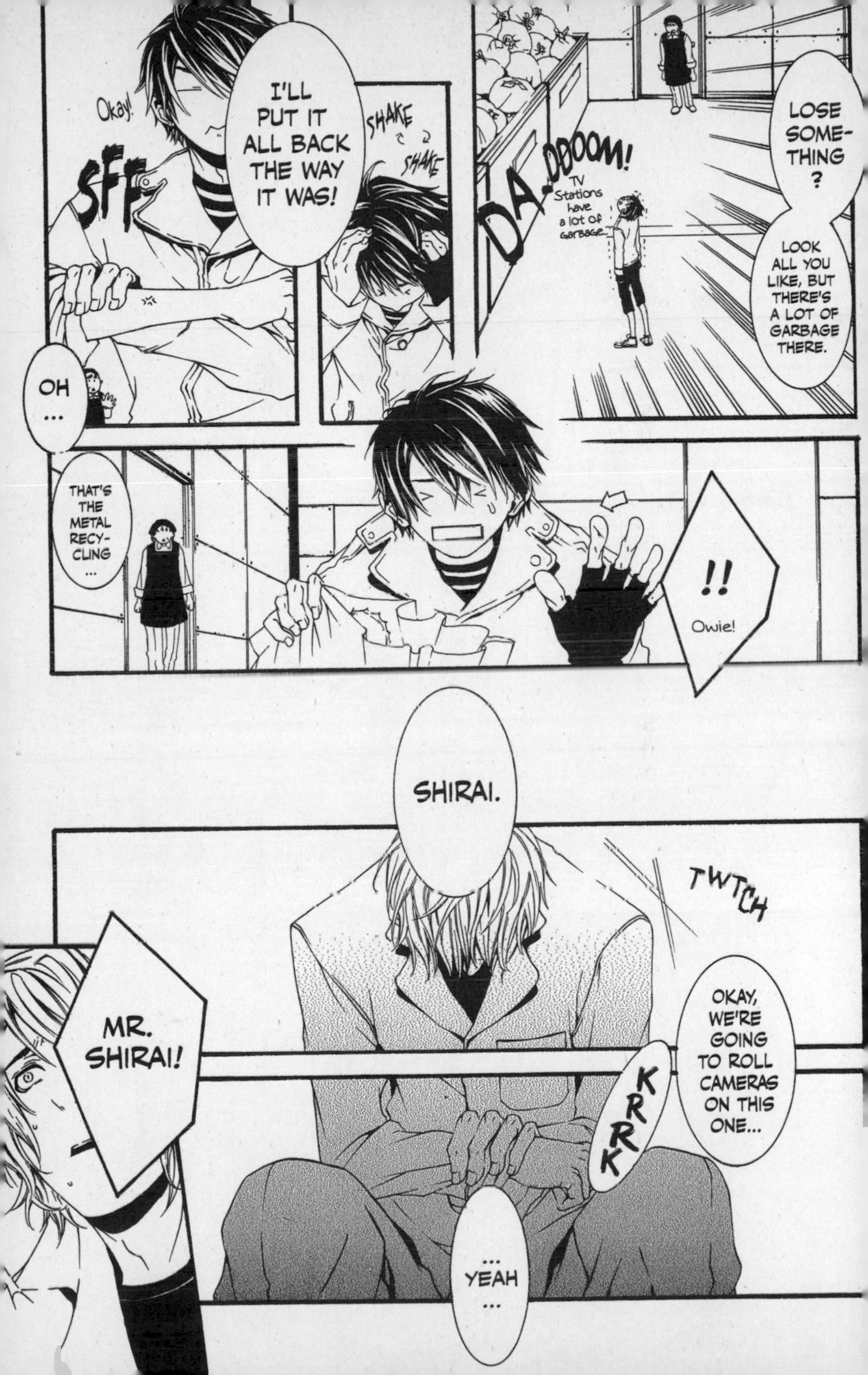
LOSE SOME-THING?
DA-DOOM!
LOOK ALL YOU LIKE, BUT THERE'S A LOT OF GARBAGE THERE.
TV Stations have a lot of Garbage...
SHAKE SHAKE
I'LL PUT IT ALL BACK THE WAY IT WAS!
Okay!
SFF
OH...
!!
Owie!
THAT'S THE METAL RECYC-LING...
SHIRAI.
TWTCH
OKAY, WE'RE GOING TO ROLL CAMERAS ON THIS ONE...
KRRK
MR. SHIRAI!
...YEAH...

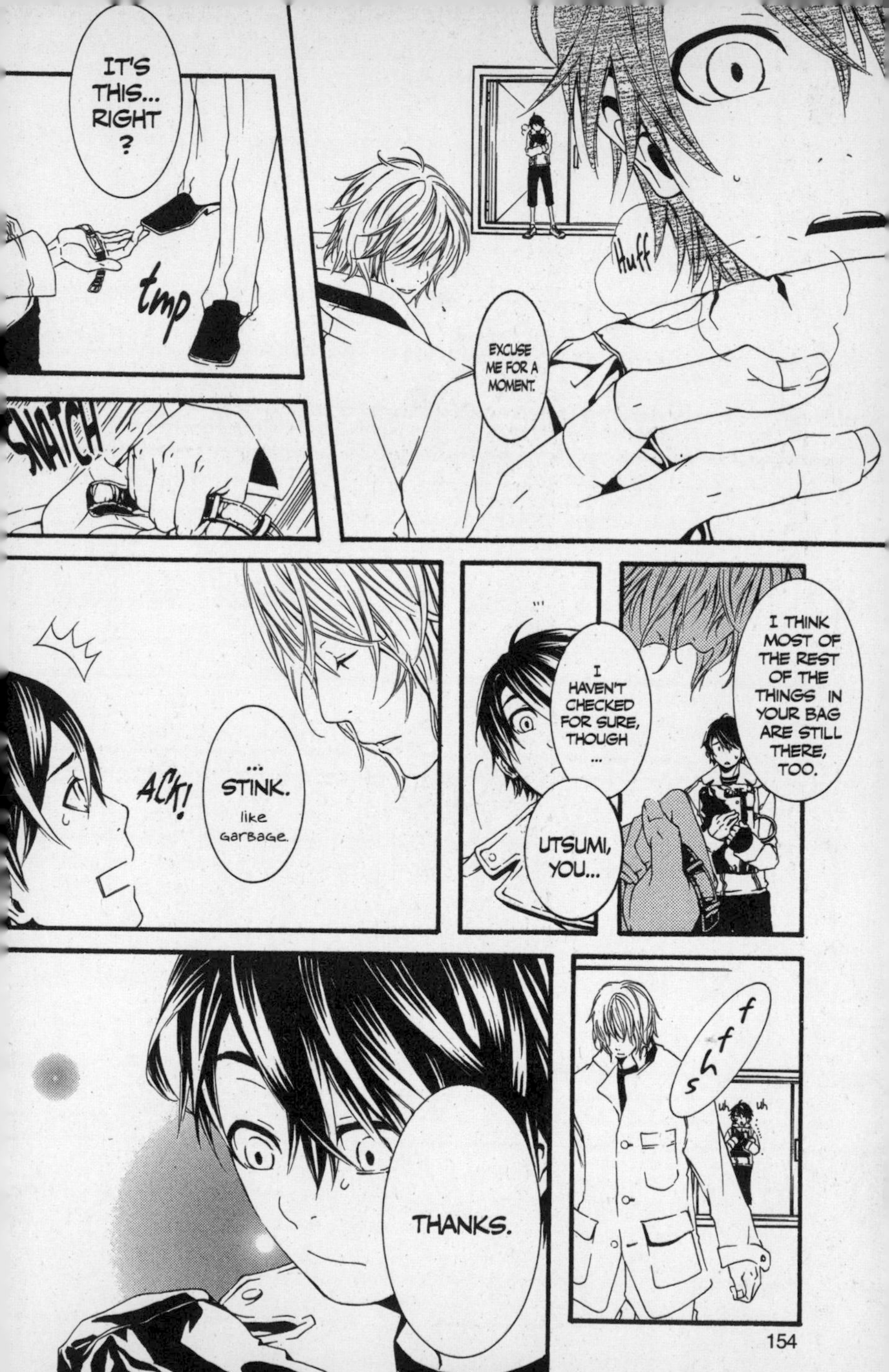
Huff
EXCUSE ME FOR A MOMENT.
IT'S THIS... RIGHT?
tmp
SNATCH
I THINK MOST OF THE REST OF THE THINGS IN YOUR BAG ARE STILL THERE, TOO.
I HAVEN'T CHECKED FOR SURE, THOUGH...
UTSUMI, YOU...
ACK!
...STINK.
like garbage.
shff
uh uh
THANKS.

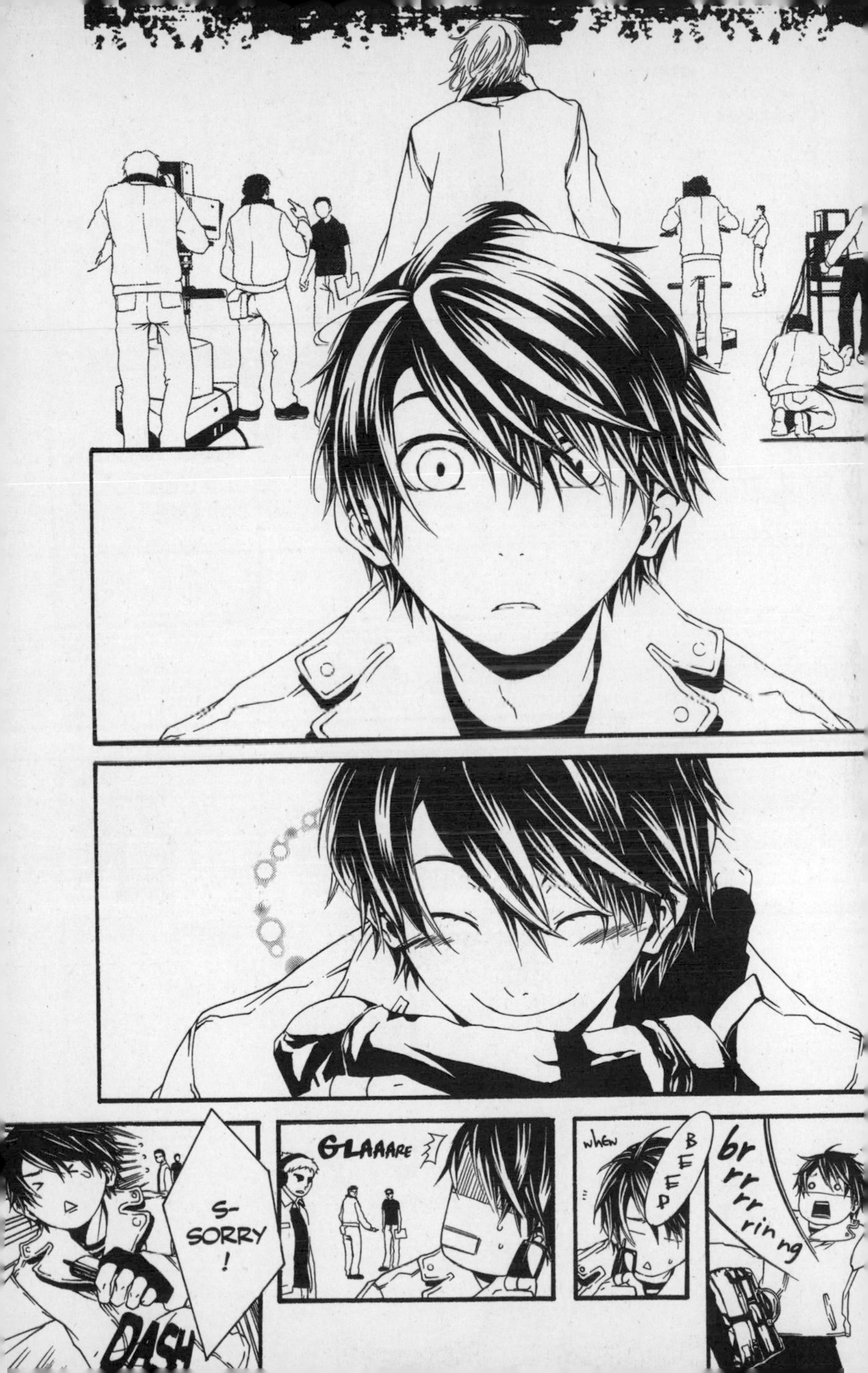
brrrrrrinng
BEEP
whew
GLAAARE
S-SORRY!
DASH

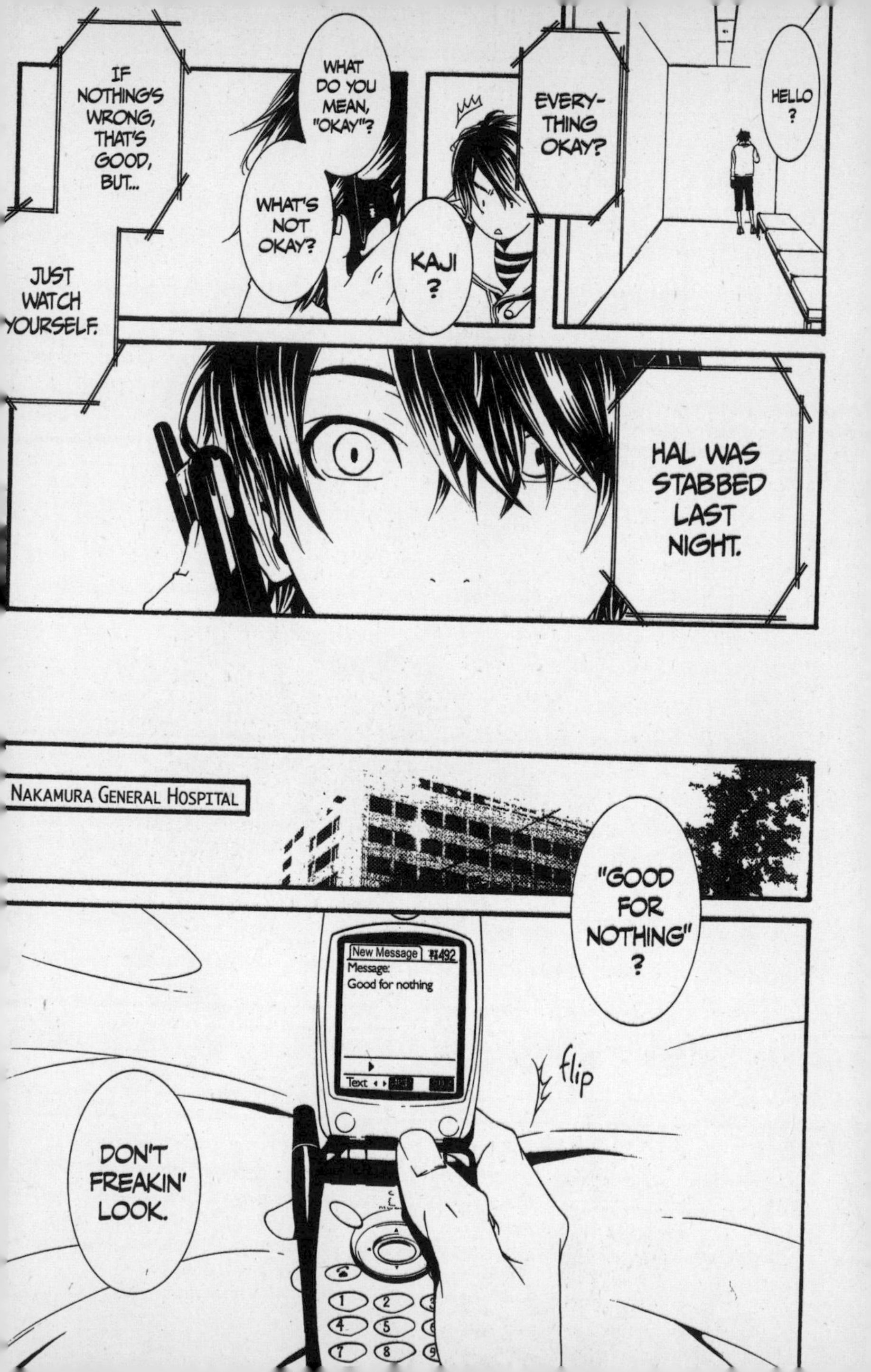
HELLO?
EVERY-THING OKAY?
KAJI?
WHAT DO YOU MEAN, "OKAY"?
WHAT'S NOT OKAY?
IF NOTHING'S WRONG, THAT'S GOOD, BUT...
JUST WATCH YOURSELF.
HAL WAS STABBED LAST NIGHT.
NAKAMURA GENERAL HOSPITAL
"GOOD FOR NOTHING"?
New Message #492
Message:
Good for nothing
Text
flip
DON'T FREAKIN' LOOK.

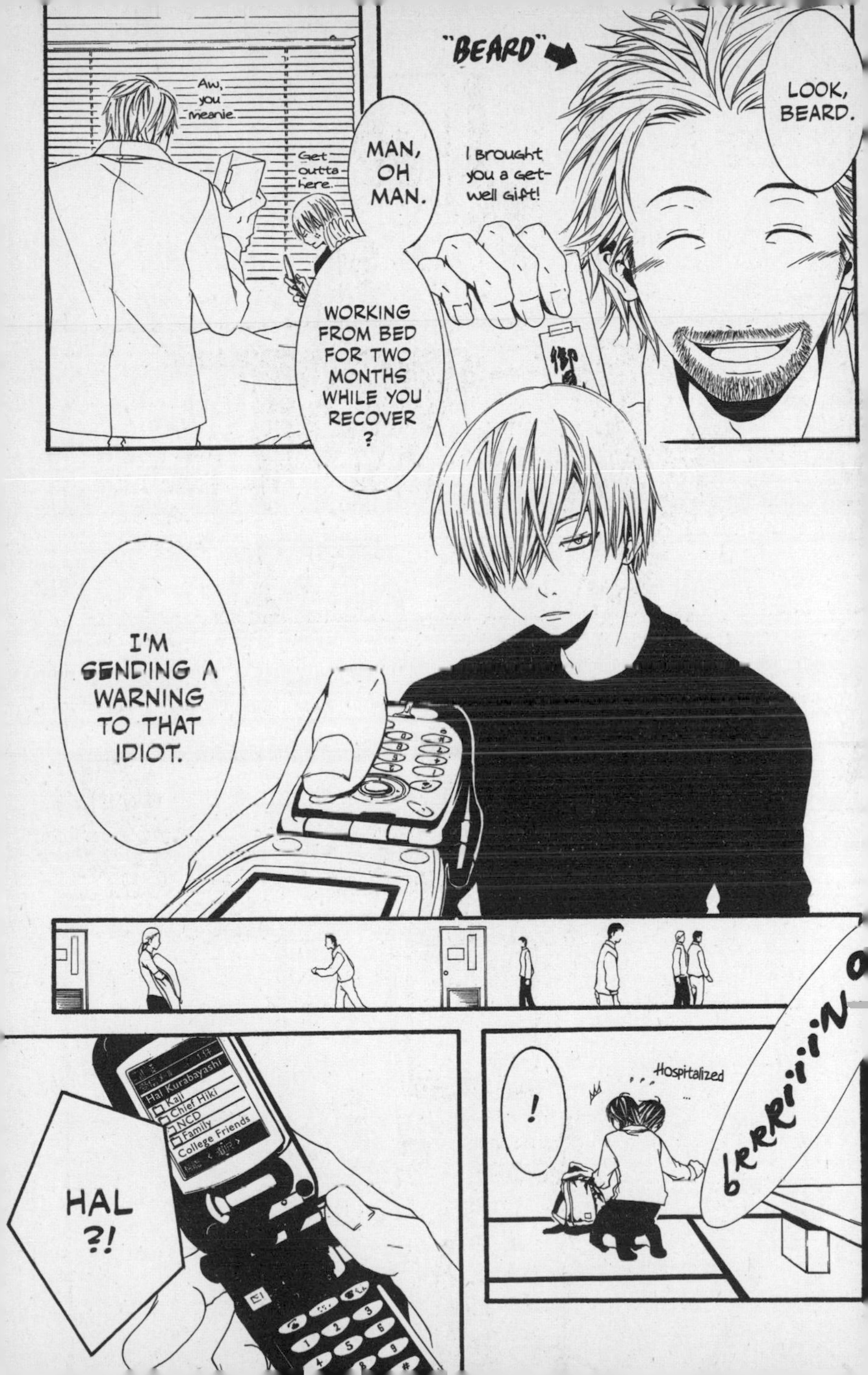
"BEARD"
LOOK, BEARD.
I brought you a get-well gift!
MAN, OH MAN.
WORKING FROM BED FOR TWO MONTHS WHILE YOU RECOVER?
Aw, you meanie.
Get outta-here.
I'M SENDING A WARNING TO THAT IDIOT.
bRRiiiNG
!
Hospitalized
...
Hal Kurabayashi
Kaji
Chief Hiki
NCD
Family
College Friends
HAL?!

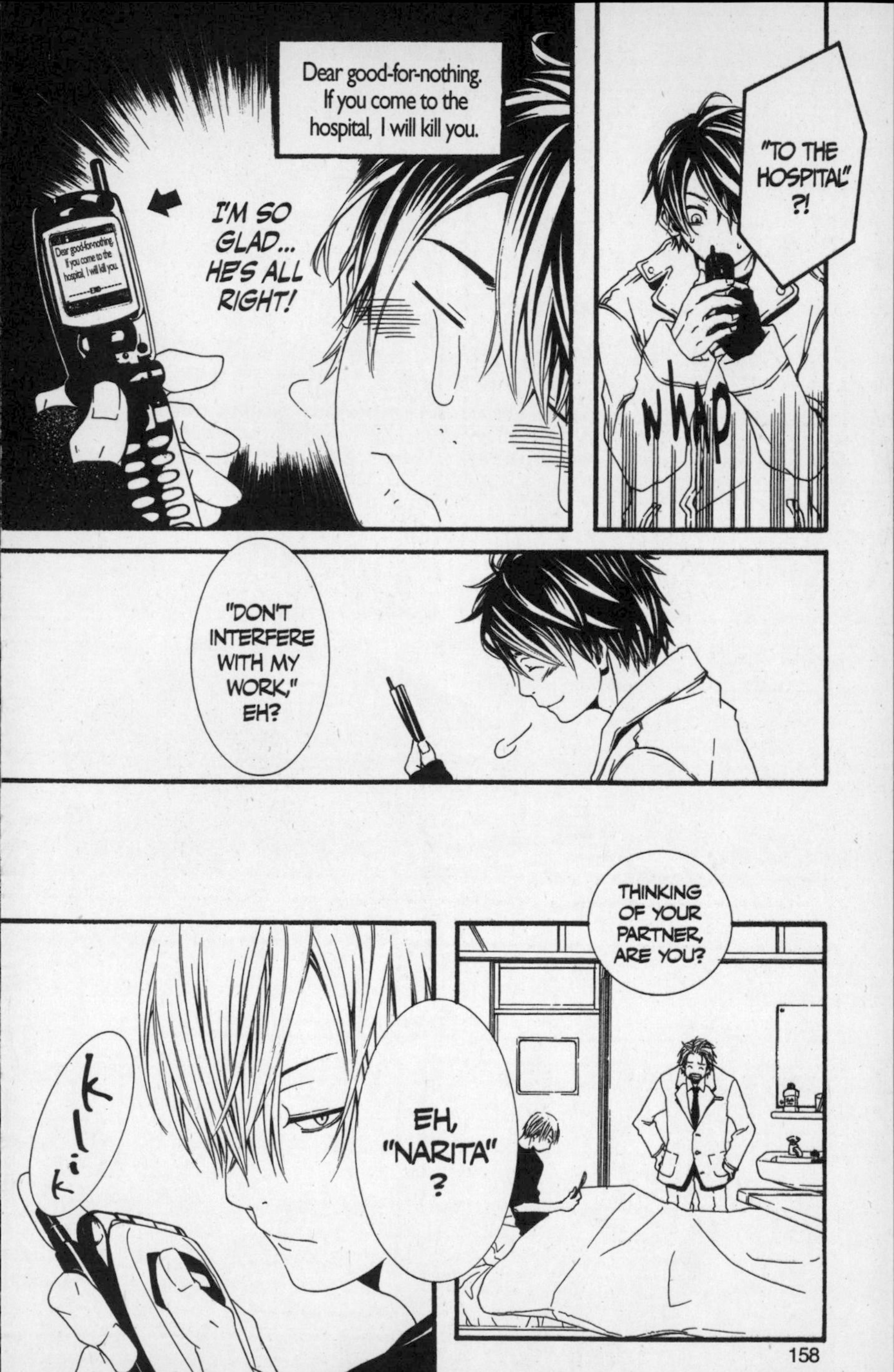
"TO THE HOSPITAL" ?!
WHAP
Dear good-for-nothing. If you come to the hospital, I will kill you.
I'M SO GLAD... HE'S ALL RIGHT!
"DON'T INTERFERE WITH MY WORK," EH?
THINKING OF YOUR PARTNER, ARE YOU?
EH, "NARITA" ?

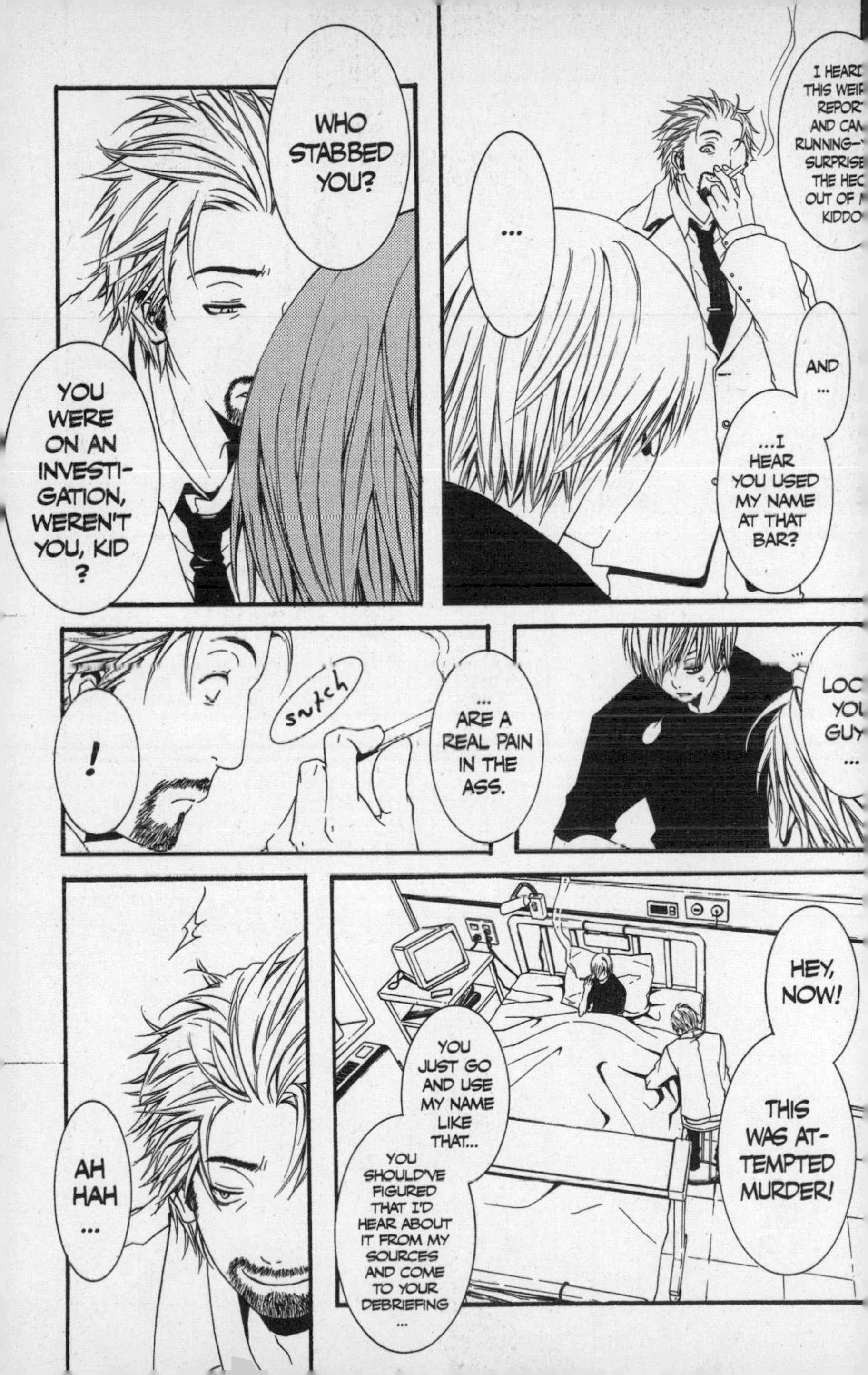
I HEAR THIS WEI REPOR AND CAM RUNNING— SURPRISE THE HEC OUT OF KIDDO
AND ...
...I HEAR YOU USED MY NAME AT THAT BAR?
...
WHO STABBED YOU?
YOU WERE ON AN INVESTI-GATION, WEREN'T YOU, KID ?
...
LOO YOU GUY ...
... ARE A REAL PAIN IN THE ASS.
snatch
!
HEY, NOW!
THIS WAS AT-TEMPTED MURDER!
YOU JUST GO AND USE MY NAME LIKE THAT...
YOU SHOULD'VE FIGURED THAT I'D HEAR ABOUT IT FROM MY SOURCES AND COME TO YOUR DEBRIEFING ...
AH HAH ...

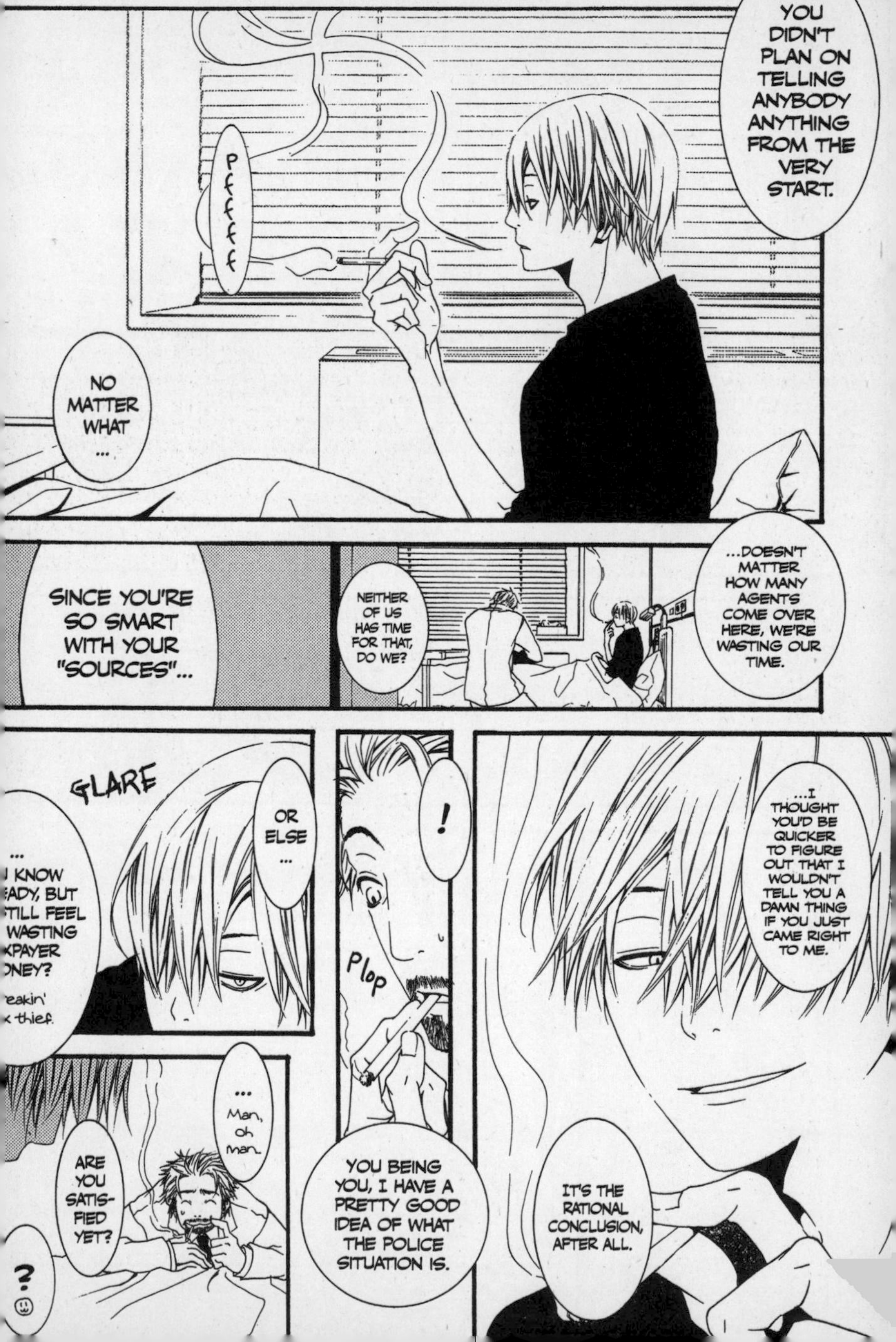
YOU DIDN'T PLAN ON TELLING ANYBODY ANYTHING FROM THE VERY START.
Pffff
NO MATTER WHAT...
...DOESN'T MATTER HOW MANY AGENTS COME OVER HERE, WE'RE WASTING OUR TIME.
NEITHER OF US HAS TIME FOR THAT, DO WE?
SINCE YOU'RE SO SMART WITH YOUR "SOURCES"...
...I THOUGHT YOU'D BE QUICKER TO FIGURE OUT THAT I WOULDN'T TELL YOU A DAMN THING IF YOU JUST CAME RIGHT TO ME.
IT'S THE RATIONAL CONCLUSION, AFTER ALL.
!
Plop
YOU BEING YOU, I HAVE A PRETTY GOOD IDEA OF WHAT THE POLICE SITUATION IS.
OR ELSE...
GLARE
... I KNOW EADY, BUT TILL FEEL WASTING XPAYER ONEY?
eakin' x thief.
... Man, oh man.
ARE YOU SATIS-FIED YET?
?

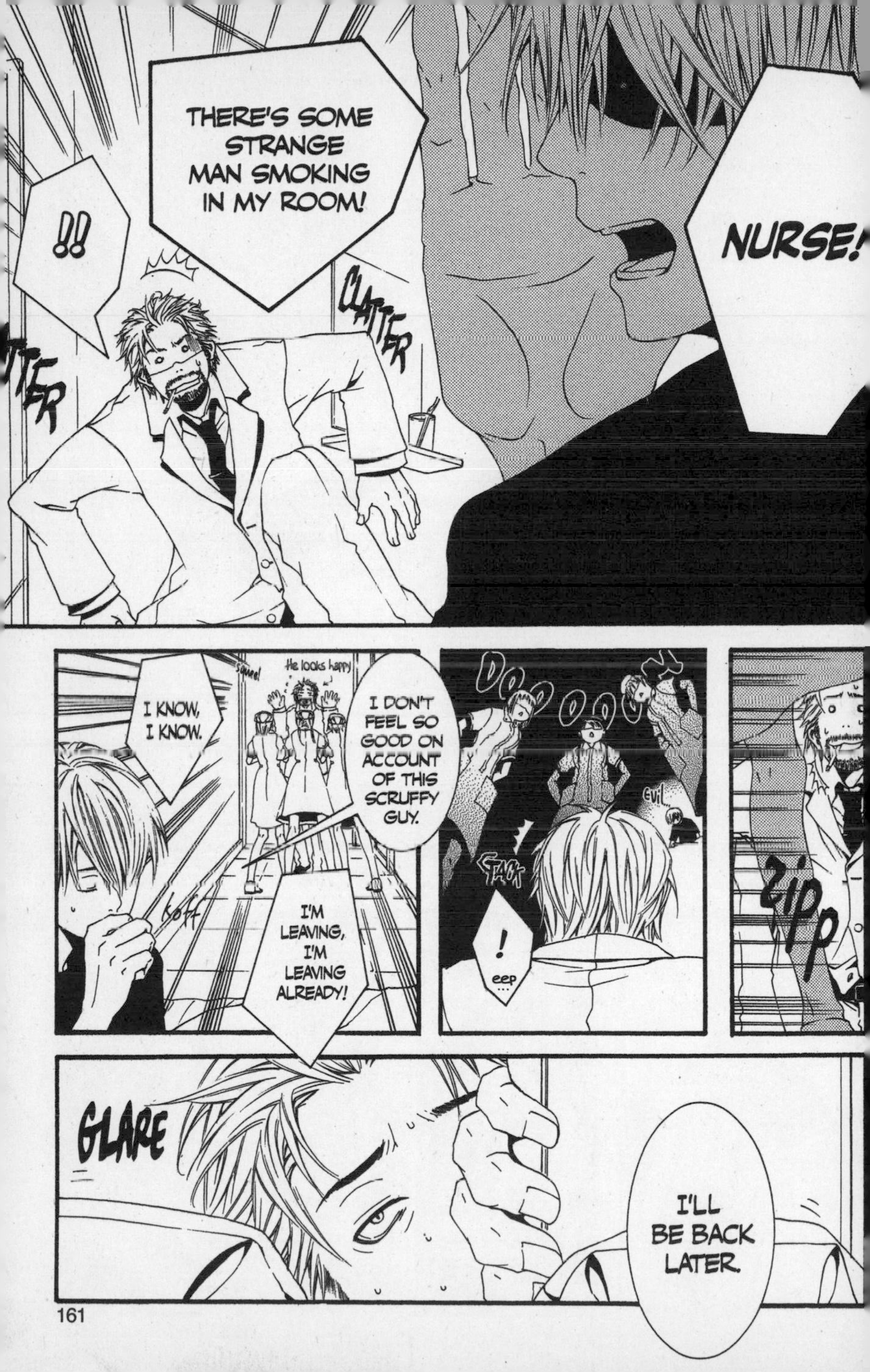
NURSE!
THERE'S SOME STRANGE MAN SMOKING IN MY ROOM!
!!
CLATTER
TTER
ZIPP
evil...
STACK
!
eep...
He looks happy
squeal
I DON'T FEEL SO GOOD ON ACCOUNT OF THIS SCRUFFY GUY.
I KNOW, I KNOW.
I'M LEAVING, I'M LEAVING ALREADY!
koff
I'LL BE BACK LATER.
GLARE

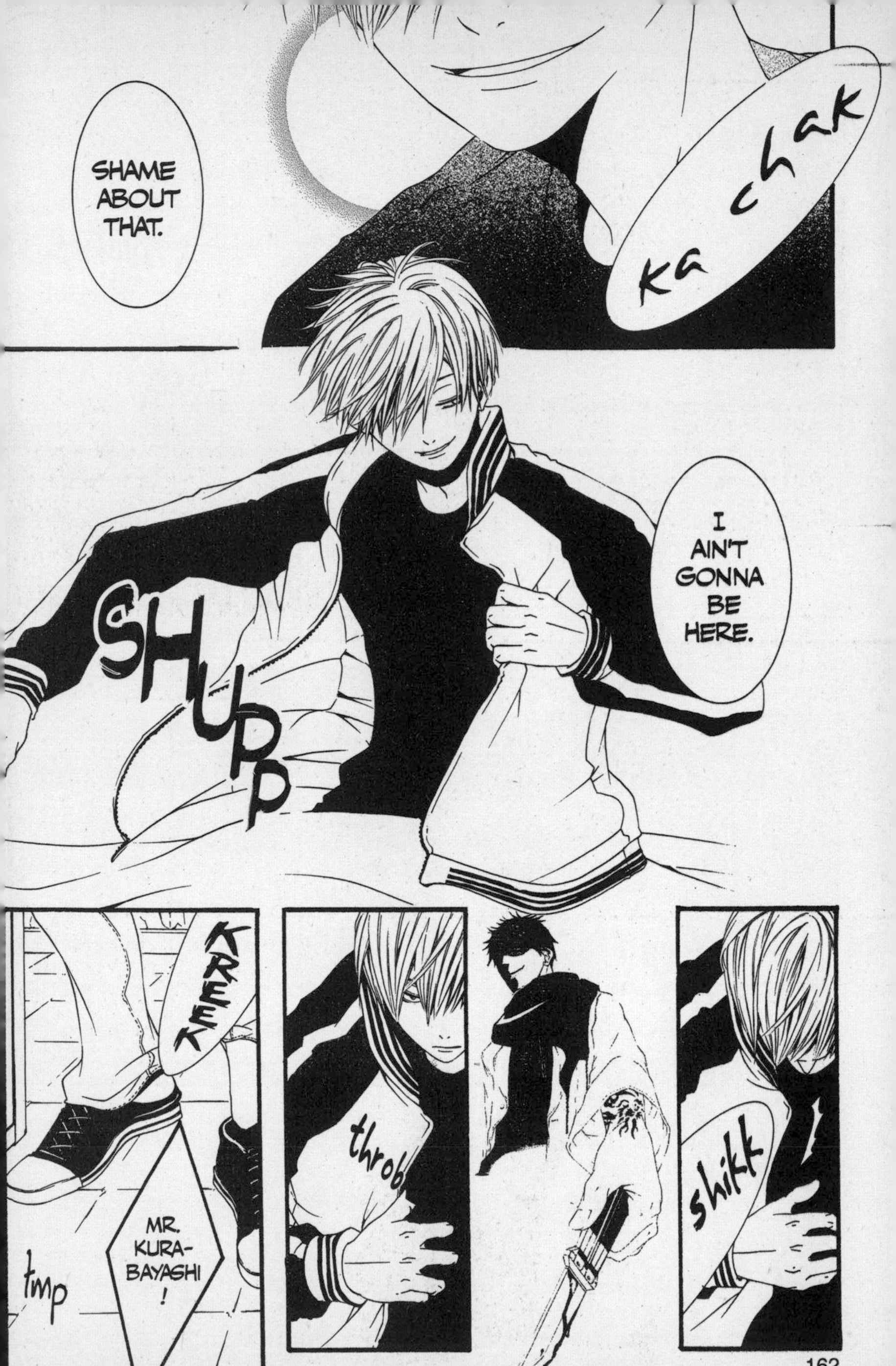
ka chak
SHAME ABOUT THAT.
I AIN'T GONNA BE HERE.
SHUPP
shikk
!
throb
KREEK
MR. KURA-BAYASHI!
tmp

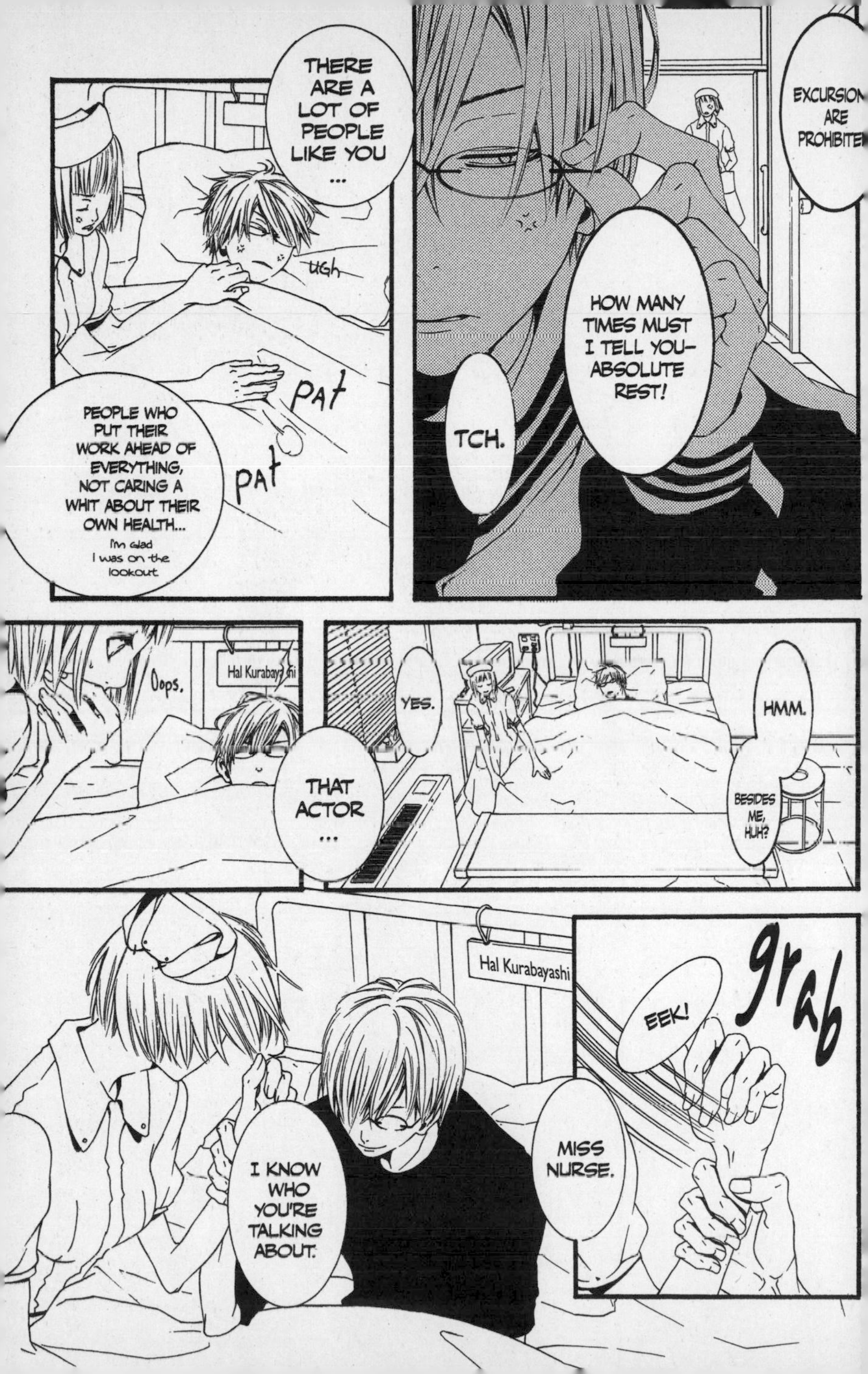
EXCURSION ARE PROHIBITE
HOW MANY TIMES MUST I TELL YOU– ABSOLUTE REST!
TCH.
THERE ARE A LOT OF PEOPLE LIKE YOU ...
UGH
PAT
PAT
PEOPLE WHO PUT THEIR WORK AHEAD OF EVERYTHING, NOT CARING A WHIT ABOUT THEIR OWN HEALTH...
I'm glad I was on the lookout.
HMM.
BESIDES ME, HUH?
YES.
THAT ACTOR ...
Hal Kurabayashi
Oops.
grab
EEK!
MISS NURSE.
Hal Kurabayashi
I KNOW WHO YOU'RE TALKING ABOUT.

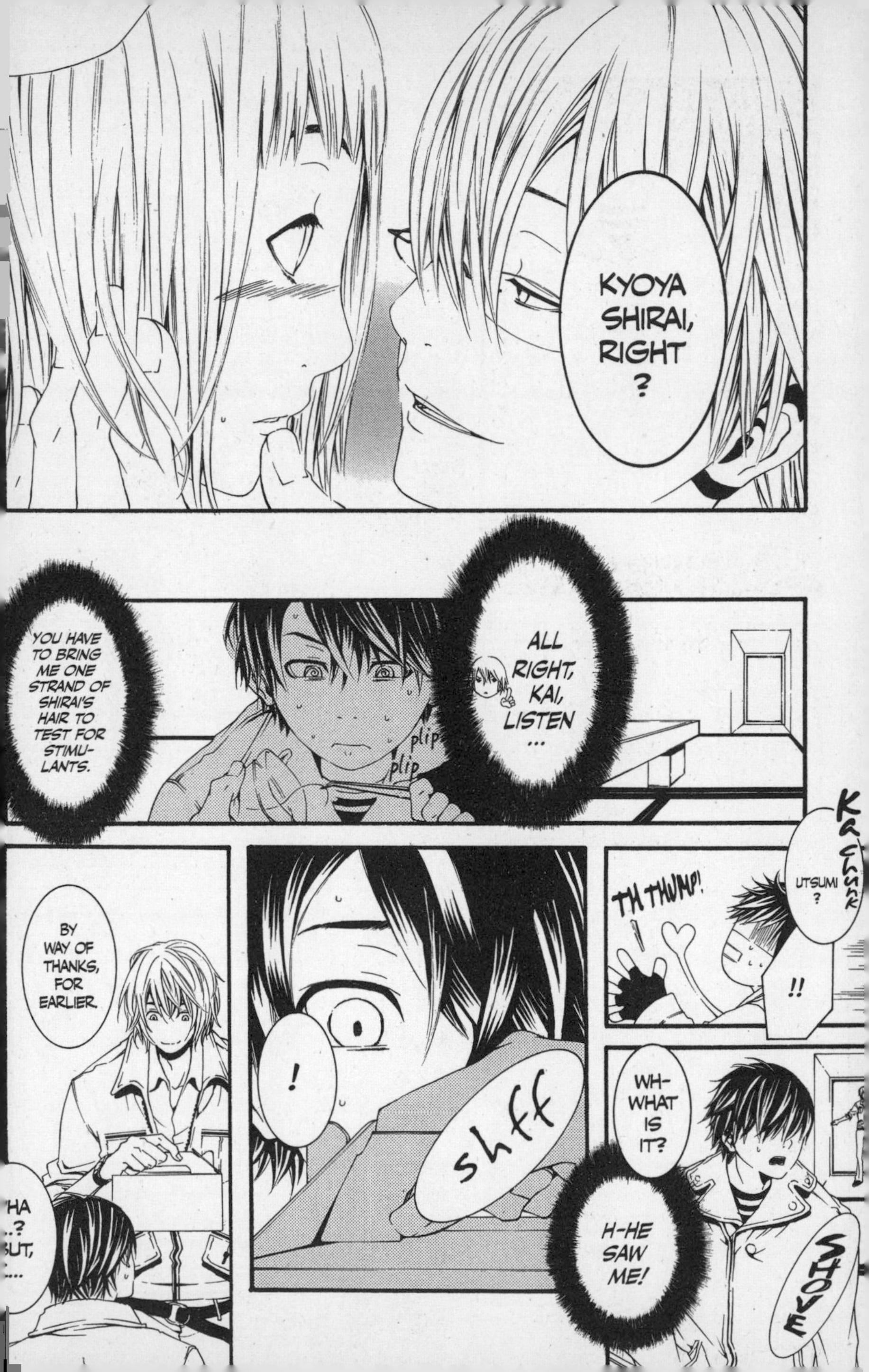
KYOYA SHIRAI, RIGHT?
ALL RIGHT, KAI, LISTEN ...
YOU HAVE TO BRING ME ONE STRAND OF SHIRAI'S HAIR TO TEST FOR STIMULANTS.
plip
plip
Kachunk
UTSUMI?
TH THUMP!
!!
WH-WHAT IS IT?
SHOVE
H-HE SAW ME!
!
shff
BY WAY OF THANKS, FOR EARLIER.

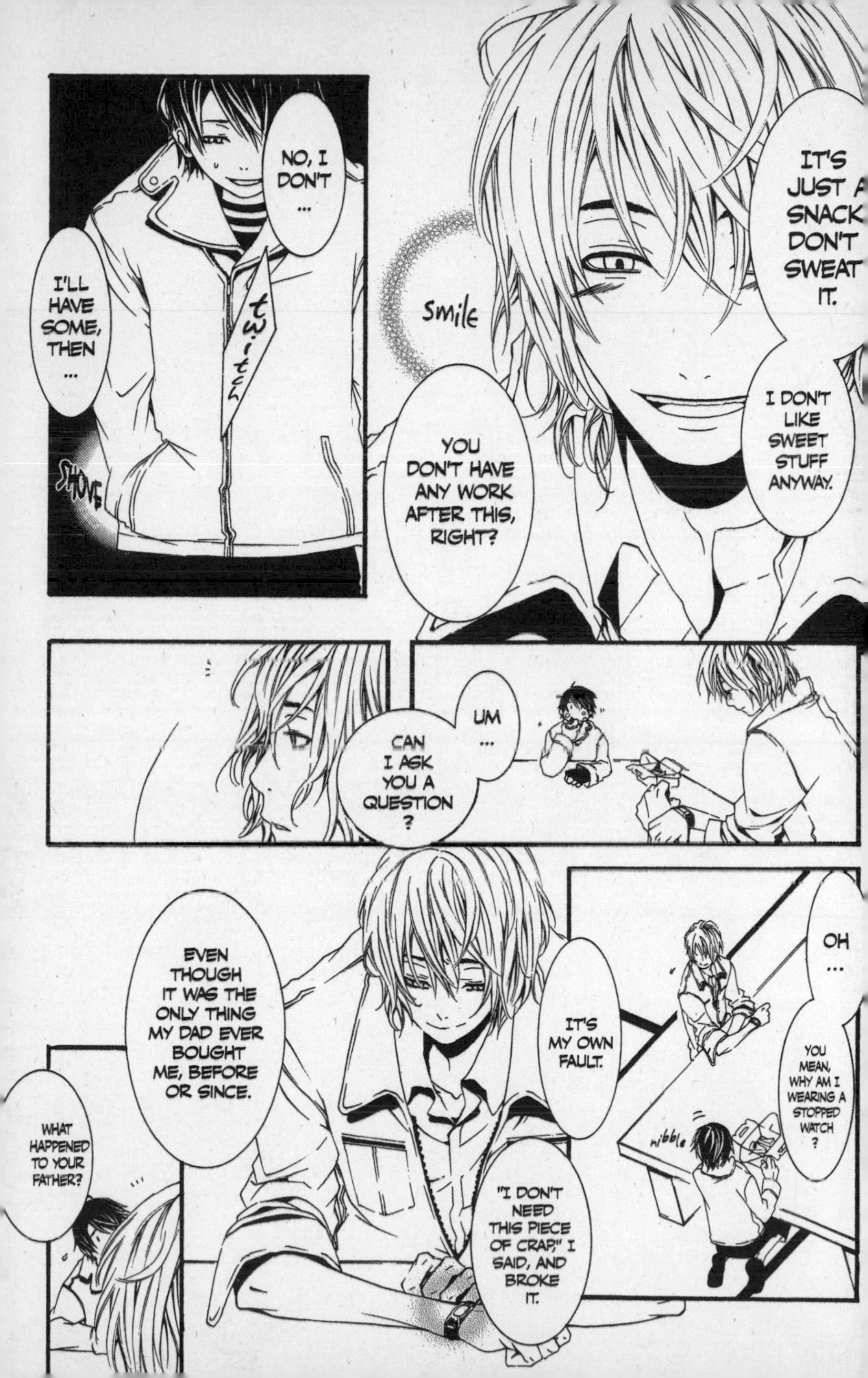
IT'S JUST A SNACK DON'T SWEAT IT.
Smile
I DON'T LIKE SWEET STUFF ANYWAY.
YOU DON'T HAVE ANY WORK AFTER THIS, RIGHT?
NO, I DON'T ...
twitch
I'LL HAVE SOME, THEN ...
SHOVE
UM ...
CAN I ASK YOU A QUESTION ?
OH ...
YOU MEAN, WHY AM I WEARING A STOPPED WATCH ?
nibble
IT'S MY OWN FAULT.
EVEN THOUGH IT WAS THE ONLY THING MY DAD EVER BOUGHT ME, BEFORE OR SINCE.
"I DON'T NEED THIS PIECE OF CRAP," I SAID, AND BROKE IT.
WHAT HAPPENED TO YOUR FATHER?

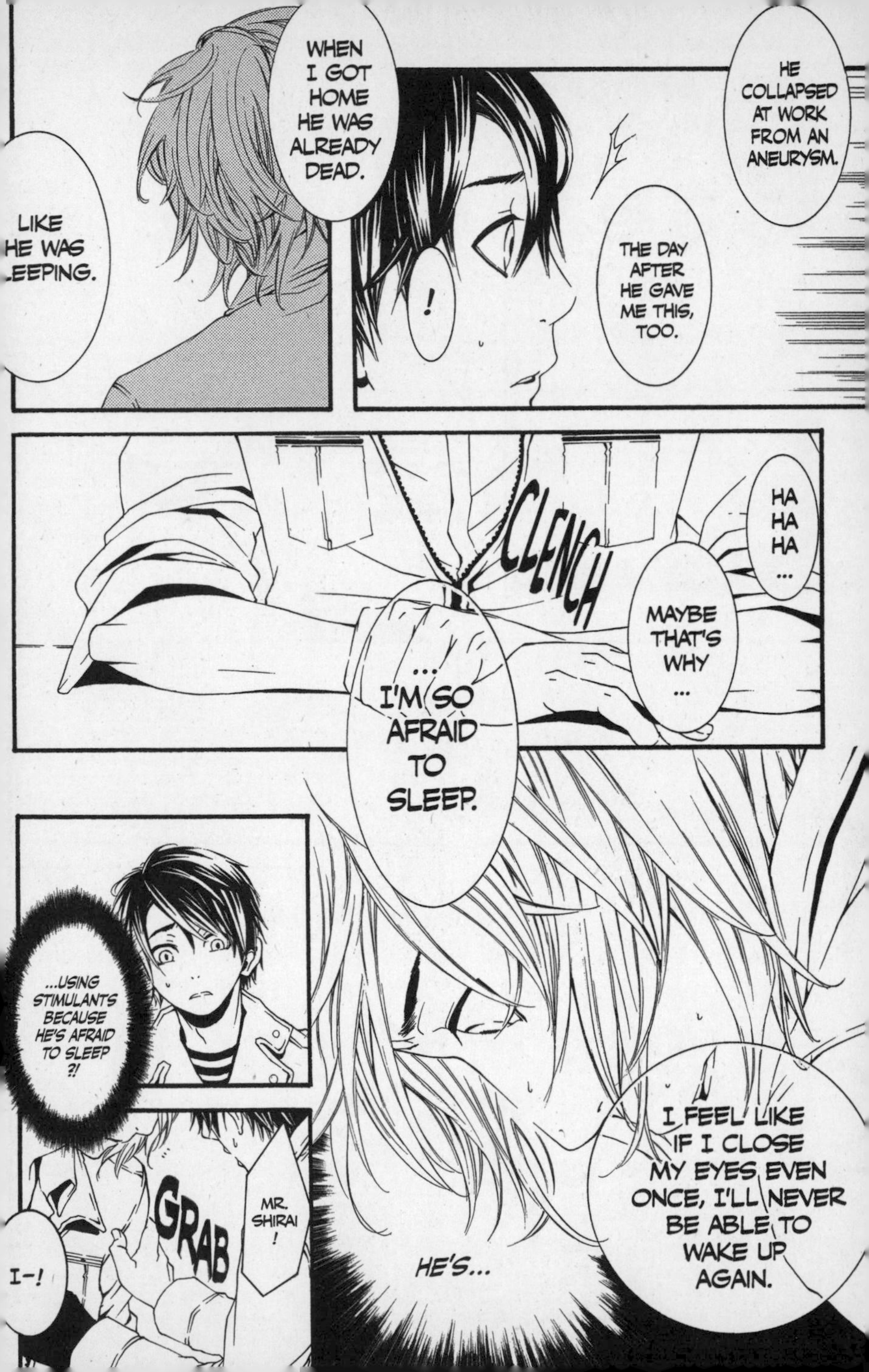
HE COLLAPSED AT WORK FROM AN ANEURYSM.
THE DAY AFTER HE GAVE ME THIS, TOO.
!
WHEN I GOT HOME HE WAS ALREADY DEAD.
LIKE HE WAS LEEPING.
HA HA HA ...
MAYBE THAT'S WHY ...
CLENCH
... I'M SO AFRAID TO SLEEP.
I FEEL LIKE IF I CLOSE MY EYES EVEN ONCE, I'LL NEVER BE ABLE TO WAKE UP AGAIN.
HE'S...
...USING STIMULANTS BECAUSE HE'S AFRAID TO SLEEP ?!
MR. SHIRAI !
GRAB
I-!

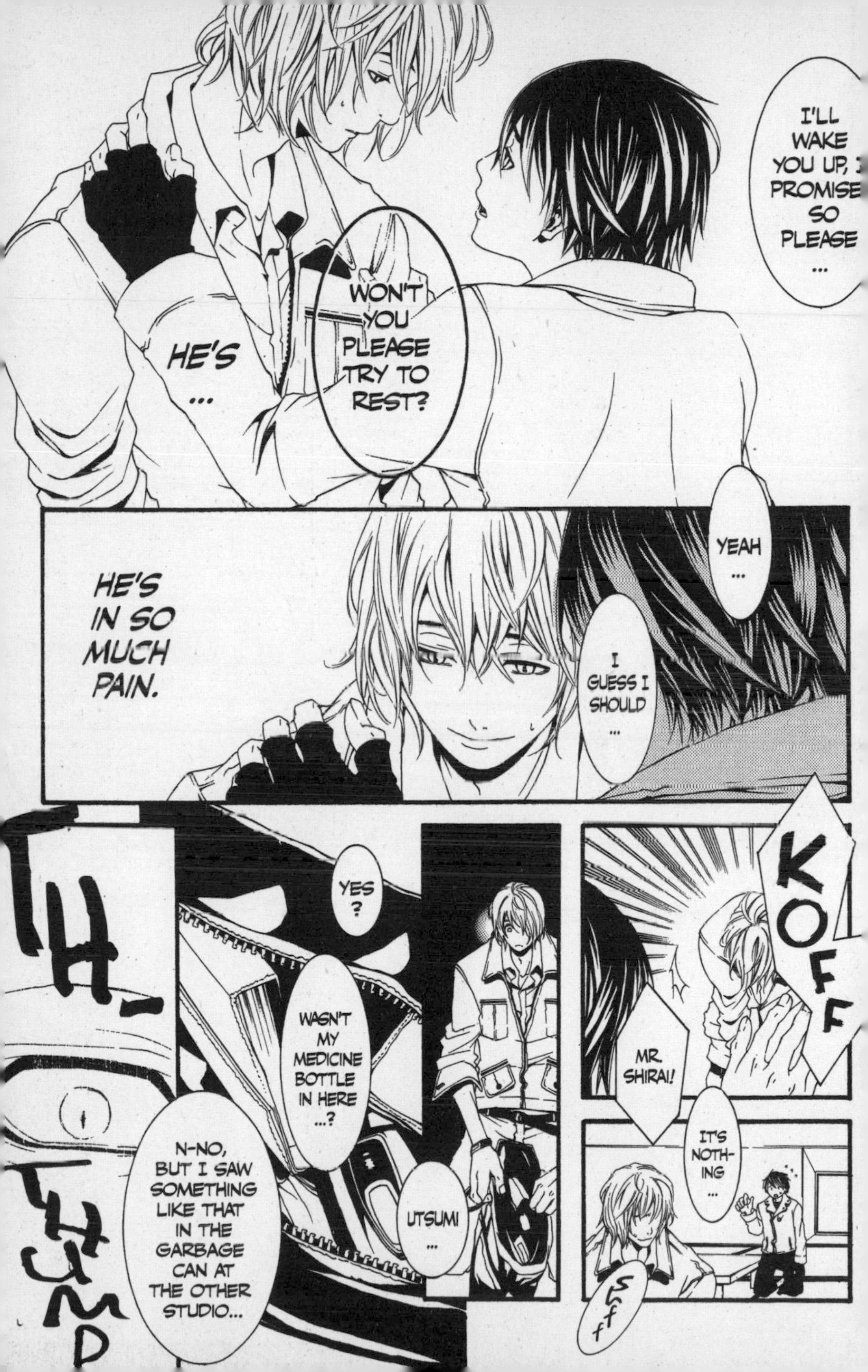
I'LL WAKE YOU UP, I PROMISE SO PLEASE ...
WON'T YOU PLEASE TRY TO REST?
HE'S ...
YEAH ...
I GUESS I SHOULD ...
HE'S IN SO MUCH PAIN.
KOFF
MR. SHIRAI!
IT'S NOTH-ING ...
YES ?
WASN'T MY MEDICINE BOTTLE IN HERE ...?
UTSUMI ...
N-NO, BUT I SAW SOMETHING LIKE THAT IN THE GARBAGE CAN AT THE OTHER STUDIO...
TH-
THUMP

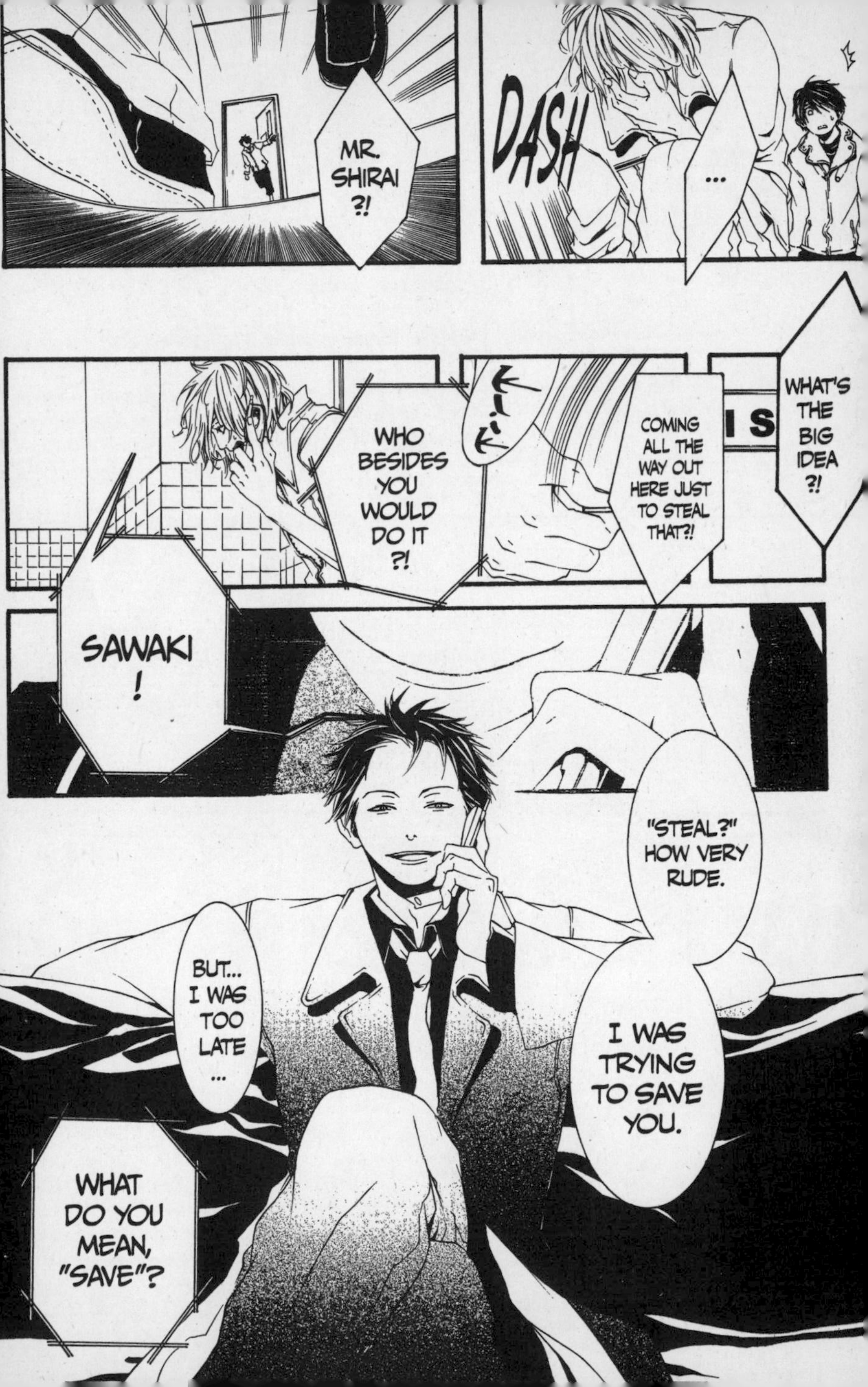
...
DASH
MR. SHIRAI ?!
WHAT'S THE BIG IDEA ?!
COMING ALL THE WAY OUT HERE JUST TO STEAL THAT?!
WHO BESIDES YOU WOULD DO IT ?!
SAWAKI !
"STEAL?" HOW VERY RUDE.
I WAS TRYING TO SAVE YOU.
BUT... I WAS TOO LATE ...
WHAT DO YOU MEAN, "SAVE"?

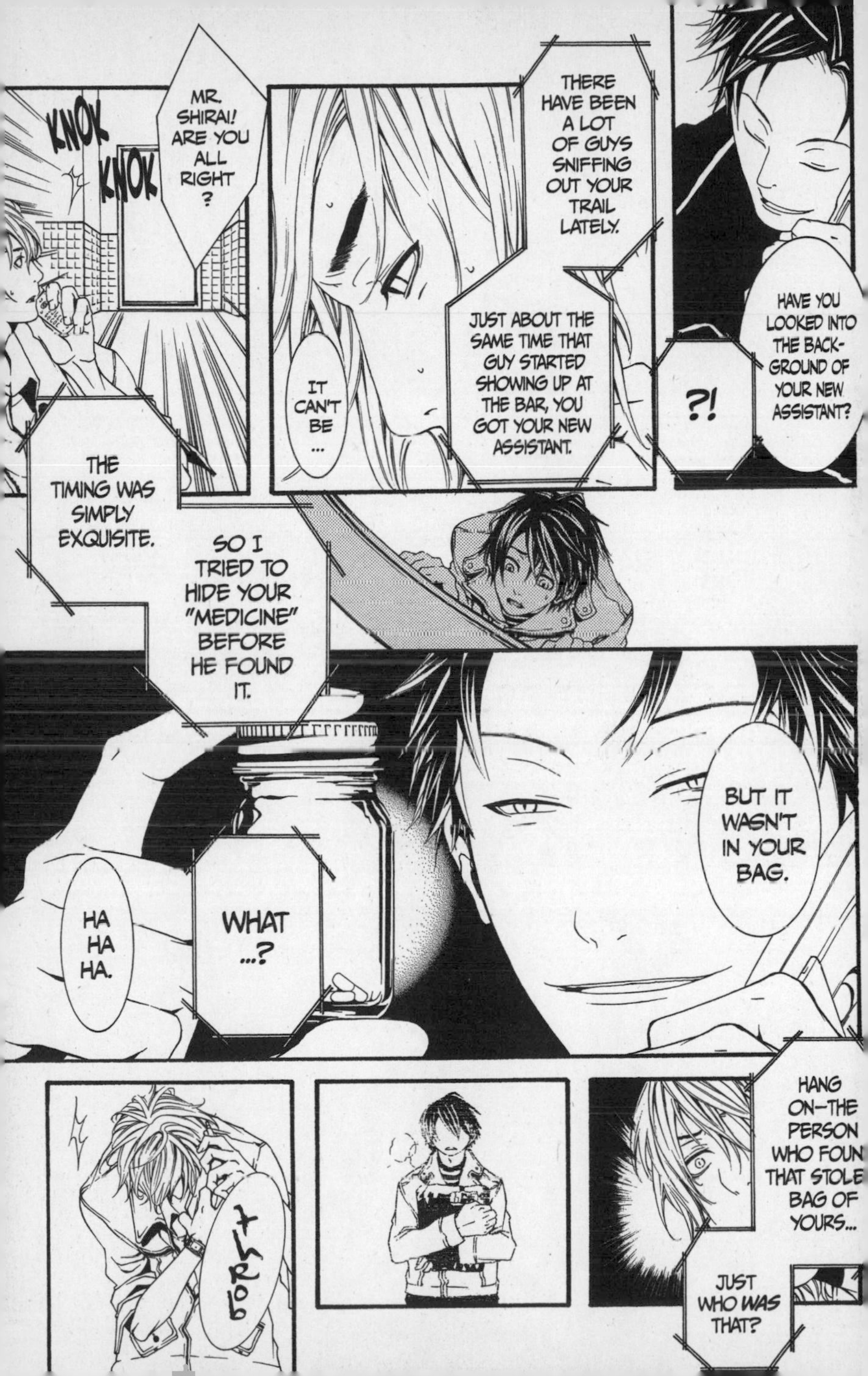
HAVE YOU LOOKED INTO THE BACK-GROUND OF YOUR NEW ASSISTANT?
?!
THERE HAVE BEEN A LOT OF GUYS SNIFFING OUT YOUR TRAIL LATELY.
JUST ABOUT THE SAME TIME THAT GUY STARTED SHOWING UP AT THE BAR, YOU GOT YOUR NEW ASSISTANT.
IT CAN'T BE ...
MR. SHIRAI! ARE YOU ALL RIGHT ?
KNOK
KNOK
THE TIMING WAS SIMPLY EXQUISITE.
SO I TRIED TO HIDE YOUR "MEDICINE" BEFORE HE FOUND IT.
BUT IT WASN'T IN YOUR BAG.
WHAT ...?
HA HA HA.
HANG ON—THE PERSON WHO FOUN THAT STOLE BAG OF YOURS...
JUST WHO *WAS* THAT?

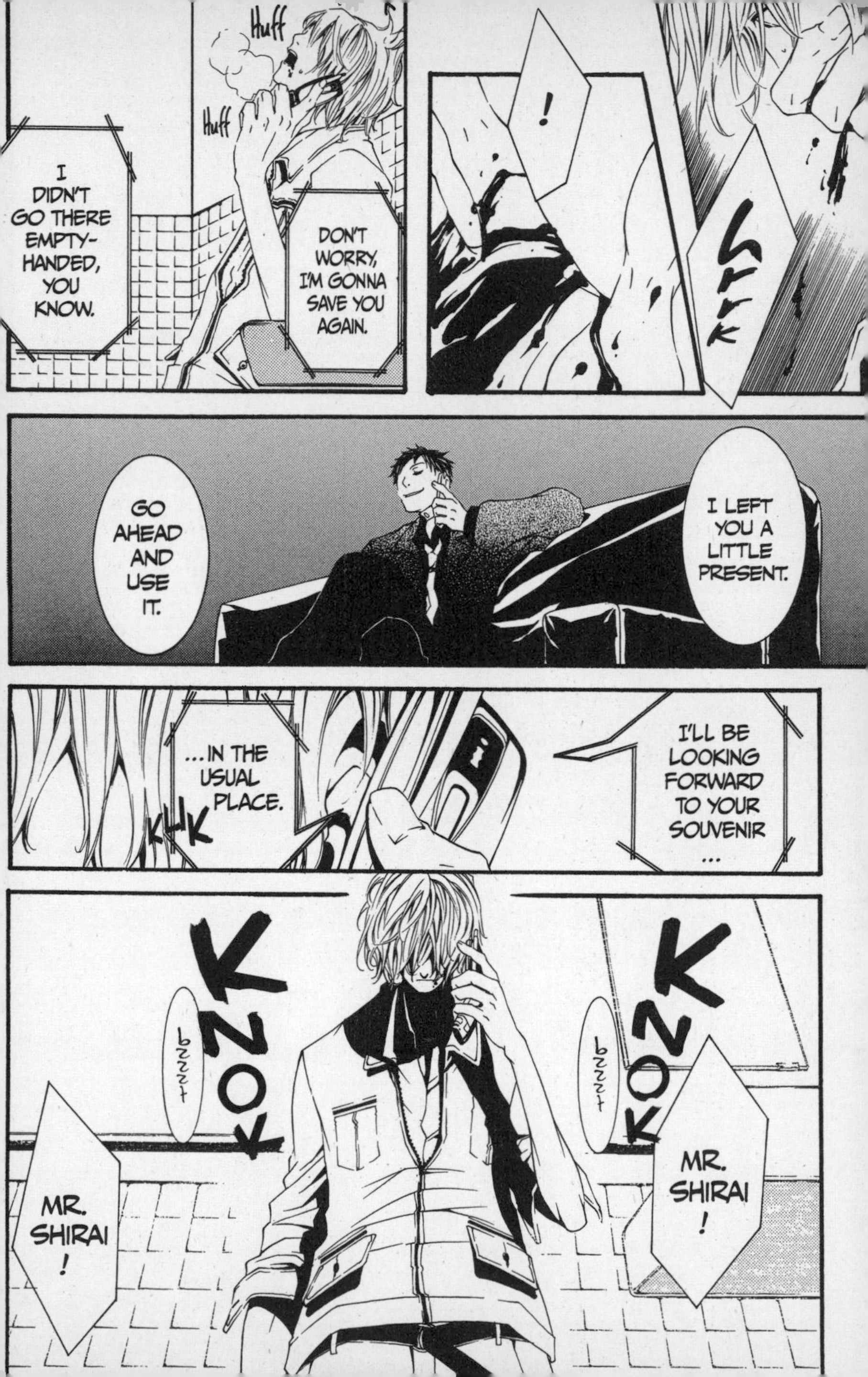
!
Huff
Huff
DON'T WORRY, I'M GONNA SAVE YOU AGAIN.
I DIDN'T GO THERE EMPTY-HANDED, YOU KNOW.
I LEFT YOU A LITTLE PRESENT.
GO AHEAD AND USE IT.
I'LL BE LOOKING FORWARD TO YOUR SOUVENIR ...
...IN THE USUAL PLACE.
KNOK
bzzzt
MR. SHIRAI!
KNOK
bzzzt
MR. SHIRAI!

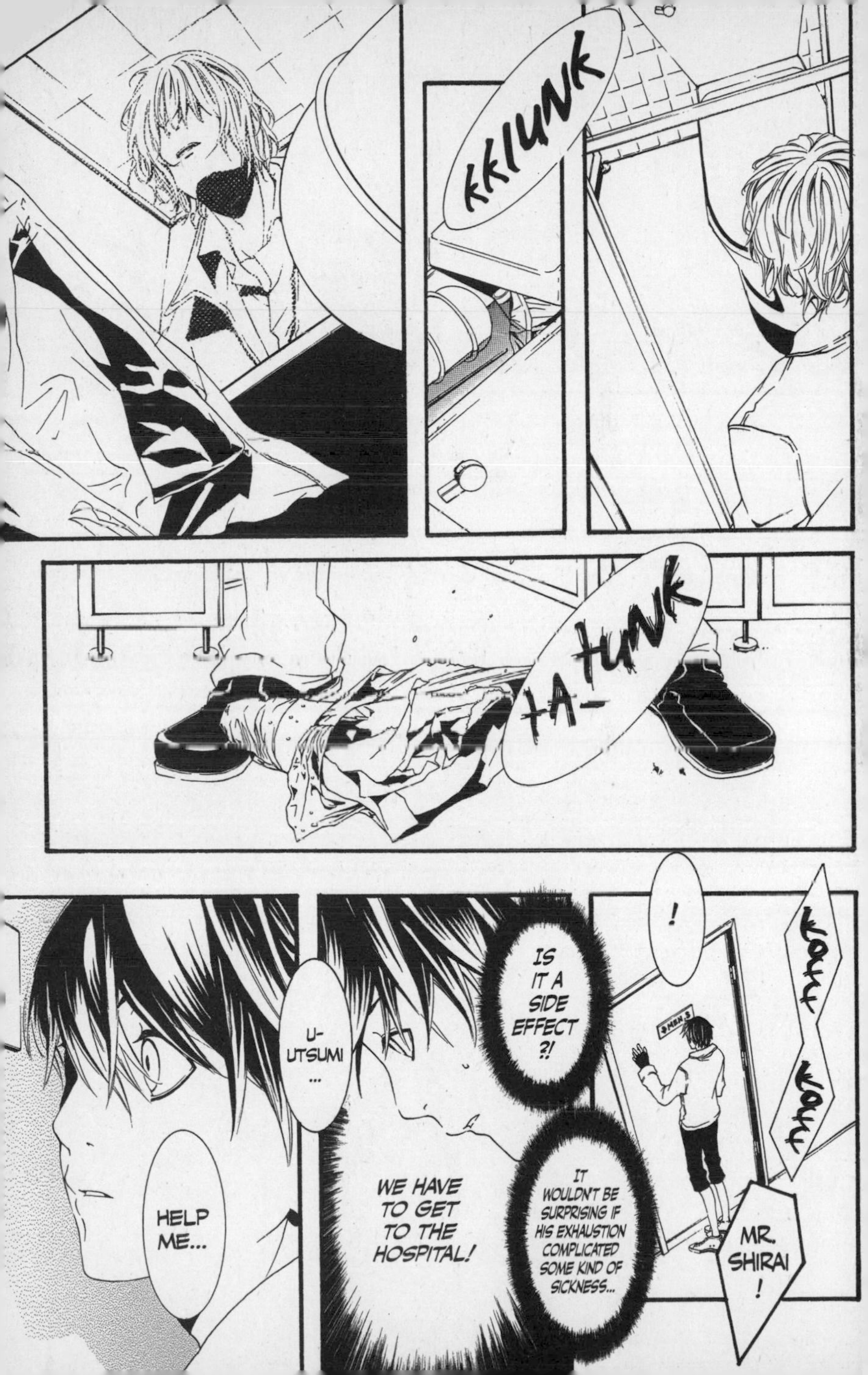
KKLUNK
TA-TUNK
!
KONK KONK
MR. SHIRAI!
IS IT A SIDE EFFECT?!
IT WOULDN'T BE SURPRISING IF HIS EXHAUSTION COMPLICATED SOME KIND OF SICKNESS...
WE HAVE TO GET TO THE HOSPITAL!
U-UTSUMI...
HELP ME...

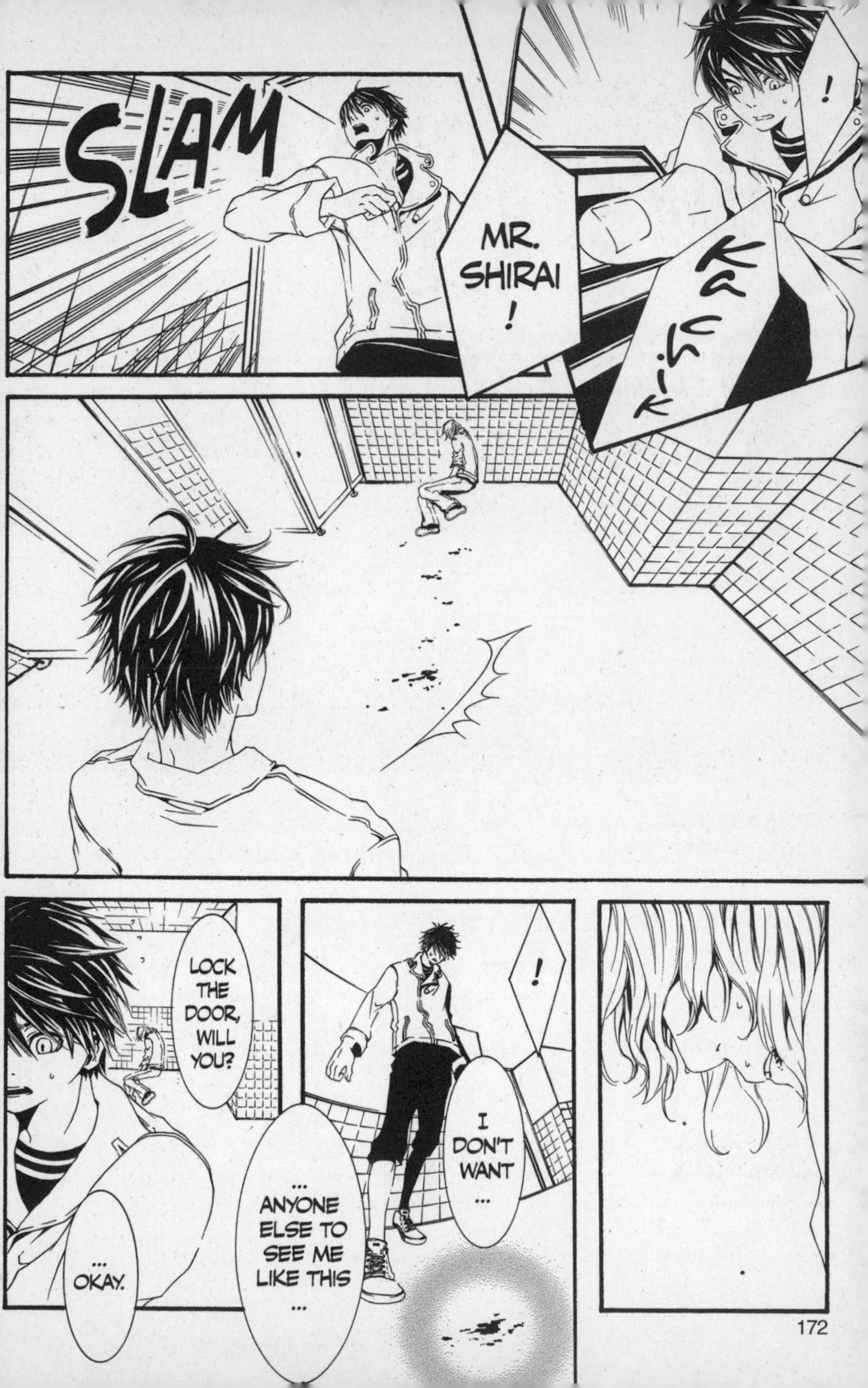
!
KA-CHUNK
MR. SHIRAI!
SLAM
!
I DON'T WANT ...
... ANYONE ELSE TO SEE ME LIKE THIS ...
LOCK THE DOOR, WILL YOU?
... OKAY.

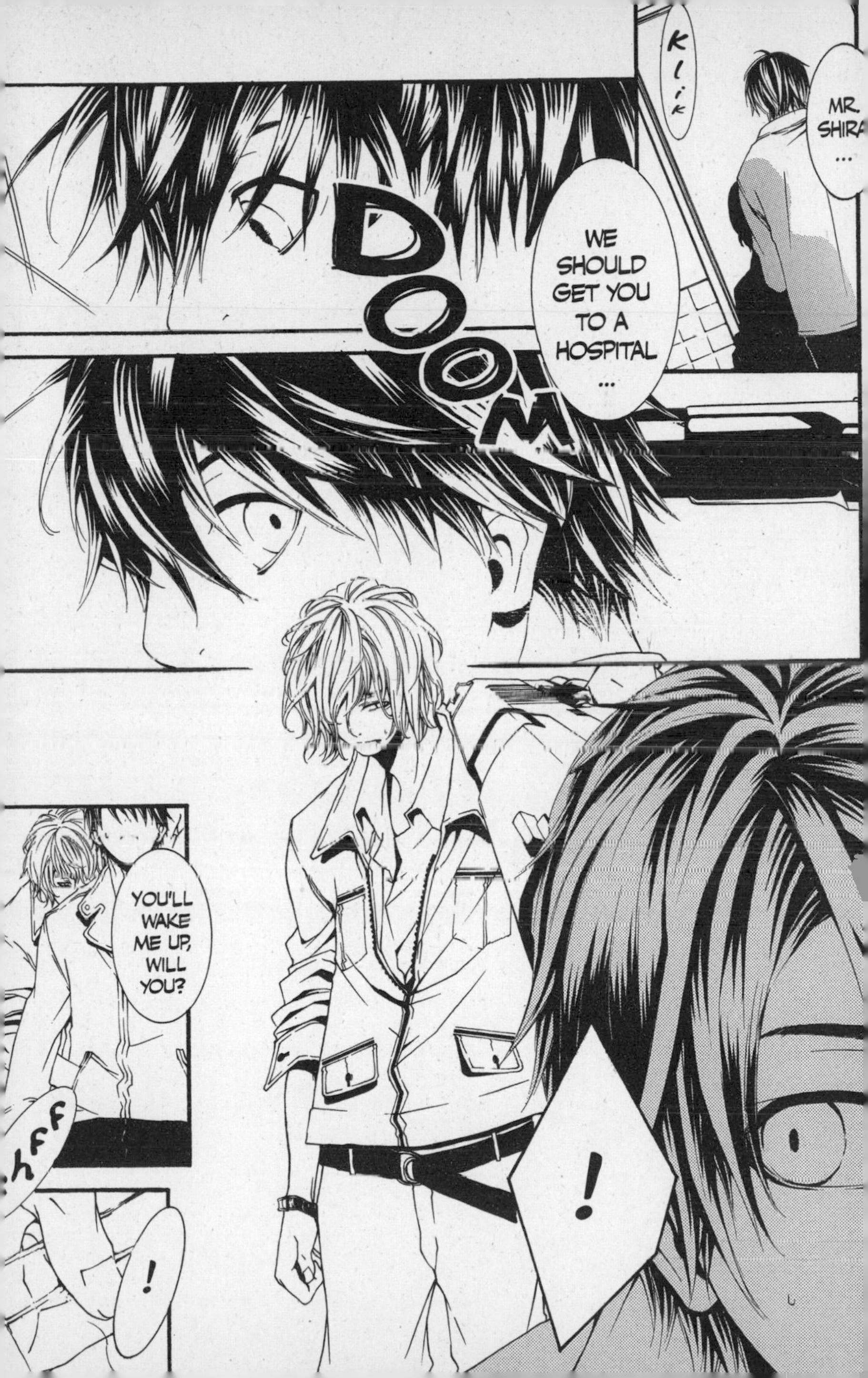
MR. SHIRA ...
Klik
WE SHOULD GET YOU TO A HOSPITAL ...
DOOOM
!
YOU'LL WAKE ME UP, WILL YOU?
hff
!

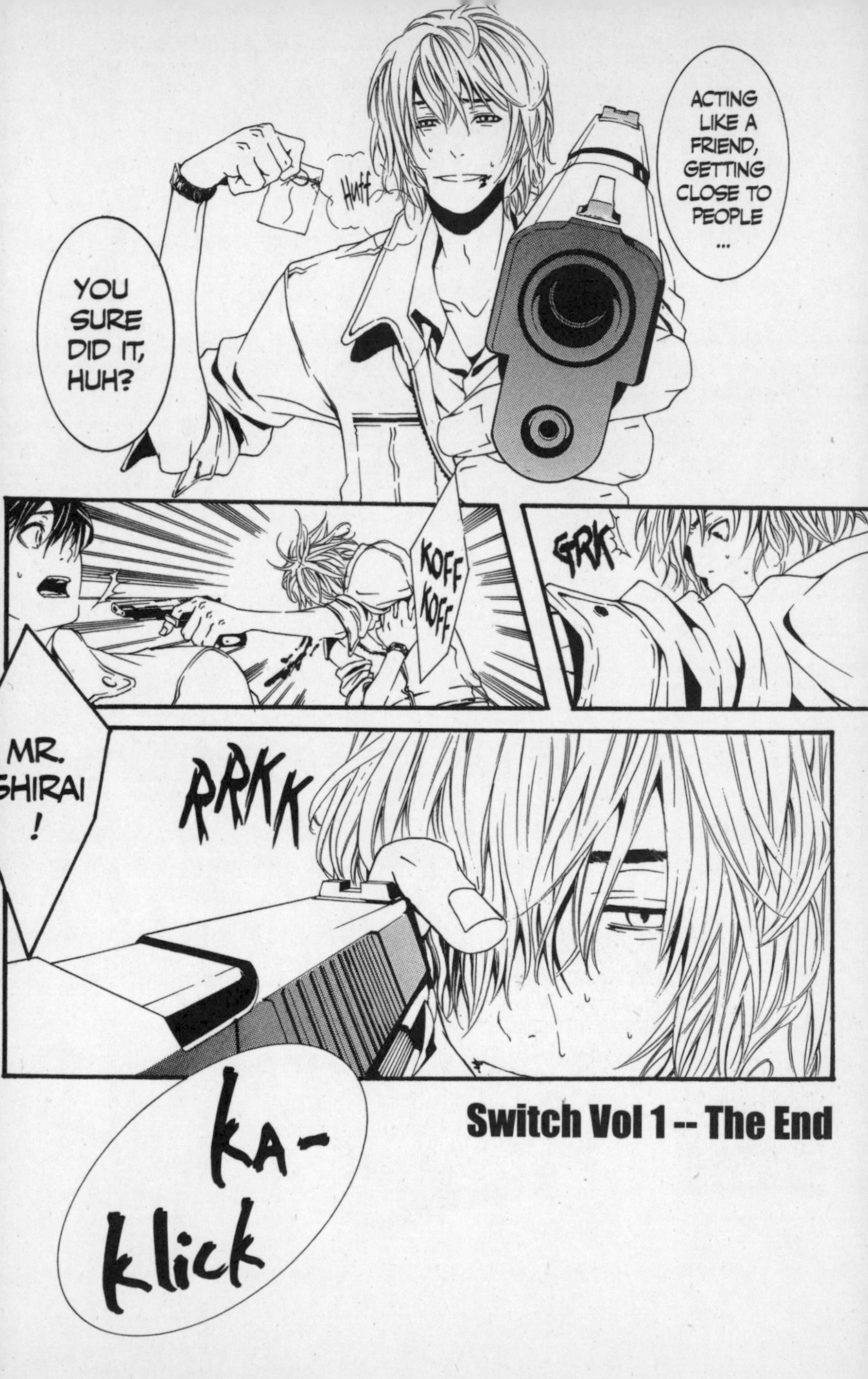
ACTING LIKE A FRIEND, GETTING CLOSE TO PEOPLE ...
Huff
YOU SURE DID IT, HUH?
GRK
KOFF KOFF
RRKK
MR. SHIRAI!
KA-klick

**Switch Vol 1 -- The End**

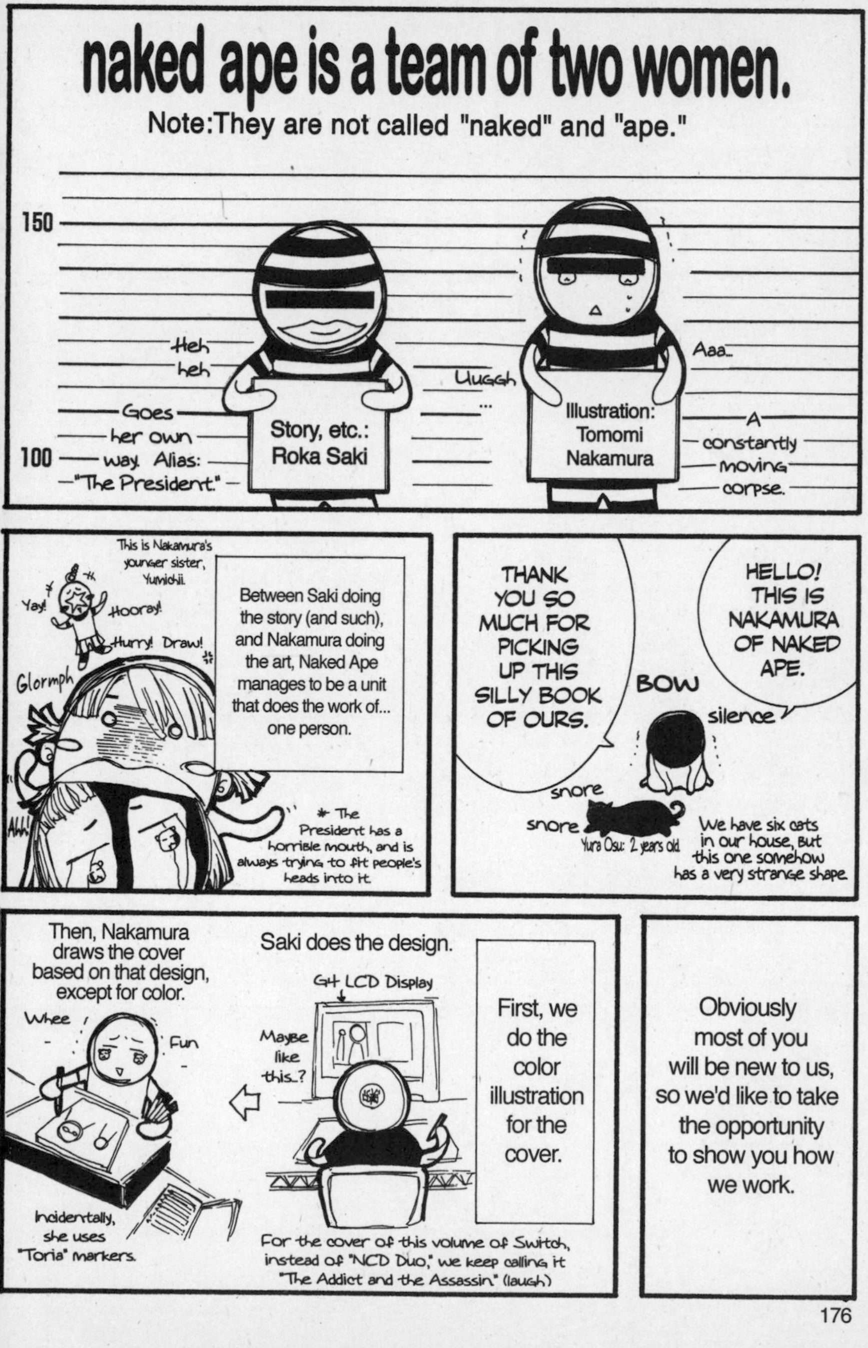
naked ape is a team of two women.
Note:They are not called "naked" and "ape."
150
100
Aaa...
A constantly moving corpse.
Illustration: Tomomi Nakamura
Uuggh ...
Heh heh
Goes her own way. Alias: "The President."
Story, etc.: Roka Saki
HELLO! THIS IS NAKAMURA OF NAKED APE.
silence
BOW
THANK YOU SO MUCH FOR PICKING UP THIS SILLY BOOK OF OURS.
snore
snore
Yura Osu: 2 years old
We have six cats in our house, but this one somehow has a very strange shape.
Between Saki doing the story (and such), and Nakamura doing the art, Naked Ape manages to be a unit that does the work of... one person.
This is Nakamura's younger sister, Yumichii.
Yay!
Hooray!
Hurry! Draw!
Glormph
Ahh!
* The President has a horrible mouth, and is always trying to fit people's heads into it.
Obviously most of you will be new to us, so we'd like to take the opportunity to show you how we work.
First, we do the color illustration for the cover.
Saki does the design.
G4 LCD Display
Maybe like this...?
For the cover of this volume of Switch, instead of "NCD Duo," we keep calling it "The Addict and the Assassin." (laugh)
Then, Nakamura draws the cover based on that design, except for color.
Whee
Fun
Incidentally, she uses "Toria" markers.

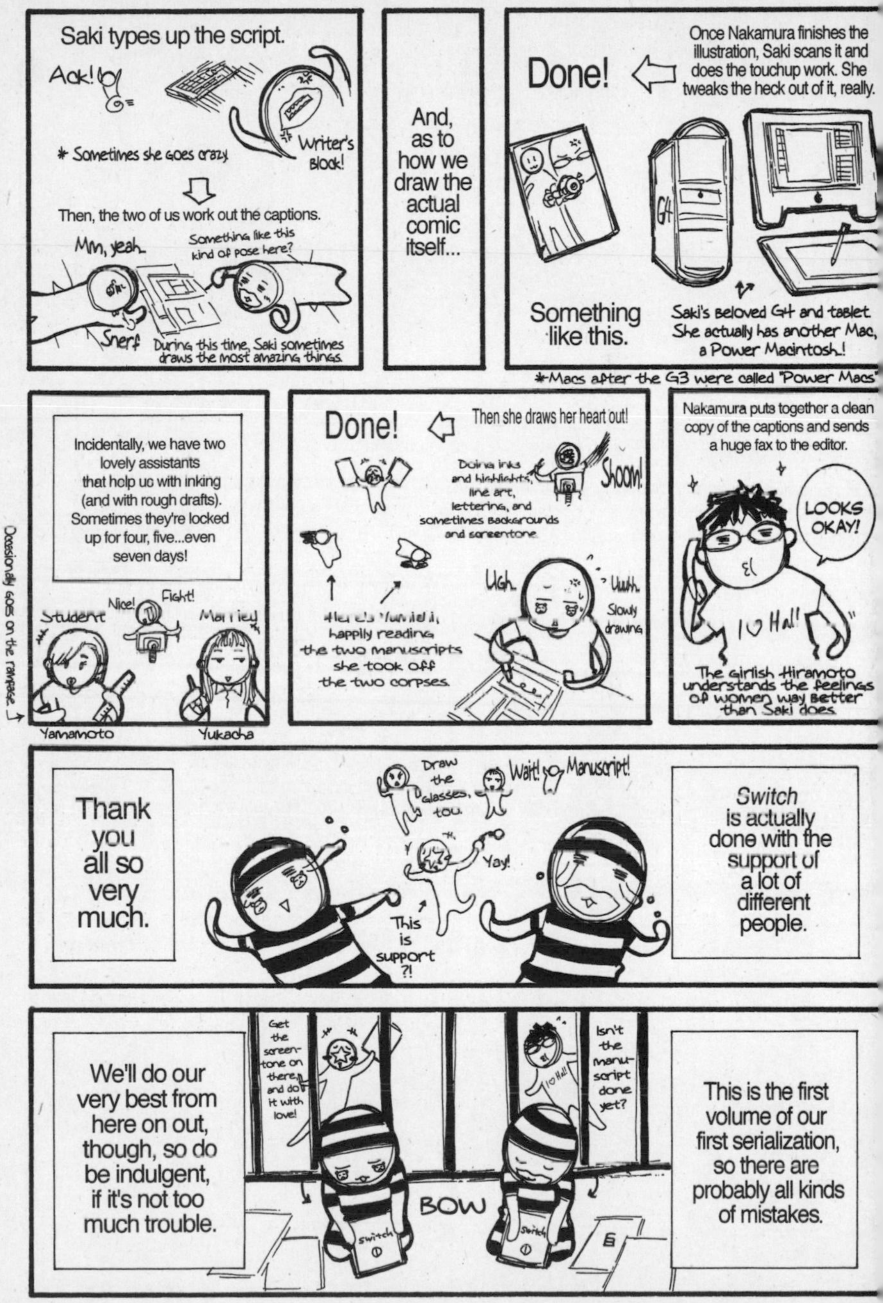
Once Nakamura finishes the illustration, Saki scans it and does the touchup work. She tweaks the heck out of it, really.
Done!
Saki's beloved G4 and tablet. She actually has another Mac, a Power Macintosh!
Something like this.
*Macs after the G3 were called "Power Macs"
And, as to how we draw the actual comic itself...
Saki types up the script.
Writer's block!
Ack!
* Sometimes she goes crazy.
Then, the two of us work out the captions.
Something like this kind of pose here?
Mm, yeah.
Snerf
During this time, Saki sometimes draws the most amazing things.
Nakamura puts together a clean copy of the captions and sends a huge fax to the editor.
LOOKS OKAY!
I ♡ Hal!
The girlish Hiramoto understands the feelings of women way better than Saki does.
Then she draws her heart out!
Done!
Shoom!
Doing inks and highlights, line art, lettering, and sometimes backgrounds and screentone.
Uuuh.
Ugh.
Slowly drawing
Here's Yumichi, happily reading the two manuscripts she took off the two corpses.
Incidentally, we have two lovely assistants that help us with inking (and with rough drafts). Sometimes they're locked up for four, five...even seven days!
Fight!
Nice!
Married
Student
Yamamoto
Yukacha
Occasionally goes on the rampage
Switch is actually done with the support of a lot of different people.
Manuscript!
Wait!
Draw the glasses, too.
Yay!
This is support?!
Thank you all so very much.
This is the first volume of our first serialization, so there are probably all kinds of mistakes.
Isn't the manuscript done yet?
I ♡ Hal!
Get the screentone on there, and do it with love!
BOW
Switch 1
Switch 1
We'll do our very best from here on out, though, so do be indulgent, if it's not too much trouble.

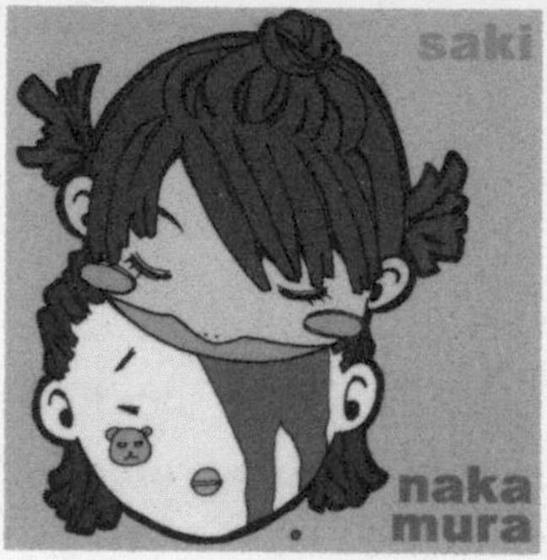
saki
naka
mura

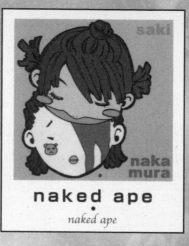

**naked ape**

*naked ape*

It's been half a year since *Switch* serialization started, and we've been able to draw what we want. At long last, we're finally able to accept this as reality and not a dream. Thank you for supporting *Switch*.

Naked ape is the collaboration of Tomomi Nakamura and Otoh Saki, who were born just three months apart. Nakamura, the artist, takes things at her own pace and feels no guilt for missing deadlines. Saki, the writer, also does cover design and inking and is called President by the assistants. Naked ape's other works include *Black tar* and the ongoing futuristic crime thriller *DOLLS*.

**SWITCH**
**Vol. 1**

Story and Art by naked ape

Translation & English Adaptation/Paul Tuttle Starr, Translation by Design
Touch-up Art & Lettering/Evan Waldinger
Design/Sean Lee
Editor/Pancha Diaz

Editor in Chief, Books/Alvin Lu
Editor in Chief, Magazines/Marc Weidenbaum
VP of Publishing Licensing/Rika Inouye
VP of Sales/Gonzalo Ferreyra
Sr. VP of Marketing/Liza Coppola
Publisher/Hyoe Narita



Printed in the U.S.A.

Published by VIZ Media, LLC
P.O. Box 77010
San Francisco, CA 94107

VIZ Media Edition
10 9 8 7 6 5 4 3 2 1
First printing, March 2008

www.viz.com

store.viz.com

**PARENTAL ADVISORY**

RATED T+ FOR OLDER TEEN

SWITCH is rated T+ for Older Teen and is recommended for ages 16 and up. Contains violence, strong language, drug use, and some sexual situations.

ratings.viz.com

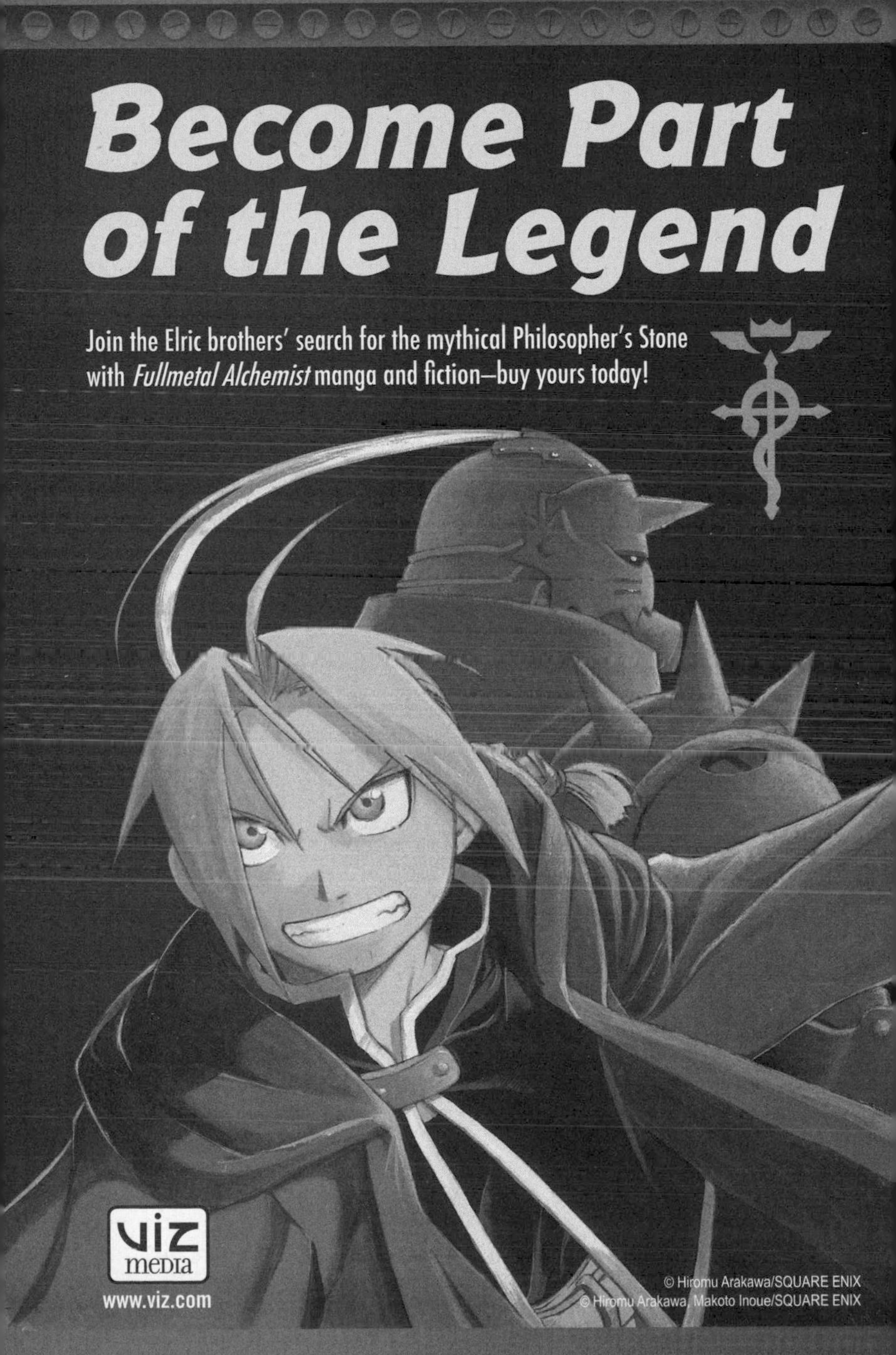
Become Part of the Legend
Join the Elric brothers' search for the mythical Philosopher's Stone with *Fullmetal Alchemist* manga and fiction—buy yours today!
viz media
www.viz.com
© Hiromu Arakawa/SQUARE ENIX
© Hiromu Arakawa, Makoto Inoue/SQUARE ENIX

# What's a Future

**Ryo thought he was normal until he learned his arm was secretly replaced with a powerful weapon. But he soon learns that there are others—teens like him—with mechanical limbs and no idea how the weapons were implanted. Now a secret organization is after the only living samples of this technology and wants to obtain their power by any means possible...**

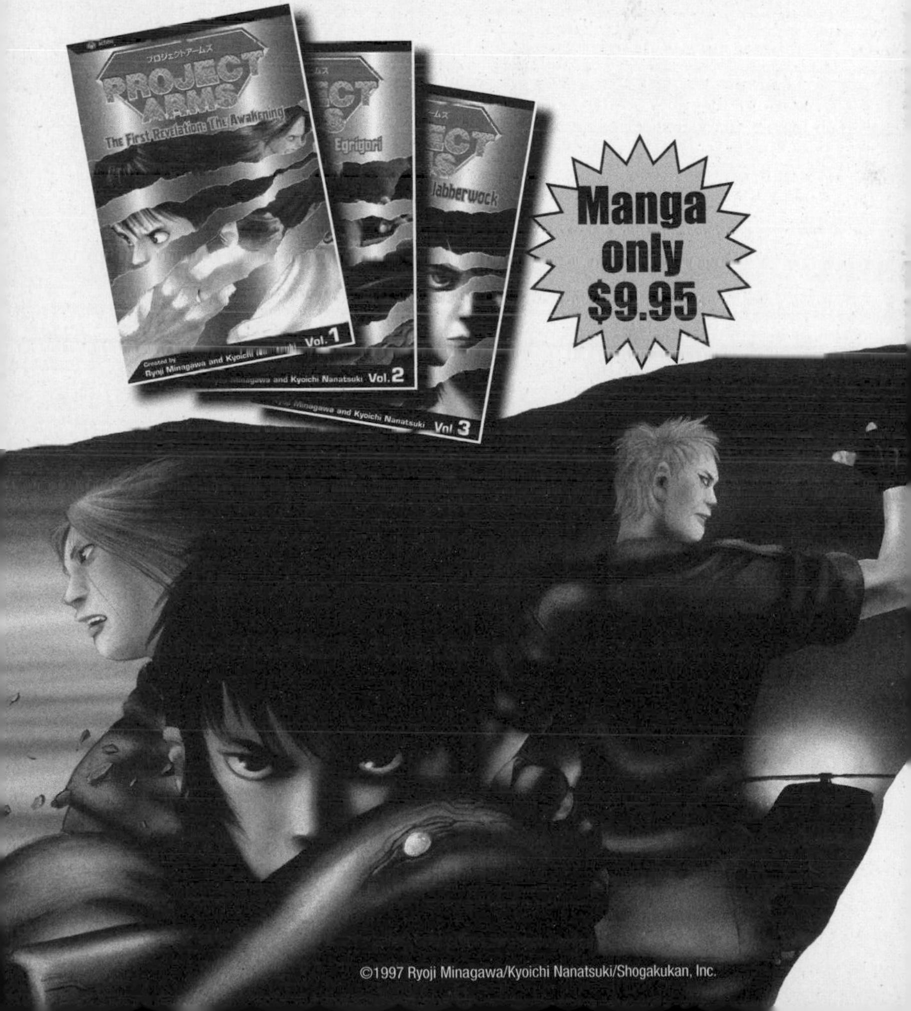

プロジェクトアームズ
PROJECT ARMS
The First Revelation: The Awakening
Vol. 1
Egrigori
Vol. 2
Jabberwock
Vol. 3
Manga only $9.95

# LOVE MANGA?
## LET US KNOW WHAT YOU THINK!